The Preemption War

The Preemption War

When Federal Bureaucracies Trump Local Juries

Thomas O. McGarity

Yale University Press
New Haven & London

Published with assistance from the Louis Stern Memorial Fund.

Set in Garamond and Stone Sans types by The Composing Room of Michigan, Inc.
Printed in the United States of America.

Library of Congress Cataloging-in-Publication Data

McGarity, Thomas O.
The preemption war : when federal bureaucracies trump local juries / Thomas O. McGarity.
p. cm.
Includes bibliographical references and index.
ISBN 978-0-300-12296-1 (cloth : alk. paper)
1. Exclusive and concurrent legislative powers—United States. 2. Federal government—United States. 3. Political questions and judicial power—United States. 4. Judicial review—United States. I. Title.
KF4600.M358 2008
342.73′04—dc22 2008021468

A catalogue record for this book is available from the British Library.

This paper meets the requirements of ANSI/NISO Z39.48-1992 (Permanence of Paper).
It contains 30 percent postconsumer waste (PCW) and is certified by the Forest Stewardship Council (FSC).

10 9 8 7 6 5 4 3 2 1

To my daughters, Kristi and Lauren

Contents

Preface

Until quite recently, the arcane law of federal preemption of state law was a topic of interest primarily to strong proponents of "federalism" and to legal scholars trying to make sense out of an amorphous body of often inconsistent quasi-constitutional jurisprudence. If it found its way into the popular press at all, it was in connection with coverage of a Supreme Court opinion or a political candidate's complaints about some recent "power grab" by the federal government. Preemption was not a matter of even passing concern to the affairs of ordinary citizens because any effects that it had on their lives were so remote as to be indiscernible.

This has begun to change in the past several years as the George W. Bush administration has attempted to implement a broader goal of limiting lawsuits, or "tort reform," by insisting that state courts dismiss an extraordinarily wide variety of traditional common law actions on the ground that the subject matter is being adequately addressed by federal regulatory agencies. As the media began to feature cases in which innocent victims of accidents caused by federally regulated products and activities were deprived of their day in court, many people began to realize that the same thing could happen to them. The Supreme Court's decision to decide the merits of the administration's aggressive position in the context of a medical device used to treat heart disease has given the topic of federal preemption of state common law claims even greater public exposure.

The legal literature on the topic of "regulatory preemption" has been growing rapidly in light of these developments, but the law review articles tend to dwell on complex analyses of narrow legal questions involving express and implied preemption under the U.S. Constitution's Supremacy Clause. Although these analyses will undoubtedly be useful in the ongoing litigation, they are of virtually no practical use to policymakers and members of the general public who want to focus on the a priori question of whether federal power should be used so aggressively in various contexts.

In this book, I have attempted to address the broader public policy questions in a way that is easily accessible to legal scholars, students of the policymaking process, and nonexperts who are interested in how federal bureaucrats in Washington, D.C., may shield negligent companies from liability when they are supposed to be protecting the public from dangerous products and activities. The preemption war is not going away anytime soon, and, as I attempt to demonstrate in Chapter 10, the courts are by and large powerless to end it. The solution must ultimately come from Congress, not the courts, and that means that the issue is ultimately a political question. It is my hope that this book will contribute to the serious deliberation and debate that should guide our representatives to a reasonable resolution of the preemption question in all of the relevant regulatory programs.

I have many people to thank for the aid and comfort that they provided while I devoted most of my time during the summer and fall of 2006 to this book. I am, as always, grateful to Dean Larry Sager and the University of Texas School of Law for supporting my research and writing through the Joe R. and Teresa Lozano Long Endowed Chair in Administrative Law. The scholars and staff of the Center for Progressive Reform have been a constant source of inspiration and ideas. My assistant Dottie Lee suffered my poor handwriting and my sometimes arbitrary deadlines with her famous good humor. My editor, Mike O'Malley, had the prescience and good judgment to see that federal agency preemption of state common law claims was an issue of sufficient public importance to warrant a book-length treatment, and his editorial advice was greatly appreciated. My debt to my wife, Cathy, for her unfailing support and patient endurance can never be adequately repaid.

Chapter 1 Introduction

Susan Halvorsen and her husband, Jim Gjebic, had planned to spend a quiet Labor Day weekend relaxing at their Grosse Pointe, Michigan, home. The weekend got off to a great start with dinner and a movie but took a minor turn for the worse just before bedtime, when Jim felt a pain in his right thigh. Susan handed him the bottle of Vioxx that he had been taking for his rheumatoid arthritis, a somewhat rare affliction for a healthy thirty-four-year-old like Jim. He told her that he would join her after the pain subsided, and he returned to the living room while she fell asleep. When Susan awoke the next morning, she discovered that Jim had not returned to the bedroom. Hurrying to the living room, she found him sitting upright on the couch, where he had died overnight of a heart attack.

Susan spent the next few years adapting to her new life as a widow and trying to reconcile Jim's death with her nagging conviction that "[p]eople don't die when they're 34 years old and have arthritis."[1] The unresolved mystery of Jim's death plagued her until September 2004, when she learned that Merck Pharmaceutical Corporation had just voluntarily withdrawn Vioxx from the market because a recent clinical study had concluded that the painkiller greatly increased the risk of heart attacks in people taking it at high doses.

SUSAN HALVORSEN'S SURPRISE

Like thousands of heart disease victims and their spouses throughout the country, Susan Halvorsen sought legal counsel in the hope of receiving compensation for Jim's loss and some degree of retribution from the large multinational corporation that, she was now convinced, had caused his untimely death. A lawyer should not have been hard to find. By early 2005, lawsuits had been filed in Alabama, California, Mississippi, New Jersey, Texas, and a number of other states, and a quick Internet search would have revealed dozens of websites inviting visitors to consult with attorneys who specialized in suing drug companies on behalf of ordinary folks like Susan.[2] Upon contacting a Michigan lawyer, however, Susan learned to her great dismay that her lawsuit was a nonstarter, not because of something she or Jim had done but because of a law that the Michigan legislature had enacted in 1995 as part of a "tort reform" package aimed at protecting a large Detroit drug company from alleged "lawsuit abuse."[3]

The Michigan statute shields from liability the manufacturer of a drug that the United States Food and Drug Administration (FDA) has approved for safety and efficacy if the drug and its labeling comply with FDA-imposed requirements and the manufacturer did not bribe an FDA official or withhold critical required information from FDA at the time of approval.[4] By the time that Susan sought legal advice, state and federal courts had already turned away several plaintiffs in Michigan cases involving different drugs,[5] and a federal court of appeals had held that the law did not infringe upon the rights of Michigan citizens under the United States Constitution to due process of law and jury trial.[6] Consequently, while lawyers for equally situated widows throughout the country were aggressively pursuing their claims, Susan was left to reflect bitterly upon her uncompensated (and unavenged) loss at the hands of what she believed to be a callous corporation that had earned billions of dollars in profits from sales of a heavily promoted but deceptively dangerous drug.

A year later, the same federal agency that had granted "fast track" approval to Vioxx in 1999 proposed to alleviate the gross inequity that vexed Susan Halvorsen. Tucked away in the seventy-seven pages of fine print in the preamble to its long-dormant but hastily revived regulations governing prescription drug labels, FDA eliminated that inequity by taking away the rights of the citizens of *all* states to sue for damages resulting from a company's alleged mislabeling of an FDA-approved drug.[7] Susan Halvorsen could now perhaps take some mild comfort in the knowledge that what the State of Michigan had denied to her, the federal government was now attempting to take away from all of the other similarly situated widows in the country.

PREEMPTION IN THE GEORGE W. BUSH ADMINISTRATION

In technical terms, the language in the FDA preamble expressed the agency's position that any lawsuits brought by plaintiffs against manufacturers of FDA-approved drugs for failure to warn doctors and patients of hazardous side effects would be "preempted" by the federal Food Drug and Cosmetics Act (FDC Act). Under the Supremacy Clause of the United States Constitution, laws enacted by Congress are the "supreme Law of the Land" and are thereby binding on both federal and state judges, state laws "to the contrary notwithstanding."[8] Although the federal law that FDA administers does not in so many words empower FDA to declare state laws null and void, the Supreme Court of the United States has interpreted the Supremacy Clause to "impliedly" preempt state laws, regulations, and common law claims that are inconsistent with federal statutes and regulations. Moreover, many federal courts have deferred to the views expressed by the agencies promulgating the relevant federal regulations in deciding whether they preempt state laws. Hence, FDA's claim that its "approval of labeling under the [FDCA] preempts conflicting or contrary State law,"[9] including state common law claims, was of no minor consequence to the attorneys filing lawsuits against Merck for damages caused by Vioxx.

FDA's preemption statement quietly implemented an important component of a longstanding and ambitious domestic policy agenda of the American business community and the Republican Party. As a presidential candidate, George W. Bush had made "tort reform" a major theme of his election campaign of 2000, and he frequently alluded in subsequent years to a "lawsuit crisis" that, he maintained, was threatening the economic vitality of American businesses and professional people by driving up their insurance costs and forcing them to engage in wasteful and expensive "defensive" practices.[10] As a former businessman who had personally experienced the threat of lawsuits and whose friends headed companies that had been forced to pay millions of dollars in compensation to victims of alleged negligent business practices and poorly designed products, President Bush was quite receptive to the business community's demands for relief from "vexatious" litigation.

Candidate Bush's long-time political guru, Karl Rove, had over the years successfully turned the business community's arcane appeal for "tort reform" into a potent political tool for winning the votes of populist conservatives and, more important, for persuading wealthy campaign contributors to open their wallets for the candidates he advised. As a $3,000-per-month consultant to the Philip Morris Company during the tobacco industry's successful tort reform efforts during George W. Bush's first term as governor of Texas, Rove had become steeped in the issues, and he soon discovered the "utility of frivolous and junk suits as a political issue." Later, during the 2000 presidential campaign, as a few fortunate private plaintiffs' attorneys were bringing in huge contingency fees from multibillion-dollar settlements in state litigation against the tobacco industry, candidate Bush discovered that forceful attacks on "greedy trial lawyers" had a degree of political salience that support for the business community's liability avoidance initiatives lacked.[11]

After the 2002 elections put the Republican Party firmly in control of both houses of Congress and solidified President Bush's political leadership, the prospect for "tort reform" at the federal level brightened considerably. Vigorously opposed by most Democrats, however, the administration's omnibus "lawsuit reform" initiative went nowhere during the 108th Congress. With a few modest single-issue exceptions, most of which related directly or indirectly to national security, the business community's demands for legislation protecting companies from state common law litigation died in Congress.[12]

As the legislative proposals languished in Congress, presidential appointees in several federal regulatory agencies launched a much less visible initiative to curb lawsuits involving products and activities regulated by the federal government. At the same time that they were reducing the stringency of federal regulations, those federal agencies urged courts to dismiss common law claims against regulated companies on the ground that they were preempted by the same federal regulations. The Chief Counsel of the FDA even went so far as to encourage defense counsel to urge courts to request amicus curiae, or "friend of the court," briefs from FDA so that he could come to their aid. Emboldened by some initial judicial receptivity to these overtures, several agencies began to tuck preemption statements into their *Federal Register* notices.[13]

In these administrative, legislative, and judicial battles at the federal level, the traditional opponents of "tort reform" (consumer advocates and plaintiffs' attorneys) have been joined by representatives of the state and local governments who oppose "one-size-fits-all" regulatory requirements emanating from the federal government. These state officials stress that the unique brand of federalism that has grown up over more than two hundred years in the United States protects diversity and encourages innovation by allowing the states to function as "laboratories" for testing new governmental theories and programs like the Michigan tort reform legislation.[14] If Michigan decides to limit the rights of its citizens to recover damages caused by federally approved drugs, that is Michigan's business. The legislation may be wise or it may be dumbfoundingly misconceived, but it can always be changed by the citizens of Michigan through legislative action. If the federal FDA successfully implements the preemption provisions of its labeling regulations, it will have imposed the policy preferences of the upper-level bureaucrats of a single federal agency on all of the citizens of all of the states, and change will be possible only through the painfully slow process of electing a new president with different policy preferences, lobbying the new administration to overrule the previous FDA position, and urging the revised position on state and federal courts. The Supreme Court of the United States will resolve this issue in the very near future.

These developments might not be troublesome if members of the general public could trust the federal agencies administering preemptive regulatory programs to perform the protective roles that Congress has assigned to them vigorously and competently. Unfortunately, the hortatory goals of the federal statutes are rarely matched by the realities of public administration in a regulatory world in which agencies constrained by limited resources are often overwhelmed by powerful economic and political interests. To the extent that the regulatory protections afforded by federal agencies are imperfect, society as a whole is the loser when federal preemption deprives the common law of its well-documented ability to "send a message" to potential wrongdoers. The regulatory history of the painkiller that Susan Halvorsen's husband took just before he died provides a useful case study in the perils of relying exclusively upon federal regulatory agencies to protect consumers from fraud and risks to their health and safety.

VIOXX AND THE REALITIES OF REGULATORY PROTECTIONS

No one knows for sure whether Vioxx killed Jim Gjebic. Thanks to the lawsuits that lawyers for alleged Vioxx victims brought in other states, however, we do know a great deal about how FDA approved Vioxx and allowed it to remain on the market, even as evidence mounted that it caused heart disease in a substantial percentage of the people taking it for pain relief. Vioxx was one of a class of "designer drugs" developed during the 1990s to address specific scientifically identified causes of human disease.[15] In the early 1990s, UCLA scientists searching for genetic causes of cancer discovered a human gene that produced an enzyme that was very similar to cyclooxygenase (COX), an enzyme that inspires the human body to produce several chemicals that contribute to pain, inflammation, and fever. The two enzymes were in fact so similar that scientists dubbed them COX-1 and COX-2. Soon thereafter, Dr. Philip Needleman, a scientist at Washington University in St. Louis, made an even more interesting discovery. Whereas the COX-1 enzyme is always in the human body and helps protect sensitive tissues in the stomach lining, the COX-2 enzyme is produced mostly during times of fever and inflammation. A drug that could inhibit COX-2 production without unduly inhibiting COX-1 production would therefore become an attractive alternative to other highly successful nonsteroidal anti-inflammatory drugs (NSAIDs), like naproxen (Aleve) and ibuprofen (Advil, Motrin), that irritate stomach linings in many people, cause bleeding ulcers in some people, and have resulted in the premature deaths of a few older arthritis patients who were also using blood thinners.[16]

FDA Regulation of Vioxx

After moving to the Searle pharmaceutical division of the nearby Monsanto Corporation, Needleman quickly discovered that the drug celecoxib (Celebrex) would do the job. Soon thereafter, scientists at the Merck Corporation discovered another COX-2 inhibitor called rofecoxib (Vioxx) that appeared to work just as well as celecoxib. Merck and the Pfizer Corporation (which had purchased the Searle assets, including the right to produce Celebrex) now pressed FDA to grant "fast track" approval to the new drugs under a program established in 1988 for speeding up approvals of drugs that could prevent life-threatening or severely debilitating diseases like AIDS.[17] The agency approved Celebrex in October 1998 and Vioxx in May 1999, both within six months of receiving the applications. Having put the COX-2-inhibiting drugs on a "fast track" because of their capacity to reduce potentially life-threatening gastrointestinal bleeding, however, the agency concluded that the companies had not proven them effective for that purpose, and it required their labels to contain the standard warning (already included on the NSAID drugs) about that side effect.

Merck then sponsored additional clinical studies aimed at demonstrating that Vioxx did in fact produce a lower incidence of gastrointestinal bleeding than did other NSAID drugs. The largest of those studies, an eight-thousand-person clinical trial called the Vioxx Gastrointestinal Outcomes Research (VIGOR) study, compared Vioxx to naproxen over an eighteen-month period. The study concluded that Vioxx did reduce the incidence of gastrointestinal problems, but it also found a four- to five-fold increase in the incidence of cardiovascular problems in the patients taking Vioxx. These results, which were shared with FDA and published in the *New England Journal of Medicine,* were consistent with a theory published by Dr. Garret A. FitzGerald in 1998 suggesting that COX-2 inhibitors, by constricting blood vessels and activating blood-clotting platelets, could cause heart attacks. Merck's public position, however, was that the difference in the incidence of adverse cardiovascular events was attributable exclusively to naproxen's ability to suppress heart disease and not to any potential that Vioxx might have to cause cardiovascular problems. Soon after receiving the VIGOR results, Merck issued a press release entitled "Merck Confirms Favorable Cardiovascular Safety Profile of Vioxx," in which it set out its position on the VIGOR study and explained that other trials had found "NO DIFFERENCE in the incidence of cardiovascular events" between Vioxx and a placebo or other painkillers.[18]

The VIGOR study convinced FDA to allow Merck to remove the gastrointestinal warning from the Vioxx label, and it was off to the races for the newest blockbuster drug. Taking advantage of 1997 changes in FDA's rules for marketing prescription drugs, both Merck and Pfizer aimed aggressive marketing campaigns directly at consumers, rather than at the doctors who wrote the prescriptions for the drugs' use. Merck's $195 million advertising campaign, featuring the former Olympic skating champion Dorothy Hamill, targeted the large population of increasingly arthritic baby boomers, rather than the population (the parents of the baby boomers) most likely to benefit from its unique ability to prevent gastrointestinal bleeding. The ads, which did not mention the risk of heart attacks, propelled sales of both drugs to blockbuster status. Before things turned sour, more than twenty million people had taken Vioxx, and Merck was grossing $2 billion in annual sales from the product.[19]

Some scientists at FDA, however, remained concerned about the potential for COX-2 drugs to cause adverse cardiovascular side effects. On the basis of the VIGOR results, an FDA scientific advisory panel, in early 2001, recommended that the agency require Vioxx, but not Celebrex, to bear a label warning that it posed a cardiovascular risk. Merck vigorously resisted this suggestion, arguing that the gastrointestinal benefits of Vioxx greatly outweighed any cardiovascular risk. After fourteen months of negotiations, Merck and the agency compromised on a warning that persons with a history of heart disease should use Vioxx with caution. FDA did not require a dramatic "black box" warning that might have neutralized Merck's extensive advertising campaign but rather allowed the warning to be hidden in the fine print of the drug label.[20]

The COX-2 drugs also moved ahead on another potentially lucrative front, as scientists explored the possibility that the COX-2-inhibiting mechanism might also function to protect people from certain cancers. A clinical study sponsored by Pfizer's predecessor and the National Cancer Institute (NCI) in the late 1990s demonstrated that Celebrex reduced the incidence of precancerous polyps in the intestines of people who were genetically predisposed to cancer of the colon. FDA approved Celebrex as a cancer preventive in 1999. Merck followed suit with three cancer-prevention studies on Vioxx, including a three-year, 2,600-patient study of the ability of Vioxx to reduce precancerous colon polyps. Although the polyps study was also successful, it ultimately sounded the death knell for Vioxx.[21]

In this randomized "double-blind" clinical study (the gold standard for clinical trials),[22] either Vioxx or a placebo was given to healthy pain patients who were genetically susceptible to polyp formation. As with all clinical studies of this nature, an independent Data Safety and Monitoring Board closely followed the progress of the study for evidence of any adverse side effects. On September 14, 2004, the Board received disturbing data indicating that after eighteen months, the group taking Vioxx was experiencing a much higher incidence of cardiovascular problems than the placebo group. In a conference call that same day with the study's principal investigator, John Baron, of Dartmouth Medical School, the Board and Dr. Baron agreed that the study should be terminated to protect the health of the patients taking Vioxx. The Merck officials overseeing the study did not resist this conclusion, and Raymond V. Gilmartin, the company's CEO, announced, on September 30, 2004, that Merck was terminating the study and withdrawing Vioxx from the market. High-level FDA officials later expressed regret that Merck had not given them an opportunity to weigh the risks against the benefits before unilaterally taking Vioxx off the market.[23]

The Merck announcement left Pfizer's two COX-2 inhibitors, Celebrex and Bextra, to dominate the market for the new class of drugs. Soon after the Vioxx polyps study results were publicized, however, Pfizer scientists examined the data from a second clinical study that it was co-sponsoring with NCI on the ability of Celebrex to reduce polyp formation. To their dismay, they discovered that patients taking Celebrex experienced similar cardiovascular side effects. Arguing that Celebrex was the "last option" for millions of arthritis patients "to live a normal life," Pfizer decided to keep on manufacturing Celebrex. FDA did not disagree with this decision, but it persuaded the company to halt its massive advertising campaign, many aspects of which FDA found to be misleading. About a month later, the company publicly acknowledged that an unpublished clinical study it had conducted in 1999 to test whether Celebrex could be used to treat Alzheimer's disease had also shown a statistically significant increase in heart attacks. Pfizer had submitted the study to FDA, but not until June 2001, four months after the agency had conducted the major review of the COX-2 drugs that resulted in the cardiovascular risk warning on Vioxx labels. The study remained in the agency's files until a public-interest group discovered a copy of it on a drug industry website in 2005.[24]

In late December 2004, two small clinical trials on Pfizer's other COX-2 inhibitor, Bextra, demonstrated an increase in strokes and heart attacks in patients who had just undergone heart bypass surgery. Within a month, FDA advised doctors to limit prescriptions for Celebrex and Bextra to patients who were at high risk for gastrointestinal bleeding or who had done poorly on other pain medications.[25] The agency did not, however, make this stipulation legally enforceable, nor could it, because it lacked authority to regulate physician prescription of drugs for nonapproved uses. It did, however, convene a special scientific advisory committee in mid-February 2005 to address whether the COX-2 drugs, including Vioxx, were safe and effective and should therefore remain on the market.

The advisory committee meeting offered Dr. David Graham, the Associate Science Director of FDA's Office of Drug Safety, an opportunity to present the results of his own retrospective analysis of the adverse health effects of Vioxx and Celebrex. Graham's small office, which was responsible for postapproval monitoring of drug safety, could draw on two large sources of data about the adverse effects of drugs in the real world. First, drug companies were required by law to forward to FDA any reports they received from doctors or medical care providers that tied an adverse health outcome to a particular drug.[26] This source, however, was not especially useful for common adverse endpoints, such as heart attacks and strokes, which have many possible causes. Second, Graham could mine the extensive records of insurance companies and health maintenance organizations (HMOs) for possible links between prescribed medications and reports of particular diseases. Relying on the second source, Graham's study reviewed information collected by the Kaiser Permanente HMO on 1.4 million patients who had received either Vioxx or Celebrex. [27]

Graham's statistical analysis, which he initially presented at a scientific meeting in France in mid-2004, showed that Vioxx posed a much higher cardiovascular risk than Celebrex. He later estimated that 88,000 to 139,000 patients may have suffered heart attacks or strokes from taking Vioxx and that 26,000 to 55,600 of them may have died as a result. After learning of the presentation, Merck complained to Graham's superiors at FDA that he should have vetted his conclusions with the company before going public with them. When Graham circulated his study to his superiors for review and approval prior to submitting it for publication in a medical journal, he was told that he should have sent it to Merck "so they can be prepared for extensive media attention that this will likely provoke." His superiors were also quite critical of the study's conclusions, and one of them characterized his analysis as "nothing more than a scientific rumor." Graham nevertheless sent the study to *The Lancet* for publication, and he was told that it would appear on the journal's website on November 17, 2004. On November 12, the editor of the journal received a call from Graham's superior, Steven Galston, warning him that the paper had been submitted in violation of the agency's clearance process and pointing him to a nine-page internal FDA critique of the study. Fearing for his job, Graham pulled the study just before it went on the website. Although the journal ultimately published it, in January 2005, Graham complained that the article had been "censored."[28]

After two days of testimony and discussion, the special advisory committee recommended that FDA allow Vioxx, Celebrex, and Bextra to remain on the market with strong warnings to doctors and users and a ban on direct-to-consumer advertising. Only the recommendation for Celebrex was clear-cut (31–1). The votes on Vioxx (17–13) and Bextra (17–15) were almost evenly split. A subsequent analysis of the backgrounds of the panel members conducted by the Center for Science in the Public Interest revealed that ten of the thirty-two panel members had served as consultants to Merck or Pfizer in recent years. Had the ten recused themselves, the outcome of the vote on Celebrex would have been the same, but the votes on Vioxx (8–14) and Bextra (8–12) would have gone the other way. FDA was aware of the past relationships, but the agency ruled that they were not a cause for concern because the committee was addressing "issues of broad applicability and there are no products being approved." The stock market apparently took a different view: on the day that the panel ruled, Pfizer's shares increased almost 7 percent in value and Merck's shares went up a full 13 percent. Mark Lanier, the Houston attorney who later won the first Vioxx lawsuit against Merck, expressed confidence that juries would be more skeptical of the panel's composition than the agency had been.[29]

In early April 2005, FDA reacted to the panel's recommendations by persuading Pfizer to withdraw Bextra from the market and to undertake a large cardiovascular study on Celebrex. The Bextra action was motivated by the fact that it causes a rare, life-threatening skin reaction with greater frequency than the other pain pills. The agency went even further, demanding that the labels of all prescription NSAID drugs, including naproxen and ibuprofen, contain "black box" warnings about their cardiovascular and gastrointestinal risks. This represented the most stringent action that FDA could take short of forcing the manufacturers to withdraw the drugs. While many scientists praised FDA's more aggressive action, industry groups and their allies in the conservative think tanks worried that "the pendulum has swung pretty far to the risk-averse side."[30]

The Rest of the Story

It is difficult to know whether or not to blame FDA for the Vioxx fiasco, because much of what the agency does is carried out behind closed doors in private meetings between FDA officials and pharmaceutical industry scientists. In this regard, the ongoing Vioxx litigation has been very revealing. The lawyers for the plaintiffs have exercised the subpoena power available to parties in civil litigation to obtain otherwise unavailable documents from Merck that document its attempts to influence FDA and manipulate the FDA approval and oversight process. The seven million documents that Merck produced for the litigation, in radio commentator Paul Harvey's memorable phrase, tell "the rest of the story."

In November 1996, almost three years before FDA approved Vioxx, an internal company memo warned that if a study comparing Vioxx with older NSAID drugs for the purpose of showing decreased risk of gastrointestinal problems was limited to patients not taking aspirin (a known inhibitor of cardiovascular disease), there was a "substantial chance that significantly higher rates" of cardiovascular disease would be observed in the Vioxx group. A February 25, 1997, internal e-mail warned that if the Vioxx patients did not also receive aspirin, "you will get more thrombotic events and kill [the] drug." In response to this e-mail, Dr. Alise Reicin (now Merck's Vice President for Clinical Research) agreed that "the possibility of increased CV [cardiovascular] events is of great concern," and she recommended that persons at high risk for cardiovascular disease be screened out of the study so that any difference in the rate of cardiovascular problems "would not be evident."[31]

Although Merck's public position has consistently been that the VIGOR clinical trial results are completely explained by naproxen's powerful ability to prevent heart disease, its internal communications paint a somewhat different picture. According to a March 9, 2000, e-mail on the VIGOR study from the company's research director to his colleagues, adverse cardiovascular events "are clearly there," and "it is mechanism based as we worried it was." Noting that other successful Merck drugs also had adverse side effects in some people, the e-mail noted that "there is always a hazard" with beneficial drugs. At that point, Merck could have learned a lot more about the Vioxx hazard if it had initiated a separate study devoted exclusively to exploring the cardiovascular effects of Vioxx. Internal Merck documents indicate that the company considered initiating just such a study at a meeting held in May 2000 but decided against it.[32]

In mid-2001, cardiologists at the Cleveland Clinic proposed a clinical trial to Merck in which they would test Vioxx in persons suffering from "acute coronary syndrome" to see whether Vioxx's strong anti-inflammatory properties would reduce the blood vessel inflammation that played a role in causing the disease. Although Merck did not react favorably to the proposal at the time, in early 2002, the company on its own developed a seventy-page protocol for a major twenty-thousand-patient clinical study, labeled the "Valor trial," along the lines suggested by the Cleveland specialists. This study would have directly probed the cardiovascular questions that the VIGOR study had raised, and it was scheduled for completion in January 2004. The company even went so far as to select several researchers and locations for the study. Just days before company scientists had planned to present the protocols to FDA for approval, however, upper-level company mangers pulled the plug on the Valor project, and it was never revived.[33]

One quite disturbing set of documents reveals an internal company interchange about a twelve-week, 5,500-patient trial called the "Advantage" study. Merck's marketing department came up with the study as a promotional tool to introduce Vioxx to the more than six hundred doctors who were paid to participate as investigators. When one of the investigators reported the death of a seventy-three-year-old patient to Merck in November 2000, the Merck scientist who originally reviewed the case ruled that she had died of a heart attack, but he cautioned that his conclusion was "not definitive." Reicin responded by e-mail that the cause of the woman's death should be characterized as "unknown" so that "we don't raise concerns." The report of the study that was submitted to FDA characterized the cause of the woman's death as "unknown." The data were published two years later in the *Annals of Internal Medicine* under the name of Dr. Jeffrey R. Lisse, of the University of Arizona, the study's ostensible principal investigator. The woman's death and two other cardiac-associated deaths were not even mentioned in that publication. In the absence of those three deaths, the difference between cardiac deaths in the Vioxx group (five deaths) and those in the group taking naproxen (one death) was not statistically significant. Dr. Lisse could not explain the missing deaths, because he did not write the article. It was in fact "ghost written" by Merck employees and merely edited and signed by Lisse, who accepted on faith the data that Merck provided to him in the original draft.[34]

Merck also aggressively challenged scientists who publicly questioned Vioxx's safety. For example, when the VIGOR study results came out, Gurkirpal Singh, a professor at Stanford University and an expert in all of the COX-2 drugs, had been delivering Merck-sponsored lectures to doctors on the benefits of those drugs. After Merck repeatedly refused his requests to see the cardiovascular data on Vioxx, he added a slide to his standard presentation criticizing Merck for hiding data. Learning of this, a Merck official called one of Singh's Stanford colleagues with the warning that Singh's career would "flame out" and Stanford itself would suffer adverse consequences if Singh continued to show the slide. The same official called doctors and professors associated with other institutions to complain when they raised the possibility that Vioxx caused high blood pressure and swelling. Merck even sued a Spanish scientist who refused to publish a "rectification" of an article repeating criticisms of Vioxx that had appeared in *The Lancet*.[35]

On September 17, 2001, FDA sent an eight-page warning letter to Merck complaining that the company had engaged in "a promotional campaign for Vioxx that minimizes the potentially serious cardiovascular findings that were observed" in the VIGOR trial and "discounts the fact that" in that trial "patients were observed to have a four to five-fold increase" in heart attacks over the patients taking naproxen. The letter went on to note that Merck's explanation that the study merely demonstrated naproxen's amazingly powerful ability to reduce heart attack risk was "hypothetical," had not been "demonstrated by substantial evidence," and ignored "another reasonable explanation, that Vioxx may have pro-thrombotic [heart attack—producing] properties." Merck's press release, titled "Merck Confirms Favorable Cardiovascular Safety Profile of Vioxx," was "simply incomprehensible" in light of the rate of heart attacks and "serious cardiovascular events compared to naproxen." Unbeknown to FDA at the time was the fact that Merck marketing officials had distributed to its field personnel an "obstacle-handling" guide to prepare them to answer difficult questions from doctors worried about Vioxx after the VIGOR trial. In response to questions about alleged cardiovascular side effects, the guide prescribed a single strategy: "DODGE!"[36]

The Vioxx Lawsuits

Several lawsuits claiming that Vioxx had caused heart attacks, strokes, and other cardiovascular problems were teed up long before Merck announced, in September 2004, that it was withdrawing Vioxx from the market. The announcement precipitated a huge second wave of filings as thousands of people who had taken Vioxx and who also suffered from cardiovascular problems became convinced that there was a causal relationship between the two events. Many of the possible victims were, like Jim Gjebic, young people in good health. Jamie Gregg, a resident of Katy, Texas, for example, was a thirty-two-year-old construction worker who took Vioxx at high doses for back pain before suffering a heart attack that left him an invalid in a nursing home. By the time that the first lawsuit went to trial in the small south Texas town of Angleton, in July 2005, more than four thousand state and federal lawsuits had already been filed, and more were on the way. Hundreds of the federal class action lawsuits were consolidated in a New Orleans federal district court prior to Hurricane Katrina. The presiding judge speculated that the Vioxx litigation could ultimately yield as many as 100,000 lawsuits. Wall Street analysts estimated that Merck's legal liability for Vioxx-induced heart attacks could exceed $10 billion.[37]

The plaintiff in the first Vioxx trial was Carol Ernst, a sixty-year-old mother of three whose second marriage to the alleged victim, Robert Ernst, occurred late in life and, sadly, lasted for less than a year. Robert had at one time been overweight and out of shape, but the fifty-nine-year-old had, toward the end of his life, become a "health nut." For several years, he had run marathons, taught aerobics, and participated in the occasional triathlon. Robert had taken Vioxx for less than seven months prior to his death, and the autopsy report stated that the cause of death was cardiac arrhythmia, not a heart attack. Merck's lawyers maintained that Robert's death was indeed unfortunate, but it had not been caused by Vioxx. Carol was convinced that her physically fit husband had died as a result of a large company's callous disregard for the health of its customers, and she "just want[ed] Merck to admit that they were wrong."[38]

Carol's attorney was the Houston "superlawyer" Mark Lanier, an experienced litigator who moonlighted as a Baptist minister. During the month-long trial, Lanier focused the twelve-person jury's attention on internal Merck documents, described earlier, showing how Merck had selectively made information available to FDA, doctors, and the public in its rush to the market, had tried to intimidate outside scientists who questioned Vioxx's safety, and had declined to undertake the studies necessary to determine whether or not Vioxx did in fact cause cardiovascular problems. In one dramatic move, Lanier rolled in 157 boxes of documents that, he alleged, Merck had "dumped" on FDA in 1999 in order to overwhelm FDA scientists struggling to give Vioxx a six-month "fast track" approval. Lanier also highlighted internal documents detailing Merck's aggressive efforts to market Vioxx to local doctors, including Robert Ernst's physician, and to the general public. Merck's attorneys attempted through cross-examination and company witnesses to explain away the documents, arguing that Lanier's selective citation of individual documents out of context did not paint an accurate portrait of Merck's efforts to understand the risks and benefits of Vioxx and to share them with FDA and the medical community. They also made frequent reference to the fact that, unlike its competitors, Merck had pulled its COX-2 product from the market as soon as a valid clinical trial unequivocally demonstrated that Vioxx caused an increased risk of cardiovascular disease.[39]

The trial also focused heavily on the cause of Robert Ernst's death as related in the county's official autopsy report. Stressing that Vioxx had not been associated with cardiac arrhythmia, Merck's expert witnesses testified that Robert's heavily calcified arteries, not his brief exposure to Vioxx, were the ultimate cause of his death. Lanier surprised everyone, however, when he located the original coroner in the United Arab Emirates and (at considerable expense) flew her back to Houston to testify about her report. In what was undoubtedly the most dramatic moment of the trial, the coroner testified that she now believed that Robert's arrhythmia was probably caused by a heart attack that occurred so rapidly that it left little evidence of tissue damage on the heart itself. Although Merck's lawyers objected to this testimony on the ground that Lanier had not listed her as a potential witness, they were hoist with their own petard when Lanier pointed out that *they* had in fact listed her as a potential witness for the defense.[40]

In his closing argument, Lanier alluded to the public perception that FDA had been lax in postapproval surveillance of drugs, and he invited the jury to "send the world a message" about the importance of drug safety. The jury did just that two days later when it returned a verdict for Ernst in the amount of $253.45 million. Although caps that the Texas legislature placed on punitive damages would limit the actual payment to no more than $26.1 million, it was still a significant verdict. Several jurors later related that they were impressed by the internal company documents that appeared to demonstrate the company's greater concern for corporate profits than for the public welfare. In fact, the punitive damages award of $229 million came directly from an internal Merck document predicting that if the company could haggle with FDA for four additional months over the label change resulting from the VIGOR clinical trial, it would net additional profits in that amount from Vioxx sales. Referring to pharmaceutical companies generally, the jury forewoman later explained: "We expect accountability; we expect them to be open with us; we expect them to be honest with us." In the jury's view, Merck had not comported itself consistently with those expectations. After winning some individual Vioxx lawsuits and losing some, Merck settled most of the more than 45,000 remaining claims for $4.85 billion in November 2007.[41]

Lessons of the Vioxx Fiasco

The picture that the Vioxx experience paints of FDA regulation of pharmaceutical products is one of an agency that has been very accommodating to the regulated industry in approving new and potentially highly beneficial drugs but not especially adept at detecting adverse side effects once those drugs are in use. At the same time, the pharmaceutical industry has been very aggressive in pushing potential "blockbuster" drugs through the approval process, and it has not been particularly forthcoming with the agency and the public when it comes upon warning signs of potential adverse outcomes. Testifying at a Senate committee hearing on the Vioxx fiasco, Dr. David J. Graham, a physician trained at Yale and Johns Hopkins who had conducted postapproval surveillance in FDA's Office of Drug Safety for twenty years, called the Vioxx episode "a profound regulatory failure," and he pessimistically concluded that "FDA as currently configured is incapable of protecting America against another Vioxx." Similarly, Dr. Wayne Ray, of the Vanderbilt University Medical School, who has done research on Vioxx, worries that "[e]verybody thinks that FDA is minding the store, but in fact, they are not." Consequently, "[t]hey have made patients guinea pigs in an experiment that hasn't turned out too well." The testimony of Graham and others at the hearing led Senator Charles Grassley (R-Iowa) to wonder whether "a too cozy relationship between the FDA and drug companies is getting in the way of public safety."[42]

Whether this portrait is properly generalized to other federal regulatory agencies (or even to other functions of FDA) is, of course, a matter for debate. Dr. Steven Nisson, of the Cleveland Clinic, correctly observes that "there is a limited amount the FDA can do under the current law," and that might not be true for other federal regulatory agencies administering other laws.[43] The extent to which the American public can trust federal agencies to protect it from dangerous and fraudulent business practices in the absence of a robust background of state common law is an underlying theme of Chapters 7 through 9. For now, the Vioxx story should sound a cautionary note in anticipation of claims detailed in those chapters that "lawsuit abuse" is wasting valuable societal resources, and it may serve as an invitation to the arcane but increasingly important world of federal preemption of state common law claims.

ROADMAP FOR WHAT FOLLOWS

Like Susan Halvorsen, most people in this country are unaware of the quiet war that has been raging for the past decade in the courts, the agencies, and Congress over federal agency preemption of state common law claims. One reason for this lack of visibility may be the fact that victims of this "stealth" variety of tort reform are not obvious to the untrained eye. The beneficiaries of preemption are invariably sophisticated economic actors who are involved in the interstate marketing of products and services and are well aware of the threat that state common law claims pose to their economic well-being. The losers are the consumers who are unable to demand compensation when they are defrauded or, worse, physically harmed by those products and services.

The outcome of the preemption war is critical to the future of the United States as a consumer-oriented society. As the leading legal treatise on products liability law notes, "[n]o issue in modern products liability law is more important, or more inscrutable, than the doctrine of federal preemption."[44] It is precisely because the issue is so important and so inscrutable that it is now critical that the American public become better informed about the terms of the debate.[45] In this book, we will relive some of the political and legal battles that corporate lawyers and lobbyists, consumer and environmental advocates, and plaintiffs' attorneys have waged at various stages of the preemption war and in various venues. At the same time, we will analyze the arguments on both sides of the battle lines in an effort to understand the nature and importance of the public policy issues that are at stake.

After brief introductions to federal regulation and common law litigation in

Chapter 2, the book turns, in Chapter 3, to the judicial principles that guide federal preemption. That chapter focuses specifically on the 1992 Supreme Court opinion in *Cipollone v. Ligget & Meyers,* a case in which the Court held that a federal statute specifying the warnings that cigarette manufacturers must include on their packaging preempted state common law claims based on the manufacturer's failure adequately to warn consumers of the risks of smoking. *Cipollone* was the first modern case in which the Court found that the deterrent function that the common law plays is close enough to the direct regulatory function that federal regulatory agencies perform to qualify as a potentially inconsistent regulatory law for purposes of preemption analysis. Much of the remainder of the book is devoted to a description and analysis of the consequences of that very limited view of the common law in the context of preemption. Chapter 3 also explores the politics of preemption. While preemption is not a topic that stirs popular political passions, the principle of "federalism" that played a large role in bringing about this country's Civil War also has a major role to play in the preemption war.

Chapters 4–6 are devoted to the battles in each of the relevant institutional settings—the courts, the agencies, and Congress. These chapters tell the stories of ordinary people who may be unwitting victims of successful efforts to preempt state common law actions and of productive companies that are struggling under the burden of what may be an uncertain and unduly arbitrary common law regime. Highlighting the strategies of the participants in the preemption battles, the chapters show how the politics of preemption occur at two levels—a vertical politics of state versus federal power and a horizontal politics of governmental versus private sector power—and how arguments framed at one level are often really about the distribution of power at the other level. Among other things, we will see how things got even worse for Michigan plaintiffs like Susan Halvorsen when the federal courts held that the Michigan statute's ban on failure-to-warn claims was constitutional but that its exception for drugs for which companies had fraudulently obtained FDA approval was preempted.[46]

Chapter 7 provides a comparative institutional analysis of federal regulatory agencies and state common law courts as regulators of undesirable private conduct and dispensers of corrective justice. Chapters 8 and 9 then analyze the broad policy arguments for and against federal agency preemption of state common law claims. Concluding that neither side should win the war outright, Chapter 10 suggests criteria for resolving preemption battles in particular substantive contexts and some rules of thumb for Congress, the agencies, and the courts to apply in individual cases.

Federal regulation, tort reform, and the allocation of governmental power between the states and the federal government are all hotly debated topics in the current political arena, and they are likely to remain so for the foreseeable future. The following pages analyze a recent development—the aggressive exercise of federal power to preempt traditional state common law claims—that is situated at a critical juncture of all three of these divisive political subjects. The subject matter of this book is also the rub of frequent and sometimes contentious institutional interactions among Congress, the federal bureaucracy, the states, and the courts. Because the law of preemption is arcane in concept, vague in articulation, and occasionally arbitrary in application, it is often avoided or marginalized in law school courses and goes virtually unmentioned in undergraduate government and political science courses. A modest investment in understanding the law and language of preemption, however, can render the recent political debates quite comprehensible. Since the outcomes of those debates will profoundly affect American society in the future, that investment should be worth the cost.

Chapter 2 Regulation and Liability: Two Well-Worn Routes to Consumer Protection

In November 1965, a thirty-year-old graduate of the Harvard Law School whose job as a low-level government bureaucrat may have suggested to some of his high-powered classmates a future as an underachiever published a rather technical book entitled *Unsafe at Any Speed: The Designed-in Dangers of the American Automobile.*[1] Drawing on depositions from lawsuits, interviews with disaffected auto industry employees, and the "crashworthiness" research of two prominent safety engineers, the book documented serious safety defects in a popular rear-engine passenger car called the Chevrolet Corvair. Concluding that American automobile manufacturers, if left to their own devices, would always allow financial considerations to trump safety concerns, the book urged Congress to enact legislation creating a federal agency that would require automakers to comply with mandatory safety standards.

As an unpaid adviser to Senator Abraham Ribicoff, the book's author, Ralph Nader, was in a good position to turn his recommendations into reality. Soon after the book was published, he testified on auto safety issues before Senator Ribicoff's committee.[2] Then the press reported that the General Motors Corporation (GM) had conducted an intensive campaign, involving private investigators and attractive women, to investigate Nader's personal life and attempt to corrupt him. After Senator Ribicoff's committee held additional hearings, featuring an apology to Nader from GM's CEO, sales of the previously obscure book took off. On September 9, 1966, Nader's work bore tangible fruit when President Johnson signed the National Traffic and Motor Vehicle Safety Act of 1966, the purpose of which was to "reduce traffic accidents and deaths and injuries to persons resulting from traffic accidents."[3] Within a decade, Congress had enacted dozens more statutes aimed at protecting consumers, workers, and the environment from products and activities that posed unnecessary risks to health and safety and from fraudulent commercial practices that posed unconscionable risks to their economic well-being.[4]

At the same time the consumer movement that Nader helped to inspire was bringing about radical changes to the federal regulatory process, a similar ferment in the law schools and state courts was bringing about a revolution in the common law of torts that governed the liability of manufacturers of potentially dangerous products and of polluters who put their neighbors' lives and property at risk. Like the consumer groups, the legal reformers were committed to changing longstanding state common law doctrines to reflect the realities of a modern mass production economy in which several intermediaries intervene between user and producer, communications between buyer and seller are indirect and impersonal, and the terms of sale (except perhaps for price) are dictated by parties far removed from the actual transaction.[5]

By the turn of the twenty-first century, however, the changes brought on by the consumer movement and the legal reformers were under heavy attack, and defenders of the changes brought about during the 1960s and 1970s were in full retreat. Nevertheless, the fundamental changes themselves remained relatively impervious to the attacks. The primary consumer and environmental protection statutes remain in place, if not always enthusiastically implemented, and the common law of torts in most jurisdictions still incorporates the powerful insights of the reformers. The preemption war is a manifestation of the latest and, in many ways, most threatening attempt to change state common law by replacing it with a body of regulatory law that is kinder and gentler to the regulated entities.

This chapter describes how both federal regulation and state common law liability are, in theory, effective legal vehicles for protecting consumers from fraud and unacceptable health and safety risks. Federal regulation and common law tort litigation share the common goal of protecting the public, but they differ greatly in how they pursue that goal, and each has other goals that at times can come into conflict with public protection. Federal regulation places direct *ex ante* constraints on private conduct through broad standards and individualized permit requirements. State common law imposes indirect constraints on corporate conduct by providing an incentive to avoid liability by adhering to the relevant standards of fair dealing, reliability, and care that the common law establishes over time through published opinions.[6] Unlike federal regulation, state common law also performs an important redistributive function by forcing those who are responsible for some risk-producing products and activities to compensate those who have been damaged by conduct that violates the standard of care.

The following description of federal regulation and state common law provides a necessary grounding in the theoretical foundations of those subjects for those who are unfamiliar with those topics. It draws upon illustrative examples involving familiar products and activities to provide a real-world context for the sometimes rather abstract theory. Readers who are familiar with administrative law and tort law should feel free to skip ahead to Chapter 3.

FEDERAL REGULATION

Congress created most federal regulatory programs in response to public demands for protection from adverse consequences of the unimpeded marketplace. Demands for government regulation of private sector products and activities also reflect a public perception that the after-the-fact protections offered by criminal codes, self-help, and the common law do not adequately protect citizens from risky business practices. The typical political impetus for establishing regulatory programs is not objective economic analyses of market imperfections but horror stories of abuses of private sector power. The congressional committees responsible for the regulatory statutes were not trying to select the "optimal" tool for fixing "market failures"; their goal was to stop the abuse and the resulting harm as quickly and effectively as possible. Consequently, federal regulatory statutes tend to employ crude but effective tools, and they often contain gaps in coverage and speak in vague language that leaves considerable room for avoidance and evasion. Despite its imperfection, federal regulation has provided many critical protections that have greatly improved the quality of life of most American citizens.

Beginning with the Interstate Commerce Commission, in 1887, Congress has created a number of regulatory agencies and charged them with protecting citizens from abusive and discriminatory business practices.[7] Agencies like the Securities and Exchange Commission (SEC), the Federal Trade Commission (FTC), and, to some extent, the Food and Drug Administration (FDA) regulate the terms and conditions of various contractual relationships to ensure that unscrupulous sellers do not take advantage of poorly informed consumers. To address abusive practices arising from unequal bargaining power inherent in some economic relationships, Congress enacted statutes like the National Labor Relations Act to establish the ground rules for important aspects of those relationships.[8]

With the enactment of the Pure Food and Drug Act of 1906,[9] Congress also began to protect citizens from products and activities that pose unacceptable health and safety risks. Congress has empowered agencies like the FDA, the Environmental Protection Agency (EPA), and the Occupational Safety and Health Administration (OSHA) to remove unhealthful or dangerous products from the market and to promulgate standards to ensure consumer safety and a clean and healthful environment. Finally, Congress has empowered several agencies to promulgate safety standards for particular industries. Examples of these agencies, which are of particular relevance to this book because of the interstate character of the regulated activities, are the National Highway Traffic Safety Administration (NHTSA), the Federal Aviation Administration (FAA), the Federal Railroad Administration (FRA), the Consumer Product Safety Commission (CPSC), and the Coast Guard, all of which are discussed in some detail in the pages that follow.[10]

Federal Regulatory Functions

The federal regulatory functions relevant to this book fall into two broad categories—standard setting and licensing. Most federal regulatory programs involve standard setting, and the resulting federal standards have an important role to play in state common law litigation, as we shall see in the second half of this chapter. A much smaller number of regulatory programs intrude more deeply into private markets by requiring advance approval by a federal agency, and these programs are more likely to give rise to the sort of serious conflicts between state common law and federal regulation that may call for federal preemption.

In federal licensing regimes, the private sector proponent of a product or activity must first obtain a permit or a license from a regulatory agency. The prospective manufacturer of a drug or medical device, for example, must demonstrate to FDA that the product will perform its function safely and effectively. This ordinarily requires the applicant to supply appropriately conducted scientific studies demonstrating that the product meets the relevant statutory test, which often requires the agency to balance the product's predicted benefits and risks. When the available information leads the agency to conclude that the product should be allowed on the market only under certain conditions, only for specified uses, or only when accompanied by certain instructions and warnings, the agency will place corresponding conditions or restrictions on the permit. A suitable warning, for example, may allow consumers to enjoy a product's benefits while avoiding the attendant risks by complying with the warnings. The manufacturers of licensed products typically have a continuing responsibility to bring to the agency's attention any information they receive indicating that the product causes adverse effects not identified in the original submissions.[11]

Regulatory agencies that administer standard setting regimes promulgate generally applicable requirements through a procedural exercise called "rulemaking."[12] Because the agency has the burden of justifying any rules that it promulgates, it must both demonstrate a need for the rule and show how the particular rule that it proposes will implement one or more of its statutory responsibilities. After developing the legal and technical basis for its rule and obtaining the views of other agencies and of the White House Office of Management and Budget, the agency publishes a notice in the *Federal Register* that includes the substance of the proposed rule and invites public comments on the proposal and the agency's supporting analysis. The agency then digests the public comments, prepares appropriate responses, and publishes another notice containing the final rule and analysis. At that point, any affected party may challenge the rule in a federal court by requesting that the court set aside aspects of the rule that it finds to be "arbitrary and capricious" or unsupported by "substantial evidence" in the rulemaking record.[13] As we shall see in Chapter 7, these opportunities for public comment and judicial review, along with other procedures that Congress and presidents have imposed on the rulemaking process, ensure that it is a resource-intensive and time-consuming affair. Agencies do not undertake rulemaking initiatives lightly, and they are usually quite hesitant to revisit existing standards once they have survived the rulemaking gauntlet.

Federal standards come in many substantive varieties that reflect the many approaches that Congress has adopted toward regulating private sector conduct. Sometimes, the agency specifies in detailed terms just how the regulatee must act in particular situations or how its products must be designed or labeled. We will refer to these as "specification standards."[14] A Federal Railroad Administration regulation that specifies the precise dimensions and wording of the "crossbuck" warning sign at railway and highway grade crossings is a good example of such a "specification standard." Many academic observers have little confidence in the ability of bureaucracies to prescribe the single best cure for a regulatory problem, and their doubts tend to grow with the geographical distance from the regulator to the regulated conduct.[15] Referring to such standards somewhat pejoratively as "command and control" standards, they believe that specification standards are likely to be inefficient or ineffective in practice.[16] More important for our purposes, any state specification standard that contains a different command rather clearly puts the regulatee in the unenviable position of choosing which standard to violate. Because of their potential for creating direct conflict between state and federal requirements, specification standards are prime targets for preemption litigation.

Like most specification standards, "design standards" are based on a model technology or approach that complies with the agency's "technology-based" statutory mandate, but they allow individual sources the freedom to adopt any other acceptable technological means that performs as well at reducing harmful residuals or increasing safety as the identified technology.[17] The agency's statute typically states in broad terms, such as "best available technology," the degree of control that it expects regulatees to achieve. The agency then examines the available protective technologies and selects an appropriate model technology. This step usually involves an exercise of engineering judgment, but economics invariably plays a critical role because cost is always a relevant consideration in determining real-world availability. Finally, the agency establishes a standard, usually expressed in units of residuals or safety per unit of the company's output, that regulatees may meet by using either the model technology or some other technology that complies with the standard. Because design standards offer the regulatee some degree of discretion in choosing the method of compliance, they present a lower potential for conflict between state and federal regulations than do specification standards.

"Performance standards" are even less prescriptive in that they allow regulatees to achieve a broad, agency-determined performance goal, expressed in units of the overall degree of protection desired (for example, no more than 150 serious injuries per year or not more that 10 million tons of sulfur dioxide emissions per year for the entire country), that all regulatees must meet, sometimes individually and sometimes collectively.[18] As such, they are more amenable to implementation tools preferred by economists, such as cap-and-trade approaches, than are design standards. Often, the trick is to identify a monitoring device that is sufficiently accurate to allow both the regulatee and the agency to determine at any given time whether the standard has been violated. Compliance with NHTSA's performance-based automobile safety standards, for example, is usually determined through crash tests employing standard dummies for which the agency has prescribed size, weight, and other relevant dimensions in a separate rulemaking exercise.

The Institutional Setting

Federal licensing and standard setting do not occur in an institutional vacuum. The federal agency must conduct its business under the watchful eye of the committees of Congress that have jurisdiction over its budget and its substantive activities. The entities most likely to be affected by the agency's actions will predictably beat a hasty path to the offices of their allies on those committees when they feel that the agency has not adequately considered their interests. Serious grievances may result in congressional hearings in which the agency head is called on the carpet to answer pointed questions about the agency's actions. Short of that, agency staffers may have to spend hours responding to lengthy letters from influential congresspersons containing dozens of questions. Agency regulatory programs are also frequent subjects of member-requested investigative reports by congressional agencies such as the Government Accountability Office and the Congressional Research Service.[19]

Executive Branch agencies must report to officials in the White House Office of Management and Budget (OMB) who are responsible for coordinating interagency reviews of important agency regulations. Every president since President Nixon has assigned to OMB the additional role of reviewing agency-prepared regulatory impact analyses for major rules. This review process gives the typically skeptical economists in OMB an opportunity to scuttle regulatory initiatives that do not conform to the policy preferences of the administration, and it sometimes gives regulatees a second bite at the apple as they lobby OMB officials for changes before the rules become final.[20]

Finally, agency actions are subject to judicial review under the "arbitrary and capricious" or "substantial evidence" tests mentioned earlier. In the context of rulemaking, the courts have crafted the "hard look" doctrine, under which a reviewing court carefully examines the agency's explanation to determine whether "the agency has relied on factors which Congress has not intended it to consider, entirely failed to consider an important aspect of the problem, offered an explanation for its decision that runs counter to the evidence before the agency, or is so implausible that it could not be ascribed to a difference in view or the product of agency expertise."[21] This broad test provides the reviewing courts with a great deal of discretion to set aside agency actions or, more typically, to remand challenged actions to the agency for more complete explanations.[22] Consequently, a regulation or license is never really final until the process of judicial review has run its course.

Enforcement

Since the most carefully designed regulatory program imaginable will have little impact if regulatees may ignore its requirements with impunity, the agency must ensure that the regulatees are in fact complying with its regulations and the permit requirements. Most agencies devote a substantial proportion of their staff resources to inspecting regulated facilities, investigating potential violations of regulatory requirements, determining whether and how to prosecute alleged violations, and adjudicating enforcement actions that they initiate. Since agency inspectors and investigators cannot possibly detect and prosecute every violation, effective deterrence depends upon the perception of members of the regulated community that sanctions will be swiftly and predictably implemented in a consistent fashion. The effectiveness of an enforcement program is therefore a function of both the probability that the government will prosecute violative conduct and the size of the likely penalty.[23]

At the same time, the enforcement stage is often the place where the agency makes a conscious (but usually unarticulated) decision to relax one or more requirements through the exercise of "enforcement discretion." When following the letter of the law would cause unanticipated or undue hardship for the regulatee, an agency may justifiably decline to prosecute. But agency officials sometimes decline to enforce regulations because they disagree with requirements imposed by their predecessors and are unwilling to undertake a rulemaking initiative to rescind them. Whatever the reason, enforcement discretion offers some "play in the joints" that permits agencies to write rules without loading them up with so many exceptions that they become unmanageable.

Congress has created a number of enforcement tools to ensure that regulated entities take their compliance responsibilities seriously, but it has not made all of the tools available for every regulatory program. Virtually all regulatory statutes provide criminal penalties, including fines and possible incarceration, for violations of regulatory requirements.[24] A criminal action, however, may be filed only by Justice Department lawyers, who must observe all of the constitutional protections available to any criminal defendant. Agencies therefore tend to rely on criminal prosecutions only as a last resort to punish the most recalcitrant scofflaws.

An equally severe penalty for agencies that administer licensing programs is revocation of the license or permit.[25] Although this penalty does not require Justice Department approval, it invariably generates fierce resistance from licensees. Because a federal permit or license is the equivalent of property, revocation ordinarily requires a formal hearing in which the agency has the burden of demonstrating that the regulatee has egregiously violated the terms and conditions of the license or that conditions have so dramatically changed that the product or activity no longer meets the statutory standards. As with criminal sanctions, agencies are generally quite reluctant to invoke the "death penalty" of license revocation.

Agencies can also request injunctive relief from federal courts.[26] In most cases, the relief consists of little more than a court order to comply with the agency's regulations, but once the injunction is issued, any future violations are immediately punishable as a contempt of court. Sometimes courts grant more innovative injunctive remedies to remediate the consequences of past practices or to ensure a proper degree of remorse. Injunctive relief does not, however, include awards of damages to compensate victims of unlawful practices.

Most regulatory agencies may also seek civil penalties from courts in amounts specified in their statutes.[27] These penalties are in the nature of fines for violations that do not reach the level of criminal conduct, and they are intended primarily to provide regulatees with an incentive to comply with the regulations. Indeed, some statutes even provide for setting the amount of the civil penalty at a level just above the amount that the regulatee saved by failing to comply with applicable regulatory requirements.[28] The goal is to take away any incentive to save money by violating the law.

A few of the modern environmental statutes empower citizens to initiate enforcement actions in court by seeking injunctive relief or civil penalties for continuing violations of federal agency regulations or permit requirements.[29] They also allow citizens to recover attorneys' fees and litigation expenses, but not compensatory damages.[30] These statutes typically require the citizen to step aside if the federal government elects to take over the enforcement action.[31] Furthermore, any civil penalties that the court assesses go to the United States Treasury, not into the pockets of the citizens who brought the actions.[32] None of the statutes of relevance to the preemption war, however, contain citizen enforcement provisions.

Finally, some agencies may address violations of their regulatory requirements by invoking special remedial tools that Congress has made available to them for particular purposes. The Food and Drug Administration, for example, may seize adulterated food and drugs and hold them out of commerce pending an adjudicatory hearing on the merits of the adulteration claims.[33] EPA may issue a "stop sale" order immediately, preventing the sale or use of a pesticide, and it may seize any pesticide that is adulterated or misbranded.[34] The National Highway Traffic Safety Administration and the Consumer Product Safety Commission can order regulatees to "recall" products with unanticipated dangerous attributes for repairs or replacement.[35] Congress has even authorized some agencies to conduct their own administrative proceedings for enforcing administrative orders and collecting administrative penalties, using administrative law judges rather than federal courts and juries.[36]

Regulatory Reform

Not long after Congress wrote the modern consumer and environmental protection statutes, the companies and trade associations that had initially opposed those laws began vigorously to resist their implementation. President Ronald Reagan, who could credit his election in part to an effective campaign against the federal bureaucracy, made "regulatory relief" one of the four primary goals of his "economic recovery program."[37] He quickly signed an executive order requiring all Executive Branch agencies to prepare a comprehensive analysis of the costs and benefits of several alternatives for every major rulemaking initiative. When not inconsistent with the agency's statute, the agency was obliged to choose the alternative with the greatest net benefits.[38] Subsequent executive orders required agencies to analyze takings, trade, federalism, and family impacts of regulations.[39] The Reagan administration's efforts to achieve substantive regulatory reforms, however, were surprisingly unsuccessful.[40]

The next wave of regulatory reform hit in 1995, after the electorate returned the Republican Party to power in the House of Representatives. The "Contract with America" that most of the Republican candidates signed during the 1994 campaign promised to enact regulatory reform legislation within the first one hundred days of the new Congress. The House passed omnibus regulatory reform legislation and a separate Unfunded Mandates Act within that time limit.[41] In the following weeks, it passed comprehensive amendments to many of the modern consumer and environmental protection statutes. The pace was much slower in the Senate, however, and the omnibus regulatory reform legislation died after a fierce floor debate in July 2005. Few of the comprehensive changes to the consumer and environmental protection statutes that passed the House even made it to the Senate floor. After President Clinton twice vetoed appropriations bills containing a group of controversial regulatory reform riders in a confrontation that closed down much of the federal government for several weeks at the end of 1995, the regulatory reform initiative in the 104th Congress fizzled.[42] Congress made a few relatively modest changes to a few statutes in 1996, but it left the basic structure of the modern regulatory state intact.

The George W. Bush administration did not undertake any comprehensive legislative regulatory reform initiatives, and Congress remained relatively inactive with respect to federal regulation during the first seven years of the twenty-first century. The Bush administration did, however, initiate a number of administrative changes designed to reduce the burden of federal regulation on American business. For example, President Bush quietly amended the Clinton administration's regulatory review executive order to force agencies to identify particular instances of "market failure" to justify promulgating regulations, and it broadened the scope of OMB review to include review of requirements and suggestions contained in policy guidance documents.[43] As we shall see in Chapter 6, most of the Bush administration's regulatory relief initiatives proceeded quietly as the politically appointed leadership of the regulatory agencies implemented less protective policies with respect to existing regulations, redirected resources away from monitoring and enforcement, and declined to put new requirements into place. Until the Vioxx fiasco placed FDA's failures in full public focus, that agency had emphasized its fast track approval process and neglected its postapproval monitoring and enforcement responsibilities. And the Occupational Safety and Health Administration did not promulgate a single significant occupational health standard during the entire first term of the George W. Bush administration.

COMMON LAW LIABILITY

The primary role of federal consumer and environmental regulation is to protect the public from fraud and risk-producing products and activities. The regulatory process focuses primarily on the entities responsible for subjecting society to risks and not on the potential victims. The interests of the victims are of course relevant to regulatory standard-setting, but they weigh into the standard-setting process only to the extent that harm to those interests is deemed "unacceptable" under the criteria specified in the governing statute. The regulatory agency does not ordinarily concern itself with assisting those who have been harmed as a result of violations of its requirements or as a consequence of the agency's determination that the risks that resulted in harm were "acceptable."

The primary function of the common law of torts, by contrast, is to force defendants to compensate plaintiffs for losses caused by the defendants' products or activities in cases where the relevant legal principles demand that the losses be shifted from the latter to the former.[44] When the legal principles require that loss be shifted on the basis of fault, this compensation function is called "corrective justice."[45] The loss-shifting function of the common law also operates indirectly to provide incentives to potential defendants to redesign their products or modify their conduct in ways that will avoid common law liability in the future. The legal literature refers to this capacity of the common law to induce modifications in products or activities as the common law's "deterrence" or "incentive" function. Because it closely parallels the protective function of federal regulation, however, we will refer to it as the "protective justice" function of the common law.[46]

CORRECTIVE JUSTICE AND PROTECTIVE JUSTICE IN THE COMMON LAW OF TORTS

The term "corrective justice" has its origin in the distinction that Aristotle drew between "distributive justice" (the just allocation of wealth among the members of a polity) and "corrective justice" (the correction of unjust changes in wealth that result from interactions among the members of a polity). The purpose of corrective justice is "to redress unjust gains and losses by means of a financial adjustment."[47] Professor Christopher Schroeder suggests that in order to achieve corrective justice, the common law of torts must meet three conditions: "(1) individual liability must be assessed consistently with moral norms of responsibility for one's actions; (2) victims must be made whole (compensated); and (3) the resources for satisfying (2) must come exclusively from the liability payments required by (1)."[48]

In some fairly rare factual settings, the common law also has an insurance-like "risk spreading" function that facilitates the transfer of wealth from the beneficiaries of a product or practice to those who are harmed by it.[49] This risk spreading role goes beyond corrective justice because it does not explicitly focus on wrongdoing. Risk spreading is a primary function of common law claims based on strict liability for abnormally dangerous activities. The defendants who engage in such activities are not wrongdoers. To the contrary, what they do contributes more to society than it takes away; otherwise, it would presumably be prohibited. Nevertheless, the enterprise should "pay its own way" by compensating the unavoidable victims. Because the conduct that gives rise to the liability does not violate moral norms, however, the risk spreading function of the common law is not corrective justice.

Prior to the 1970s, judges and legal scholars emphasized the corrective justice function of tort law.[50] By providing a comprehensible analytical vehicle for predicting how different rules of tort law might affect incentives, the "law and economics" movement of the 1970s offered an instrumental approach to structuring liability rules in ways that could provide a degree of protective justice, as well. For many law and economics scholars, however, economic analysis could also play the normative role of achieving an *efficient* allocation of limited societal resources. In their view, an interaction between two individuals that results in a gain of wealth by one and a loss of wealth by the other is a good one if the gain exceeds the loss, irrespective of the moral norms that underlie corrective justice.[51] Put simply, society is better off after such an interaction from the standpoint of allocative efficiency (overall wealth maximization) if the winner wins more than the loser loses.

From this perspective, the primary role of the common law of torts is to readjust wealth in cases in which the defendant has acted inefficiently by manufacturing a product or engaging in an activity for which the risks imposed on society exceed the benefits to society. The point of compensation in such lawsuits is not to achieve corrective justice but to steer private conduct in the direction of an efficient allocation of resources. Thus, the role of the common law is precisely the same as the role that the law and economics scholars would allow for regulatory law—to provide incentives for those engaged in risk-producing activities to act efficiently. Indeed, if the common law rules are clear enough, lawsuits should be necessary only on rare occasions to reinforce the efficiency-enhancing message of the common law.[52] Likewise, if regulatory law is working properly, there should be no need for common law at all, because there will never be a case in which regulation has not already achieved an efficient allocation of resources, and any resulting losses are efficient losses for which compensation is not needed to achieve greater efficiency. In a world in which efficiency is the only goal and the regulatory system is functioning efficiently, preemption of an entirely duplicative and potentially conflicting state common law regime appears quite sensible.[53]

It is possible, however, to imagine a more modest role for protective justice that recognizes the power of the common law to steer private sector conduct in socially desirable directions without limiting that power to the single goal of achieving allocative efficiency. Professor Gary T. Schwartz notes that "[i]f accident prevention is an economic goal, it is also a generous, warm-hearted compassionate and humane goal" that exceeds the limits that some economists would place on it.[54] The common law can pursue corrective justice goals by making victims of risk-producing products and activities whole at the expense of those who profit from those products and activities while at the same time structuring the rules governing compensation to provide incentives to protect future victims. One of the goals of protective justice might be allocative efficiency, but another might be to achieve a precautionary margin of safety or even to attain some degree of wealth redistribution beyond that required by corrective justice by "spreading the risk" of socially desirable but risky activities across all of the beneficiaries and victims of those activities.

The foregoing admittedly dense analysis is relevant to the preemption war for two reasons. First, insofar as the federal government's regulatory standards preempt state common law remedies without providing an alternative compensation regime, preemption completely eliminates the corrective justice role that common law courts have played in this country since its founding. Congress may have valid reasons for denying injured citizens the corrective justice to which the common law entitles them. For example, Congress may decide that corrective justice is not a proper social goal in situations where private entities have complied with regulatory standards. Or, Congress may decide that some victims do not deserve corrective justice at the expense of some risk producers. Because a robust system for obtaining corrective justice is critical to a polity's health, however, this is not a decision that Congress should make lightly, and we should not presume that Congress has delegated that critical decision to a regulatory agency that does not concern itself at all with corrective justice goals.

Second, when federal regulatory standards preempt the common law, they also deprive the polity of the reinforcing role that the common law courts play in providing protective justice. Without the incentive provided by common law rules, private entities will be guided only by the incentives provided by the regulatory laws. A decision to preempt the common law not only presumes that the federal standard is the only appropriate standard but also assumes that the regulatory agency has accurately reflected congressional intent in promulgating the standard, that the agency is actively enforcing the standard to minimize violations, and that the penalties for the violations that are detected are steep enough to provide an acceptable degree of protective deterrence. As we shall see in Chapter 7, neither the presumption nor the attendant assumptions are necessarily warranted in today's less-than-robust regulatory state.

Five Theories of Common Law Liability

The common law of torts has been an evolving body of largely judge-made law since at least the fourteenth century. The courts of England were empowered to dispense the King's justice through an arcane system of writs that limited judicial power to specifically crafted claims. A plaintiff claiming to be damaged by the act or omission of the defendant or one of the defendant's agents petitioned the King's courts for relief. If the plaintiff proved that the facts fit the requirements of the relevant writ, the court would order relief, ordinarily in the form of damages compensating the plaintiff for his loss but occasionally in the form of an injunction requiring the defendant to behave differently in the future.[55] By the mid-nineteenth century, the common law of torts had evolved into three broad substantive bodies of law that imposed liability for intentionally caused harm, for negligently caused harm, and, in some special cases, for innocently caused harm. A fourth body of tort law imposing liability on manufacturers and sellers of consumer products emerged in the mid-twentieth century.

Two elements of American tort law have traditionally distinguished it from the tort law of most other developed countries. The first is the unique and powerful role played by the common law jury. Enshrined in the Seventh Amendment to the United States Constitution and in virtually every state constitution, the right to a jury trial in civil cases ensures that the entity that determines the facts and applies the relevant legal principles to those facts is a group of six to twelve adult men and women chosen by the parties from a pool of randomly selected citizens. The jury dispenses justice between private litigants on the basis of testimony presented at trial pursuant to instructions on the applicable law provided by judges, who are appointed in some states and elected in others.

A second distinguishing element of American common law is the freedom with which the principles of common law liability have evolved over time as courts apply legal principles derived from previously decided cases to the unique facts presented in the cases before them. Although legislatures can, and occasionally do, determine the general rules to be applied in various situations, they rarely attempt to codify an entire body of tort law into a static set of rules to be applied in all cases. Most important, from the perspective of this book, legislatures never delegate to a subordinate executive branch agency the power to prescribe the substantive rules for courts to apply in individual cases.

When a federal statute or regulation completely preempts state common law, the evolving system of common law is replaced by a legislative or administrative judgment about the legal acceptability of a product or activity. A plaintiff who has suffered harm because of products or activities that comply with the statutory or regulatory requirements may seek a remedy only if the legislature has provided an alternative vehicle for seeking relief. Otherwise, a damaged plaintiff must bear the loss or seek relief through extralegal means. As a procedural matter, a defendant who thinks that a plaintiff's claim is preempted will raise that issue early in the litigation, by way of either a motion to dismiss the case or a motion for "summary judgment" on the applicable law. The parties will brief the issue, and sometimes the court will hear oral argument. All of this typically happens long before a jury is empaneled. If the trial court agrees with the defendant, it will dismiss the case, and a jury will never address the plaintiff's complaint.

Intentional Torts. When a person has intentionally caused another to suffer loss, the case for compensation is strongest. Absent some good reason for regarding that intentional imposition of loss as privileged or otherwise socially acceptable, the damaged victim should be able to invoke the civil justice system to shift his loss to the one who intentionally caused it. The common law of torts will yield this result if the plaintiff proves that the defendant acted intentionally and that the relevant facts fit the elements that the common law has established for battery, assault, false imprisonment, trespass, or intentional infliction of severe emotional distress.[56] The fact that all of these torts have analogues in the criminal law of assault and battery, false imprisonment, trespass, and extortion has never motivated the courts to abandon the common law, even though both systems are intended to discourage the same conduct. Corrective justice considerations keep the common law courts open to civil claims, and those courts have not been noticeably concerned about any "overdeterrence" that might result from forcing intentional tortfeasors to compensate damaged plaintiffs for conduct that also subjects them to criminal sanctions.

Likewise, while federal statutes and regulatory programs certainly encompass many kinds of conduct that also constitute intentional torts, defendants rarely argue that common law claims for intentional torts are preempted by federal statutes or regulations. Only the tort of intentional infliction of severe emotional distress has resulted in significant preemption litigation. Interestingly, that tort is a relatively recent addition to the arsenal of claims available to plaintiffs, having come into its own only during the second half of the twentieth century. According to the generally accepted definition provided by the *Re-*

statement (Second) of Torts, a person who "by extreme and outrageous conduct intentionally or recklessly causes severe emotional distress to another is subject to liability for such emotional distress."[57] As we shall see in Chapter 4, defendants have argued that claims for intentional infliction of emotional distress are preempted by the National Labor Relations Act and the Labor Management Relations Act in the context of disputes between workers and employers and by various other statutes in the context of employer retaliation against whistleblowers. With these limited exceptions, the intentional torts are only marginally relevant to the preemption war.

Negligence. The "garden variety" common law tort action is one in which the plaintiff claims that the defendant has behaved negligently. To prevail, the plaintiff must establish that the defendant owed a duty to the plaintiff, that the defendant breached that duty, and that that breach proximately caused damage to one or more of the plaintiff's legally protected interests.[58] Ordinarily, a person has a duty to behave reasonably with respect to the interests of others in conducting his activities but does not have a duty to come to another's aid.[59] A duty may arise, however, when a person realizes or should realize that his conduct "involves an unreasonable risk of harm to another through the conduct of . . . a third person who intended to cause harm, even though such conduct is criminal."[60] Plaintiffs have alleged that manufacturers of assault handguns, for example, negligently marketed them to criminals through dealers who were known to be unscrupulous violators of firearms sales laws.[61] As we shall see in Chapter 5, Congress, in 2005, decided to preempt most of these claims in the Protection of Lawful Commerce in Arms Act.

The standard of care that the jury ordinarily applies in a negligence action is that of the reasonable person in the same or similar circumstances.[62] When a statute or regulation is applicable to the defendant's conduct, the fact that the defendant violated the statute is usually evidence of negligence. In most states, a showing by the plaintiff that the purpose of the statute or regulation was to protect a class of persons that includes the plaintiff and to protect the interest that was invaded will shift the burden to the defendant to show that the violation was excused.[63] The defendant may likewise introduce evidence that it has complied with an applicable statute or regulation, but the generally accepted common law rule is that "[c]ompliance with a legislative enactment or an administrative regulation does not prevent a finding of negligence where a reasonable man would take additional precautions."[64] The rationale for this important difference in treatment is that since "legislatures and regulatory agencies normally set safety standards at minimally acceptable levels," juries should be allowed to conclude that the defendant should have taken additional measures to protect potential plaintiffs.[65]

Defendants have never been especially happy with this state of the law, because it allows important decisions about the usefulness of valuable products with national markets to turn on the assessment not "of pharmacologists at the FDA, or toxicologists at the EPA, or mechanical engineers at the FAA, but of the juror, pulled off the voter lists at random."[66] A 1991 study commissioned by the American Law Institute (ALI) recommended that common law courts recognize a "government standards" or "regulatory compliance" defense that would provide a liability shield for products that comply with the regulatory requirements of a state or federal agency.[67] The ALI did not pursue this recommendation, however, and the courts have not moved perceptibly in that direction.[68]

Nuisance. The common law of nuisance is a rather nebulously defined catch-all category of common law liability that permits courts to address activities that create conditions that are annoying or harmful to others. A "public nuisance" action may be filed by a representative of the public or an individual who has suffered unique harm against one who engages in conduct that constitutes an "unreasonable interference with a right common to the general public." One important consideration in determining whether an activity constitutes a public nuisance is "whether the conduct is proscribed by a statute, ordinance or administrative regulation." Beyond that, the fact finder must consider the extent to which the conduct "involves a significant interference with the public health, the public safety, the public peace, the public comfort or the public convenience."[69] A "private nuisance" action is available to an owner of land who has suffered significant interference with his use and enjoyment of his property due to the defendant's intentional or unreasonable conduct.[70] Since the remedy for a public nuisance is typically an order requiring the defendant to take particular action designed to abate the nuisance, the law of public nuisance offers perhaps the most easily accessible route for plaintiffs seeking to persuade judges to create regulatory regimes to supplement, or even replace, existing regulatory programs. Private nuisance, on the other hand, is of little relevance to the preemption war.

Strict Liability for Abnormally Dangerous Activities. Strict liability for abnormally dangerous activities has its origins in the common law rules that govern the liability of owners of animals other than pets that are likely to do harm to someone (or his crops) if they leave the owner's property. The famous nineteenth-century British case *Rylands v. Fletcher* extended that liability to uncommon uses of private property that result in the escape of water or other material that may cause great harm.[71] In both cases, the landowner was liable irrespective of the degree of care that he exercised to keep the animals or other materials on his property. Reflecting the evolution of the rule in many states, the *Restatement (Second) of Torts* provides that "[o]ne who carries on an abnormally dangerous activity is subject to liability for harm to the person, land or chattels of another resulting from the activity, although he has exercised the utmost care to prevent the harm."[72] The courts are responsible for determining whether activities are "abnormally dangerous," and the *Restatement* suggests five factors for the judges to consider in that regard.[73] In the preemption context, defendants have maintained that federal regulatory programs preempted strict liability claims involving the use of radioactive materials, a classic example of an abnormally dangerous activity, and claims involving the use of assault handguns by criminals, a relatively novel use of the concept.

Products Liability. Adhering strictly to the principle of caveat emptor, the nineteenth-century common law did not impose liability on sellers of products outside of express or implied warranties made to consumers of those products. American courts in the 1960s and early 1970s adapted implied warranty concepts from the law of contracts to the tort law governing liability for negligently designed and manufactured products to create a law of strict liability for defective products.[74] Under the widely relied upon articulation of this doctrinal merger in the *Restatement (Second) of Torts,* a person who "sells any product in a defective condition unreasonably dangerous to the user or consumer or to his property is subject to liability for physical harm thereby caused to the ultimate user or consumer, or to his property," even though the seller "has exercised all possible care in the preparation and sale of his product."[75] In an explanatory comment, the *Restatement* clarifies that a defective condition is "a condition not contemplated by the ultimate consumer."[76] The importance of "consumer expectations" in applying the rule reflected the warranty-like considerations that influenced the evolution of tort law, and it rapidly became the dominant test for product defectiveness. The test was "objective" in that it turned not on what any particular plaintiff expected but on what a reasonable consumer in the plaintiff's position would have expected in the way of safety or warnings.[77]

Another explanatory comment created an important qualifier for "unavoidably unsafe" products. The comment noted the existence of "some products which, in the present state of human knowledge, are quite incapable of being made safe for their intended and ordinary use" and cited drugs and vaccines as examples. When "properly prepared, and accompanied by proper directions and warning," these products are not defective and should not be regarded as unreasonably dangerous.[78] Since the courts have for the most part followed this advice, the primary focus in products liability cases involving food, drugs, cosmetics, cigarettes, and the like has been on the manufacturer's duty to provide proper warnings and instructions. Consequently, a claim that a federal regulation governing the warnings that must accompany such products preempts state common law actions is effectively a claim that the entire field of products liability is preempted.[79]

By the mid-1990s, the American law of products liability was, in the words of Professor Jean Stapleton, a "bewildering array of conflicting cases" that reflected a continuing disagreement among the courts and legal scholars over the extent to which the law of products liability should give effect to consumer expectations or should attempt primarily to achieve economically efficient outcomes through a "risk-utility" test that closely paralleled the cost-benefit paradigm that economists advocate for federal regulatory programs.[80] Proponents of the risk-utility test argued that consumer expectations could be ill informed or reflect biases and prejudices that lead to irrational results when incorporated into an after-the-fact test for liability. The risk-utility test, in their view, relied "less on intuition and more on a balancing of articulated considerations regarding the relative advantages and disadvantages of the product as designed and as it alternatively could have been designed."[81] The risk-utility advocates prevailed in one important forum when the American Law Institute appointed two strong critics of the consumer expectation test to undertake an effort to "restate" the common law of products liability.[82]

The *Restatement (Third) of Products Liability,* published on May 20, 1997, demotes consumer expectations to a relatively minor consideration in most product design cases and elevates the risk-utility test to prominence.[83] Avoiding any reference at all to "strict liability," the *Restatement (Third)* articulation subjects to liability anyone "engaged in the business of selling or otherwise distributing products" for harm to persons or property damage caused by "a defective product." A "defect" must fall into one of three fairly restrictive categories—(1) a "manufacturing defect" that occurs when the product "departs from its intended design"; (2) a design defect that results "when the foreseeable risks of harm posed by the product could have been reduced or avoided by the adoption of a reasonable alternative design . . . and the omission of the alternative design renders the product not reasonably safe"; or (3) a warning defect that occurs "because of inadequate instructions or warnings when the foreseeable risks of harm posed by the product could have been reduced or avoided by the provision of reasonable instructions or warnings . . . and the omission of the instructions or warnings renders the product not reasonably safe."[84] Only the latter two types of defect are relevant to the preemption war.

The *Restatement (Third)* also departs from its predecessor in specifically addressing prescription drugs and medical devices. It provides that a drug or device is inadequately designed only if "the foreseeable risks of harm" are sufficiently great in relation to its foreseeable therapeutic benefits "that *reasonable health-care providers,* knowing of such foreseeable risks and therapeutic benefits, would not prescribe the drug or medical device for *any* class of patients." Similarly, a prescription drug or medical device is unreasonably unsafe due to inadequate instructions or warnings only "if reasonable instructions or warnings regarding foreseeable risks of harm are not provided to . . . prescribing and other health-care providers who are in a position to reduce the risks . . . or the patient when the manufacturer knows or has reason to know that health-care providers will not be in a position to reduce the risks of harm in accordance with instructions or warnings."[85]

In a comment providing their rationale for the very limited role that they assign to tort law in the special case of drugs and devices, the *Restatement* authors express their view that the courts had traditionally been reluctant to impose liability for inadequate design and warnings on manufacturers of prescription drugs and devices because prescribing physicians were "learned intermediaries" who could ensure that "the right drugs and medical devices reach the right patients" and because "government regulatory agencies adequately review new prescription drugs and devices, keeping unreasonably dangerous designs off the market."[86] Thus, to the extent that such claims are not preempted at the outset, the fact of FDA approval powerfully affects the standard of care for drugs and devices under the *Restatement (Third)* approach. Another comment, however, cautions that manufacturers of drugs and devices "have the responsibility to perform reasonable testing prior to marketing a product and to discover risks and risk-avoidance measures that such testing would reveal," thereby opening the door to liability for inadequate testing and surveillance on the part of drug manufacturers.[87]

The judicial and scholarly reception accorded the *Restatement (Third)*'s substitution of the risk-utility test for the consumer expectation test has been decidedly mixed. While some courts have embraced the change, others have remained "deeply suspicious" of what many scholars view as a thinly veiled attempt to enhance the role of experts and limit the role of juries.[88] The comparative advantage of experts over juries in determining the adequacy of consumer warnings is especially controversial, because "warnings are indisputably *supposed* to be understandable by a member of the general public."[89] As we shall see in Chapter 7, this dispute parallels the battle in the preemption war over whether the judgments of experts in federal agencies should preempt those of common law juries.

Critics also argued that the ALI "virtually without debate" reversed "thirty-five years of safety-advancing products-liability law" when it prescribed a separate test for drugs and devices that depended upon whether a reasonable doctor would prescribe it for *any* use, whether or not the use for which the plaintiff took the drug was a use for which a reasonable physician would prescribe it. This allowed a drug manufacturer to escape liability even in cases in which it knew full well that doctors would prescribe the drug for uses that had not received FDA approval. In their view, the special liability standard was "a kind of 'super-negligence,' requiring plaintiff to establish that the product should not have been marketed at all."[90] One of the *Restatement* reporters, however, responded that the courts owed "substantial deference to a marketplace for prescription drugs that appears to function almost perfectly," a proposition with which Susan Halverson might disagree.[91]

A much less controversial provision of the *Restatement (Third) of Products Liability* addresses the effect of statutes and regulation on common law litigation. A product's noncompliance with an applicable safety standard or regulation automatically "renders the product defective with respect to the risks sought to be reduced by the statute or regulation." Compliance with a statute or regulation, on the other hand, "is properly considered" in determining whether the product is defective, but "such compliance does not preclude as a matter of law a finding of product defect."[92] This provision has drawn little criticism because it so clearly reflects the existing precedent in nearly every state.[93] It is, however, entirely inconsistent with the FDA's claim that all common law actions based on a drug manufacturer's failure to warn are preempted when the warnings comply with FDA's requirements.

Three Forms of Common Law Relief

Having concluded that the plaintiff is entitled to relief, a common law court has the power to administer a wide variety of remedies, ranging from compensatory damages to sophisticated injunctive relief that can look very much like the regulations that agencies typically promulgate. If the court decides that compensatory damages are appropriate, the jury will determine the amount of the damages. If it decides to award injunctive relief, the court itself will fashion the remedy on the basis of its assessment of the equities of the situation. Finally, the court has the option of allowing the jury to consider awarding the plaintiff punitive damages on top of compensatory damages to punish a defendant for especially egregious conduct. Juries determine the amount of punitive damages, but courts frequently reduce awards that they believe to be out of line.

Compensatory Damages. The purpose of compensatory damages is to achieve corrective justice by compensating the plaintiff for his loss. Compensatory damages are available for medical expenses and loss of income due to personal injury, for losses due to temporary and permanent disability, for objectively determinable mental distress, for wrongful death, and for property damage.[94] Some courts even allow recovery for extra medical monitoring required by exposure to toxic substances that subject plaintiffs to chronic risks. Purely economic loss, however, is ordinarily not recoverable.[95]

Injunctive Relief. An injunction is a command issued by a court to a defendant to act or refrain from acting in a particular way. The order is backed up by the court's power to hold the defendant in contempt of court and to fine or incarcerate him as a sanction. In the common law context, the purpose of injunctive relief is to achieve protective justice by preventing the defendant from harming the plaintiff and/or others in the future. The traditional common law rule was that injunctive relief was not appropriate when relief in the form of damages was "adequate." Although this rule of thumb is honored more in its breach in modern times, it is nevertheless rare for a court to provide injunctive relief in run-of-the-mill common law cases. In the rare cases in which courts do so, sophisticated injunctive relief can be virtually indistinguishable from regulatory standards.[96]

Punitive Damages. The purpose of punitive damages is to punish defendants who engage in especially egregious conduct and to send a strong message to potential future defendants that similar conduct will not be tolerated. They also ensure that consumers are fully compensated for their loss, including attorneys' fees, which are ordinarily not recoverable as a separate item of damages. Punitive damages are available in the case of intentional torts, but, for claims based in negligence or strict liability, the plaintiff must prove that the defendant "was guilty of flagrantly disregarding" the plaintiff's legally protected interests.[97]

Because large punitive damage awards are often highly publicized, even though they are nearly always subsequently reduced by the courts, they are an easy target for the tort reform efforts described later. Many state legislatures have limited the availability of punitive damages in cases where the defendant has complied with an applicable statutory or regulatory requirement, and others have placed explicit caps on punitive damages in cases in which they are allowed. Moreover, the U.S. Supreme Court has interpreted the Due Process Clause of the United States Constitution to require trial courts to instruct juries properly on the functions of punitive damages and to allow appellate courts to review such awards with special care to ensure that the ratio of punitive damages to compensatory damages is reasonable.[98]

THE PREEMPTION WAR AS TORT REFORM

The companies that found themselves subject to the threat of multiple damage awards in the wake of the rapid development of law in the 1960s and 1970s did not take these changes lying down. By the early 1980s, various industry trade associations joined the Chamber of Commerce and industry-funded think tanks to launch a broad "tort reform" initiative in Congress and state legislatures aimed at relieving American business of what they regarded to be "frivolous" common law claims. In 1996, for example, President Clinton vetoed a comprehensive bill, entitled the Common Sense Product Liability Legal Reform Act, that would have "significantly altered" many aspects of state common law and preempted any state law to the contrary. Advocates of tort reform were more successful in state legislatures, where they secured the enactment of a number of substantive "reforms," including brief statutes of limitations, caps on punitive damages, restrictions on the liability of doctors, retailers, and other favored constituencies, and regulatory compliance defenses like the Michigan law discussed in Chapter 1.[99]

The changes achieved through tort reform legislation had a powerful impact on some substantive areas, including medical malpractice and mass torts, but they left most of the substance of negligence and products liability law relatively untouched. More important, the tort reform movement did not have a significant impact at all in some states where legislatures were not especially receptive to the demands of business interests for relief from lawsuits brought by local plaintiffs. By the end of the 1990s, it was clear that serious change would have to come at the national level and that it would have to preempt state common law. While the business community continued to press for national legislation preempting both entire fields of tort law and discrete but highly contested areas of law, such as liability for leaking gasoline additives, it also expanded the preemption war to a new battle front occupied by regulatory agencies. At the same time, tort reform organizations were filing amicus curiae, or "friend of the court," briefs in individual cases urging federal courts to expand longstanding legal doctrine to preempt state common law claims that arguably conflicted with federal agency licenses and regulations.

According to the respected torts scholar David G. Owen, "the defense of federal preemption in recent years has grown from little more than a blip on the radar screen to one of the most powerful defenses in all of products liability law." This has not been a desirable development, in his view, because "the law on federal preemption has obstinately refused to set anchor in enduring principles" but has instead continued to "wallow in a state of utter chaos."[100] Most experts in the law of preemption agree with Professor Owen.[101] It is to that chaotic body of law that we now turn.

Chapter 3 The Law and Politics of Preemption

Before proceeding to the battlefields of the preemption war, we must first ascend to a nearby hill to obtain a broader view of the lay of the land. In this case, the relevant terrain is the arcane federal law of preemption. Since Congress can change nearly any judicial resolution of a preemption issue, the primary focus of this book is on the debates over whether federal agency preemption of state common law claims is a good or bad idea in various regulatory contexts. Some familiarity with judicial doctrine is necessary, however, to understand how the preemption war has been waged in the courts and to figure out how Congress could change the relevant laws to fix some of the unfortunate messes that the combatants have left behind on the judicial battlefield.

THE POWER TO PREEMPT AND THE PRESUMPTION AGAINST PREEMPTION

Under the Supremacy Clause of the United States Constitution, laws duly enacted by the Congress of the United States are the "supreme Law of the Land" and therefore binding on state and federal courts, state laws "to the contrary notwithstanding."[1] Hence, when Congress in the valid exercise of its constitutional powers enacts legislation, it is "empowered to pre-empt state law by so stating in express terms,"[2] and it has exercised that power hundreds of times since the dawn of the Republic.[3] According to a 2006 report issued by the National Academy of Public Administration, "[f]ederal preemption of state and local responsibilities has grown rapidly in the past 40 years and will likely continue to grow."[4] Congress can also expressly delegate the power to preempt to federal agencies, but it does so only very rarely.[5]

If the principles underlying express preemption were the only law applicable to the preemption war, the following discussion would be difficult enough for a reader who is unfamiliar with the Supreme Court's preemption jurisprudence. Unfortunately, the Court has also created an entirely separate body of "implied preemption" law in which the courts divine congressional intent not by interpreting an express preemption clause but by comparing the federal statute's overall language and purpose to the operative aspects of the applicable state law. The fact that both the Supreme Court and the courts of appeals have applied both bodies of law inconsistently further complicates the following analysis.[6] Thus, in addition to providing the underlying legal setting for the preemption war, the following pages should clarify why the judicial branch will remain a critical battlefield in that war.

Under the well-known 1938 case *Erie Railroad Co. v. Tompkins*,[7] federal courts must apply state law to state common law claims. The Court stated in no uncertain terms that "Congress has no power to declare substantive rules of common law applicable in a State, whether they be local in their nature or 'general,' be they commercial law or a part of the law of torts."[8] Congress may, however, exercise its power under the Commerce Clause to create a federal regulatory regime to govern interstate commerce in various products and/or activities. Under the Supremacy Clause, Congress may preempt state common law that is inconsistent with federal law as articulated in a statute or by a federal agency pursuant to congressionally delegated powers. The bottom line is that the federal courts must apply state law in adjudicating common law claims, unless Congress has preempted state common law.[9]

The Supreme Court has, however, created a presumption against preemption when Congress legislates in "a field which the States have traditionally occupied."[10] Thus, "[i]n areas of traditional state regulation," the courts "assume that a federal statute has not supplanted state law unless Congress has made such intention 'clear and manifest.'"[11] The presumption applies with special force when defendants contend that Congress has preempted state common law remedies and Congress has not replaced the state common law regime with a federal cause of action or some other alternate administrative compensation regime.[12] Most students of preemption, however, agree with Professor Viet Dinh that the "actual strength" of the presumption against preemption "is a matter of considerable doubt."[13] If all of the "howevers" in the preceding two paragraphs suggest that the law of federal preemption lacks a clear guiding compass, we may perhaps gain a better sense of the lay of the land from the statutes and foundational Supreme Court cases.

EXPRESS PREEMPTION OF STATE COMMON LAW CLAIMS

When Congress expressly preempts state common law, neither state nor federal courts may entertain claims based on the preempted law. Until quite recently, however, Congress never expressly preempted state common law without providing an alternative route to corrective justice by creating either a separate federal cause of action or an alternative administrative compensation regime.[14] Congress typically created a national compensation regime because it concluded either that the common law of some states inadequately advanced important public policies or that a national system with uniform rules was necessary to ensure the continued availability of valuable products and activities. The discussion in this chapter briefly explores the wide variety of federal compensation regimes and how they fit into the federal regulatory programs to which they are attached. We take up in Chapter 5 more recent congressional efforts to enact express preemption legislation not to provide more effective corrective justice for victims but to shield the business community completely from alleged "lawsuit abuse."

Congress has over the years created several compensation programs to supplement or replace state common law for federally regulated products and activities. One of the earliest was the Federal Employees Liability Act, enacted in 1908 to replace regressive state common law doctrines that shielded railroads from liability with a more "enlightened" federal common law cause of action for workers of interstate common carriers.[15] This progressive model "was not widely influential," and more recent statutes generally serve the dual role of providing limited corrective justice to victims and preventing state common law from discouraging favored industries from manufacturing valuable products.[16]

The National Childhood Vaccination Injury Act (NCVI Act) of 1986, for example, created "a remedial program designed to provide swift compensation for persons injured by vaccines, while ensuring that the nation's supply of vaccines isn't unduly threatened by the costs and risks of litigation."[17] Even though vaccines have always been heavily regulated through a federal licensing regime administered by the Food and Drug Administration, compensation is necessary because most vaccines pose some risk to a small number of susceptible individuals. The statute established a fund from general revenues and a surtax on vaccines that provides compensation on a "no fault" basis to all persons (not just children) who are injured by covered vaccines. Plaintiffs must initially file their claims against vaccine manufacturers and the fund in the Federal Court of Claims, and the vast majority of such claims are resolved in that forum.[18] In cases that involve "avoidable" side effects or noncompliance with Food and Drug Administration requirements, plaintiffs may opt out of the federal system and pursue state common law remedies, with some restrictions on punitive damages.[19] The statute expressly preempts all other state claims, but it also prohibits any state legislature from eliminating state common law claims based on violations of FDA requirements.[20]

The Price-Anderson Act of 1954 established a complex hybrid compensation regime to encourage a reluctant electric utility industry to get into the business of generating nuclear power.[21] The statute explicitly preempts all state law claims arising out of activities that are subject to the comprehensive regulatory regime run by the Nuclear Regulatory Commission (NRC) and replaces them with a hybrid federal cause of action. The common law of the state in which the accident occurs provides the content of the law that the federal court applies, except that no claim may be based on conduct that complies with NRC requirements and no defenses are available at all. Instead, the law provides a general cap on liability of $560 million for any single accident, $500 million of which the federal government agrees to pay.[22] The courts have interpreted the statute to allow claims based on intent and negligence to proceed so long as the standard of care does not vary from NRC standards, but claims based on strict liability are barred because they "act the opposite of a federal safety regulation."[23]

Some modern statutes rely upon administrative compensation regimes run by federal agencies to provide the alternative to state common law.[24] For example, eleven days after the terrorist attacks on the World Trade Center and the Pentagon, Congress created the September 11 Victim Compensation Fund.[25] The fund established an administrative process through which victims and their families might claim on a no-fault basis medical expenses, economic compensation, and limited damages for pain and suffering. Compensation was determined by a judicially supervised "Special Master" on the basis of guidelines that his office developed under the statute. The law preempted all common law claims against defendants other than Al Qaeda and Osama Bin Laden if a claimant accepted compensation from the fund, but potential claimants could opt out of the administrative system and pursue common law remedies subject to prescribed liability caps.[26]

EXPRESS PREEMPTION OF INCONSISTENT STATE "REQUIREMENTS"

Although Congress expressly preempts state common law claims only very rarely, it has enacted dozens of express preemption provisions specifically designed to substitute a federal regulatory regime for potentially inconsistent state laws and regulations.[27] These provisions typically employ terms like "requirements" or "prohibitions" to identify the particular state or federal actions that Congress intended to preempt. Since "'the purpose of Congress is the ultimate touchstone' in every preemption case," the critical preemption question for our purposes is whether such words manifest a congressional intent to preempt state common law claims as well as laws enacted by state legislatures and regulations promulgated by state agencies.[28] In a case involving the federal labor laws, the Supreme Court, in 1959, announced that state regulation "can be as effectively exerted through an award of damages as through some form of preventive relief," because "[t]he obligation to pay compensation can be, indeed is designed to be, a potent method of governing conduct and controlling policy."[29] The Court then opened the door to expansive common law preemption claims in the landmark 1992 case that precipitated the preemption war, *Cipollone v. Liggett Group, Inc.*[30]

For most of the nation's history, the federal government studiously avoided regulating tobacco and tobacco-related products, despite a growing body of scientific evidence that smoking caused lung cancer, heart disease, and other deadly afflictions. This all changed in 1965, when the Federal Trade Commission (FTC) promulgated a regulation requiring cigarette manufacturers to disclose on package labels and advertising the fact that "smoking is dangerous to health and may cause death from cancer and other diseases." Congress reacted to this development by enacting the Federal Cigarette Labeling and Advertising Act of 1965, which voided the FTC regulation and replaced it with a requirement that all packaging (but not advertising) contain a specific warning that "cigarette smoking may be hazardous to your health."[31] Four years later, Congress strengthened the warning requirement and banned cigarette advertising on radio and television. Both the 1965 and the 1969 laws contained express preemption provisions that clearly encompassed state statutes and regulations but did not explicitly mention state common law claims.[32]

Years later, an intrepid lawyer named Marc Edel attempted to recover damages from the tobacco industry for the damage that smoking had caused to a fifty-seven-year-old homemaker named Rose Cipollone. By the time he contacted Cipollone, the pack-a-day smoker had already had two lung cancer operations and was undergoing chemotherapy.[33] In his filings, Edel claimed that the Liggett Company had defectively designed its cigarettes, failed adequately to warn Cipollone of the health risks of cigarette smoking, fraudulently misrepresented its product by using advertising to "neutralize" government-required warnings, conspired with other tobacco companies to hide from state and federal authorities scientific information on the adverse health effects of smoking, and breached express warranties made in advertising and elsewhere that cigarettes did not present any significant health risks.[34]

The extensive discovery that Edel undertook in preparation for the *Cipollone* trial provided the first public glimpse into the hidden world of industry research on the addictive effects of tobacco. Although it was closely followed by health advocates hoping for a breach in the heretofore impenetrable wall of tobacco industry secrecy, the case ultimately turned on the issue of federal preemption of state common law claims. Edel persuaded the jury that Cipollone's heirs (she died before the trial) deserved compensation, but the Supreme Court held that the claim was preempted. A plurality opinion (written by Justice Stevens for four justices) concluded that the purpose of the 1965 Act, which preempted any state law-imposed "statement" related to smoking and health, was to prohibit "state and federal rulemaking bodies from mandating particular cautionary statements," not to preempt "state-law damages actions." However, the language of the 1969 Act preempting state-imposed "requirements or prohibitions," in the plurality's view, "easily encompass[ed] obligations that take the form of common-law rules."[35]

Three dissenting justices (Blackmun, Kennedy, and Souter) and many legal scholars have concluded that the *Cipollone* plurality opinion went off track at precisely this point. The words "prohibition or requirement" call to mind a legal obligation to take or refrain from taking a particular course of action. They do not naturally encompass a latent common law duty to pay damages to someone who is harmed by a violation of the broad common law standard of reasonable care. Indeed, insofar as a common law action seeks damages, rather than injunctive relief, the defendant need not alter its conduct at all so long as it is willing to "accept damages awards as a cost of doing business." Furthermore, the plurality opinion ignored the fact that "tort law has an entirely separate function—compensating victims—that sets it apart from direct forms of regulation." Unlike statutes that replace preempted state common law with an alternative federal compensation regime, the 1969 Act, as construed by the plurality opinion, would divest plaintiffs of *any* compensation for any of the preempted claims.[36] Since Justices Scalia and Thomas agreed with the plurality opinion on this point, however, it represented the conclusion of a majority of the Court.

Prior to *Cipollone,* the Supreme Court had been extremely reluctant to conclude that Congress meant to leave tort victims without a remedy, and it was therefore "willing to tolerate a certain amount of tension between federal regulatory objectives and state tort law." Common law defendants viewed the *Cipollone* opinion as their pathway to deliverance from burdensome common law obligations, and the preemption war was soon under way.[37]

IMPLIED PREEMPTION AND THE DIFFICULTIES OF DIVINING CONGRESSIONAL INTENT

When Congress fails to mention preemption one way or the other in the statute establishing a regulatory program, one might naturally conclude that Congress did not intend for the agency's actions to preempt state law. The Supreme Court, however, has been unwilling to expand the presumption against preemption into a general requirement that Congress speak its mind if it intends to preempt. Instead, the Court has crafted an ornate, and often inconsistent, body of law to decide whether Congress has *impliedly* preempted state law. Not surprisingly, the confusing terrain of implied federal preemption is where the Executive Branch has launched its most aggressive assaults in the preemption war.

The factual setting for one of the most important Supreme Court opinions on implied preemption provided the plot for one of the more memorable dramatic performances of the actress Meryl Streep.[38] On November 5, 1974, a laboratory analyst named Karen Silkwood set off an alarm after she had been grinding and polishing samples composed of the highly radioactive transuranic element plutonium in a glove box at the Kerr-McGee Corporation's plutonium fabrication plant near Crescent, Oklahoma. Tests conducted by the company determined that Silkwood, her roommate, and several rooms of her apartment were contaminated with plutonium. A week later, Silkwood was killed in what the Supreme Court later characterized as an "unrelated automobile accident." Although conspiracy theorists (including the movie's screenwriters) have suggested more sinister explanations for the accident, Silkwood's father sued Kerr-McGee not for her death but for damages to her person and property caused by the plutonium contamination prior to her death.

The trial was a contentious affair in which Silkwood's lawyer presented evidence that the company had frequently violated Nuclear Regulatory Commission (NRC) safety regulations and the company alleged that Silkwood had intentionally removed plutonium from the plant to embarrass it. Despite a formal NRC report exonerating Kerr-McGee, the jury found the company liable to Silkwood's estate for compensatory damages in the amount of $505,000. To this, the jury added $10 million in punitive damages on the basis of its finding that the company was guilty of "oppression, fraud or malice." The trial judge later rejected Kerr-McGee's posttrial contention that its compliance with the relevant federal regulations insulated it from any punitive damages awards.

The Supreme Court began its analysis with a summary of the law of implied preemption that nicely captures that branch of preemption law.[39] First, "[i]f Congress evidences an intent to occupy a given field, any state law falling within that field is pre-empted." This form of implied preemption, referred to as "field preemption," is rarely applicable to state common law claims. Second, "[i]f Congress has not entirely displaced state regulation over the matter in question, state law is still pre-empted to the extent it actually conflicts with federal law." The courts generally subdivide "conflict preemption" into two subcategories. The least controversial type of conflict preemption, called "impossibility" preemption, exists when compliance with both the state law and the federal law is impossible because compliance with state law will cause the actor to violate federal law and visa versa. Under the more contentious form of conflict preemption, called "obstacle preemption," state law is preempted to the extent that it conflicts with federal law because "the state law stands as an obstacle to the accomplishment of the full purposes and objectives of Congress." Most of the legal battles in the preemption war are fought on this exceedingly treacherous terrain of obstacle preemption.

Turning to the Atomic Energy Act, the Court found "no indication that Congress even seriously considered precluding the use of [common law] remedies."[40] This silence took on "added significance in light of Congress' failure to provide any federal remedy for persons injured by" violations of the federal safety requirements. The Court found it "difficult to believe that Congress would, without comment, remove all means of judicial recourse for those injured by illegal conduct." If Congress had intended to preempt state common law claims altogether, why would it have limited the plants' liability under the Price-Anderson Act (described earlier in this chapter)?

The Court also rejected Kerr-McGee's attempt to distinguish punitive damages from compensatory damages. Noting that "[p]unitive damages have long been a part of traditional state tort law," the Court reasoned that Congress must have "assumed that traditional principles of state tort law would apply with full force unless they were expressly supplanted." The Court noted the "tension between the conclusion that safety regulation is the exclusive concern of the federal law and the conclusion that a State may nevertheless award damages based on its own law of liability." It concluded, however, that even if "the award of damages based on the state law . . . is regulatory in the sense that a nuclear plant will be threatened with damages liability if it does not conform to state standards," that "regulatory consequence was something that Congress was willing to accept."

The Department of Justice filed an amicus curiae brief in which it argued that the Atomic Energy Act preempted Oklahoma common law actions because a state jury award of punitive damages would conflict with the NRC's power to impose civil penalties on its licensees for violations of federal standards. The Supreme Court often requests such briefs to obtain the views of the agencies charged with administering the statutes at issue, and the briefs frequently have a powerful influence on the Court's thinking. The four dissenting Justices agreed with the government, concluding that it was "not reasonable to infer that Congress intended to allow juries of lay persons, selected essentially at random, to impose unfocused penalties solely for the purpose of punishment and some undefined deterrence." The majority concluded, however, that paying both civil penalties and punitive damages was certainly not impossible and that exposing licensees to punitive damage awards would not "frustrate any purpose of the federal remedial regime."

Although the Supreme Court in *Silkwood* appeared to take a fairly narrow approach to obstacle preemption, we shall see in Chapter 4 that it has not done so consistently in the ensuing years. Scholars from across the political spectrum have strongly criticized the Supreme Court's jurisprudence in this critical area, and the former Solicitor General Kenneth Starr has suggested that the Court should jettison it altogether.[41] For the time being, however, there is little likelihood that the Court will discard obstacle preemption or that it will offer clear and consistent guidance on the meaning of that malleable concept. Consequently, the treacherous terrain occupied by the law of obstacle preemption will also continue to be highly contested terrain.

THE HORIZONTAL AND VERTICAL POLITICS OF PREEMPTION

The preemption war is by no means limited to the judicial battlefield described earlier. Since Congress has the last word on preemption when it is legislating on questions within its constitutional powers, the preemption war is fundamentally political in nature. Politics also plays a profound role in forming the positions of the Executive Branch on the preemption question, a fact that is clearly demonstrated by the speed with which the agencies change their positions on the issue as administrations change. Thus, an initial foray into the politics of preemption is appropriate at this point to set the stage for the descriptions of the preemption war in the following three chapters and the analysis of the preemption issue in the more analytical chapters that follow them.

The politics of preemption are complex because they operate in two dimensions. The first dimension addresses the *extent* of governmental power over the *private sector* and should be quite familiar to any student of government regulation. It ranges from a "weak government" approach to the relationship between government and private economic actors at one end of the spectrum to a strongly interventionist government approach at the other. Regulatory programs along this dimension range from laissez faire approaches at the weak end of the spectrum to so-called command-and-control approaches, in which a regulatory agency specifies in great detail exactly how private sector actors must go about their business. In between are various "mixed" approaches in which the government promulgates "performance" standards or attempts to steer private sector conduct by creating and applying various positive or negative incentives like subsidies and excise taxes.

When tort law performs its protective justice function through injunctive relief, it is usually operating at the command-and-control end of the government control dimension. When judicial relief is entirely unavailable to victims of private sector risks for either doctrinal reasons (e.g., the absence of a common law duty) or institutional reasons (e.g., the available court's lack of jurisdiction over the defendant), the common law is operating at the laissez faire end of the government control dimension. In between are various doctrinal vehicles for determining whether the courts will force private sector actors to compensate others (i.e., negligence, strict liability, products liability) that operate indirectly to influence private sector conduct through the incentive of avoiding common law liability.

The second dimension of the politics of preemption addresses the *locus* of governmental power and is familiar to students of American federalism. Assuming that that sum total of available governmental power remains constant at any point on the governmental power dimension, that power is divided between the federal government and the state governments. This federalism dimension therefore ranges from a centralized approach to government in which the federal government exercises all of the available governmental power at one end of the spectrum to a decentralized approach in which state and local governments exercise all available governmental power at the other end. Thus, the spectrum ranges from federal regulatory programs that completely preempt state and local regulations at one end to the complete absence of any federal regulatory program at the other. In between are various mixed programs in which both state and federal regulatory agencies are allowed to exercise some (perhaps overlapping) controls.[42]

According to the *Erie* doctrine discussed earlier in this chapter, the common law of torts ordinarily operates at the weak central government end of the federalism dimension. Because there is no federal common law to govern private disputes, federal courts exercising jurisdiction over those disputes must apply the relevant state common law. Congress does, however, have the power to create a federal common law to govern private disputes in federal courts (e.g., the Federal Employers Liability Act for rail workers) or in administrative institutions. And it has the power to preempt state common law with no law at all, thereby eliminating all claims for compensation in both state and federal courts. In between, Congress can create compensation mechanisms that give victims the option to file a claim for compensation in a federal court under certain restrictions or in state court under other restrictions (e.g., the September 11 Victim Compensation Fund).

The crosscutting politics of preemption play out against these two intersecting dimensions. The "vertical" politics of preemption have to do with the allocation of governmental power between the federal government and state governments. The "horizontal" politics of preemption have to do with the allocation of power between the government and the private sector. The horizontal and vertical politics of preemption are somewhat simplistically illustrated in Figure 3.1:

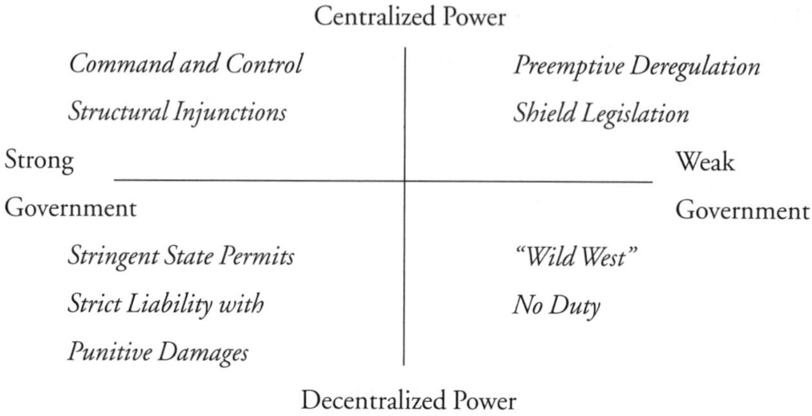

Figure 3.1

The upper left quadrant contains regulatory and common law approaches that involve strong exercises of centralized power. In the regulatory sphere, these are sometimes pejoratively referred to as "Soviet-style command-and-control" regulatory regimes.[43] Since injunctive relief is an especially intrusive intervention in the litigative context, structural federal injunctions of the sort that federal courts have issued to reform schools, jails, and mental institutions belong in this quadrant. The upper right quadrant of weak government and centralized power contains deregulatory statutes that preempt more stringent state regulatory programs or shield particular defendants (e.g. firearms manufacturers) from state tort liability. The lower left category, in which strong government controls are applied on a decentralized basis, contains regulatory programs like the permits issued by states under the Clean Water Act, which can contain requirements that are more stringent than the applicable federal permit requirements and state common law based upon strict liability backed up by easily obtainable punitive damages. The lower right quadrant contains weak controls exercised on a decentralized basis. In the regulatory context, this is the "wild west" of little federal regulation and weak state government. In the litigative context, this is an area in which federal courts are powerless and state courts are reluctant to recognize or give effect to common law duties.

Lurking beneath arguments framed as issues of vertical power between the federal government and the states are often more serious but less politically attractive concerns about the horizontal distribution of power between government and the private sector. In principle, federalism is about locating governmental power at the most appropriate place on the federalism dimension. Principled advocates of federalism examine the comparative advantages and disadvantages of state and federal institutions and seek to lodge governmental power in the state or federal institutions that are best positioned to exercise that power appropriately. The criteria for determining "appropriateness," however, are invariably vague and contestable. Whether a state or federal entity will provide "better" governmental intervention depends upon how one defines "good" and "bad" governmental intervention. For some, the only "good" intervention is no intervention, whereas, for others, "good" intervention means command and control. Arguments about federalism therefore inevitably overlap with arguments about governmental power.

Business interests generally prefer limited government. They would rather go about their business without worrying about "intrusive" governmental regulations and "abusive" lawsuits. Business interests also prefer to avoid uncertainty. All other things being equal, a company that markets a product nationally would prefer uniform safety regulations and liability standards to rules and standards that vary from state to state. But other things rarely are equal. When federal regulatory agencies are powerful and intrusive, business interests support weak state regulatory programs, even if that means dealing with the uncertainty of variable requirements from state to state. In deregulatory periods, when federal agencies are generally unobtrusive, business interests prefer the uniformity of weak federal regulation to the uncertain business risks posed by varying state regulatory and common law liability regimes. Thus, business interests generally prefer the right two quadrants of Figure 3.1 when it comes to government regulation. Public interest groups and victim advocates, by contrast, generally prefer strong governmental protections, and they are not especially concerned about uniformity in national markets. They prefer the left two quadrants of Figure 3.1.

Now comes the interesting part. When it comes to the preemption war over federal regulation versus state *common law*, business entities consistently argue in favor of federal agency preemption of state common law claims. Why the sudden consistency in the vertical dimension? Because, as we saw in Chapter 2, state common law tends to give more weight to noncompliance with regulatory requirements than it does to compliance. Since most state courts do not recognize a regulatory compliance defense but do give a significant procedural advantage, under the doctrine of negligence per se, to a plaintiff who can demonstrate noncompliance, potential defendants are always better off in the horizontal dimension by arguing for preemption of state common law claims in the vertical dimension. If a jury at the state level can always apply a common law standard that is more stringent than either a federal or state regulatory standard, then potential defendants are always better off in the horizontal dimension if they can avoid the state common law standard. They have an obvious economic incentive as potential defendants to avoid paying damages to people they have injured, but they could avoid paying damages by complying with the common law standard. If the common law standard is always equal to or more stringent than the federal regulatory standard (and in the absence of a regulatory compliance defense that is generally the case), then preemption saves them the difference between the investment required to comply with the federal regulatory standard and that required to comply with the state common law standard.

Preemption advocates in the business community rarely frame their arguments for federal agency preemption of state common law claims in the horizontal dimension, because it is difficult to craft such horizontal claims on the defendant's side of the issue as anything other than self-interested attempts to escape accountability for damage caused to others. Moreover, horizontal claims from the business community are typically met with horizontal arguments from plaintiffs' advocates cast in corrective justice terms that pit greedy corporate defendants against innocent injured victims. Consequently, business interests generally prefer vertical arguments, however makeweight they might appear upon close analysis, in preemption battles.

This unique aspect of the preemption war makes it especially difficult to divine the extent to which a vertical argument about the applicability of the law is in reality a politically attractive cover for a less attractive horizontal position on the substance of the law. For example, a strong argument favoring preemption is the desirability of uniformity in government requirements for products that move about in a national marketplace. As we shall see in Chapter 8, this argument makes a great deal of sense in the context of state regulatory requirements but is much less plausible in the context of state common law claims. It is, however, a politically attractive argument because it plays so well in the former context. Thus, arguments based on uniformity in the vertical dimension may in fact be a cover for less attractive positions in the horizontal dimension, in this case the desire to avoid paying damages for harm caused.

Now that we have a rudimentary understanding of the often confusing law and unique politics of federal preemption in the context of state common law, it is time to descend from the hillside to the battlefields where the combatants are waging the preemption war. The first battlefield we shall visit is the judicial battlefield where the war broke out. Because the war has been raging for much longer here, there is more to see. The battles in the courts also provide a rich source of information on the strengths and weaknesses of the arguments for and against agency preemption of state common law in a wide variety of regulatory settings. Therefore, we will spend more time observing the judicial battles than we spend on the battles in Congress and the agencies.

Chapter 4 The Preemption War in the Courts

The Supreme Court has decided hundreds of preemption cases during the past fifty years, and the pace appears to be accelerating. Yet, prior to the *Cipollone* case, in 1992, the Court had never held that a federal statute or regulation preempted state common law claims where the effect of the holding was to leave plaintiffs without a remedy.[1] Courts in subsequent cases could easily have limited that case to its unique institutional and historical setting. Instead, they turned it into the opening salvo of a preemption war that has continued unabated into the twenty-first century and has spread from the judiciary to Congressional and Executive Branch agencies. On the judicial front, federal preemption became the favored defense for regulated companies seeking to avoid liability and accountability for harm caused by their products and activities. If, as many legal scholars believe, the Supreme Court "took a wrong turn in *Cipollone*," it was in retrospect an exceedingly influential one, because it invited the lower courts to view common law litigation almost exclusively in protective justice terms and to ignore the corrective justice role that the Court clearly recognized in *Silkwood*.[2] As we shall see in this chapter, the

Court continues to send mixed signals in this regard. A 2005 opinion in a case involving pesticide regulation appeared to signal a shift back in the direction of corrective justice, but a powerfully worded 2008 opinion in a case involving medical devices suggested that the presumption against preemption may be honored more in the breach when state common law threatens nationwide commercial interests.[3]

TRANSPORTATION REGULATION

The most active front in the judicial preemption battles has been litigation over whether the regulatory programs established by federal transportation laws preempt state common law claims. This is unsurprising, because the transportation sector has traditionally been heavily regulated, transportation is an important aspect of interstate commerce, and transportation-related accidents are one of the most frequently litigated classes of common law claims. In the following pages, we examine the preemption war in the context of litigation involving motor vehicles, motor boats, trains, and airlines in a variety of regulatory (and deregulatory) contexts.

Automobiles

The Federal Motor Vehicle Safety Act (FMVS Act), enacted in 1966, was one of the very first of the federal regulatory statutes inspired by the nascent consumer movement of the 1960s.[4] It empowers the National Highway Traffic Safety Administration (NHTSA) to promulgate "objective" motor vehicle safety standards that are "practicable" and that "meet the need for motor vehicle safety."[5] Once NHTSA promulgates a federal motor vehicle safety standard, the FMVS Act provides that no state or local government may "establish or . . . continue in effect . . . any safety standard applicable to the same aspect of performance" that is not "identical" to the federal standard.[6] While this express preemption provision does not specifically address state common law claims, a "savings clause" provides that "[c]ompliance with" an NHTSA-promulgated safety standard does "not exempt a person from any liability at common law."[7]

At roughly the same time that Congress was enacting the FMVS Act, the common law courts were also expanding the duty of auto manufacturers to reduce the risks of the "second collision" that occurs when passengers are propelled by the force of a collision into objects within the vehicle's interior. In *Larsen v. General Motors Corp.*,[8] the plaintiff claimed that General Motors had defectively designed the Corvair he was driving because the rigid steering wheel shaft that extended from the front of the vehicle through the dashboard was, in effect, a spear aimed at the driver's chest, ready to be launched at the moment of a head-on collision. In a well-reasoned opinion that initiated a sea change in the common law, the court rejected General Motors' argument that it had "no duty whatsoever to design and manufacture a vehicle . . . which is otherwise 'safe' or 'safer' to occupy during collision impacts." Applying the accepted principle that the manufacturer of a product has a duty to design "a product that is reasonably fit for its intended use and free of hidden defects that could render it unsafe for such use," the court concluded that protecting the occupants during collisions was one of an automobile's "intended uses."[9]

The *Larsen* court easily, too easily in retrospect, dismissed General Motors' argument that common law crashworthiness claims were preempted by the recently enacted FMVS Act.[10] While the common law crashworthiness doctrine became "almost universally accepted,"[11] the tension between that doctrine and NHTSA's responsibility to promulgate occupant protection standards remained unresolved for three decades, until the Supreme Court took it up it in the seminal 2000 case *Geier v. American Honda Motor Co.*[12] In that case, the Court had to decide whether Standard 208, the "occupant protection" regulation that NHTSA promulgated in 1967 and revised on several occasions thereafter, preempted state common law claims that automobile designs were defective even though they complied with the standard.

The original Standard 208, which the agency derived from existing industry guidelines, required manufacturers to install lap and shoulder belts for the driver and passenger positions and either lap belts or lap and shoulder belts for all other positions.[13] NHTSA soon discovered, however, that surprisingly few occupants were making the effort to fasten the belts. For activist consumer groups, the solution to this problem was a new technology, called the "airbag," which consisted of a device concealed in the steering column or the dashboard that would inflate automatically when a sensor detected that the vehicle was rapidly decelerating and that would prevent the victim from coming into contact with interior objects. In 1969, NHTSA invited public comments on whether it should mandate "passive restraints" like airbags for all passenger vehicles. As Henry Ford II denounced airbags as "a bunch of baloney," the industry sponsored a series of television advertisements portraying the horrible consequences of a prematurely deploying airbag.[14]

The agency nevertheless revised Standard 208 to require that manufacturers provide either airbags or "automatic seatbelts" for front seat occupants by August 1975.[15] Ford and the company president, Lee Iacocca, headed for Washington, D.C., where they privately lobbied the White House to allow the industry to use "ignition interlock" devices that would prevent the driver from starting the vehicle until all front seat occupants had buckled up. In what turned out to be a disastrous concession, NHTSA yielded to White House pressure and allowed the industry to use ignition interlock devices instead of passive restraints from 1973 until 1975.[16] The driving public hated the interlock contraption because it was difficult to figure out and frequently failed, leaving the occupants either stranded or unprotected.[17] Reacting to a huge public outcry, Congress, in 1974, amended the FMVS Act to forbid the use of ignition interlock devices.[18] NHTSA then suspended the passive restraint standard and initiated a government-sponsored airbag demonstration program.[19]

The Carter administration, in 1977, lifted the suspension but gave the industry until the 1982 model year to begin implementing the passive restraint standard.[20] With the 1981 arrival of the Reagan administration, however, the newly appointed head of NHTSA overrode his staff and rescinded the standard altogether. The agency explained that instead of airbags, the auto industry had decided to rely exclusively upon easily detached automatic seatbelts that would provide few safety benefits over the seatbelts currently in use.[21] Rather than require an ineffective technology, the agency would adopt an $8 million education campaign in which it would, among other things, produce a guide on how to pray for auto safety on "Safety Sabbaths" and put messages in fortune cookies encouraging people to wear their seat belts.[22]

Unwilling to rely upon preachers and Chinese food to ensure auto safety, consumer groups and the insurance industry challenged the rescission in federal court. The Supreme Court, in *Motor Vehicle Manufacturers Ass'n of the United States v. State Farm Mutual Automobile Ins. Co.*,[23] found the agency's action to be "arbitrary and capricious" because the agency did not explain why it had not reacted to the industry's ploy by simply requiring airbags without the detachable seat belt option. In response to this devastating defeat, Secretary of Transportation Elizabeth Dole imposed a complex solution that provided the regulatory background for the *Geier* preemption litigation. The new regulation required auto manufacturers to install passive restraints (either airbags or non-detachable automatic seat belts with shoulder harnesses) on a phased basis beginning in the 1986 model year, unless states representing two-thirds of the U.S. population enacted and enforced legislation requiring all drivers of passenger cars to wear seat belts. To mollify consumer advocates and the insurance industry, the rule allowed manufacturers to count any car containing airbags as 1.5 cars toward the phase-in quotas.[24]

Pleased with this solution, the industry initiated a multi-million-dollar campaign to lobby state legislatures to enact mandatory seat belt laws.[25] Although airbag proponents were not happy, they could not overtly oppose the industry lobbying effort because they had always been strong advocates of seat belt use as well. They were, however, able to sabotage the effort by urging state legislatures to pass laws that did not meet the requirements that NHTSA had specified for such laws. The net result was that the passive restraint standard at long last went into effect.[26]

Plaintiffs' attorneys were well aware of the fact that the airbag technology had been available for installation in automobiles long before NHTSA's standard had run its tortuous course through the bureaucracy and the courts. Armed with a rapidly growing body of information on the ease of installation and efficacy of airbags, some of which came from the industry's own files, they argued that automobiles manufactured before the passive restraint requirement became effective were nevertheless defectively designed under the *Larsen* test because they lacked airbags. One of those plaintiffs, a young woman named Alexis Geier, was seriously injured despite the protection offered by a combined shoulder harness and lap belt when her 1987 Honda Accord collided with a tree. The Supreme Court, in *Geier v. American Honda Motor Co.*,[27] held that her claim was impliedly preempted because the NHTSA standard explicitly gave manufacturers of 1987 model year automobiles a choice as to whether to install airbags or nondetachable seatbelts.

The Court initially found that the statute's common law "savings clause" rendered its express preemption provision inapplicable to Geier's common law claims.[28] This did not, however, resolve the question whether her claims were impliedly preempted under "ordinary conflict preemption principles." Although the savings clause definitely "preserve[d] those actions that seek to establish greater safety than the minimum safety achieved by a federal regulation intended to provide a floor," it did not necessarily "'save' all state-law tort actions, regardless of their potential threat to the objectives of federal safety standards." The express preemption provision, after all, suggested a congressional "intent to avoid the conflict, uncertainty, cost, and occasional risk to safety itself that too many different safety-standard cooks might otherwise create." This policy favoring uniformity that the Court derived from the express preemption clause argued in favor of implied preemption of state common law claims, "for the rules of law that judges and juries create or apply in such suits may themselves similarly create uncertainty and even conflict, say, when different juries in different States reach different decisions on similar facts."

Relying heavily upon the agency's statement in the preamble that it intended to give manufacturers a range of choices regarding passive restraints, the Court found that Geier's lawsuit, if successful, would stand as an obstacle to attaining that goal. By allowing a mix of technologies to be implemented over time, the standard's flexibility would "lower costs, overcome technical safety problems, encourage technological development, and win widespread consumer acceptance," all of which would promote the standard's safety objectives. The Court noted that the agency had specifically rejected the airbags-only option because it might lead to a consumer "backlash" against all passive restraints not unlike the backlash against ignition interlock devices. The key to attaining the safety goal was the agency's desire for a "*gradual* phase-in of passive restraints" from 1986 through 1989. Finally, the Court noted the agency's position, as articulated in an amicus curiae brief, that "safety would best be promoted if manufacturers installed *alternative* protection systems in their fleets rather than one particular system in every car." Compliance with the duty alleged by Geier to install airbags in 1987 vehicles would therefore have "presented an obstacle to the variety and mix of devices that the federal regulation sought" and to the "passive restraint phase-in that the federal regulation deliberately imposed." Years later, the agency effectively conceded that this had been an exceedingly foolish policy choice when it estimated that if all manufacturers had installed airbags from the outset, as many as 63,000 additional lives might have been saved.[29]

The four dissenting justices were convinced that the agency's regulatory objectives "would not be frustrated one whit by allowing state courts to determine whether in 1987 the lifesaving advantages of airbags had become sufficiently obvious that their omission might constitute a design defect in some new cars."[30] The "gradual change" and "variability" policy arguments had all of the hallmarks of a makeweight position formulated after the fact for purposes of the preemption litigation. If gradual change and variability were so critical, the agency would have capped the phase-in rate instead of accelerating it, would not have given manufacturers extra credit for installing airbags, and would not have referenced the "potential liability" of manufacturers in the preamble as a response to consumer concerns that manufacturers would install the cheapest (rather than the safest) passive devices.

Although the *Geier* decision effectively ended the "airbags-only" litigation against manufacturers of pre-1992 automobiles, the lower courts could easily have limited its holding to cases in which NHTSA has either expressly rejected the technology that the plaintiff offers as a safer alternative or explicitly determined that the FMVS Act's safety goal requires regulatees to choose from among a discrete and limited set of allowable options. Such situations should be fairly rare, because NHTSA typically promulgates "performance" standards that allow manufacturers to select any technology that is capable of meeting prescribed tests with dummies in simulated crashes.[31]

Several lower courts, however, have interpreted *Geier* broadly to preempt any common law claim that would have the effect of narrowing the range of options available to a manufacturer, whether on not the agency has concluded that the availability of specific options is necessary to advance the statute's safety goals. Thus, in the influential 2002 case *Griffith v. General Motors Corp.,*[32] the court of appeals held that when a NHTSA standard "leaves a manufacturer with a choice of safety device options, a state suit that depends on foreclosing one or more of those options is preempted."[33] Unlike the *Geier* opinion, however, the *Griffith* court did not emphasize the FMVS Act's overarching safety goal or explain how maximizing the options available to manufacturers in this instance would advance that goal. Instead, the court appeared to substitute for the statute's safety goal a new "meta-policy" of maximizing manufacturer choice that effectively trumps that safety goal. Several other lower courts have subsequently employed this new meta-policy to preempt common law design defect claims in the context not just of Standard 208 but of all NHTSA standards promulgated under the FMVS Act.[34]

This new meta-policy ignores the congressional concern, as reflected in the savings clause, for preserving the corrective justice function of the common law. In the specific amendment to Standard 208 involved in *Geier,* the agency concluded that it would be preferable if all manufacturers did not adopt the airbags option. In most cases, however, the agency does not care how manufacturers meet its performance standards, so long as they are met. Thus, a common law rule that would effectively require manufacturers to employ a technology that did not meet an applicable performance-based standard would be preempted, because it would be impossible for the manufacturer to meet both the state and the federal requirements. If, however, a common law claim that the manufacturer was negligent in selecting a single option from among the many options that are ordinarily capable of meeting NHTSA's performance standards is impliedly preempted because it poses an "obstacle" to the new meta-policy identified by some lower courts, then very few common law claims will be left for the statute's "savings clause" to save.

Trains

For more than 150 years, railroads have contributed to the nation's commerce and economic well-being. Today, railroads transport approximately 42 percent of the country's freight.[35] At the same, trains derail with distressing regularity, and the "grade crossing" at which a highway intersects with a railroad track continues to be one of the country's deadliest locations. About once a year, the release of hazardous materials from a derailed train requires a major evacuation of surrounding neighborhoods, and trains collide with motor vehicles and pedestrians at grade crossings about ten times a day.[36] Except for very rare cases of sabotage, train derailment is largely a function of the degree of care that the railroads and their employees exercise in track and air brake inspection and maintenance, rail traffic control, and avoidance of engineer fatigue. Despite huge expenditures on the construction of overpasses, more than 150,000 grade crossings still remain in this country. The vast majority of them are protected not with automatic gates or even bells and lights but with the all-too-familiar X-shaped "crossbuck" warning sign.[37] Grade crossing accidents are usually attributable either to lack of care on the part of the driver in approaching rail crossings or to lack of care on the part of the railroad's employees in managing train speeds, sounding horns when approaching intersections, maintaining signaling devices, and keeping vegetation and railroad equipment from obscuring motorists' views of oncoming trains.

Throughout most of the nation's history, conduct at grade crossings was governed by a combination of state laws, local ordinances, and common law duties that evolved over time as courts reacted to changes in technologies and population growth. The common law initially placed primary responsibility for grade crossing safety on the railroads.[38] The Supreme Court, in 1892, held that a railroad had a duty to exercise reasonable care at grade crossings that could require extraordinary measures, such as the use of flagmen or gates at especially hazardous grade crossings, "even though it may have complied literally with the terms of a statute prescribing certain signals to be given, and other precautions to be taken by it, for the safety of the traveling public at crossings."[39] The introduction of the automobile into the mix in the early twentieth century, however, persuaded the Court, by the mid-1930s, that "[t]he railroad has ceased to be the prime instrument of danger and the main cause of accidents" and that "[i]t is the railroad which now requires protection from the dangers incident to motor transportation."[40] Dramatic increases in automobile use and overland freight by truck during the 1940s and 1950s yielded an equally dramatic increase in the carnage at grade crossings. Although the massive interstate highway system that went into place in the 1950s and 1960s generally avoided highway-railway intersections, accidents at existing grade crossings "increased rather sharply" again during the 1960s.[41]

Concluding that "there can be, should be and must be a substantial upgrading of the level of railroad safety," Congress enacted the Federal Railroad Safety Act of 1970 (FRS Act).[42] The purpose of the statute is "to promote safety in every area of railroad operations and reduce railroad-related accidents and incidents."[43] The statute authorizes the Federal Railroad Administration (FRA) "as necessary" to prescribe "appropriate rules, regulations, orders and standards for all areas of railroad safety."[44] A complex express preemption provision states that "[l]aws, regulations, and orders related to railroad safety . . . shall be nationally uniform to the extent practicable." A state may prescribe a "law, regulation, or order related to railroad safety" until FRA "prescribes a regulation or issues an order covering the subject matter of the State requirement." Otherwise, a state "may adopt or continue in force an additional or more stringent law, regulation, or order related to railroad safety or security" when it is "necessary to eliminate or reduce an essentially local safety or security hazard," is not "incompatible with" the federal law, and "does not unreasonably burden interstate commerce."[45]

Soon after the FRS Act was enacted, FRA promulgated regulations establishing maximum train speeds for different classes of track. Not long thereafter, the agency promulgated regulations setting the conditions under which states could obtain funds for grade crossing improvements under the Highway Safety Act of 1973.[46] The safety regulations provide that federally funded warning devices at grade crossings must conform to detailed standards set out in the agency's "Manual on Uniform Traffic Control Devices for Streets and Highways" (MUTCD). The MUTCD requires, at a minimum, that the roadway approach to a grade crossing must contain a crossbuck sign with the words "RAILROAD CROSSING" on the crossed panels. The regulations also require automatic gates with flashing light signals (a $1.15 million improvement that reduces the incidence of serious injury and death by 80 to 89 percent) at major crossings or sites where high speed trains may approach with limited visibility. Otherwise, either the state or the railroad may determine the appropriate device, subject to FRA approval.[47]

The full preemptive effective of these regulations did not become clear until the preemption war ignited, near the end of the twentieth century. In December 1989, a group of defense attorneys who specialized in representing railroads formed a "Special Advisory Committee on Grade Crossing Litigation" to come up with a strategy for "demonstrat[ing] that claims based on the theory of a railroad's failure to provide additional grade crossing warning devices are preempted under federal law." In March 1990, the Committee sent to the members a package containing an extensive background document on preemption, a "punch list" of "necessary items," a "Model Brief with Form Affidavit," and a set of model jury instructions.[48] Less than two years later, the Supreme Court agreed to hear its first case on the extent to which the FRS Act preempted state common law claims.

The case originated on a clear winter day in 1988 when a veteran delivery driver, Thomas Easterwood, loaded up his long-bed truck and headed for his first delivery of the day, in Cartersville, Georgia. When he came to the Cook Street railroad crossing, in the center of the business district, he was driving about 10 miles per hour and heading east toward the rising sun. A CSX Railroad engine was pushing a train toward the same intersection at a speed of between thirty-two and fifty miles per hour. The crossing was equipped with flashing lights and bells that activated just as Thomas entered the intersection, but it did not have an automatic gate. A curve in the track obstructed the view of oncoming trains that were more than 150 feet away, and vegetation growing along the track further obstructed the view. No one knows whether Easterwood saw the train, because he was instantly killed in the seventh grade crossing collision at that busy intersection in seven years.[49]

Easterwood's wife sued CSX Corporation for negligence in failing to install gate arms at the crossing and for failing to reduce the speed of the train as it moved through the Cartersville business district. In an opinion that followed the federal government's amicus curiae brief almost to the letter, the Supreme Court, in *CSX Transportation, Inc. v. Easterwood*,[50] allowed the first claim to go forward but found the second to be preempted.[51] Relying on the fountainhead *Cipollone* case, the Supreme Court first found that the statutory phrase "law, rule, regulation, order or standard" in the FRS Act preemption section easily included common law duties imposed by courts. Easterwood's inadequate-warning claim was not preempted by the FRA grade crossing regulations, however, because they technically did not "cover" the Cook Street grade crossing. The regulations applied only to grade crossings receiving federal funds, and the Cook Street crossing had not received any federal funding.

The FRA maximum speed regulations, on the other hand, did "cover" the CSX train as it approached the Cook Street grade crossing. Since its fifty-two-miles-per-hour speed clearly complied with the sixty-miles-per-hour maximum speed for the class 4 track in Cartersville, the regulations preempted any claim based on an asserted common law duty to travel less rapidly. The Court noted that, unlike highway speed limits, the railroad speed limits set by FRA regulations were not intended to ensure that trains traveled at speeds that would permit them to stop quickly enough to avoid an accident after spotting a dangerous situation. They were instead aimed at ensuring that the available warning devices would be triggered in time to prevent drivers from entering grade crossings when a train was coming. The regulations focused on regulating the conduct of drivers, rather than of train engineers, because trains "offered far fewer opportunities for regulatory control (e.g., a freight train traveling sixty miles per hour takes almost two miles to stop) and because the agency had concluded that "[n]early all grade crossing accidents" were "attributable to some degree of 'driver error.'"[52] The Court did not address the argument that a slower moving train approaching a busy intersection in the middle of a town would give lengthy vehicles like Easterwood's long-bed truck more time to clear the grade crossing after the lights began to flash. According to the Court, the regulations placed the responsibility for staying out of grade crossings on drivers of motor vehicles, not on the engineers of trains. In a footnote, however, the Court noted that CSX Transportation conceded that a claim that a company breached its common law duty "to slow or stop a train to avoid a specific, individual hazard" would not be preempted.[53]

Seven years after its *Easterwood* decision, the Court, in *Norfolk Southern Railway Co. v. Shanklin,*[54] held that FRA's grade crossing regulation preempted common law inadequate warning claims for crossings that had received federal funding. The only real surprise in the case was the changed position of the government. Whereas the George H. W. Bush administration had taken the position that the grade crossing regulations were applicable to *any* federally funded grade crossing sign, the Clinton administration took the narrower view that preemption would occur only for federally funded grade crossings where the states and the FRA had made "site-specific engineering judgments," not where the state or the railroad company had merely installed the bare-minimum crossbuck signs that the aging MUTCD allowed as a fallback.[55] This time, however, the Supreme Court rejected the administration's position. The Court explained that the states were certainly free to install more protective devices than the bare minima required by the FRA regulations on their own nickel, but state courts were not free to "hold the railroad responsible for the adequacy of those devices."[56]

The *Easterwood* and *Shanklin* decisions did not relieve the railroads of all common law responsibilities at grade crossings. The *Shanklin* plaintiff's claim that the railroad had been negligent in allowing the vegetation in its right-of-way to obstruct the view, for example, was still a viable claim so long as vegetation growth was not governed by FRA regulations.[57] After deciding, in 1998, that it would be too difficult to write generic vegetation regulations for all grade crossings, FRA concluded that such claims were not preempted.[58] Some courts have held that FRA's admittedly incomplete regulations still completely preempt all negligence claims not based on violations of those regulations at federally funded grade crossings.[59] Others have allowed some claims, especially those involving failure to remove vegetation and similar obstructions in the railroad's right-of-way, to proceed.[60] Most courts have allowed claims based on alleged violations of FRA regulations to proceed, thereby allowing plaintiffs to reinforce FRA regulations through the added incentive of common law liability.[61] A few courts, however, have concluded that all common law claims involving conduct that falls within the scope of FRA's regulations are preempted, reasoning that "Congress gave the Secretary of Transportation 'exclusive authority' to impose civil penalties and request injunctions for violations of the railroad safety regulations."[62]

Although the Supreme Court has not decided a train derailment case, most of the lower courts have found all claims, including those based on violations of FRA regulations, to be preempted. Thus, in the litigation over the notorious Scottsbluff, Arizona, derailment in which eighteen derailed cars leaked toxic chemicals into the air, soil, and groundwater, the Eighth Circuit Court of Appeals held that the common law claims of 1,100 Scottsbluff evacuees were completely preempted. The plaintiffs had alleged that company inspectors negligently failed to discover a faulty coupler during a routine inspection conducted pursuant to FRA's lenient inspection regulations two days prior to the derailment. The plaintiffs' expert maintained that a thirty-minute examination of the entire eighty-four-car train from a moving all-terrain vehicle was wholly inadequate. Because FRA's nonspecific inspection regulations were "intended to prevent negligent inspection," however, they preempted the plaintiffs' common law claims, even in the absence of any evidence that the inspectors had in fact performed their inspection in accordance with the FRA requirements. The court reasoned that "a regulatory framework need not impose bureaucratic micromanagement in order to substantially subsume a particular subject matter" for purposes of preemption.[63] Two separate district courts entertaining cases involving the disastrous 2002 Minot, South Dakota, derailment, which released 200,000 gallons of anhydrous ammonia that killed one person and injured 1,442 others, followed the Eighth Circuit precedent. One of them, however, expressed its regret that "the judicial system is left with a law that is inherently unfair to innocent bystanders and property owners who may be injured by the negligent actions of railroad companies."[64]

There is, at the end of the day, a certain irony to the grade crossing story. The unacceptable incidence of grade crossing fatalities that Congress identified in 1970 was attributable in large part to inadequate incentives provided by a common law strongly influenced by a Supreme Court opinion that viewed the problem as one of motorists putting trains at risk. Congress therefore empowered a federal agency to promulgate standards forcing railroads to do more to improve railroad safety. The federal agency, however, also concluded that the problem was primarily attributable to driver error. It then wrote regulations allowing trains to cruise through the business districts of small cities at sixty miles per hour while depending exclusively upon the requirements of a related federal funding program to ensure that proper warning devices were installed at low visibility intersections. Completing the circle, the Supreme Court held that the federal regulations took away the power of state courts to address the problem through an evolving common law that by then had placed greater responsibility for ensuring grade crossing safety on the railroad companies.

The derailment story is not so much ironic as it is just plain unfair. The facts of the *Scottsbluff* case fairly screamed negligence. If the railroads are in fact responsible for ensuring that the couplers on fast-moving trains carrying dangerous cargo are working properly, it does not take an expert to know that a thirty-minute whirlwind tour of an eighty-four-car train cannot possibly do the job. If the FRA regulations permit railroads to cut corners to this degree at the expense of innocent neighbors, then the regulatory system is failing badly and needs all the help it can get from the common law in encouraging the railroads to take their responsibilities to their neighbors more seriously. As it stands, the railroads' responsibilities to the neighbors are in fact minimal, and they are likely to remain so until either the FRA or Congress declares that the agencies' imperfect regulatory requirements are not preemptive.

Motor Boats

During the 1950s, a newly prosperous American middle class discovered the pleasures of recreational boating on the country's abundant rivers and lakes. By the early 1960s, the number of registered motorboats and yachts had increased from around 300,000 at the end of the Great Depression to more than five million. Inexpensive fiberglass construction and powerful outboard motors turned water skiing into a popular sport as suburban driveways filled with easily towed ski and fishing boats. With this greatly increased use came a correspondingly large increase in the number of boating accidents. Reports of needless deaths and injuries inspired calls for action at the national level.[65] Congress responded by enacting the Federal Boat Safety Act of 1971 (FBS Act) "to improve boating safety," to authorize "the establishment of national construction and performance standards for boats and associated equipment," and to encourage greater "uniformity of boating laws and regulations as among the several States and the Federal Government."[66]

The FBS Act empowered the Department of Transportation to promulgate "minimum safety standards for recreational vessels and associated equipment" after consulting with a twenty-one-member National Boating Safety Advisory Council. The Secretary of Transportation, in turn, delegated this power to the Coast Guard, which over the years promulgated several safety standards. The statute contains a preemption clause and a savings clause that are very much like those contained in the FMVS Act empowering the same department to regulate automobile safety. Unless the Coast Guard determines otherwise, "a State or political subdivision . . . may not establish, continue in effect, or enforce a law or regulation establishing" a standard or "imposing a requirement" that is "not identical to a regulation prescribed under" the federal law. An associated savings clause provides that compliance with Coast Guard standards "does not relieve a person from liability at common law or under State law."[67]

In 1988, the agency asked a subcommittee of the Advisory Council to examine the existing information on propeller guards and to make recommendations. The subcommittee concluded that the guards might interfere with engine performance at speeds in excess of ten miles per hour and would not increase overall safety because they would increase the surface area of the propeller casing and thereby increase the risk of striking potential victims with that larger object. Even at speeds as slow as ten miles per hour, collision with such a blunt object would tear tissue, crush bones, and create wounds potentially more serious than the series of evenly spaced cuts that a spinning propeller blade would produce. The agency, in 1990, accepted the Advisory Council's recommendation that it "should take no regulatory action to require propeller guards." In the intervening years, however, reports of injuries and deaths attributable to leisure boat propellers mounted, and the Injury Prevention Center at Johns Hopkins University estimated that propeller accidents were responsible for as many as three thousand injuries and deaths per year.[68]

Rex and Jeanne Sprietsma were enjoying an afternoon spin in their eighteen-foot ski boat on a hot July day in 1995 when the boat took a sharp turn and Jeanne was thrown overboard. Although the fall itself caused no serious injuries, Jeanne was killed when the rear of the boat passed directly over her and the propeller of the 115-horsepower Mercury outboard motor struck her in the head.[69] Rex sued the manufacturer of the motor in an Illinois state court. His lawyers alleged that the motor was defectively designed because it lacked a propeller guard to protect people who would foreseeably come into contact with the spinning blade. The Illinois Supreme Court, however, held that the claim was impliedly preempted because the FBS Act occupied the entire field of motorboat equipment regulation. The United States Supreme Court concluded otherwise in *Sprietsma v. Mercury Marine.*[70]

The Court first held that the claims were not expressly preempted, because the preemption provision of the statute applied only to a state or local "law or regulation," and this rather clearly indicated an intent not to include state common law claims. Since compensation for victims was "the manifest object of the saving clause," it "would have been perfectly rational for Congress not to preempt common-law claims, which—unlike most administrative and legislative regulations—necessarily perform an important remedial role in compensating accident victims." Thus, on the question of express preemption, the Court's result did not differ from the result that it reached on the similar language at issue in *Geier.* The difference in the opinions was the *Sprietsma* Court's explicit recognition of the importance of the common law's corrective justice role.

The Court then rejected the conclusion of the Illinois Supreme Court and several federal courts of appeals that the agency's decision not to regulate propellers impliedly preempted common law claims based on the manufacturer's failure to install propeller guards. The Court found it "quite wrong to view that decision as the functional equivalent of a regulation prohibiting all States and their political subdivisions from adopting such a regulation." The Coast Guard's decision not to regulate "left the law applicable to propeller guards exactly the same as it had been before the [Advisory Council] subcommittee began its investigation."[71] Importantly, the Coast Guard had "never taken the position that the litigation of state common-law claims relating to an area not yet subject to federal regulation would conflict with 'the accomplishment and execution of the full purposes and objectives of Congress.'" And the government's amicus curiae brief made it clear that the agency still did not regard its "1990 refusal to regulate . . . as having any pre-emptive effect."

Finally, the Court turned to the Illinois court's holding that the regulatory regime established by the FBS Act so completely occupied the field of recreational boat regulation that it foreclosed state common law remedies altogether. Acknowledging the possibility that the statute "might be interpreted as expressly occupying the field with respect to state positive laws and regulations," the Court held that its "structure and framework" did not convey a clear intent "to go even further and implicitly pre-empt all state common law relating to boat manufacture." While uniformity was "undoubtedly important to the industry," the Court agreed with the Coast Guard that it did not "justify the displacement of state common-law remedies that compensate accident victims and their families and that serve the Act's more prominent objective, emphasized by its title, of promoting boating safety."

In the years following the *Sprietsma* Court's 2002 holding, the Coast Guard has promulgated no new regulations of any significance, and the lower courts have not concluded that the regulations that the agency has promulgated in the past impliedly preempt common law claims. Thus, on this small battleground of the preemption war, the dust has apparently settled with the opponents of preemption in firm control.

TRANSPORTATION DEREGULATION

During the last quarter of the twentieth century, Congress took the unusual step of partially deregulating the transportation sector of the economy in several important regards. It directed most of its attention in these reforms to complex "economic" regulation of rates, routes, and services that was by and large unrelated to public safety. The deregulation statutes had a direct impact on state consumer fraud litigation and an indirect impact on common law tort litigation in less familiar areas such as nuisance and tortious interference with business relations. Since Congress usually meant for the deregulatory aspects of the federal statutes to preempt any intrusive regulation at the state level that was inconsistent with its overall deregulatory goals, defendants in post-*Cipollone* common law litigation argued that the deregulatory statutes barred plaintiffs' common law claims.

Airline Deregulation

From the advent of commercial air travel until the present, the Federal Aviation Administration (FAA), an Executive Branch agency located in the Department of Transportation, has regulated various safety-related aspects of air travel.[72] In 1958, however, Congress created an independent federal agency called the Civil Aeronautics Board (CAB) to regulate air fares, routes, and deceptive trade practices with respect to interstate flights.[73] By 1978, Congress had concluded that the 1958 program was inefficient and was keeping air fares too high. It therefore decided to "deregulate" certain aspects of airline regulation.

The Airline Deregulation Act of 1978 (AD Act) did not address safety regulation at all, but it abolished the CAB, took away the federal government's power to regulate the economic aspects of air travel, and transferred CAB's remaining functions to FAA. Fearing that states would simply "re-regulate" the airlines by enacting their own programs, Congress expressly prohibited states from "enact[ing] or enforc[ing] any law, rule, regulation, standard, or other provision having the force and effect of law relating to rates, routes, or services of any air carrier."[74] The AD Act did not, however, repeal a preexisting "savings clause" stating that nothing in the statute would "in any way abridge or alter the remedies now existing at common law or by statute."[75]

After the Supreme Court's 1992 *Cipollone* opinion, defendants began to argue in dozens of cases that a wide variety of common law tort claims were attempts to impose standards "relating to" airline "services" and were therefore preempted. In the absence of definitive Supreme Court guidance, the lower courts have developed two broad approaches to the issue, both of which are fairly inhospitable to the preemption argument. The Fifth Circuit Court of Appeals, in 1995, interpreted the word "services" to "represent a bargained-for or anticipated provision of labor from one party to another." The term includes "items such as ticketing, boarding procedures, provision of food and drink, and baggage handling, in addition to the transportation itself." Since the statute did not "displace state tort actions for personal physical injuries or property damage caused by the operation and maintenance of aircraft," the plaintiff's claim for damages resulting from an airline's alleged negligence in failing to prevent a box full of bottles of rum from falling on him from an overhead bin was not preempted.[76] Two other courts of appeals followed the Fifth Circuit's approach.[77]

Three years later, the Ninth Circuit Court of Appeals concluded that the statute meant "to preempt only state laws and lawsuits that would adversely affect the economic deregulation of the airlines and the forces of competition within the airline industry." Unlike the Fifth Circuit, the Ninth Circuit concluded that the two words "rates" and "routes" that immediately preceded "service" in the preemption clause referred to such things as "the frequency and scheduling of transportation" and "the selection of markets to or from which transportation is provided (as in, 'This airline provides service from Tucson to New York twice a day.')." To the Ninth Circuit, this strongly suggested that Congress meant to protect the airlines from further economic regulation by the states but did not intend to shield them from run-of-the-mill common law actions. Like the Fifth Circuit, the Ninth Circuit relied on the savings clause, and it further noted that the statute still required airlines to obtain insurance to cover liability for personal injury and death caused by their operations.[78]

Under both approaches, the courts have allowed most common law claims to proceed. Claims for false imprisonment, assault, battery, and the like related to conduct that takes place at the airport prior to boarding are unrelated to service and are therefore not preempted.[79] Likewise, claims for intentional infliction of mental distress suffered as a result of discrimination based on race or disability are generally not preempted.[80] Claims based on negligence for failing to remove a hijacker, failing to provide a defibrillator, defectively designing passenger seats, providing incompetent assistance for disabled passengers, and training pilots are also not preempted.[81] Similarly, an airline's refusal to allow a passenger to board a plane for security reasons is clearly related to the provision of airline services, and a claim for resulting mental distress was therefore preempted.[82] Under the Fifth Circuit approach, claims related to baggage handling and claims by travel agencies for tortious interference with business advantage are preempted.[83] The courts are split on whether claims for punitive damages are preempted.[84]

ICC Termination Act

From 1877 through 1976, railroads were heavily regulated by the Interstate Commerce Commission (ICC) with regard to the rates they could charge and the services they provided. This began to change with the enactment of the Railroad Revitalization and Regulatory Act of 1976, and it culminated with the outright repeal of many of the government's regulatory functions and the abolition of the ICC in the Interstate Commerce Commission Termination Act (ICCT Act).[85] The 1995 statute transferred the agency's remaining regulatory functions to a new agency, called the Surface Transportation Board. According to an express preemption provision, "the remedies provided under" the statute "with respect to regulation of rail transportation are exclusive and preempt the remedies provided under Federal or State law."[86] The statute's legislative history made it clear that Congress intended for the word "remedies" to include common law remedies, and the statute never contained a savings clause. The primary question for the preemption war was not whether the statute preempted common law claims but what kinds of common law claims Congress meant for it to preempt.[87]

The Supreme Court has not yet provided an answer to these questions. Some kinds of tort claims, such as those alleging tortious interference with business advantage, provide incentives related to rates and services that closely resemble economic regulation in nature. The lower courts have found such claims to be inconsistent with the primary purpose of the statute, which is to free the railroads from governmental control, and therefore expressly preempted.[88] The incentives provided by common law claims, like negligence and nuisance, that provide compensation for harm to person or property less easily fit the economic regulation mold. The rule of thumb is that a claim that "will directly affect railroad transportation" is preempted, but, "where adjudication of a claim will address garden variety issues of negligence, without significant 'regulation' of the railroad, then preemption generally will not be appropriate."[89]

Some examples may help. Claims that a railroad's greatly increased activities on a particular local line produced vibrations, noise, and fumes that damaged the plaintiffs' property were preempted because they would provide an incentive to cease the operations altogether or to conduct them in a different manner.[90] On the other hand, a claim that a railroad created a nuisance by piling debris into a drainage ditch that caused periodic flooding of the plaintiffs' property was not preempted because "a generally applicable state law regulating the disposal of detritus" does not "collide with the Federal scheme of economic regulation or deregulation."[91] Property damage claims based on loss of access due to blocked grade crossings were preempted because the only way to avoid liability was for the railroad to change its methods of service.[92] But an action for damages to one railroad's property resulting from a derailment caused by another railroad's negligence was not preempted, because "it would be illogical to conclude that the mere fact that financial liability must be allocated between two railroads is tantamount to regulating the railroads."[93]

The preemption war thus continues to rage in the lower courts on the transportation deregulation front without any clear victor. In the cases of both airline and railroad deregulation, a "common law of preemption" has evolved in the lower courts. In the case of railroads, a single broad approach has guided the courts to fairly consistent results. In the case of airlines, two lines of authority have evolved, and it will probably take a Supreme Court opinion to resolve the matter. In the meantime, some degree of uncertainty persists in both areas of the law.

MEDICAL DEVICES AND FRAUD ON THE AGENCY

In the 1976 Medical Device Amendments to the Food, Drug, and Cosmetic Act (FDC Act), Congress gave FDA authority to regulate medical devices, like artificial limbs and electronic pacemakers, that doctors frequently use in treating illness. The statute contains an express preemption provision that we will examine in the following pages. After that, we will look at a broader body of preemption litigation involving claims that a licensee committed a fraud on the federal agency in obtaining its license, because the seminal Supreme Court case in this important area of litigation involved an FDA-approved medical device.

Medical Devices

On February 1, 1970, the *American Journal of Obstetrics and Gynecology* published a paper by Dr. Hugh Davis, a professor of gynecology at the prestigious Johns Hopkins Medical School, demonstrating the effectiveness of an intrauterine contraceptive device (IUD) he had designed, called the Dalkon Shield. The paper was at best deceptive and at worst fraudulent. Soon thereafter, Davis and his co-inventor sold the rights to the shield to the A. H. Robbins Corporation, and he continued his devious practices as an employee of the company. Robbins soon became aware of the misleading aspects of the paper and, more important, of the critical fact that Davis had added copper sulfate to the version of the device that Robbins manufactured. This addition turned the otherwise unregulated device into a regulated drug, but Robbins did not seek FDA approval as required by the FDC Act. The company also ignored its quality control supervisor's strong recommendation that both ends of the device's "sheath" be sealed to prevent "wicking" of bacteria-laden fluids from the vagina into the uterus. When two Dalkon Shield users died within a month of each other in May 1973 because of infections resulting from the devices, things began to unravel for Robbins. Nevertheless, the company continued to market the device for another year, at which point it stopped selling it but declined to assist in removing the 3.6 million devices that had already been installed.[94] In the common law litigation that followed, the company's successor paid out nearly $3 billion in claims to more than 200,000 women who had used the device.[95]

In response to the Dalkon Shield fiasco, Congress enacted the Medical Device Amendments of 1976.[96] That statute created a comprehensive regulatory regime in which medical devices are divided into three classes according to the risks that they pose to the user. A manufacturer may not market a Class III medical device, which is one that is likely to cause death or serious adverse effects if it fails or otherwise poses potentially serious direct risks, until FDA has approved a Premarket Application for Approval (PMA) providing "reasonable assurance" that it is both safe and effective. During the Class III approval process, the FDA staff examines both the device and the manufacturer's proposed labeling in great detail and offers suggestions for improving both. Once FDA has approved a device, the manufacturer may make changes in the device that affect safety or efficacy only after obtaining FDA approval of a Supplemental PMA. Changes to the label that enhance safety, however, may be made unilaterally, subject to subsequent FDA disapproval.[97]

These stringent requirements are subject to two gaping loopholes. First, Congress "grandfathered" medical devices that existed prior to 1976 for as long as it took for the manufacturers to undertake the necessary studies and for FDA to approve the devices. Second, Congress greatly expanded the grandfather clause to include new devices that did not exist prior to 1976 but that are "substantially equivalent" to such preexisting devices. If a manufacturer decides that its device is "substantially equivalent" to an existing device, it need only provide FDA with advance notice of its intent to market it. If FDA does not object after an abbreviated review in which it quickly compares the new device to the existing device, the manufacturer is free to market it. More than 80 percent of the new devices that have entered the market since 1976 have received this abbreviated form of approval.[98]

The Medical Device Amendments contain an express preemption clause providing that no state or political subdivision "may establish or continue in effect" with respect to a medical device "any requirement" that is "different from, or in addition to, any requirement applicable under this Act to the device" and "which relates to the safety or effectiveness of the device or to any other matter included in a requirement applicable to the device under this Act."[99] The statute does not contain a savings clause. For the first few years of the statute's existence, defendants in medical device litigation rarely raised the preemption defense in state common law litigation, and when they did, the outcomes were decidedly mixed. The Supreme Court's *Cipollone* opinion, however, combined with the disastrous failures of several widely used medical devices to produce a mini-industry of preemption litigation in the mid-1990s. During this round of litigation, the lower courts nearly always found the claims to be preempted."[100]

In 1987, Lora Lohr, a twenty-seven-year-old cardiac ultrasound specialist, received the bad news that her own heart was not well. Fortunately for her, a widely available and frequently used medical device called a pacemaker could solve her problem with few associated risks. She readily agreed to a surgical procedure in which a pacemaker manufactured by Medtronics, Inc., was installed in her chest cavity and wires called "leads" were inserted into her heart to deliver a signal from the device to that critical organ. The pacemaker quietly did its job for the next three years when, after laying her baby daughter down for a nap and sitting down to watch television, Lohr suddenly felt dizzy. Her alert husband called 911, and she was rushed to the hospital as her condition rapidly worsened. Correctly surmising that the pacemaker had failed, Lohr's doctor performed an emergency medical procedure that saved her life. Without the protection that the pacemaker afforded, Lohr's heart had suffered a blockage. Lohr's doctor later concluded that the device had failed because of a defect in the lead. Four more operations were required to repair the resulting damage to her heart.

When Lohr called her deceased father's former law partner to inquire into the possibility of a lawsuit, she learned that she was not the first victim of a failed Medtronic pacemaker. Medtronic was in fact aware of other similar failures at the time that it sold the device to her doctor. While Lohr certainly wanted compensation for her medical expenses, which came to about $15,000, she also strongly believed that a lawsuit was necessary to send a message to the company. To Medtronic she may have been just "a statistic . . . a nothing," but she was also "a mom, a daughter, a sister," and a "good person" who "shouldn't be treated like that." Lohr's attorney filed a lawsuit in a Florida state court alleging that Medtronic was negligent in using defective materials and in failing to warn her and her physician of the device's tendency to fail. Her complaint also alleged that Medtronic was strictly liable because the product was in a defective condition and unreasonably dangerous to potential users. Medtronic argued that the claim was preempted by the Medical Device Amendments.[101]

A divided Supreme Court (5–4) held, in *Medtronic, Inc. v. Lohr,*[102] that the Medical Device Amendments preempted some but not all of Lohr's claims.[103] Like *Cipollone,* the case turned on the meaning of the word "requirement" in the express preemption provision. In a plurality opinion joined by three other justices, Justice Stevens (the author of the Court's *Cipollone* opinion) observed that to interpret "requirement" to encompass all state common law claims would "require far greater interference with state legal remedies, producing a serious intrusion into state sovereignty while simultaneously wiping out the possibility of remedy for Lohr's alleged injuries." Given the "ambiguities in the statute," the plurality could not conclude that Congress had "clearly signaled its intent to deprive States of any role in protecting consumers from the dangers inherent in many medical devices." Justice Stevens also found support for his conclusion in the overall protective purpose of the Medical Device Amendments and in its legislative history.

Justice Stevens concluded that Lohr's defective design claims were clearly not preempted, because FDA had not "required" Medtronic to use any particular design for its pacemakers. In fact, the abbreviated "substantial equivalence" procedure under which the agency approved the device gave FDA very little to say about the its design. Likewise, any claims based on Medtronic's violation of FDA's regulations were preserved, because a damages remedy merely provided "another reason for manufacturers to comply with" the federal requirements. On this point, the plurality's interpretation was "substantially informed" by FDA's own preemption regulations, which provided that state requirements would be preempted only when FDA had established "specific requirements applicable to a particular device" that were inconsistent with the state requirements. The FDA preemption regulations also informed the plurality's analysis of Lohr's claims relating to the manufacturing process and the adequacy of the warnings for the pacemaker. The FDA labeling and good manufacturing practices regulations were quite general in nature and did not establish a "specific mandate" for manufacturers to follow. Similarly, state common law "requirements," such as they were, did not require any specific manufacturing practice or label that was inconsistent with the general FDA regulations. Thus, the plurality concluded that "few, if any, common law duties have been pre-empted by this statute" and that none of Lohr's specific claims were preempted.

Justice Breyer, who provided the needed fifth vote for a majority, agreed with the plurality that Lohr's claims should go forward, but he did not dwell on the word "requirements." He agreed with the plurality's analysis of the FDA preemption regulations in this particular case, but he disagreed with its broader conclusion that "future incidents of MDA pre-emption of common-law claims will be 'few' or 'rare.'"[104] The four dissenting justices (Justices O'Connor, Rehnquist, Scalia, and Thomas) agreed that Lohr's claims based on defective design were not preempted because the "substantial equivalence" procedure did not require companies to employ particular designs. They also agreed with the plurality that claims based upon alleged violations of FDA regulations and requirements were not preempted. They concluded, however, that the defective manufacture and failure-to-warn claims were preempted by FDA's good manufacturing practices regulations and its label requirements.[105] The justices were thus unanimous in concluding that design defect claims regarding devices that received only the abbreviated "substantial equivalence" approval were not preempted.

Although most medical devices still go through the abbreviated approval process, a large proportion of the more innovative devices entering the market in recent years, like drug-coated stents, are sufficiently innovative to require full FDA approval.[106] The critical question whether the express preemption clause preempted common law claims regarding devices receiving full FDA approval remained open for more than a decade. Although most legal scholars who examined the issue concluded that full approval should not preempt such claims,[107] the Supreme Court on February 20, 2008 held otherwise in *Riegel v. Medtronic, Inc.*[108]

The facts in *Riegel* were not especially compelling from the plaintiff's perspective.[109] Shortly after Charles Riegel suffered a heart attack, his doctor attempted to dilate his partially blocked coronary artery by dilating it with a medical device called a "balloon catheter" that could be inserted into the artery and then blown up like a balloon while in the artery. This was not an especially good idea, because the device's label clearly stated that the procedure was contraindicated for patients with Riegel's condition. The label also warned against inflating the catheter beyond eight atmospheres, but the doctor inflated it five times to a pressure of ten atmospheres. On the fifth try, the balloon exploded, and Riegel developed a heart blockage that required additional surgery. Riegel had the option, of course, of suing the doctor and leaving it at that, but understandably he did not want to sue the man who saved his life.[110] He decided instead to sue the Medtronic Corporation, the manufacturer of the catheter, for negligence and strict products liability in the design, testing, inspection, distribution, labeling, marketing and sale of the device.

In an opinion authored by Justice Antonin Scalia and joined by seven of the other justices, the Court held that the full FDA approval process imposed "requirements" on device manufacturers within the meaning of the express preemption clause. Unlike the abbreviated process at issue in *Lohr,* the full approval process focused on "safety, not equivalence." In particular, "the FDA requires a device that has received premarket approval to be made with almost no deviations from the specifications in its approval application."[111] The Court further held that Riegel's common law claims came within the meaning of the word "requirement" in the statute's express preemption clause. In broad dicta that defendants will no doubt cite in future cases involving statutes using that word, the Court stated that "[a]bsent other indication, reference to a State's 'requirements' includes its common-law duties."[112] The Court explained that "State tort law that requires a manufacturer's catheters to be safer, but hence less effective, than the model the FDA has approved disrupts the federal scheme no less than state regulatory law to the same effect."[113] The Court did not address the argument that the state common law that Riegel invoked did not in fact "require" Medtronic's catheter to be safer; it only required the company to pay damages if a jury held that its catheter was defectively designed or unreasonably labeled (a perhaps unlikely prospect in Reigel's case).

Justice Scalia's opinion did not stop there. It further speculated that "one would think that tort law, applied by juries under a negligence or strict-liability standard, is less deserving of preservation," because a state agency "could at least be expected to apply cost-benefit analysis similar to that applied by the experts at the FDA: How many more lives will be saved by a device which, along with its greater effectiveness, brings a greater risk of harm?"[114] The Court pointed out that the jury "sees only the cost of a more dangerous design, and is not concerned with its benefits; the patients who reaped those benefits are not represented in court."[115] To the extent that a plaintiff's claim was based on a company's violation of FDA's regulations, however, there was no variance between the duty imposed by the federal government and that imposed by the common law. Therefore, such claims were not preempted.[116] The Court pointed out that its reading of the statute squared with the FDA's position on the preemption question.

As with the railroad grade crossing litigation, there is a certain irony in the Court's holding that design defect and failure-to-warn claims regarding fully approved medical devices are preempted. Professors Adler and Mann note that "had preemption been applied to the Dalkon Shield, A. H. Robins would have succeeded in operating incompetently and illegally, [and] hundreds of thousands of injured women would have been denied recompense and justice."[117] Moreover, Congress would probably not have enacted the Medical Device Amendments in the first place. Another irony, noted by Professor David Vladeck, lies in FDA's mysterious "shift in position" just prior to a "stream of highly publicized recalls of defective medical devices."[118] Yet, if FDA and the medical device manufacturers prevail on this front of the preemption war, innocent victims of fully approved devices will have no remedy against device manufacturers, and the common law will play no role in ferreting out past malfeasance and discouraging future abuse in what appears to be a fairly risky business.[119]

Fraud on Federal Agencies

On December 2, 1971, the parents of eight-month-old Harrikah Stanton checked her into Harrisburg Hospital for bone marrow tests.[120] Her doctor injected a 2-percent solution of Xylocaine into Harrikah's posterior to anesthetize the area from which he would take the marrow. Soon thereafter, Harrikah began convulsing, and she later experienced cardiac and respiratory arrest that resulted in severe brain damage. During the lawsuit that Harrikah's parents brought against the manufacturer of Xylocaine, their lawyers discovered that the company had received more than two hundred reports of adverse reactions ranging from minor health effects to death but had failed to forward those reports to FDA as required by the agency's adverse effects reporting regulations. The trial court instructed the jury that, absent some good excuse, it should find the company negligent if it determined that the company had in fact violated the FDA reporting regulations. It then upheld a jury verdict for $2,367,032. The Stantons' case was decided in 1983. In 2003, the outcome would probably have been different because the court would have found that their claim, which was based largely on the defendant's alleged fraud on FDA, was preempted.

An entity subject to a federal licensing requirement, like the FDA drug and device approval process, usually has many opportunities to determine the direction of the regulatory process by manipulating the information available to the agency and managing public perceptions about the implications of the relevant information. First, a regulated entity may engage in overt fraud by submitting fraudulently conducted studies to the agency or by withholding relevant information. Second, it can covertly "massage" or otherwise manipulate the scientific, economic, and statistical information in misleading ways to fit the company's view of the scientific facts. Third, it can affect agency decision making by finding flaws with or otherwise attempting to undermine scientific, economic, and statistical studies from sources over which the company has no control. Finally, it can attempt to bring pressure to bear on an agency to take lenient regulatory action through public relations exercises aimed at manipulating public perceptions of publicly available scientific information.[121] Some of these techniques are clearly unlawful under federal law; others are clearly lawful; still others fall into grey areas that require further analysis and investigation.

In most cases, the federal agency will not know that it is being misled or defrauded, and it may never uncover the deception. After-the-fact prosecution of fraud that agencies do detect can protect the government's interest in the integrity of the regulatory process and provide incentives to regulatees not to dissemble with federal agencies in the future. That strategy will be effective, however, only to the extent that agencies make a serious effort to uncover that deception and heavily penalize the responsible companies. The Vioxx story, related in Chapter 1, suggests that the public should not place a great deal of faith in the regulators to detect and prosecute such fraud. Furthermore, this strategy does nothing to provide corrective justice to those who are injured by fraudulently licensed products and activities.

Proponents of preemption, including the United States government, argue that common law claims that depend on proving fraud on regulatory agencies unduly interfere with the right and responsibility of the agencies to decide whether they have been defrauded and, if so, what to do about it. They also fear that plaintiffs' lawyers on "fishing expeditions" for possible evidence of fraud will file burdensome discovery requests and subpoena busy agency decision makers to testify in state common law trials.[122] In the context of federal licensing regimes, such intrusions could cause delays in agency approvals of valuable or even life-saving products and activities.[123]

The Supreme Court first resolved the question in the context of FDA device regulation in a fairly unusual factual setting in *Buckman Co. v. Plaintiffs' Legal Committee*,[124] a case in which a class consisting of more than 2,300 plaintiffs claimed that its members had been damaged by defective orthopedic bone screws that doctors had installed in the pedicles of their spines. Like the pacemaker in *Lohr,* the bone screws went through the "expedited" FDA approval process that is available for devices that are "substantially equivalent" to "predicate" devices that were on the market prior to 1976.[125] During the approval process, the submitter had to certify that "all data and information submitted" during the expedited process were "truthful and accurate" and that "no material fact" had been omitted.[126]

After FDA twice found that the screws were riskier than pre-1976 spinal-fixation devices and therefore were not substantially equivalent, the manufacturer hired the Buckman Company, a consultant with experience in the expedited approval process, to assist in a third try. On Buckman's advice, the manufacturer split the device into its component parts, renamed them, and filed separate applications for use in the long bones of the arms and legs instead of in the spine. Both Buckman and the manufacturer fully expected that doctors would prescribe the screws for "off-label" use in spinal-fixation systems, an outcome that was perfectly legal so long as the company did not directly promote them for that unapproved use.[127] This time, FDA approved the devices as substantially equivalent to predicate devices used in long-bone surgery. The agency much later approved the bone screws for use in spinal-fixation systems.[128]

After settling their claims against the manufacturer,[129] the plaintiffs sued Buckman, claiming that its misleading manipulation of the regulatory process violated its common law duty to the plaintiffs as foreseeable victims. The Supreme Court held that the Medical Device Amendments impliedly preempted the plaintiffs' claims. The Court first found that the general presumption against preemption, which depended upon the "historic primacy of state regulation of matters of health and safety," was inapplicable to state common law claims based on fraud on the FDA because policing fraud against federal agencies was not a field that the states had traditionally occupied. Next, the Court held that, while not clearly inconsistent with FDA's authority to regulate medical devices, the plaintiffs' claims presented a subtler conflict with the "delicate balance of statutory objectives" that the agency had to strike in deciding whether or not to investigate and punish fraud. In particular, the agency's flexibility to decide which, if any, of the available antifraud provisions to invoke was "a critical component of the statutory and regulatory framework under which the FDA pursues difficult (and often competing) objectives." Since doctors could lawfully prescribe approved medical devices for unapproved uses, FDA faced an especially difficult balancing job in "regulating the marketing and distribution of medical devices without intruding upon decisions statutorily committed to the discretion of health care professionals." The Court concluded that Congress did not intend to allow common law juries to second-guess the agency's discretion in striking this balance.

The Court also found that state common law claims based upon alleged fraud on the FDA could increase the regulatory burdens on potential applicants, who might "be discouraged from seeking expedited approval of devices with potentially beneficial off-label uses for fear that such use might expose the manufacturer or its associates (such as petitioner) to unpredictable civil liability." In addition, they could "deter off-label use despite the fact that the [MDA] expressly disclaims any intent to directly regulate the practice of medicine . . . and even though off-label use is generally accepted." Finally, a common law claim based on fraud on the FDA would "cause applicants to fear that their disclosures to the FDA, although deemed appropriate by the [agency], will later be judged insufficient in state court." Alternatively, massive prophylactic submissions by applicants concerned about state tort liability could tie up the agency and slow down the flow of approved predicate devices, thus impeding competition and delaying health care professionals' ability to prescribe appropriate off-label uses. Since all of these possibilities had the potential to erect serious obstacles to the agency's efforts to implement the statutory goals, the Medical Device Amendments impliedly preempted the plaintiffs' claims.

The Court's holding in *Buckman* was consistent with the position set out in the government's amicus curiae brief defending the "important federal interest in permitting FDA to decide for itself whether it has been defrauded, and, if so, what sanction is appropriate."[130] At the same time, the Court's preemption analysis focused heavily on the adverse effects that state common law claims might have on *regulatees.* Apart from its rather speculative "deluge of information" concern, the Court did not cite any evidence suggesting that the plaintiffs' claims would interfere with the agency's regulatory efforts. Significantly, the Court's opinion did not pay even passing deference to the statute's *primary* purpose, which is "to provide for the safety and effectiveness of medical devices intended for human use."[131]

Although the Court did not identify the factors that weighed into the "delicate balance" the government employs in deciding whether to enforce the statutory antifraud provisions, one careful observer of the FDA's enforcement process suggested long before the *Buckman* case that FDA enforcement officials should consider such factors as the seriousness of violations, the level of knowledge or intent, the resources available to the agency, and the potential benefit to consumers of successful pursuit of the prosecution.[132] In the case of fraudulent withholding or misrepresentation of data, this balance does not seem especially "delicate." Fraud on an agency is very serious, because it undermines the integrity of the regulatory process, and the level of knowledge or intent is very high. The potential benefit to consumers of ensuring that the data underlying agency safety determinations are complete and reliable is exceedingly high. The only factor arguably militating against prosecuting cases of fraudulent manipulation of the regulatory process is therefore the ever-present limitations on the agency's enforcement resources. Yet, this is the very limitation that a common law action for fraud on a federal agency would most clearly help alleviate.

The interests of consumers in corrective justice and corporate accountability would be better served by limiting *Buckman* to the particular statutory and factual context in which it arose—a claim against a consultant that assisted in a fraud perpetrated by a drug or device manufacturer. Most lower courts have in fact been careful not to extend *Buckman* beyond the narrow confines of fraud on the agency itself. The courts have not, for example, interpreted *Buckman* to prevent failure-to-warn claims to go forward,[133] and they have refused to extend *Buckman* to claims based on fraud and misrepresentation to doctors and consumers.[134] A few courts, however, have extended *Buckman* far beyond its factual confines. In *Morgan v. Brush Wellman, Inc.*,[135] for example, the essence of the plaintiffs' claim was not that the company had defrauded the regulatory agencies, which were allegedly co-conspirators, but that it had hidden potential risks to workers and neighbors who were exposed to the undisclosed hazards of beryllium. The court nevertheless found the claims to be preempted because they would conflict with the Department of Energy's ability to set nuclear policy consistent with its own judgment and objectives."[136] Another court interpreted *Buckman* to require it to exclude any evidence offered of fraud on the agency to support claims based on negligence, defective product design, and failure to warn, even though the complaint did not include a specific fraud on the agency claim.[137]

The Supreme Court in 2007 agreed to address the scope of fraud-on-the-agency preemption in a case involving the Michigan liability shield statute, featured in Chapter 1, that prohibited common law claims against manufacturers of certain federally approved products unless the approval was procured by fraud. In that case, a large number of plaintiffs in Michigan and California sued the manufacturer of the FDA-approved diabetes drug Rezulin. The claims in all of the cases were consolidated in a New York federal district court where the Michigan plaintiffs argued that their claims were appropriate under Michigan law because the company had misled the FDA in reporting on the clinical trials upon which the agency based its approval. In this regard, the plaintiffs relied on a series of articles in the *Los Angeles Times* reporting that the company knew that Rezulin could cause liver damage, but concealed that information from FDA in its New Drug Application. A safety update submitted soon after FDA approved the drug in 1997 reported that no patients taking the drug in the clinical trials had liver enzymes in excess of three times the upper limit of normal. The company knew at the time (and later admitted in a letter to the *New England Journal of Medicine*) that 20 patients in the study had in fact demonstrated elevated enzyme levels. Ultimately, the company was forced to pull the drug from the market, but only after an FDA medical officer told it that the agency would not have approved the drug in the first place if it had been privy to the information that the company had withheld.

The Second Circuit Court of Appeals, in an opinion written by former Yale Law School Dean Guido Calabrese, held that the plaintiffs' claims could go forward because they came within the fraud exception to the Michigan law. Because the plaintiffs' common law claims and the state statute limiting common law liability were clearly areas that had traditionally been regulated by the states, the court applied the presumption against preemption. The court noted that FDA approval was relevant to the cases only if the defendant elected to assert the Michigan statute as an affirmative defense. The case was therefore not like *Buckman,* a case in which the alleged fraud against FDA, standing alone, was sufficient to impose liability on the defendant. Responding to the defendant's concern that allowing the claim to go forward would inspire pharmaceutical companies like itself to deluge FDA in irrelevant information (a concern raised by the *Buckman* court), the court pointed out that this incentive existed *any* time evidence of a company's misbehavior with respect to a regulatory agency is relevant to a plaintiff's claim. The court was unwilling to conclude that the Supremacy Clause required common law courts to exclude all evidence of fraud on federal agencies. In allowing the plaintiffs to proceed, however, the court refused to follow the contrary holding of the Sixth Circuit Court of Appeals, the court that ordinarily has jurisdiction in cases arising in Michigan.[138]

Less than a week after hearing oral arguments in the case, the Supreme Court found itself equally divided 4-4 (Chief Justice John Roberts had recused himself). The Court therefore affirmed the Second Circuit court's holding in a one sentence unsigned opinion.[139] This meant that the Michigan plaintiffs in that case (and presumably future cases in which plaintiffs from Michigan and states with similar statutes can locate their cases in that circuit) can continue to pursue their claims against Wyeth. At the same time, plaintiffs in states within the sixth circuit (Ohio, Michigan, Tennessee and Kentucky) remain in the worst of all possible worlds: drug companies are immune from failure-to-warn claims, and the fraud on the FDA exceptions that the legislatures added to prevent scofflaws from taking advantage of the immunity are also unavailable.

PESTICIDES

Rachel Carson's path-breaking book, *Silent Spring,* focused on an environmental hazard that the federal government had been regulating for twenty years.[140] Unlike the risks posed by polluted water, dirty air, and hazardous wastes, all of which until the 1970s had been primarily the responsibility of the states, the risks that pesticides posed to humans and the environment had been a federal responsibility from the time that Congress enacted the Federal Insecticide, Fungicide, and Rodenticide Act of 1947 (FIFR Act).[141] Since most of the modern organochlorine and organophosphate pesticides on the market entered commerce after World War II,[142] the tragic destruction of wildlife and the looming risks to human health portrayed in *Silent Spring* had resulted from the failure of a *federal* regulatory program.[143] Spurred on by an activist environmental movement in the early 1970s, Congress completely overhauled the federal program in 1972, and it has continued to refine that program in the ensuing years.[144]

The FIFR Act requires the manufacturer of any chemical that is intended to kill any "pest" to obtain a "registration" for that product from the Environmental Protection Agency (EPA). An applicant for registration must provide a proposed label and comprehensive studies on the health and environmental effects of the pesticide sufficient to demonstrate that: (1) its composition is such as to warrant the proposed claims for it; (2) its labeling complies with the provisions of the statute governing misbranding; and (3) it will not generally cause unreasonable adverse effects on the environment.[145] A pesticide is misbranded if its label contains any statement that is "false or misleading in any particular" or if it does not contain "a warning or caution statement which may be necessary, and if complied with . . . is adequate to protect health and the environment."[146]

Since a pesticide registrant has a continuing obligation to ensure that its product is not misbranded, it must be prepared to update the label as information relevant to the misbranding criteria becomes available.[147] On the other hand, the law does not require that all labels for the same pesticide convey the same information. It is therefore not uncommon for different registrants of the same pesticide to use different labels. Moreover, registrants are free to include on labels information that EPA does not require.[148] Indeed, the fact that EPA has approved a label is no defense against a claim that it is misbranded.[149] When amendments to the statute in 1978 authorized EPA to waive data requirements for pesticide efficacy,[150] EPA ceased all of its efficacy reviews and let it be known that it was no longer interested in whether or not the pesticide label was truthful with respect to whether the pesticide worked as promised and whether it would "damage crops or cause other property damage." EPA explained that "pesticide producers are aware that they are potentially subject to damage suits by the user community if their products prove ineffective in actual use."[151]

The FIFR Act has an express preemption provision stating that a state "may regulate the sale or use of any federally registered pesticide . . . , but only if and to the extent that the regulation does not permit any sale or use prohibited by" EPA.[152] In addition to this "floor preemption" provision allowing more stringent state regulation, however, the statute also provides that a state may "not impose or continue in effect any requirements for labeling or packaging in addition to or different from those required under" the statute.[153] State and federal courts entertained common law actions against pesticide companies for damage caused to human health, property, and crops long before the FIFR Act was enacted in 1947, and they continued to do so after it was modernized in 1972 without any thought to dismissing such actions as preempted by the FIFR Act's regulatory regime.[154]

The Supreme Court's holding in *Cipollone,* however, prompted defendants in pesticide litigation to raise the preemption defense, and nine of the twelve federal courts of appeals held that the FIFR Act did in fact preempt common law failure-to-warn claims.[155] Indeed, some courts held that the FIFR Act's comprehensive regulatory regime preempted virtually all common law claims against manufacturers of registered pesticides, including claims based on adverse health effects suffered by innocent third parties.[156] Several courts even found claims based on the pesticide's failure to perform as advertised to be preempted, despite EPA's 1978 announcement that it was no longer in the business of regulating pesticide efficacy.[157] One of these cases came to the Supreme Court's attention in 2005.

As west Texas peanut farmers prepared for the 2000 growing season, they were invited to a series of "Field Days" sponsored by Texas A & M University, where they learned from representatives of Dow Agrosciences Company of a revolutionary new herbicide that would be available for soybeans and peanuts just in time for the May plantings. The new product, called "Strongarm," would be a "pre-emergent" herbicide that could be applied to the soil before the seeds were planted. The Dow salespersons assured the farmers that Strongarm would kill the weeds that typically infested peanuts without harming the peanut plants themselves. Although Dow scientists knew that herbicides like Strongarm were not actively absorbed by soils having a pH level above 7.0, the Dow representatives did not relate that critical fact, nor was it on the Strongarm label. Excited about its ease of application, many west Texas farmers applied Strongarm to the soil containing their crops, much of which had a pH of 7.2 or greater.[158]

Within weeks after they planted their seeds, the farmers noticed signs of herbicide damage in the emerging leaves. Dow representatives agreed with the farmers that their crops were "burning," and they promised that the company would provide compensation for any extra expenses caused by Strongarm. As time went on, it became clear that Strongarm also failed to kill the weeds that began to strangle the peanut crops. The much-delayed harvest was a disaster, and the farmers pressed their claims for compensation on the company. By this point, Dow had secured from EPA an amended registration with a special label telling farmers in Texas, Oklahoma, and New Mexico not to apply Strongarm to soils with a pH of 7.2 or greater and to apply it only after planting. Nevertheless, Dow denied many of the claims, blaming "[e]xtreme heat, a prolonged drought, and heavy fall rains."[159]

When the farmers notified the company of their intent to sue, Dow strongarmed them by filing a preemptive lawsuit in federal court asking for a declaratory judgment that their claims were all preempted. The farmers then counterclaimed, demanding compensation for their economic losses and alleging that Dow had committed breach of warranty and fraud, had negligently failed to test Strongarm in high pH soils, and had marketed a defectively designed and manufactured product. The district court and court of appeals holdings that the FIFR Act preempted the plaintiffs' claims were inconsistent with the position that EPA had taken in an amicus curiae brief filed in 2000, but the agency had changed its position after the change of administration in 2001.[160]

The Supreme Court, in *Bates v. Dow Agrosciences, LLC,*[161] held (7–2) that the farmers' claims were not preempted. The Court first agreed with Dow that, under *Cipollone,* the term "requirements" in the FIFR Act's preemption clause "embrace[d] common law duties." Noting that the provision extended only to requirements for labeling and packaging, however, the Court clarified that product design claims were clearly not preempted. The Court further noted that, since the preemption provision encompassed only state-imposed requirements that were "in addition to or different from" federal requirements, claims based on conduct that violated EPA-imposed requirements were likewise not preempted. The Court concluded that "[r]ules that require manufacturers to design reasonably safe products, to use due care in conducting appropriate testing of their products, to market products free of manufacturing defects, and to honor their express warranties or other contractual commitments" were "plainly" not preempted.

The Court next rejected the "effects-based" test, employed by several courts of appeals, under which a common law claim is preempted if it would induce the company to alter its federally approved label. The Court observed that "[a] requirement is a rule of law that must be obeyed; an event, such as a jury verdict, that merely motivates an optional decision is not a requirement." The proper judicial inquiry is into the elements of the common law duty and not "speculation as to whether a jury verdict will prompt the manufacturer to take any particular action (a question, in any event, that will depend on a variety of cost/benefit calculations best left to the manufacturer's accountants)."

The Court then addressed the concerns raised by Dow and the government that allowing juries in fifty different states to conclude that pesticides are improperly labeled would result in "a crazy-quilt of anti-misbranding requirements different from the one defined by FIFRA itself and intended by Congress to be interpreted authoritatively by EPA." The problem with this argument was that it failed to recognize that the statute preempted only state requirements (common law or otherwise) that were "different from or in addition to" EPA-imposed requirements. Noting that the government had taken a different position on this question five years previously, the Court reasoned that "FIFRA contemplates that pesticide labels will evolve over time, as manufacturers gain more information about their products' performance in diverse settings." Furthermore, "the specter of damage actions may provide manufacturers with added dynamic incentives to continue to keep abreast of all possible injuries stemming from use of their product so as to forestall such actions through product improvement." Conceding that "properly instructed juries might on occasion reach contrary conclusions on a similar issue of misbranding," the Court could see no reason to conclude that "such occurrences would be frequent or that they would result in difficulties beyond those regularly experienced by manufacturers of other products that every day bear the risk of conflicting jury verdicts."

Given the long history of tort litigation by victims of badly designed and poorly labeled pesticides, the Court believed that Congress would have been more explicit about preempting state common law if it had intended to do so. Indeed, the common law cases had emphasized "the importance of providing an incentive to manufacturers to use the utmost care in the business of distributing inherently dangerous items" like pesticides. The "over-enforcement" that might result from common law claims based on misbranding created "a risk of imposing unnecessary financial burdens on manufacturers," but "under-enforcement creates not only financial risks for consumers, but risks that affect their safety and the environment as well." The Court was unwilling to conclude that Congress intended that result.

The *Bates* case put an end to an industry-encouraged movement in the lower courts toward expanding the FIFR Act's preemption beyond product label cases to all design defect cases.[162] The Court also recognized the important role that common law liability can play in reinforcing the incentive of pesticide manufacturers to meet their continuing obligation under the FIFR Act to ensure that their products are not misbranded. In 1994, EPA's Assistant Administrator for Pesticides and Toxic Substances cried out for help from the common law, noting that "[i]f tort actions are not preempted by FIFRA, manufacturers' concern about possible tort liability may well lead them to take additional steps to provide users with information about their products," and that information "could, in turn, enable users to choose and use pesticides in ways that are safer for themselves, others, and the environment."[163] The Supreme Court in *Bates* ensured that the common law would continue to encourage manufacturers to provide consumers with this much-needed information.

JOB-RELATED ACTIONS AND HAZARDS

Many federal statutes address many aspects of the critical relationship between employers and employees. The well-known National Labor Relations Act (NRL Act),[164] as amended by the Labor Management Relations Act of 1947 (LMR Act),[165] for example, pervasively regulates the employer/employee relationship in unionized workplaces. Some of the earliest preemption cases established that these statutes occupy the entire field of covered labor-management issues and therefore preempt all state regulatory and common law in that field.[166] Congress has made its intentions less clear in other statutes, some of which regulate conduct that threatens employee health and well-being more directly.

Job-Related Emotional Distress

The NLR Act and the LMR Act govern the creation and enforcement of collective bargaining agreements (CBAs) between employers and unions. They also specifically address various aspects of the employment relationship, including the conditions under which employees may be hired, disciplined, and fired. Congress delegated the day-to-day administration of the statutes to an independent federal agency called the National Labor Relations Board (NLRB). Employees who believe that their employers have violated the terms of a CBA may file grievance actions and secure the remedies provided for in the CBA. Most CBAs provide for private arbitration of these disputes, but the NLRB is the ultimate arbiter of disputes covered by CBAs. Over the years, the NLRB and the federal courts reviewing NLRB decisions in individual cases have developed a sophisticated body of common law derived from the statutes and the language that is common to most CBAs.[167]

The Supreme Court, in the fountainhead 1959 case of *San Diego Building Trades Council v. Garmon,*[168] recognized that "[w]here the exercise of state power over a particular area of activity threatened interference with the clearly indicated policy of industrial relations, it has been judicially necessary to preclude the states from acting." At the same time, the federal labor laws do not withdraw from the states the "power to regulate where the activity regulated [is] a merely peripheral concern" to the federal statutes.[169] The test for preemption under the LMR Act is "whether an evaluation of the tort claim is inextricably intertwined with consideration of the terms of the labor contract."[170] Even if a dispute under the LMR Act would involve the same facts as the common law claim, the state action may go forward "so long as the state-law claim can be resolved without interpreting the agreement itself."[171]

Because state claims for intentional infliction of severe emotional distress by their very nature require a showing of an additional element of extreme outrage that goes "beyond all possible bounds of decency" so as to be considered "utterly intolerable in a civilized community,"[172] the courts have been reluctant to find that emotional distress claims arising out of workplace conduct are preempted. Thus, the Court, in *Farmer v. United Brotherhood of Carpenters and Joiners of America,*[173] held that an employee's claim that officials of his union had intentionally caused him severe emotional distress when they engaged in a "campaign of personal abuse and harassment" against him as a result of disagreements over various internal union policies was not preempted. The Court recognized that a state has "a substantial interest in protecting its citizens from the kind of abuse" that the plaintiff had suffered.[174]

The lower courts have held that emotional distress claims resulting solely from adverse employment actions such as firing or suspension, however arbitrary the actions might be, are preempted because the lawfulness of the action is ordinarily determined by the CBA.[175] On the other hand, CBAs do not ordinarily envision outrageous or defamatory conduct,[176] and courts have allowed plaintiffs to pursue state common law claims for mental distress resulting from termination for especially outrageous reasons, such as in retaliation for filing legitimate workers compensation claims.[177] Claims alleging emotional distress from actions occurring during the pendency of the employment relationship are not generally preempted because CBAs rarely address such activities. Thus, courts have allowed employees to pursue claims for emotional distress caused by outrageous and untrue statements about the plaintiff's wife, coerced sex with a supervisor, heterosexual and homosexual advances by co-workers, and verbal harassment (called "mad-dogging") designed to induce the employee to resign.[178] Other courts have held such harassment claims to be preempted on the questionable ground that it would be impossible for a court to determine whether an employer had "acted outrageously or was merely insisting on his legal rights" without reference to the CBA.[179]

The cases leave the strong impression that the lower courts' preemption analysis turns to some degree on their assessments of the validity of the underlying claims for emotional distress. If a court is not convinced that the employer's conduct is truly outrageous so as to pass all possible bounds of decency, they are more likely to find the claims preempted.

Occupational Safety and Health

Congress enacted the Occupational Safety and Health Act of 1970 (OSH Act) "to assure so far as possible every working man and woman in the Nation safe and healthful working conditions."[180] The statute empowers the Occupational Safety and Health Administration (OSHA) to promulgate standards to protect workers from workplace risks, and it allows states to set their own standards and to administer their own programs if they receive OSHA approval.[181] OSHA may approve a state program if it finds that it "will be at least as effective in providing safe and healthful employment and places of employment as the standards promulgated" under the OSH Act.[182] The statute also contains an express preemption provision stating that a state may assert jurisdiction over "any occupational safety or health issue with respect to which no standard is in effect" under the Act.[183] Read together, these provisions mean that a state may establish standards in areas that OSHA has not addressed, but it cannot set standards in areas where OSHA has promulgated its own standards in the absence of an approved state program.[184] A savings clause provides that nothing in the Act "shall be construed to supersede or in any manner affect any workmen's compensation law or to enlarge or diminish or affect in any other manner the common law or statutory rights, duties, or liabilities of employers and employees under any law with respect to injuries, diseases, or death of employees arising out of, or in the course of, employment."[185]

The Supreme Court addressed the preemptive effect of OSHA standards on state regulatory requirements in *Gade v. National Solid Wastes Management As-*

sociation, where it held that a state's licensing requirements for hazardous waste disposal operators and laborers, which were not part of an OSHA-approved program, were impliedly preempted by an OSHA standard for hazardous waste operations that contained detailed regulations on worker training requirements.[186] Given the breadth of the savings clause, it is not surprising that no lower court has found an OSHA standard to expressly preempt a state common law claim.[187] Somewhat more surprising, perhaps, is the fact that no court has seized upon *Geier's* invitation to find state common law claims impliedly preempted in spite of the savings clause.[188] So far, the OSH Act does not pose a significant barrier to injured workers seeking compensation under state workers compensation laws or state common law.

Employee Drug Testing

Congress enacted the Federal Omnibus Employee Testing Act of 1991 (FOTET Act) to address a growing problem of illicit drug and alcohol abuse among employees in the transportation sector.[189] Although some of the federal transportation agencies, including the Federal Aviation Administration (FAA), had already promulgated regulations requiring employers to conduct random drug testing of employees in positions for which sobriety was needed to protect public safety, the FOTET Act reaffirmed their authority to promulgate those regulations and required the other transportation agencies to promulgate similar regulations.[190] The agencies then promulgated regulations prescribing in some detail exactly how employers and the laboratories that test the randomly collected samples must go about those tasks.[191] The statute contains an express preemption provision stating that a state or local government "may not prescribe, issue or continue in effect a law, regulation, standard, or order that is inconsistent with regulations prescribed" pursuant to the Act, except that criminal laws imposing sanctions for "reckless conduct leading to loss of life, injury, or damage to property" are not preempted.[192] Although the Supreme Court has not addressed this statute, the lower courts have interpreted its preemption clause quite narrowly.

When LabOne, a company specializing in testing urine samples for evidence of drug use, reported that a sample taken from Yasuki Ishikawa, a Delta Airlines flight attendant, at the end of a nine-hour trip from Japan to Oregon was a "substituted" specimen, Delta fired her. Ishikawa successfully challenged Delta's action after a different company reported that the other half of the "split" sample was within the FAA regulation's tolerances for determining substitution and tested negative for drugs. Ishikawa then sued LabOne alleging common law negligence, and a jury awarded her $400,000 in economic and noneconomic damages. A federal court of appeals, in *Ishikawa v. Delta Airlines,*[193] rejected LabOne's argument that the FOTET Act preempted the action. The court could not "see how the duty the state common law imposed, that LabOne test urine and report the results with due care, could be inconsistent with the federal guidelines, which require the same thing with more specificity."[194] Most courts have followed this line of reasoning in similar cases against testing laboratories alleging negligence in conducting drug testing on employees covered by the FOTET Act.[195] Although the FOTET Act's preemption provision probably shields airlines from negligence claims regarding the administration of random drug testing programs conducted in accordance with agency regulations, the opponents of preemption have apparently won the battle over negligence claims against testing companies.

Whistleblower Retaliation

The common law rule governing an employer's termination of the employment relationship, called the "employment at will" doctrine, is that an employee may be fired for a good reason, a bad reason, or no reason at all.[196] This harsh rule was gradually softened during the twentieth century as courts recognized that a job was a valuable resource and that employees often made substantial investments of their time and resources in reliance on the legitimate expectation that they would not be fired arbitrarily. The courts further recognized that the public interest was sometimes best served by protecting an employee from arbitrary job actions taken in retaliation for public-spirited conduct like blowing the whistle on fraud, corruption, or other misconduct on the part of other company officials or for taking other actions that were "strongly rooted in public policy."[197]

At the same time, Congress was enacting various labor laws that, among other things, protected certain covered employees from arbitrary retaliation for whistleblowing, exercising their collective bargaining rights, and engaging in other specified actions. The Atomic Energy Act of 1954, for example, makes it unlawful for an employer in the nuclear industry to "discharge any employee or otherwise discriminate against any employee with respect to his compensation, terms, conditions of privileges or employment" because the employee has initiated an enforcement proceeding under the Act, testified in such a proceeding, or otherwise participated in such a proceeding.[198] Similarly, the Occupational Safety and Health Act of 1970 (OSH Act) provides that no employer "shall discharge or in any manner discriminate against any employee because such employee has filed any complaint . . . because of the exercise by such employee . . . of any right afforded by" the Act.[199] Both statutes allow employees to bring administrative actions in the Department of Labor to correct and redress violations of their whistleblower protection sections.[200]

In *English v. General Electric Co.*,[201] the Supreme Court found that the Atomic Energy Act's whistleblower protection provision did not preempt a discharged employee's state common law claim for intentional infliction of severe emotional distress associated with the same adverse employment action. The Court could find no "'clear and manifest' intent on the part of Congress . . . to preempt all state tort laws that traditionally have been available to those persons who . . . allege outrageous conduct at the hands of an employer."[202] Although the Supreme Court has not addressed the OSH Act's whistleblower protection provision, the lower courts have uniformly applied the *English* reasoning to hold that it does not preempt state common law actions addressing the same conduct.[203] Likewise, the courts have uniformly held that the LMR Act does not preempt state common law claims for emotional distress based upon alleged retaliation for filing workers compensation claims or reporting violations of safety, civil rights, and other protective statutes.[204] On the whistleblower front, the opponents of preemption have thus far prevailed in the preemption war.

CONSUMER PRODUCTS

Since the early 1970s, consumer products have been subject to federal regulation by the Consumer Product Safety Commission (CPSC) under a statute that applies broadly to all consumer products and two narrower laws that cover hazardous substances and toys that pose safety risks to children. The agency has never lived up to its potential, at first because of limitations imposed by federal courts and later because of amendments to the statute during an era of "regulatory reform" and the agency's subsequent reluctance to assert its remaining power in ways that might stir up controversy. Thus, while products liability is a very active area of common law litigation, relatively few cases have raised the preemption question, and the Supreme Court has not decided a single case involving a CPSC regulation. This could, of course, change in the future if CPSC becomes more aggressive, a very likely possibility in light of the scandal that erupted in late 2007 over the safety of toys imported from China.[205]

Consumer Product Safety Generally

The Consumer Product Safety Act (CPS Act) was enacted in 1972 to "protect the public against unreasonable risks of injury associated with consumer products" and to "develop uniform safety standards for consumer products and to minimize conflicting State and local regulations."[206] The statute empowers CPSC to promulgate "consumer product safety standards," which can be stated as either performance or labeling requirements, that are "reasonably necessary to prevent or reduce an unreasonable risk of injury associated with" such products.[207] The agency, however, ran into a judicial roadblock in the late 1970s in the form of a court of appeals holding that CPSC had to meet a high evidentiary threshold for demonstrating that the benefits of its standards exceeded their costs.[208]

An express preemption clause provides that whenever a consumer product safety standard "is in effect and applies to a risk of injury associated with a consumer product," no state may promulgate or implement "any provision of a safety standard or regulation" prescribing requirements with respect to that right, unless they are identical to the federal requirements.[209] On its face, this provision appears to preempt only "standards or regulations" that prescribe "requirements," and not state common law claims that might indirectly "require" defendants to take some action inconsistent with the standard. A savings clause provides that "[c]ompliance with consumer product safety rules . . . shall not relieve any person from liability at common law or under State statutory law to any other person."[210] Another section of the statute creates a new federal cause of action for victims of knowing or willful violations of consumer product safety rules, but it also contains a savings clause making it clear that "[t]he remedies provided for in this section shall be in addition to and not in lieu of any other remedies provided by common law or under Federal or State law."[211]

Despite the clarity of the CPS Act's two savings clauses, the Supreme Court's *Cipollone* opinion inspired defendants to raise the preemption defense in cases involving the few standards that CPSC has promulgated. In the most important of these post-*Cipollone* cases, a seventeen-year-old named Brian Moe was mowing a neighbor's lawn on a damp morning when his MTD lawnmower clogged up with grass. He released the blade clutch on the handle, waited the three seconds that it was supposed to take for the blade to stop spinning, and reached into the side grass chute to pull out the clogged grass. Unbeknown to Brian, the clutch cable had frayed and broken, and the clutch device had not engaged. As a result, he lost all of the fingers on his right hand. The court of appeals, in *Moe v. MTD Products, Inc.*, concluded that the express preemption clause in the CPS Act preempted "not only positive enactments of state standards, but also common law tort actions that would have the effect of creating a state standard."[212] Furthermore, since one of the stated statutory purposes was uniformity in product standards, the court found that the savings clause did not save Brian's claim.[213]

The *Moe* court's analysis was poorly received in the academic literature, and with good reason.[214] The court either missed or ignored the obvious difference between a standard or regulation, which courts never promulgate in common law litigation, and "requirements," which the Supreme Court in *Cipollone* found the common law could impose indirectly through liability determinations.[215] It also allowed its conception of the "goals and policies" of the CPS Act to trump the clear language of the savings clause. Indeed, it is difficult to conceive of any language that could have expressed Congress's intent not to preempt state common law more clearly than the words that it used in the CPS Act's savings clause. Nevertheless, the *Moe* opinion proved quite influential in the lower courts for several years.[216] Only after the Supreme Court in *Geier* made it clear that savings clauses need not play second fiddle to express preemption clauses did some courts begin to allow failure to warn claims to proceed against companies that complied with CPSC's standards.[217] Other courts have adhered to the *Moe* analysis.[218] Until the Supreme Court takes up a case involving the CPS Act, litigation over CPSC-required warnings is likely to remain a limited but active front in the preemption war.

Hazardous Substances and Child Safety

The Federal Hazardous Substances Act (FHS Act) empowers CPSC to declare a substance or mixture of substances to be a "hazardous substance" subject to the Act's requirements and to ban such substances when necessary to protect public health and safety.[219] The statute itself prescribes the contents of labels for packages for consumer products containing listed hazardous substances. Such labels must contain the common name for the chemicals contained therein, the signal word "DANGER" for substances that are extremely flammable, corrosive or highly toxic, the signal word "WARNING" or "CAUTION" for all other hazardous substances, and an affirmative statement of the nature of the hazards presented.[220] CPSC may, however, promulgate regulations deleting or refining these requirements.[221] The Child Safety Protection Act (CSP Act, not to be confused with the previously described CPS Act) specifies similar statutory warnings for toys and games to be used by young children, with a similar grant of authority to CPSC to delete or refine the requirements.[222]

The preemption provisions of both the FHS Act and the CSP Act are of the traditional variety that applies to all "requirements." The FHS Act prevents states from establishing or implementing "a cautionary labeling requirement" that is "designed to protect against the same risk of illness or injury" unless the state or local requirement is identical to the federal requirement.[223] The CSP Act likewise prevents states from establishing or enforcing "a requirement relating to cautionary labeling" of the toy hazards subject to the statute unless it is identical to the requirement specified in the statute or CPSC regulations.[224] The FHS Act allows a state to petition CPSC to promulgate a regulation waiving the preemptive effect of the federal requirement if the state requirement provides a "significantly higher degree of protection" than the federal requirement and does not "unduly burden interstate commerce."[225] The CSP Act does not provide for such petitions. The statutes do not contain savings clauses for common law actions, and the Supreme Court has addressed neither statute's preemptive effect on common law actions.

The lower courts have interpreted the FHS Act to permit common law claims based on violations of the statutory labeling requirements and agency regulations, but they have uniformly found failure to warn claims aimed at labels that comply with the statute or regulations to be preempted.[226]

In the only case that has been decided under the CSP Act, the statutory warning specified that, for balls or toys containing balls of less than 1.75 inches in diameter, the label had to contain a specified symbol and say: "WARNING: CHOKING HAZARD—This toy is [or contains] a small ball. Not for children under 3 yrs." The victim was an autistic seven-year-old who choked on a 1.72-inch Pokemon Power Bouncer ball and died of asphyxiation. Arguing that the statutory warning was not written with children like their son in mind, the victim's parents were prepared to offer expert testimony that the label should have at least informed parents of the general nature of the hazard posed by the ball. Relying on prior holdings under the FHS Act, the court, in *Brazier v. Hasbro, Inc.*,[227] found the common law warning defect claims to be preempted because they would have indirectly imposed "requirements" within the meaning of the CPS Act's express preemption clause that were different from the warning that the statute required.[228]

The *Brazier* case illustrates a dilemma that is endemic to all attempts to capture in a single statute or regulation every conceivable situation in which a hazard might arise from a regulated product or activity. The statutory warnings required by the FHS Act and the CSP Act are no doubt quite effective in communicating in a simple and dramatic way the nature of the hazard posed by the product and the importance of avoiding exposure to that hazard in cases that the drafters envisioned. The drafters could not, however, anticipate every possible hazard that might arise from the regulated products. Robert Brazier was not under three years old, but he was definitely at risk because of his unique disease. Perhaps his parents should have treated him like a three-year-old for purposes of allowing him to join in his younger brothers' games with the Pokemon Power Bouncer, and, if a jury so concluded, the defendant would have avoided liability to the extent that they were at fault.[229] But they were not provided an opportunity to make their case to a jury because their claim was preempted by a statute that never envisioned their son's situation.

CREDIT REPORTING AND IDENTITY THEFT

Congress enacted the Fair Credit Reporting Act (FCR Act) in 1970 to address the growing problem of inaccuracy in credit reports on individual consumers prepared by "credit reporting agencies" (CRAs) for banks, mortgage companies, and other lenders.[230] The FCR Act originally focused almost exclusively on CRAs, requiring them "to maintain 'reasonable procedures' designed 'to assure maximum possible accuracy of the information' contained in credit reports and to 'limit the furnishing of [such reports] to' certain statutorily enumerated purposes."[231] The law empowered the Federal Trade Commission to write rules and regulations to implement these broad prescriptions. In addition to empowering federal agencies to seek civil or criminal penalties, the statute also empowered private individuals to sue in federal court for actual and punitive damages suffered as a result of negligent and willful violations of the statute and implementing regulations.[232] Having provided this private remedy, the statute then preempted all state common law claims "in the nature of defamation, invasion of privacy, or negligence with respect to the reporting of information," but it did not preempt claims based on "false information furnished with malice or willful intent to injure."[233]

The 1970 law succeeded in making credit more freely available to consumers, and they, in turn, became more dependent upon the availability of credit for purchases of day-to-day necessities, as well as for large items like cars and homes. As horror stories of inaccuracies and abuses by furnishers of information heightened consumer awareness of the great risks that inaccurate credit reports posed to their creditworthiness, pressure grew to impose additional restrictions on those who gathered and used credit-related information.[234] By the mid-1990s, enough states had enacted their own regulatory programs that, in the view of the credit industry, they were "beginning to threaten the efficiency and cost-effectiveness of the national credit reporting system."[235] The time was therefore ripe for an overhaul of the FCR Act, and Congress amended the statute in 1996 in several important regards.

The amendments expanded the scope of several new requirements beyond CRAs to include creditors and private investigating agencies (the so-called "furnishers" of credit information) that voluntarily provide data to the CRAs.[236] Among other things, the amended FCR Act prohibits a furnisher from transmitting information to a CRA that it knows or has "reasonable cause to believe" is inaccurate, and the statute further imposes a duty to correct inaccurate information that furnishers have already provided. Furnishers must also comply with regulations issued by FTC and other federal banking and credit agencies to implement the new requirements.[237] After a consumer has provided proper notice of a dispute to a CRA and the CRA has in turn informed the furnisher, the furnisher has an additional duty to "reinvestigate" the accuracy and completeness of the information that it provided to the CRA and to report back any alleged inaccuracies. The furnishers' "duty to reinvestigate" is backed up by the statute's private right of action for damages, but their obligation to furnish accurate information in the first place is not.[238] Congress amended the FCR Act once again, in 2003, to allow consumers to block furnishers from conveying to CRAs any information resulting from identity theft.[239]

To meet the demands of CRAs and furnishers for protection from multiple state laws, the 1996 amendments expressly prohibited states from imposing any "requirement or prohibition" with respect to the "subject matter regulated" by, among other things, the requirements "relating to the responsibilities of persons who furnish information to consumer reporting agencies."[240] This express preemption provision is ambiguous with respect to the extent to which Congress meant to preempt state common law actions. Because it uses the word "requirement," the *Cipollone* analysis would indicate that Congress meant for common law claims to be preempted. On the other hand, the word "prohibition" seems more applicable to state legislatures and regulatory agencies than to common law courts that rarely prohibit malfeasance in advance.

Insofar as CRAs and users of credit information are concerned, this ambiguity in the preemption provision is a matter of minor consequence, because the statute gives consumers a *federal* cause of action for actual and punitive damages against those entities for violations of the statute and implementing regulations. In the case of furnishers, however, the matter is more complicated. Since there is no federal private right of action against furnishers for violating their duty to provide accurate information, the question remains whether consumers may file defamation-like actions against furnishers under state common law. The 1970 express preemption of defamation-like common law claims against CRAs, users, and furnishers would seem to bar claims for negligence but leave open the claims for willful or malicious conduct that the 1970 law declined to preempt. However, if the phrase "requirement or prohibition" in the general preemption section added by the 1996 amendments is applicable to state common law claims, then even claims for willful or malicious misconduct would be preempted.

Not surprisingly, this complex question has generated a great deal of very confusing litigation. The courts are in utter disagreement, and it will probably take a Supreme Court opinion to iron it all out. The facts of *Vasquez-Garcia v. Trans Union de Puerto Rico*[241] offer a comprehensible vehicle for sorting these cases out. In that case, Jose Vasquez-Garcia (the consumer) received a telephone call out of the blue from Sears, Roebuck & Co. (the furnisher and an alleged creditor), advising him that he had an overdue payment on his Sears credit card. Since Jose had never applied for a Sears card, this came as a shock to him. He then requested an update of his credit report from Trans Union (the CRA) and discovered several other suspicious entries. Upon investigating the matter further, Jose discovered that he was the victim of a rather transparent identity theft by an unknown person in Nevada (Jose lived in Puerto Rico), and he demanded that Trans Union investigate the situation and correct his report. Trans Union did revise the report but left the Sears debt on the report. A second request for a revision yielded the same result, Sears having apparently concluded that the debt was genuine. Consequently, Jose's applications for credit continued to be rejected by numerous credit card companies. Jose's lawyers filed suit against both Sears and Trans Union under the FCR Act and state common law.

Many courts have sensibly concluded that the term "requirement or prohibition" in the 1996 preemption provision does not include a state common law claim and therefore does not preempt any common law claim for willful or malicious conveyance of inaccurate information to a CRA.[242] Under this view, Jose would have a federal private right of action against Trans Union for not correcting his credit report after repeated requests to do so and a state common law defamation claim against Sears for willfully or maliciously continuing to provide inaccurate information to Trans Union. Quite a few courts have held that the term "requirement or prohibition" in the 1996 preemption provision does include state common law claims and that the newer section therefore preempts all common law claims by consumers against furnishers.[243] Under this approach, Jose would have a federal private right of action against Trans Union but no claim at all against Sears for violating its statutory duty to reinvestigate. Still other courts have attempted to reconcile the two preemption provisions by holding the original 1970 specific preemption provision applicable to furnisher conduct occurring before the consumer provides notice to the CRA and the 1996 general preemption provision applicable to furnisher conduct after the consumer provides notice.[244] The court in Jose's case adopted this approach, holding that Jose could pursue a state law claim against Sears for malice or willful intent to injure with respect to information provided before Trans Union received Jose's notice but not with respect to information received after Trans Union received that notice.[245]

It should be clear from this discussion that Congress can unintentionally create some severe interpretational problems when it does not specifically address state common law claims at the same time that it addresses state laws and regulations. The original preemption provision of the 1970 Act did address state common law claims, and the law was fairly well settled on that issue. The 1996 addition muddied the waters considerably by failing to address common law claims in the new general preemption provision and by failing to amend the existing preemption provision to make its desires clear. We will return to the need for clarity in preemption provisions with respect to common law claims in Chapter 10.

CONCLUSIONS

The preemption war has inspired more battles in the courts than anywhere else. Major fronts in the war opened up along the doctrinal lines drawn by the law of express preemption and obstacle preemption, and a minor front briefly flared up in the domain of field preemption. Litigation across many fields of federal regulation has in turn yielded a great deal of inconsistent and muddled law. Both proponents and opponents of preemption have won some clear victories, and trends along some fronts are visible over time. The serpentine nature of some of these trends is both a contributor to and a result of the generally muddled state of preemption law.

The initial battle resulted in a huge victory for the manufacturers of consumer products when the Supreme Court held, in the *Cipollone* case, that the word "requirement" in an express preemption clause could include state common law duties. The front quickly expanded to encompass common law claims addressing the subject matter of any federal regulatory statute with an express preemption clause. Defendants rapidly captured the terrain occupied by the many statutes, such as the Federal Hazardous Substance Act, that contain express preemption clauses using the word "requirement," and the battle moved on to statutes employing different but arguably equivalent language.

The Supreme Court, in *Easterwood* and *Shanklin,* agreed with defendants that the phrase "law, rule, regulation, order or standard" in the Federal Railroad Safety Act clearly encompassed state common law claims involving railroad safety. The lower courts then quickly extended those holdings to common law cases involving activities covered by more recent statutes deregulating railroads and airlines and statutes governing random drug testing. The focus then shifted from the battle over the objects of the preemption (now presumed to include common law claims) to salvos over statutory phrases and regulatory provisions defining the scope of the preemptive federal regulatory activity, and plaintiffs prevailed in many of these limited encounters.

It appeared for a time that plaintiffs would recapture some of the lost terrain when the Supreme Court, in *Lohr,* held that the term "requirement" in the Medical Device Amendments did not include common law design and warning defect claims involving medical devices that had undergone FDA's abbreviated approval process. On the perhaps more important question of whether the statute preempted similar claims against manufacturers of more recently developed medical devices that had undergone FDA's more extensive full approval process, however, the Court, in *Riegel,* closed the door on common law claims that did not allege violations of FDA-imposed requirements. Plaintiffs won another battle on the express preemption front when the Supreme Court, in *Sprietsma,* concluded that the very similar term "law or regulation" in the Federal Boating Safety Act did not preempt state common law claims related to motor boat safety. The plaintiffs won a major victory on the express preemption front when the Supreme Court, in *Bates,* held that the word "requirement" does not automatically include all common law duties, thereby casting doubt on a number of lower court opinions in regulatory areas that the Supreme Court has yet to address.

Plaintiffs in litigation involving express preemption provisions were far more successful when they could rely upon savings clauses expressing a congressional intent to preserve state common law claims even as they preempted state statutes and regulations. Workers injured in workplace accidents, for example, persuaded lower courts to allow state common law and workers compensation claims to go forward despite the Supreme Court's holding, in *Gade,* that state regulatory requirements were preempted. The Court, in *Geier,* reinforced the savings clause defense when it held that the Federal Motor Vehicle Safety Act's savings clause trumped its express preemption clause with respect to common law claims. Reacting to *Geier,* the lower courts then reversed a trend in which they had consistently found common law defective warning claims to be preempted by CPSC labeling requirements.

The Court, in *Geier,* opened up a new front in the preemption war when it held that a statute could impliedly preempt a common law claim even after Congress specifically addressed the preemption issue with an express preemption provision and a savings clause. Thus, even though the plaintiff's airbags-only common law claim was saved from express preemption by the Federal Motor Vehicle Safety Act's savings clause, it was still preempted because it stood as an obstacle to two implicit statutory policies favoring diversity and gradualness in implementation. The Court, in *Sprietsma,* solidified the *Geier* holding when it strongly suggested that a direct Coast Guard regulation requiring a safety technology would impliedly preempt common law claims. Still later, the Supreme Court, in *Buckman,* referred to the "delicate balance of statutory objectives" inherent in the agency's enforcement discretion in holding that the medical device regulatory program impliedly preempted state common law claims based exclusively on a manufacturer's fraudulent activities in obtaining FDA approval. Some eager lower courts have extended the holding to reach almost any common law claim regarding almost any product that needs federal agency approval if fraud on the agency is an essential element of that claim.

The Supreme Court has applied field preemption sparingly to state common law claims, and the lower courts have followed suit. In the context of labor/management relations, where the concept originated in early Supreme Court opinions interpreting the National Labor Relations Act, the Court, in *Farmer,* allowed an employee's common law emotional distress claim against his union to go forward, even though it involved disagreements over union representation. Following the Supreme Court's injunction, in *Garmon,* to examine "whether an evaluation of the tort claim is inextricably intertwined with consideration of the terms of the labor contract,"[246] the lower courts have generally declined to find that emotional distress claims arising out of interactions between employees and managers or fellow employees in the workplace are preempted. Similar claims against employers in the context of adverse job actions, however, are much more likely to fall within the preempted field. The Supreme Court, in *English,* limited the range of field preemption under the Atomic Energy Act to allow an employee's whistleblower retaliation claim to go forward, and the lower courts have allowed similar claims to proceed under the Labor Management Relations Act. The Court has not extended field preemption to common law claims outside the area of labor/management relations and nuclear power regulation, and it explicitly declined to do so in *Sprietsma* when it held that the Federal Boating Safety Act did not occupy the field of motor boat safety.

Throughout this chapter, we have seen many examples of courts giving short shrift to the corrective justice function of the common law. They approach the cases as regulators who have no corrective justice role to play, rather than as judges for whom corrective justice should be an important goal. Even when Congress expresses a clear desire to preserve the corrective justice role of the common law courts by including a savings clause in a regulatory statute, the Supreme Court has often concluded that threats posed by common law actions to the federal statute's general purposes trump concerns over corrective justice. In the absence of a savings clause, even unexpressed or secondary goals such as market uniformity or gradualness in implementation easily trump corrective justice concerns. The elevation, in *Bates,* of corrective justice concerns over the protective justice goals implicit in the federal pesticide law's express preemption provision is, thus far, a singular exception to this general trend. Congress, in theory, has the power to end the preemption war in the courts if it is willing to articulate with special clarity its desire to preserve the common law's corrective justice function when it drafts regulatory statutes. We will see in the next chapter why Congress rarely takes that simple step.

Chapter 5 The Preemption War in Congress

Congress has only very rarely expressly preempted common law claims, and it ordinarily substitutes a cause of action in federal court or some alternative administrative regime to provide corrective justice when it does take away the common law rights of injured citizens. Preemption rarely entered into the debates over the landmark protective legislation of the 1960s and 1970s. Express preemption clauses were contained in the original bills, explained by a sentence or two in the relevant committee reports, and forgotten. To the extent that preemption came up at all, the debates were over whether federal regulatory programs should trump state regulatory programs and not over whether injured plaintiffs should be allowed to sue.

This benign neglect of common law preemption began to change in the 1990s with the launch of a major effort by the business community to relieve itself of liability and accountability in state courts. In the vertical dimension of the politics of preemption, business entities complained of the negative impact of varying liability rules on interstate commerce. In the horizontal dimension, they complained of "vexatious litigation" brought by "greedy" plaintiffs' attorneys against "deep pocket" companies. The ultimate goal was legislation that would for the first time take away existing common law rights without providing an alternative route to corrective justice for damaged parties.[1] The usual justification for such legislation was the assertion that a federal regulatory agency was already protecting the public adequately and that any additional protection afforded by the common law would be overly burdensome on the regulatees. They did not, however, attempt to show that the protective justice provided by federal regulatory programs was an adequate substitute for corrective justice.

Although the business community's "tort reform" initiatives had been proceeding apace since the early 1980s in state legislatures, it did not undertake a major preemption initiative at the federal level until the 104th Congress of 1995–96. One of the promises contained in the Contract with America that propelled the Republican Party into power in 1995 was that it would "put justice back in our civil justice system" by enacting "common sense legal reforms."[2] Congress passed a bill in May 1996 that would have sharply limited punitive damages in all state products liability actions and preempted any state common law to the contrary, but President Clinton vetoed it.[3] With the election of George W. Bush in 2000, the prospects for preemptive tort reform legislation increased dramatically. Although most of these efforts also failed, Congress did enact a few laws that for the first time took away common law rights and replaced them with nothing at all.

This chapter describes the battles in Congress over these recent efforts to pass legislation preempting state common law claims with respect to federally regulated products and activities. It highlights two successful efforts to enact laws shielding manufacturers of firearms and certain vaccines from liability and an unsuccessful effort by the petroleum industry to shield itself from liability for damages caused by a fuel additive that leaked out of underground storage tanks into groundwater. We then examine an ambitious attempt by victims of HMO and insurance company negligence to persuade Congress to fix an unanticipated and highly inequitable preemption situation by enacting a Patients' Bill of Rights. With one exception, the battles discussed here were the subjects of major lobbying initiatives, attracted a great deal of public attention, and called for large expenditures of political capital. Although Congress devoted scant attention to federal preemption of common law claims in the 1960s and 1970s, the congressional front of the preemption war at the turn of the century was both heavily contested and highly visible.

THE BATTLE OVER GUN LIABILITY

The manufacturer of the TEC-DC9 semiautomatic assault pistol designed it to have the look and feel of the assault weapons used by the military. It was not especially useful for hunting and target practice because of its questionable accuracy and the risks that it posed to the person firing the weapon. It did, however, have an impressive capacity to produce an intense spray of bullets over a very short period of time.[4] It also came with a "combat sling" that allowed two guns to be fired simultaneously, Rambo-style, by anyone who desired to bring a great deal of firepower to bear on a hostile situation. An advertisement for a TEC-DC9 in sporting magazines claimed that it "deliver[ed] a more gutsy performance and reliability than ANY other gun on the market." It also broke down into easily concealed components and (according to the advertising) had a finish that provided "excellent resistance to fingerprints." Statistics compiled by the federal Bureau of Alcohol, Tobacco, and Firearms (BATF) showed that one out of every five guns used in crimes involving assault weapons was either a TEC-DC9 or its predecessor, the TEC-9. While it may not have been an ideal tool for teaching aspiring young hunters the simple pleasures of outdoor life, it was a popular item at gun shows and suburban gun shops.

In early 1993, Gian Luigi Ferri purchased a TEC-9 assault handgun from a Nevada pawn shop after asking the clerk to show him "something relatively compact that holds a lot of rounds."[5] Although the employee attempted to steer him toward more accurate guns that were somewhat more expensive, Ferri purchased a used TEC-9. Later that spring, Ferri bought a brand-new TEC-DC9 from a pawn shop in Las Vegas after telling the salesperson that he wanted a gun for target practice. He made this purchase despite a warning from a fellow customer that if he took the gun to a shooting range, the patrons would probably laugh at him for using such a notoriously inaccurate pistol. Ferri purchased still another new TEC-DC9 at a Las Vegas gun show from a Utah dealer.

On July 1, 1993, in an act of revenge that inspired the opening scene of the movie *Runaway Jury*, Ferri entered a San Francisco office building with his three pistols equipped with "Hell Fire" trigger systems that allowed the weapons to be fired in rapid bursts and preloaded with forty- and fifty-round magazines. Proceeding to the thirty-fourth floor offices of the target law firm, Ferri began to fire randomly at people with his high-powered weapons. In each case, he used the rapid-fire capacity of the weapons to "lay down" a field of fire that greatly reduced the victims' opportunities to escape. Before he turned a gun on himself, Ferri had killed eight people and wounded six more on three different floors of the building.

Opponents of gun control regulation repeatedly remind us that "guns don't kill people; people kill people." But guns indisputably increase the risk that people, either accidentally or intentionally, will kill and maim other people. Guns like the TEC-DC9 increase that risk dramatically, and they may well have been designed with criminal purchasers in mind.[6] Irresponsible gun dealers operating out of suburban pawn shops and itinerant gun shows, like those that serviced Gian Ferri, can ensure that these guns get into the hands of the people who are most likely to use them illegally. Statistics compiled by the BATF show that powerful guns are channeled to criminals through a very small number of "rogue" dealerships, and testimony presented in litigation reveals that gun manufacturers can easily ascertain the identities of these dealerships. For example, only 1.2 percent of licensed retail gun dealers were responsible for the sale of more than 57 percent of the guns traced to crimes between 1996 and 1999.[7]

Because guns are also a big business in this country, large gun manufacturers like Smith & Wesson have deep pockets that are attractive to attorneys for victims of gun violence.[8] Indeed, in cases of injuries caused by firearms in the hands of criminals, the manufacturer may be the only solvent potential defendant. Yet, the plaintiff's attorney who would impose common law liability on the manufacturer must be prepared to prove that the manufacturer violated the relevant standard of care, that the violation caused the plaintiff's harm, and that the intervening acts of dealers, previous owners, and the criminal are not "superseding intervening causes." Consequently, gun manufacturers have paid out few actual judgments. Nevertheless, the prospect of "ruinous" liability inspired them, in the early 2000s, to demand legislation from Congress shielding them from liability on the ground that the manufacture and the sale of firearms are already heavily regulated by the BATF under federal law.

When it comes to Congress, the firearms industry is "the fortunate son of American industry" in that it can elicit at a moment's notice the support of a vocal and politically powerful populist movement. With a membership in excess of four million, the National Rifle Association (NRA) is a political powerhouse that routinely spends tens of millions of dollars on presidential and congressional campaigns. It has lobbied against every piece of federal gun control legislation from the 1934 ban on machine guns to the 1993 Brady Act requiring background checks on purchasers of firearms. It has also opposed bans on hollow-point "cop killer" bullets and plastic bullets that can escape detection in airport screening. The NRA has sponsored a continuous campaign to demonize the federal agency that administers the modest firearms control programs that have survived its legislative attacks. President George H. W. Bush resigned from the organization after an NRA fundraising letter written during his presidency referred to BATF agents as "Nazi storm troopers." The backing of a highly ideological movement that regards the consumer's right to purchase firearms with an intensity bordering on religious fervor can be a mixed blessing, however, when gun manufacturers seek compromise solutions in legislation or lawsuit settlements.[9]

The Regulatory Regime

Given the hazardous nature of its product, the firearms industry is surprisingly thinly regulated. The existing federal regulatory regime consists largely of outright prohibitions on sales of certain especially dangerous kinds of guns and modest attempts to keep other kinds of guns out of the hands of people who will use them inappropriately through specified background checks and sales restrictions. These requirements are implemented and enforced by the BATF through a comprehensive licensing and recordkeeping regime designed to enhance the likelihood that state and federal authorities will detect violations of the sales restrictions and prohibitions. Gun manufacturers must obtain a federal license, but BATF lacks authority to write substantive regulations governing gun design or to order recalls of defectively manufactured or designed guns. Licensed manufacturers are free to sell their wares to licensed distributors without inquiring into their distribution practices. No federal law requires gun manufacturers to oversee dealer behavior or to report adverse information that they receive about their products to BATF. Subject to some rather limited registration requirements, a licensed distributor is free to sell a gun to anyone, no matter how likely that person is to use it inappropriately, so long as that person does not fall within a prohibited category. The federal laws do not even prohibit intentional diversion of firearms from legal channels into unlawful channels.[10]

With a tiny budget that it must stretch to include its tobacco and liquor regulatory responsibilities as well, the BATF is the weak sister of federal agencies. Virtually all objective observers have concluded that BATF has "far too few resources to fully investigate the dealings of" licensed manufacturers. In a good year, BATF can inspect only about 10 percent of the more than 100,000 licensed dealers, and it typically detects noncompliance at an astonishing rate of around 34 percent. The BATF is limited by statute to a single inspection per year at any given manufacturing establishment, and it must give advance notice of even that inspection.[11] The Department of the Treasury's inspector general reported that the 134,832 violations that the BATF inspectors detected in FY 2002 yielded only thirty dealer license revocations, and 149,832 violations in FY 2003 yielded only thirty-two revocations.[12] According to a twenty-three-year veteran of the Bureau's enforcement staff, the general rule of thumb is: "No cases, no waves. Little cases, little waves. Big cases, big waves."[13] Thus, BATF enforcement officials concentrate on helping local officials prosecute small-time illegal possession cases against individuals, rather than launching large-scale initiatives against the gun manufacturers, dealers, and traffickers who provide a virtually inexhaustible supply of guns to those individuals.[14]

Prosecution of rogue dealerships is further hampered by restrictions imposed by the McClure-Volkmer Firearm Owners Protection Act of 1986, which, according to Professors Jens Ludwig and Phillip J. Cook, "establishes near-impossible evidentiary requirements for successful prosecution." Consequently, when BATF does decide to revoke a rogue dealer's license, the process takes five years on average to complete. In one instance involving a Baltimore dealer who was a member of the NRA Board of Directors, BATF inspectors first discovered a large number of violations in 1997, returned two years later to find that things had gotten worse, returned a year later to discover that one hundred guns were unaccounted for, and returned two years after that to discover that 28 percent of the store's inventory had gone "missing." The store's license was finally revoked a decade after the initial inspection, but the owner was allowed to move the inventory to a newly incorporated gun dealership located next door on land owned by his eighty-year-old mother. It would appear that the threat of a BATF enforcement action does not provide a serious incentive to comply with the law.[15]

The Common Law Litigation

Litigation against firearms manufacturers, distributors, and retailers has come in two distinct varieties: (1) claims brought by individual victims against individual companies seeking compensation for losses sustained through accidental or intentional use of firearms; and (2) claims brought by governmental entities or public interest groups against firearms manufacturers, distributors, and dealers seeking compensation for public monies expended on treating and supporting indigent gun victims and for broad injunctive relief aimed at reducing the incidence of future gun violence. Litigation in the first category, which we will refer to as "private interest litigation," is wholly unremarkable and fits easily within traditional common law doctrines and remedies. Litigation in the second category, which we will refer to as "public interest litigation," asks the courts to expand traditional tort doctrine and to exercise their equitable powers widely and aggressively.[16] Litigation in the former category has achieved some degree of success; litigation in the latter category has generally gone nowhere, in part because of restrictions imposed by state legislatures.

Private Interest Litigation. Like consumers of most products, plaintiffs who can prove that they have been damaged by improperly functioning guns have been able to call on state common law courts to require the manufacturers of those products to compensate them for their losses, and individual victims of gun malfunctions have been successfully suing gun manufacturers since the early 1900s. Gun manufacturers and their insurance companies typically settle lawsuits based on specific malfunctions, such as hair triggers and poorly functioning safety devices, because they are very difficult to justify. As the courts expanded the reach of products liability doctrine in the late twentieth century, however, victims of gun violence attempted to hold gun manufacturers responsible for damages caused by third party use of properly functioning guns. Plaintiffs in these lawsuits relied on several theories of liability, including strict products liability, strict liability for abnormally dangerous activities, negligent marketing, and negligent entrustment.[17]

Most of these more recent products liability claims have foundered on the plaintiffs' inability to identify a specific "defect" in the product. When a criminal uses a TEC-DC9 assault pistol to kill someone, the gun is functioning precisely as designed and expected.[18] Plaintiffs have had some success, however, in persuading courts and juries that the defect lies in the manufacturer's failure to incorporate easily available safety technologies like childproof safety locks, accidental discharge prevention devices, loaded gun indicators, and "smart" technologies that render guns inoperable by nonowners.[19] By contrast, strict liability claims based on abnormally dangerous activities have universally failed because the manufacture and sale of firearms are "a common activity that poses no abnormally high risk to the public."[20]

Under the negligent marketing theory, plaintiffs have claimed that manufacturers have (1) marketed products directly to foreseeable criminals through mail order or Internet sales; (2) marketed guns indirectly to foreseeable criminals through gun shows and known rogue dealers; (3) saturated poorly regulated markets knowing that the guns will wind up in the hands of urban criminals; and (4) "overpromoted" guns designed primarily to kill people by stressing firepower, resistance to fingerprints, and military accoutrements such as "combat slings."[21] Many of these cases rely on complex statistical analysis not unlike the epidemiological studies that scientists use to draw connections between chemical exposures and particular human diseases. Others depend upon the testimony of industry whistleblowers who tell tales of "see-no-evil" strategies on the part of gun company executives and a "culture of evasion of firearms laws and regulations."[22] Most negligent marketing claims, however, have stumbled on the well-settled common law rule that one person has no duty to control the actions of another in the absence of a preexisting relationship that expressly or impliedly creates such a duty.[23]

The narrowly confined negligent entrustment theory subjects a defendant to liability if he directly or indirectly supplies an item to someone whom the defendant should know is likely to "use it in a manner involving unreasonable risk of physical harm to himself and others."[24] Although several courts have applied this theory to dealer sales of firearms to children, drunks, and ex-convicts, the courts have declined to extend it to gun manufacturers. In the one case in which the court allowed the plaintiff to proceed with the claim, the jury found that the defendant had not in fact been negligent.[25]

Under any of these theories, private litigants face a major stumbling block in establishing a causal link between manufacturing and marketing firearms and damage caused by violent crime. It is, for example, difficult for plaintiffs to prove that the criminal would not have simply purchased another manufacturer's gun from some other dealer. Plaintiffs have also been unable to persuade courts that gun manufacturers' marketing practices are a "proximate cause" of the damages suffered by gun violence victims when the defendants can always point to another human actor who is a much more direct and immediate cause of that harm. Finally, courts have stressed the fact that a federal regulatory program already exists to "ensure seller 'responsibility' through licensing requirements and buyer 'responsibility' through background checks."[26]

Although most of the attempts by private parties to impose liability on gun manufacturers for harm caused by gun violence have failed, a few have survived. Most of these have involved clear attempts to circumvent state and federal laws aimed at regulating the marketing of firearms to potential criminals. Courts have also approved a number of relatively modest settlements, such as the $2.5 million settlement agreed to by the manufacturer and seller of one of the guns used in the 2002 Washington, D.C., sniper killings.[27]

Public Interest Litigation. Drawing upon the successful model of state attorney general litigation against the tobacco industry, several municipalities in the late 1990s initiated a series of major lawsuits against the gun industry in what became "one of the most notable legal trends of the decade."[28] Since the lawsuits sought broad injunctive relief as well as compensation, they raised two critical policy issues: (1) the role that regulation of firearms industry practices could play in reducing gun violence; and (2) the role that the courts should play in regulating the firearms industry.[29] Because the firearms industry had not been effectively regulated by the BATF, the first question remained unanswered decades after Congress enacted the first modern gun control legislation in 1968 following the Martin Luther King and Robert F. Kennedy assassinations. The tobacco litigation offered at best a very mixed answer to the second question. Despite paying tens of billions of dollars to the states and agreeing to various advertising and marketing restrictions, the tobacco industry continued to flourish, and the money as often as not wound up in the general revenue pool and therefore amounted merely to a large excise tax on cigarettes.[30]

The first of the public interest cases, filed by the City of New Orleans in October 1998, was the brainchild of the same ad hoc group of lawyers that initiated the first of the major class action lawsuits against the tobacco industry. It named fifteen gun manufacturers, five local pawnshops, and three firearms trade associations as defendants, and it demanded compensation for the costs of police protection, emergency services, medical care, lost tax revenue, and other losses that were, in the City's view, caused by gun violence.[31] Soon thereafter, more than thirty other municipalities made similar arrangements with trial lawyers to bring similar claims in state and federal courts under the same basic theories of liability. In addition to the theories underlying the private interest litigation, the municipalities added much broader claims for public nuisance, unjust enrichment, deceptive advertising, civil conspiracy, and fraud that could effectively be pursued only by representatives of the general public.[32] Some East Coast cities added claims based on the alleged industry practice of flooding weakly regulated markets in southern states knowing that the guns would wind up in the hands of urban criminals.[33]

These lawsuits met with very limited success. The New Orleans suit went down in flames after a legislature dominated by rural legislators enacted a statute prohibiting municipalities from bringing lawsuits against gun manufacturers.[34] Courts dismissed lawsuits by the Cities of Bridgeport, Miami, Atlanta, Camden, Philadelphia, and Newark and by the City and State of New York. In some cases, the claims were barred by similar state legislation; in others, the court concluded that federally permitted marketing practices could not constitute a public nuisance or that a causal connection between negligent marketing practices and illegal gun sales had not been established.[35] Although the Ohio Supreme Court allowed the City of Cincinnati's lawsuit to proceed, the City ultimately dropped the case in the face of mounting legal costs and the failure of its attorneys to locate "smoking gun" documents in industry files.[36] In the one successful case, the Indiana Supreme Court reinstated a public nuisance action by the City of Gary after concluding that a public nuisance action can be based on an otherwise lawful activity if it is carried out in a manner that imposes unreasonable costs on others.[37]

The City of Chicago's lawsuit departed from the New Orleans model.[38] Based on evidence gathered in an undercover sting operation, the City claimed that several suburban firearms dealers were engaged in a number of practices that constituted a public nuisance.[39] The Supreme Court of Illinois, however, rejected the theory, holding that gun manufacturers and wholesale distributors had no duty to members of the general public to protect them from the misuse of firearms by criminals. Finding that "[s]tate and federal regulation of handgun sales is extensive," the court concluded that "[l]itigation should not be used to achieve legislative goals."[40]

Finally, the National Association for the Advancement of Colored People (NAACP) filed a major class action lawsuit in a New York federal district court based on public nuisance.[41] The NAACP claimed that gun manufacturers had made a large number of guns easily available to criminals, juveniles, and others who were prohibited by law from possessing them and that their marketing practices negligently and intentionally endangered the citizens of New York. The court accepted the factual basis for the NAACP's claims, finding that "[t]he flow of guns into criminal hands in New York would substantially decrease if manufacturers and distributors insisted that retail dealers who sell their guns be responsible"; it also found that "[m]embers of the industry continue to fail to take many obvious and easily implemented steps, such as requiring retailers to avoid multiple or repeat sales to the same customers." It ultimately concluded, however, that the NAACP had failed to establish that it or its members had suffered the unique harm that is an essential element of a public nuisance claim brought by a private entity. A jury later ruled against the NAACP on its remaining claims.[42]

The Scene Shifts to Congress

The gun industry and its powerful allies were not willing to rely on their rout of the municipalities and public interest groups in state courts and state legislatures. Determined to seal their position into federal law, they launched a major lobbying effort in 1998 to enact a federal "shield" law called the Protection of Lawful Commerce in Arms Act. A major player in the congressional debates was the National Shooting Sports Foundation, an entity that the gun industry created to intervene in lawsuits and to lobby state legislatures and Congress. Each of the largest manufacturers agreed to contribute a portion of its income to the Foundation, which over a five-year period raised more than $100 million to fund its initiatives.[43] The bill made little progress in the 107th Congress, but it gained traction during the 108th Congress and was enacted in the 109th Congress.

The bill's proponents argued that federal legislation was needed to prevent "frivolous" lawsuits from driving legitimate gun manufacturers and distributors out of business, thereby reducing citizens' access to an essential tool required to exercise their constitutional right to bear arms. Lawsuits by deep-pocketed municipalities were illegitimately putting financial pressure on small gun manufacturers to settle unmeritorious cases to avoid crushing litigation costs.[44] Proponents even invoked national security interests, stressing the importance of keeping domestic gun manufacturers in business to supply weapons to the armed forces.[45] Unless halted immediately, this litigation would become another instance of "greedy trial lawyers" and misguided "do-gooders" persuading "activist judges" to engage in "regulation through litigation" in an area where Congress had decided to allow the market to function with only a modest degree of regulatory intervention. If Congress allowed state common law to proceed down this slippery slope, the next victims would be the manufacturers of knives, automobiles, and even baseball bats.[46]

Opponents of the bill complained that it represented a brute force legislative intrusion into the common law process that risked undermining the integrity of the entire civil justice system by "determining liability on the basis of political muscle rather than judicial procedure."[47] Forcing gun manufacturers to internalize some of the costs that the industry imposed on firearms victims and urban municipalities would not threaten the availability of firearms to the military or anyone else.[48] To the contrary, passing the bill would destroy the last remaining incentives for a poorly regulated industry to maintain high quality control and to develop more effective safety technologies. It would also deprive innocent individuals of corrective justice in traditional private litigation.[49] Finally, opponents noted that the overall number of firearms lawsuits against manufacturers was quite small, and the fact that courts were rapidly dismissing those that lacked merit was powerful evidence that judges could be trusted not to allow the litigation to become a substitute for the legislative process.[50]

The bill was reported out of two House committees and placed on the calendar for floor action in October 2002 with more than one-half of the House members listed as cosponsors. A few days later, however, the Washington, D.C., area was terrorized by two snipers who used illegally obtained high-powered rifles to kill their victims from a distance. Although the bill was the top priority of the National Rifle Association (NRA) and seemed virtually assured of enactment prior to that tragedy, the House leadership quietly tabled it in the expectation that the public's attention would move on to other things by the time the next Congress took it up.[51]

Under the careful supervision of House Majority Leader Tom DeLay (R-Texas), the gun shield bill moved rapidly through the House the next year. A single committee hearing ended after three hours when, to the consternation of the bill's opponents, the chairman gaveled the proceedings to a close. Only one of the five witnesses testified against the bill.[52] The full committee markup, which occurred the following day, ended prematurely. After the sponsor of the first of about a dozen proposed amendments asked to read the one-page amendment into the record, the chairman forced committee members to vote on the main bill before considering the rest of the amendments. A heated exchange ensued, but the chairman quickly ended it by taking an oral vote and gaveling the hearing to a close.[53] When the bill came to the floor of the House, a few days later, the leadership limited debate and amendments, and it passed by an overwhelming 285–140 vote.[54]

The bill did not have as easy a time in the Senate, where several prominent Democrats promised a filibuster. Other Democrats, however, cut a deal with the Republican leadership to allow a vote on the bill if the Senate could also vote on amendments renewing the expiring ban on military-style assault weapons and requiring gun show operators to conduct instant background checks on their customers. The amendments then passed by slim majorities. Within minutes of those votes, lobbyists for the National Rifle Association e-mailed urgent messages to the BlackBerry pagers of supporters of the original bill stating in no uncertain terms that the NRA, which adamantly opposed the amendments, now wanted the entire package killed. The bill's chief sponsor, Senator Larry Craig (R-Idaho), then took the floor to urge supporters to vote against his bill, and it was defeated by a 90–8 vote. Senator Dianne Feinstein (D-California), a supporter of the amendments, later expressed her amazement that a single organization "had the power to turn around at least 60 votes in the Senate." Wayne LaPierre, the executive vice president of the NRA and the author of the NRA e-mail, explained that "[w]e believe in what we are doing, and we never go away."[55]

Gun shield proponents received a boost when freshly re-elected President

George W. Bush announced, on January 5, 2005, that tort reform would be a high administration priority.[56] The House Judiciary Committee held a brief hearing on the bill in mid-March and reported it out in late May.[57] Concluding that the "numbers were right" in mid-July, Senate Majority Leader Bill Frist (R-Tennessee) interrupted debate on the Defense Department appropriations bill to schedule a Senate vote on the gun shield bill before the upcoming August recess. The White House added to the sense of urgency by announcing that the bill would "safeguard our national security by preventing frivolous lawsuits against an industry that plays an important role in fulfilling our military procurement needs."[58] With twelve Democratic senators supporting the bill, it easily passed by a 65–31 vote with only a single amendment requiring dealers to include a child safety or locking device with every handgun sold.[59] The House passed the same bill in late October by a vote of 283–144 after an hour of debate in which the leadership permitted no amendments.[60] A week later, President Bush signed the Protection of Lawful Commerce in Arms Act (PLCA Act) into law.[61]

The PLCA Act went far beyond most state gun shield laws in the extent to which it eliminated state common law claims.[62] Unlike most state laws, it retroactively banned private interest actions brought by victims of negligent marketing and distribution practices, as well as public interest lawsuits. The statute also protected a broader class of potential defendants, including manufacturers, importers, distributors, dealers, and even trade associations.[63] Only one of the statute's five very narrow exceptions (the exception for any action based on a violation of a state statute "applicable to" the sale or marketing of firearms) is likely to have any continuing significance. Finally, the shield extended beyond common law litigation to any "administrative proceeding," an undefined term that arguably included even BATF license withdrawal proceedings. Depending on how the courts interpret it, the bill may have reached beyond "regulation through litigation" to eliminate "regulation through regulation."[64]

The PLCA Act represented a strong congressional response to a new brand of "public interest" common law litigation. The public interest litigation was an ideal target for an industry attempting to avoid responsibility for the adverse consequences of its products, because it allowed manufacturers and their politically powerful allies in the NRA to focus the debate on greedy trial lawyers and not on innocent victims of gun violence who were not parties to that litigation. The overly broad and perhaps unintended result was a statute that retroactively eliminated not only the protective justice possibilities of the targeted public interest litigation but also the corrective justice function of the private interest litigation that had been quietly evolving in state common law courts for a century without stirring up any significant public controversy. The irony is that by the time that Congress enacted the PLCA Act, the public interest litigation was "considered an almost total failure" as a vehicle for advancing protective justice.[65]

The public interest lawsuits were consciously designed to "pursue gun control policies" that municipalities and gun control advocates had "failed to achieve through the political process."[66] They produced a number of "smoking gun" documents and some very revealing testimony from former industry officials supporting the plaintiffs' claims that manufacturers knew that a few rogue dealers were selling guns to known criminals, that codes of conduct had been drafted and rejected by gun manufacturers, and that the NRA strongly retaliated against any company that broke ranks on gun control issues.[67] The litigation therefore had the potential to fill many of the gaps left open by federal regulation, but only at the expense of forcing common law courts into the unaccustomed role of continuing regulator of an entire industry. In dismissing public interest lawsuits, courts frequently observed that the issue of gun violence was more appropriately resolved by legislative bodies than by unelected judges, and Congress apparently agreed.[68]

The full impact of the statute is difficult to predict. The first court to address its continuing vitality concluded that the exception for actions based on a violation of a state statute "applicable to" the sale or marketing of firearms was broad enough to encompass the City of New York's public nuisance action against gun manufacturers and distributors based on alleged violations of a New York criminal nuisance statute.[69] A California district court, however, disagreed with the New York court's broad reading of the word "applicable" to include all statutes that are "capable of being applied" to the sale or marketing of firearms and limited the term to statutes that state legislatures have made "specifically applicable to the firearms industry."[70] If municipalities are allowed to bootstrap criminal nuisance statutes to fit common law nuisance claims by interpreting the word "applicable" broadly, then the PLCA Act may not serve as a complete bar to public interest lawsuits. But it will still bar the more deserving private interest claims for corrective justice that are not likely to have an analog in state nuisance statutes.

VACCINES IN EMERGENCIES

Congress established a comprehensive regulatory program for human vaccines under the Virus, Serum, and Toxin Act of 1902 and the Food, Drug, and Cosmetics Act of 1938 that, if anything, is more pervasive than the regulatory regime for pharmaceuticals and medical devices.[71] A manufacturer desiring to distribute a new vaccine in interstate commerce must first submit a Product Licensing Application to the Food and Drug Administration (FDA), along with the proposed label and supporting information related to safety, efficacy, and the manufacturing process.[72] Once the vaccine is approved, the manufacturer may not change either the vaccine or the label without FDA approval.[73] Neither statute contains an express preemption provision, and courts have been unwilling to find implied "obstacle" preemption. As one court noted, "[v]accine regulation . . . is primarily, but not exclusively, a federal concern," and "[s]tate regulation of these products plays an important and legitimate role and should not be displaced unless exceptional circumstances warrant it."[74]

As related in Chapter 3, the National Childhood Vaccination Injury Act of 1986 (NCVI Act) created a federal compensation regime to replace state common law design defect claims addressing "unavoidable" side effects and failure-to-warn claims for FDA-approved vaccines. The statute in fact prohibits any state from establishing or enforcing any law that "prohibits an individual from bringing a civil action against a vaccine manufacturer for damages for a vaccine-related injury or death" to the extent that it is not expressly preempted.[75] By all accounts, the program appears to be working reasonably well from the standpoint of both vaccine manufacturers and the relatively rare victims of vaccine-related injuries. Since anyone allegedly injured by a vaccine must file a claim with the government before electing to file an action in state court, one measure of claimant satisfaction with the system is the percentage of claimants who in fact opt out. According to a recent Department of Health and Human Services report, that percentage has been exceedingly low, ranging from 0 percent to 1.5 percent between 2002 and 2005.[76]

Vaccine manufacturers, however, were not satisfied with the program established by the NCVI Act, despite the indirect subsidy it provided to the industry. They decided to take advantage of numerous frightening reports of vaccine shortages during the 1994–95 flu season, the ongoing risk of bioterrorism, and the ominous new threat of avian flu to seek legislation providing further insulation from liability.[77] In the waning moments of the first session of the 109th Congress, both houses of Congress passed the Department of Defense Emergency Supplemental Appropriations Act. Attached as "Division C" to the appropriations act was a previously unknown provision called the Public Readiness and Emergency Preparedness Act of 2005 (PREP Act).[78] That provision had not been the subject of any congressional hearings, and it was not debated on the floor of either house of Congress when the members voted on the appropriations bills that went to the conference committee for resolution on a Sunday afternoon as the session drew to a close. The forty-page document that was inserted into the appropriations bill by the conference committee was the product of a meeting held a month earlier and attended by representatives of Senate Majority Leader Bill Frist, the White House, the Departments of Justice and Health and Human Services, and the biotechnology and pharmaceutical industries.[79]

After rumors about the possible addition of a liability shield rider surfaced, one of the members of the conference committee that assembled that Sunday afternoon asked for and received both verbal and written assurances that it would not be inserted at that late hour into the appropriations act, which was desperately needed to continue financing the Iraq war and to provide an additional $29 billion in hurricane relief for victims of Hurricane Katrina.[80] When the committee had completed its work and adjourned later that afternoon, the bill did not contain Division C. Late that evening, however, Senator Frist paid a visit to House Majority Leader Dennis Hastert (R-Illinois) and urged him to add the measure to the bill before sending it to the House floor for a final vote, even though the conferees had not voted in favor of that move. Hastert agreed, and the appropriations bill that went to the House floor at 4:30 the next morning contained the rider that became the PREP Act. Both houses favorably voted on the amended bill without debating the PREP Act, and President Bush signed it on December 30, 2005.[81]

The PREP Act declares that any "covered person" shall be "immune from suit and liability under Federal and State law" with respect to "all claims for loss" caused by, arising out of, or even "relating to" the "administration" or individual "use" of a "covered countermeasure" if the Secretary of Health and Human Services (HHS) has issued a "declaration" reflecting the Department's "determination" that a "disease or other health condition" or some other "threat to human health" constitutes or may in the future constitute a "public health emergency."[82] The sole exception to the immunity granted by such a declaration is for a very limited claim to be filed in a three-judge federal court in which the plaintiff has the burden of proving by "clear and convincing evidence" that the defendant's act or omission constituted "willful misconduct."[83] If, however, that act or omission is "subject to regulation" under the Food, Drug, and Cosmetic Act, it cannot constitute "willful misconduct."[84] The statute establishes a "Covered Countermeasure Process Fund" to provide compensation for injuries caused by covered countermeasures, but that provision will kick in only if and when Congress appropriates money for the fund in a separate statute.[85]

The breadth of the power that this law gives the HHS Secretary to exempt drug, vaccine, and device manufacturers from liability for damage caused by defectively designed and manufactured products is apparent in the definitions of the critical statutory terms. A "covered person" is virtually anyone who has anything to do with the production, dispensation, and use of a "covered countermeasure."[86] The critical term "covered countermeasure" is defined to include any drug, biological, or device that FDA has authorized for emergency use under section 564 of the FDC Act or that is designed or used for diagnosing, mitigating, preventing, treating, curing, or limiting the harm from a pandemic or epidemic or from another covered countermeasure.[87] The most critical term of all in terms of limiting the Department's discretion, "public health emergency," is not defined at all. Since the statute explicitly precludes judicial review by any state or federal court of "any action by the Secretary" under the law, Congress has apparently left the scope of the Department's discretion in this regard to the Department's own discretion.

Since the Secretary of HHS has not yet exercised this new power, the impact of this new law is difficult to assess. Its potential to wreak havoc on the common law of the fifty states should, however, be apparent. All that is required for a Secretary of HHS to bestow an enormous windfall on any favored medical constituency is to make an unreviewable declaration of an undefined "public emergency." The statute provides no guidance whatsoever on what should trigger the declaration and when it should end. Although the PREP Act lacks any legislative history, given its secretive and procedurally questionable origins, the fact that it was enacted not in the wake of the September 11 attacks but, instead, in midst of speculation about a possible outbreak of bird flu suggests that a public health emergency need not involve terrorism or even any serious present risk to public health. One could imagine, for example, a declaration of a "public health emergency" resulting from an announced threat by one of the four manufacturers of childhood vaccines, in the wake of a large jury verdict, that it will regrettably have to cease production in the near future if liability relief is not immediately forthcoming.

MTBE

In June 1995, the North Carolina Division of Environmental Protection began deliveries of bottled water to eleven homes on Horne Place Drive in Wrightsboro, North Carolina, after discovering that their well water had become contaminated with gasoline. It appeared to state environmental investigators that the gasoline came from a filling station across the street, but it was not at all clear how the gasoline had gotten into the groundwater in the first place. The state agency had known about the problem for several months but had not taken any action until the residents started complaining of "funny"-tasting drinking water. Several months later, representatives for the company that provided the gasoline reported that the foul taste was probably caused by a little-known gasoline additive called MTBE.[88]

A group of subdivision residents sued the company in March 1996 seeking a permanent solution to their drinking water supply problems and compensation for increased medical expenses needed to monitor for diseases they were at risk of incurring as a result of their past exposure to the contaminated water. Scott Summy, a Texas lawyer who had agreed to take the plaintiffs' case on a contingency-fee basis, knew that it would be very difficult to prove that the gasoline in the plaintiffs' wells came from any particular source, particularly in the absence of any information suggesting that any filling station in the vicinity had suffered a large spill of gasoline in the not-too-distant past. He did, however, learn during the discovery phase of the trial that MTBE was a fuel additive that many refining companies had recently been using to replace tetraethyl lead in gasoline to prevent engine knocking. He further learned that MTBE had some unique properties that allowed it to travel farther and faster in groundwater than other gasoline constituents and that gasoline sellers knew of these properties.[89]

As the case went to trial, Summy achieved a breakthrough when he called Richard Powell, a former group manager for the company. Powell told him that there had been a three-hundred- to four-hundred-gallon leak at the suspect filling station in 1983 that had saturated the surrounding soil. Later that evening, in a recorded interview, Powell told Summy that he had reported the 1983 event to company officials in 1995 when the stories appeared in the local press about the subdivision's contamination and that he had flown to Houston to talk with company officials about it. None of this had been revealed to Summy during discovery.[90] A few days later, Powell told the jury in open court how the filling station had suffered the large leak, how gasoline had "saturated" the surrounding soils, and how he dug a new water well for the filling station after he discovered gasoline in the toilets. At the trial's end, the jury awarded the plaintiffs $9.5 million in damages. Before the punitive damages phase of the trial went forward, the company settled with the plaintiffs for an undisclosed amount.[91]

Within days of obtaining the North Carolina verdict, Summy received a phone call from lawyers for the City of Santa Monica, California, asking for help with possible litigation against companies responsible for leaks of MTBE-containing gasoline into the city's drinking water supplies.[92] Within another few years, MTBE had become a household word in some states as more and more individuals and communities discovered that their drinking water had become contaminated by the bitter-tasting and foul-smelling chemical. The chemical drew national attention during the preemption war of the early 2000s when a battle over whether Congress should shield the petroleum industry from liability killed the George W. Bush administration's high-priority energy legislation not once but twice.

The MTBE Problem

Although petroleum companies had been using MTBE to replace lead in gasoline since the late 1970s, they began to use more of it in the mid-1980s to meet the winter oxygenate requirements that several states had imposed to enable them to meet air quality standards for carbon monoxide.[93] Its use increased rather dramatically during the late 1980s as two of the major oil companies serving the huge California market began to blend MTBE into gasoline that they marketed as "environmentally friendly" because emissions from cars that burned it did not produce as many smog-producing pollutants. Soon the other major oil companies were, in the words of the head of EPA's fuel regulation office, "to some extent tripping over themselves coming out with cleaner products," and MTBE had become "the fastest-growing chemical in the world."[94] Its use increased even more in the mid-1990s as localities strove to meet the requirement of the 1990 Clean Air Act Amendments that reformulated gasoline (RFG) be sold in the nation's ten most polluted metropolitan areas. As of 2000, more than 30 percent of the gasoline sold in the United States was reformulated, with about 87 percent of RFG containing MTBE and 12 percent containing ethanol, an alternative to MTBE that is distilled from corn.[95]

While MTBE is no more toxic than some of the other familiar gasoline constituents, such as benzene, it is carcinogenic in laboratory animals. The primary problem is that it smells and tastes so bad, even in the tiniest concentrations, that MTBE contamination ruins drinking water supplies.[96] The industry discovered in the late 1970s that MTBE moves very rapidly in groundwater from spills and leaking underground storage tanks (LUSTs) to aquifers that are often used by municipalities and individuals as a source of drinking water. The LUSTs were arguably the responsibility of the major petroleum distribution companies that had originally installed most of them at local gas stations. EPA estimated in 1999 that there were 825,000 LUSTs nationwide, approximately

550,000 of which were located at retail gasoline stations. Although EPA had required all tanks to be upgraded by 1998, progress was slow and releases were continuing from some upgraded systems due to inadequate design, installation, maintenance, and/or operation. Since MTBE was used in about one-third of U.S. gasoline, this meant that groundwater throughout the United States was continuing to be contaminated with MTBE. When MTBE releases do occur, according to EPA, they "require much more aggressive management and remediation than do spills of conventional gasoline."[97]

The MTBE Litigation

When Scott Summy arrived in Santa Monica, he joined an already burgeoning litigation team seeking to recoup the monies the city had expended trucking in safe water and to recover damages for the loss of a valuable groundwater resource. While the Santa Monica case was pending, an environmental group called Communities for a Better Environment sued the major oil companies operating in California under several state statutes for negligence and reckless contamination of groundwater throughout the state.[98] Many of the attorneys who contributed pro bono to this effort were also working on a major case involving widespread contamination of the groundwater supplies for South Lake Tahoe, California. Most of the defendants settled the *Communities for a Better Environment* case in August 2001 by agreeing to remediate about seven hundred sites throughout the state. The *South Tahoe Public Utility District* case went to trial in 2002 and resulted in jury findings that all of the defendants were responsible for contaminating the groundwater and that two of them were well aware of MTBE's dangerous properties but withheld that information from consumers and the government. The plaintiff recovered in excess of $69 million in total damages.[99]

By the turn of the century, litigation involving MTBE-contaminated groundwater had spread throughout the country, and most of the cases had been consolidated in a single federal district court in New York. In August 2001, that court held that none of the claims were preempted by the Clean Air Act.[100] The express preemption provision of the statute, which prohibited any state from prescribing any controls on fuels or fuel additives, was not applicable because it was explicitly limited to controls imposed "for purposes of motor vehicle emissions control," and the lawsuits had nothing whatsoever to do with motor vehicle emissions. The court also rejected the implied preemption argument that holding the defendants liable for the consequences of groundwater contamination would present an obstacle to achieving the objectives of the

Clean Air Act's reformulated gasoline program. Unlike the *Geier* case, in which the plaintiffs had argued that auto manufacturers should have installed airbags, the plaintiffs in this case did not argue that the defendants had a common law duty to implement any particular technology. They merely contended that the additive that the defendants selected to meet the nonspecific reformulated gasoline requirements was defective. The court reached the same result five years later when the defendants filed a similar motion for summary judgment on preemption grounds.[101]

Congress Debates Liability Relief

Faced with the prospect of hundreds of millions of dollars in cleanup costs and saddled with a convincing judicial holding that the Clean Air Act did not preempt the still-growing number of claims being filed by landowners, municipal water utility districts, and state attorneys general, the petroleum industry headed for the one institution that could solve its litigation problem for good. It launched a massive lobbying campaign to persuade Congress to insert an express MTBE preemption provision in an energy bill that President George W. Bush badly wanted to see enacted during his first term.

Three months after Vice President Dick Cheney's Energy Policy Task Force issued a report to the president containing several recommendations for major energy legislation, the House of Representatives passed the five-hundred-plus page Securing America's Energy Future Act in early August 2001. In the process, the House specifically rejected an amendment to allow states to waive the Clean Air Act's reformulated gasoline requirement so that California could implement a ban on MTBE that EPA had recently disapproved.[102] The legislation moved at a more leisurely pace in the Senate, where the leadership was unable to prevent the debates from becoming enmeshed in the politics of fuel additives, but its progress came to a complete halt on September 11, 2001, as Congress turned its attention to national security and terrorism.[103]

In early February 2002, Senate Majority Leader Tom Daschle introduced a Democratic counterpart to the Bush administration's energy bill. A radical departure from the House bill, Daschle's bill contained a complete ban on MTBE by 2006 and required a tripling of the use of ethanol in fuels. Ostensibly for the purpose of increasing energy supplies while protecting air quality, the requirement would have vastly increased nationwide demand for ethanol, thereby shifting about $1 billion per year from urban purchasers of reformulated gasoline to midwestern corn-growing farmers. Observing the problems that the petroleum industry had encountered as a result of LUSTs, farm-state senators also added a provision shielding ethanol producers from any liability for groundwater contamination resulting from ethanol use in fuels. These aspects of the Democratic bill attracted the support of farm-state Republicans and the Bush administration, which was concerned about the upcoming midterm elections, and the bill was easily approved by the full Senate over the strong opposition of the senators from oil-producing states and California.[104]

As the House-Senate conference committee took up the two quite dissimilar bills in September 2002, the House negotiators resigned themselves to the ethanol mandate, but some of them demanded a similar liability shield for MTBE manufacturers and petroleum refiners. This demand, however, fractured the fragile coalition on the Senate side of the negotiating table. Some of the Senate negotiators from farm states were happy to add a liability shield for MTBE if the shield for ethanol remained in the bill, but senators from MTBE-contaminated states strongly resisted any liability shield for MTBE. The conference committee was unable to reach any agreement on the shield issue, and the bill went nowhere for the remainder of the 107th Congress.[105]

The House got off to a much earlier start in the 108th Congress, and it quickly passed an energy bill that had now blossomed to 772 pages. This time the bill contained both the ethanol liability shield and the MTBE liability shield that the petroleum industry desperately wanted in return for its loss of the cheaper MTBE additive. By this point, the industry had finely honed its argument that "[t]hese companies should not be punished for doing what they were commanded to do under the Clean Air Act."[106] This was, however, a mischaracterization of the Clean Air Act's reformulated-gasoline requirement. In implementing that requirement, EPA did not require the petroleum industry to use MTBE or any other additive; it simply promulgated a broad performance standard requiring that reformulated gasoline be 2 percent oxygen by weight. Indeed, the industry had been moving strongly in the direction of using MTBE in the late 1980s as a component of "environmentally friendly" gasoline without the impetus of the then-nonexistent federal program.[107]

Now under Republican control after the 2002 elections, the Senate could not come to agreement. In August 2003, the leadership abandoned its efforts to write a new bill and simply substituted the previously passed Senate bill. When the conference committee took up the bill in September, the same dispute over the MTBE liability shield, now dubbed the "Fuels Safe Harbor," created the same obstacle to agreement. An attorney for several city municipal water districts in the MTBE litigation complained that the provision would "let the worst polluters off the hook and shift the remediation to the taxpayers." A report issued by Representative Henry Waxman of California predicted that the liability shield would shift $29 billion in clean-up costs from the oil industry to state taxpayers. The provision was also opposed by a coalition of fourteen state attorneys general and the U.S. Conference of Mayors. It was, however, an extremely high priority for House Majority Leader Tom DeLay.[108]

In early October 2003, a coalition of forty-two senators sent a strong letter to the senators on the conference committee urging them to hold out for a bill that did not contain an MTBE liability shield. The fact that forty-two senators could prevent the full Senate from putting an end to a filibuster was not lost on the conferees. After the Republican committee members from both houses decided to shut the Democratic members out of the negotiations, they were able to come to an agreement, in November 2003, on a bill that contained a phase-out of MTBE by 2015, a $2 billion tax subsidy for petroleum refiners to ease the transition from MTBE, and an MTBE liability shield that would apply to all future lawsuits and any pending claims filed since the previous September. Supporters of the bill defended the retroactive aspect of the liability shield as necessary to prevent a "rush to the courthouse, even with the most frivolous of claims," and they argued that potential plaintiffs had been put on notice of the liability shield in April, when the bill passed the House.[109]

The House quickly passed the conference committee bill, but it stalled in the Senate. As the previously shut-out Democrats and the press began to parse the huge bill, several other odd subsidies began to emerge into the daylight, including $227 million in taxpayer financing for a riverfront shopping mall in Shreveport, Louisiana, featuring a fourteen-screen cinema complex and a Hooter's restaurant. This was too much for Senator Maria Cantwell (D-Washington), an opponent of the MTBE shield, who dubbed the bill the "Hooters, Polluters, and Corporate Looters" Act. House Majority Leader DeLay responded in kind, arguing that the MTBE liability provision had been an unfair target of "trial lawyers" who "don't create anything—they just suck blood." The filibuster threat became very real on the eve of the Thanksgiving recess when the full Senate failed by two votes to shut off debate, thereby killing the bill for that session of Congress. Senate Minority Leader Tom Daschle, who strongly supported the bill, placed the blame squarely on the House Republican leadership for not yielding on the MTBE shield provision. An unrepentant Representative DeLay claimed that the senators who blocked the bill were using the liability shield as a "scapegoat to block the comprehensive energy package."[110]

Senate Republicans in early 2004 attempted to revive a scaled-down version of the energy bill, minus the MTBE liability shield, but Representative DeLay and other oil-state representatives would have none of it. Even when pressed by President Bush to try to reach a compromise, DeLay made it clear that House supporters of the MTBE shield "were not interested in renegotiating this bill." He continued to blame the bill's failures on "trial lawyers and environmental extremists."[111]

With an even larger Republican majority in the Senate after the 2004 elections, the prospects for enacting energy legislation during the 109th Congress grew. The House Energy and Commerce Committee once again approved a bill that included the MTBE liability shield. After a very close vote on the shield provision, the House passed a thousand-page bill with the MTBE shield intact. The Senate passed a bill with no MTBE shield in June 2005, and the bills headed to conference committee for the third time. House Republicans on the committee attempted a compromise by agreeing to create an $11 billion cleanup fund funded by the federal government, the states, and a tax on petroleum products, but the proposal went nowhere after the industry would not agree to pick up $4 billion of that amount.[112]

With Representative DeLay in serious political trouble over alleged campaign law violations, the House leadership finally relented and agreed to drop the MTBE liability shield provision. The conference committee quickly reported out the compromise bill, and both houses of Congress passed it soon thereafter. The final bill, which was signed by President Bush, eliminated the 2 percent oxygenate requirement for reformulated gasoline, but it did not include a liability shield for manufacturers and users of MTBE. In February 2006, EPA announced that it would no longer specify the oxygen content for reformulated gasoline in nonattainment areas, and MTBE manufacturers began to phase out production of this once high-volume product.[113]

UNDOING PREEMPTION—THE PATIENTS' BILL OF RIGHTS

When Buddy Kuhl suffered a serious heart attack, the designated primary care physician under his employer's medical benefits plan placed him in the care of a heart specialist who recommended heart surgery. A second specialist agreed with this diagnosis. Since the local Kansas City hospitals lacked the proper equipment for the prescribed surgery, the primary care physician arranged for the surgery at a St. Louis hospital. The surgery was scheduled for July 6, 1989, but the plan's "utilization reviewer" refused to approve Kuhl's precertification request, and the surgery was canceled. After a third specialist concurred in the need for the surgery, the plan finally agreed to precertify the operation. By then, however, Kuhl's heart had deteriorated to the point at which surgery was no longer possible. The St. Louis specialist recommended a heart transplant, but the plan also refused to precertify that surgery. Kuhl died three months later as a result of his heart disease. His outraged family filed a lawsuit against his employer's plan for malpractice, negligent infliction of emotional distress, and tortious interference with contract, but the suit was dismissed by a federal court because it was preempted by the Employee Retirement Income Security Act of 1974 (ERIS Act).[114]

Congress enacted the ERIS Act to address the very serious problem of abuse of employee pension funds by employers, unions, and other entities with fiduciary responsibilities for administering those funds.[115] Congress delegated to the Department of Labor (DoL) broad authority to promulgate regulations defining relevant terms and establishing standards for administering pensions and other employee benefit plans, including those that, "through the purchase of insurance or otherwise," provide medical care for covered employees through insurance companies and health maintenance organizations (HMOs).[116] The statute's preemption clause is quite broad in scope, providing that the Act's provisions "shall supersede any and all State laws insofar as they may now or hereafter relate to any employee benefit plan." The savings clause provides that nothing in the Act "shall be construed to exempt or relieve any person from any law of any State which regulates insurance, banking, or securities." Neither clause explicitly mentions state common law claims.[117] The statute also establishes a fairly elaborate civil enforcement regime that empowers the federal government, employer participants, and beneficiaries to obtain relief when fiduciaries violate such plans or otherwise mishandle their fiduciary responsibilities. In particular, a participant or beneficiary may bring a civil action in federal court "to recover benefits due to him under the terms of his plan, to enforce his rights under the terms of the plan, or to clarify his rights to future benefits under the terms of the plan" and "for appropriate relief under" the section establishing the fiduciary duties of plan administrators.[118]

The Supreme Court Interprets the ERIS Act

The Supreme Court early on concluded that the ERIS Act's broad preemption clause was one of those "superpreemption" provisions that completely substitute the specified federal remedies for any state common law remedies.[119] In *Pilot Life Insurance Co. v. Dedeaux,*[120] the Court, in 1987, discerned a clear congressional intent that "all suits brought by beneficiaries or participants asserting improper processing of claims under ERISA-regulated plans be treated as federal questions governed by" the ERIS Act's civil action provision. Congress meant to establish "a federal common law of rights and obligations under ERISA-regulated plans" that displaces state common law on any issue "related to" such plans.[121] Moreover, the Court held, in *Metropolitan Life Insurance Co. v. Massachusetts,* that Congress intended the ERIS Act and its implementing regulations "to displace all state laws that fall within its sphere, even including state laws that are consistent with ERISA's substantive requirements," thereby displacing even state common law claims based on gross violations of the ERIS Act's requirements.[122] The Court greatly expanded the ERIS Act's preemptive "sphere" when it broadly construed the words "related to" quite literally to reach any law or common law claim that "has a connection with or reference to such a plan."[123]

The reach of the ERIS Act's preemption provision quickly exceeded the statute's substantive grasp, however, because Congress had drafted the Act with pensions in mind and addressed "employee welfare benefit plans" providing medical and disability coverage only as an afterthought.[124] The Department of Labor could have filled this gap by promulgating protective substantive regulations for welfare benefit plans, but it consistently failed to do so, fearing that too many restrictions would discourage employers from adopting such plans in the first place.[125] Since welfare benefit plans clearly "relate to" employee benefit plans, there is a disconnect between the limited scope of the substantive requirements relating to medical coverage in welfare benefit plans and the much broader scope of its express preemption provision. Consequently, the statute has substituted a virtually content-free regulatory regime for a rich body of common law in which fiduciaries who negligently fail to perform their fiduciary obligations are subject to injunctive relief and liability for damages caused by such failures.[126]

To make matters worse, the Supreme Court interpreted the ERIS Act to limit drastically the relief available under the "federal common law" remedies that the statute substituted for state common law remedies.[127] Most important, the Supreme Court held that the "equitable relief" available to a plaintiff did not include monetary damages, relying on the hypertechnical rationale that nineteenth-century equity courts did not entertain claims for consequential damages attributable to a violation of fiduciary obligations.[128] According to Professor John Langbein, the holding was probably wrong as a historical matter, but it nevertheless "rendered the protections of ERISA illusory in any case in which the victim of ERISA-proscribed wrongdoing needs damages for consequential injury in order to be made whole."[129]

These judicial trends converged with disastrous consequences for some beneficiaries in the 1990s when traditional insurance policies providing "fee-for-service retrospective pay" were largely replaced with health maintenance organizations (HMOs), preferred provider plans (PPOs), and other types of "prospective pay" managed care plans.[130] The latter plans were popular with employers because they purported to reduce unnecessary treatment, but, according to one federal court, they "often ignore[d] the individual needs of a patient in order to improve the HMOs' bottom lines."[131] The critical cost-containment aspect of this new approach was the simple fact that the fiduciary determines whether or not to pay for the prescribed health care in advance of treatment.[132] As another court noted, "a system of prospective decisionmaking influences the beneficiary's choice among treatment options to a far greater degree than does the theoretical risk of disallowance of a claim facing a beneficiary in a retrospective system."[133]

When plaintiffs who are damaged by gross mismanagement of employee medical benefit plans sue under the exclusive "federal common law" created by the ERIS Act and its implementing regulations, they first encounter an empty body of substantive law, because the statute and implementing regulations by and large ignore such plans. The rare plaintiffs who can prove violations of the regulations can sue for reimbursement but cannot recover compensatory damages for bodily injury or emotional distress or punitive damages.[134] Beneficiaries who consider opting out of a system that is clearly rigged against them quickly discover that the statute's preemption provisions deprive them of any state common law remedies, as well. When coupled with the absence of any effective regulatory program at the federal level, the result is that health care for thousands of Buddy Kuhls throughout the country is determined not by their doctors but by anonymous nurses working phone banks for HMOs and insurance companies who have every incentive to deny expensive medical procedures and no incentive to allow them.

The ERIS Act provides a strong incentive to HMOs and insurance companies to deny legitimate requests for coverage in violation of their fiduciary obligations to patients who are, in the words of one court, "often in the throes of medical crises and entirely unable to assert what meager rights they possess."[135] HMOs and insurance companies receive a fixed income stream that they may invest as it comes in from employers, but the outgo depends on the number of claims that they pay and the amount that they pay for each claim. Thus, an HMO or insurance company can make money by denying or delaying claims because the money otherwise paid to satisfy the claims remains in the company's account to be invested by the company. The only serious consequence of even gross breaches of fiduciary obligations is the highly unlikely prospect of injunctive relief or the contingent prospect of a court order to reimburse the rare beneficiary who elects to undergo the treatment at his own expense. While the matter is being litigated, the employer's premiums are still piling up interest in the HMO's account. If the interest is sufficient to cover the litigation expenses, opportunistic breaches can become a profit center.[136]

The HMOs and insurance companies are, of course, well aware of this asymmetry. A training video for one company's claims handlers of the late 1990s featured a panel of company attorneys instructing claims handlers on the critical difference between ERIS Act-covered claims and non-ERIS Act claims. The lawyers stressed that claims in the latter category required a "reasonable investigation" and review by a "Specialty Review Team" before being denied because wrongful denials could result in "bad faith failure to settle" lawsuits, with attendant punitive damages. Handlers of ERIS Act-covered claims, on the other hand, should make the claimants undertake the investigation. If the beneficiary did not present precisely the proof required or filed the claim after the deadline, the claim should be denied. Since ERIS Act beneficiaries cannot sue at common law and cannot receive compensatory damages under federal law, "[a]fter we send the final letter, it doesn't matter what they send us any more."[137]

When an HMO employee renders a prospective judgment about whether or not the treatment recommended by a beneficiary's doctor is "medically necessary," the employee is not simply interpreting the contract between the employer and the provider. As the American Medical Association and numerous state medical examination boards have concluded, that employee is making a medical decision that should be subject to the same ethical and common law principles that constrain the prescribing physician's judgment.[138] In the absence of common law liability, an HMO employee with little or no expertise in the relevant area can second-guess highly credentialed medical experts, constrained only by the knowledge that a claim denied or delayed is money in the bank for his employer. Thus, by the late 1990s, this badly broken but preemptive federal regulatory regime had produced literally hundreds of horror stories, a sampling of which follows:

- The family of a patient with lung cancer who begged the plan administrator to authorize the treatment recommended by her oncologist watched helplessly as her cancer metastasized to her brain while the company equivocated.[139]
- After his wife's employer's insurance company abruptly stopped paying for a drug that was adequately treating a construction manager's multiple sclerosis symptoms, his symptoms returned with a vengeance as he took the drug that the insurer was willing to pay for, and he became permanently disabled.[140]
- A mentally ill patient was severely burned in an attempt at self-immolation after her insurance company twice refused to authorize a stay at the hospital recommended by her physician where she had been successfully treated in the past.[141]
- After a plan-approved doctor prescribed physical therapy for a patient following knee replacement surgery, the plan's approval nurse decided that therapy was unnecessary, and the patient suffered permanent injury to her knee as a result.[142]

It looked for a time as if the Supreme Court would take steps to eliminate these obvious injustices when it agreed, in 2004, to hear two consolidated appeals in *Aetna Health, Inc. v. Davila.*[143] In one of the cases, Juan Davila's treating physician prescribed the painkiller Vioxx for his arthritis pain, but his employer-provided HMO refused to pay for that drug on the ground that it was too expensive. When Davila took the generic drug Naprosyn that the HMO specified as a suitable alternative, he suffered a severe reaction that required extensive hospitalization and left him unable to take any orally administered painkillers.[144] Davila sued the HMO under a Texas statute that authorized a common law claim for tort damages against HMOs for failure to use ordinary care in making coverage determinations. Twenty states, the National Council of State Legislatures, and a number of consumer groups weighed in with their own amicus curiae briefs urging the Court to correct its past mistakes and allow the lawsuits to go forward.[145] The federal government's amicus curiae brief joined that of the United States Chamber of Commerce in support of the HMO.[146]

Mimicking the federal government's brief, the Court held that the ERIS Act preempted all of Davila's claims. The majority opinion reasoned that the "limited remedies available" under the ERIS Act "are an inherent part of the 'careful balancing' between ensuring fair and prompt enforcement of rights under a plan and the encouragement of the creation of such plans."[147] State common law tort claims against HMOs, even for violations of the statute's substantive requirements, could undermine that "careful balance" by recognizing rights or providing remedies that might discourage employers from creating such plans in the first place. This outcome was not unfair because, as the government's brief pointed out, the ERIS Act's enforcement tools were equal to the task of protecting the legitimate rights and expectations of the beneficiaries of such plans.[148] The Court noted that Davila could have invoked the ERIS Act's civil enforcement mechanism in advance of the denial of the benefits to seek an injunction requiring the HMO to provide those benefits, or he could have "paid for the treatment [himself] and then sought reimbursement" in an action under the ERIS Act's claims procedures.[149]

To anyone at all familiar with how managed care plans operate in the real world, the Court's analysis of the plaintiffs' rights under the ERIS Act's procedures borders on the Pollyanna-ish. It was hardly realistic to expect Davila to forgo the generic drug proffered by his HMO, hire a lawyer at his own expense, and endure his arthritis pain while the lawyer sought injunctive relief.[150] Maybe it would not have been too burdensome to expect him to dip into savings and purchase his own Vioxx until he could sue for reimbursement after the fact, assuming that he could persuade a lawyer to take the case for what would have been a very small contingency fee. Perhaps that is the way things work in the rarified world of Supreme Court Justices and their families, but the reason that most employees join their employers' health benefits plans is that they cannot afford to pay for medical treatment in advance.[151] As one doctor noted, "[t]he economic reality is that, if these insurance companies are not going to pay for something, it won't get done."[152] Taking the time to write a special concurring opinion, a frustrated Justice Ruth Bader Ginsburg "join[ed] 'the rising judicial chorus urging that Congress . . . revisit what is an unjust and increasingly tangled ERISA regime.'"[153]

Justice Ginsburg's plea was in its own way Pollyanna-ish. Reform legislation in the regulatory arena runs the risk of disrupting settled expectations and upsetting existing allocations of economic power in the private sector. When the demand for reform comes from a diffuse or economically disadvantaged segment of society and status quo arrangements are congenial to a concentrated and economically powerful segment, the prospects for reform are best in periods of social ferment following a long history of past injustice. Proponents for the victims of managed care abuse thought the late 1990s and early 2000s were a propitious time to address the injustices brought on by the Supreme Court's broad interpretation of the ERIS Act's preemption provisions. Their efforts to enact a "Patient's Bill of Rights" that would, among other things, amend the ERIS Act's express preemption provision to allow state common law claims against managed care providers for unreasonable denial of coverage precipitated the fierce legislative battle to which we now turn.

The Scene Shifts to Congress

By early 1997, most American working people received medical benefits from employer-sponsored managed care providers, and they were beginning to realize that the absence of any legal recourse against negligent providers could result in grave injustices.[154] Perhaps more important, doctors had become virtual prisoners of a system that effectively took away much of their discretion to treat ailing patients and turned it over to the "utilization management coordinators" who were deciding what treatments were "medically necessary" and therefore reimbursable. Combined with a genuine concern for patient well-being, the doctors' desire for greater control over medical decisions yielded a potent political demand from the medical community for significant change.[155]

Sensing that the time was ripe for managed care reform, Senator Edward Kennedy (D-Massachusetts) introduced a comprehensive "Patients' Bill of Rights." A companion bill was introduced in the House by two Republican representatives, Charles Norwood and Greg Ganske, a dentist and a doctor who had both crossed swords with the managed care industry in their practices. Soon thereafter, the Clinton administration introduced still another managed care reform bill.[156] The Republican congressional leadership warned its allies in the managed care industry that "we are in a war and need to start fighting like we're in a war." Not one to mince words, Senator Trent Lott (R-Mississippi) told the industry to "[g]et off your butts" and "[g]et out your wallets."[157] Joined by perennial business allies like the United States Chamber of Commerce, the industry formed two groups, called the Health Benefits Coalition and the Coalition for Patient Choice.[158]

The opponents warned that the patients' rights legislation would spawn "frivolous lawsuits" that would drive up medical costs, and they predicted that the resulting increases in managed care and insurance fees would force most employers to drop medical benefits altogether. This was a frightening prospect for workers who would then find themselves without any protection against potentially catastrophic medical expenses in the event of a major illness.[159] Opponents also accused doctors of advancing a hidden agenda of returning to the old fee-for-care system in which doctors faced no downward pressure on fees and made out like bandits by overprescribing treatments for which they received a cut of the profits.[160] Citing polls indicating that most patients were happy with the care they were receiving, opponents warned against "legislation by anecdote."[161]

Consumer groups and labor unions pressing corrective justice arguments were joined by politically potent medical organizations like the American Medical Association that were interested in retaining the power to make medical decisions in the hands of doctors. A manifesto signed by two thousand doctors declared that "[p]hysicians and nurses are being prodded by threats and bribes to abdicate allegiance to patients, and to shun the sickest, who may be unprofitable."[162] In response to the "frivolous lawsuit" claim, proponents observed that very few lawsuits had in fact been filed in states like Texas and California that had enacted laws permitting suits against managed care providers.[163]

The Health Benefits Coalition quickly "blew past" its $1 million advertising budget and was "well into the second million" by May 1998. It used the money to launch a major television advertising "blitz" targeting the districts of the House Republican leaders and committee chairpersons. The theme of the ads was "[w]hen politicians play doctor, real people get hurt," a suggestion that the thousands of real doctors who supported the legislation found especially galling.[164] One large California HMO hired a Virginia firm called Direct Impact to conduct a "grass roots" lobbying campaign. Armed with a list of the HMO's patients arranged by congressional district, the HMO asked "champions" that Direct Impact identified from the list to call critical congresspersons just prior to important votes.[165] In September 1998, nine major insurance companies and health management providers formed a new coalition, called the Coalition for Affordable Health Care, and committed $18 million more to a three-year advertising campaign.[166]

House Speaker Newt Gingrich (R-Georgia) appointed a special task force to critique the Norwood bill and to come up with a "bolder" and "more visionary" substitute bill that was less comprehensive and less burdensome for the managed care industry. Unsure of exactly what the Speaker had in mind, the task force wrote a bill that allowed patients to appeal coverage denials to an independent external review board but did not amend the ERIS Act to allow patients to sue managed care companies. To win over the doctors, it also included some highly controversial extraneous provisions, including nationwide limits on damages that plaintiffs could recover in malpractice actions against physicians. Playing the good soldier, Representative Norwood abandoned his bill and endorsed the task force's substitute.[167] When the House passed the task force bill on a mostly party-line vote, however, President Clinton threatened to veto it if it passed the Senate.[168]

As the 105th Congress wound down, President Clinton offered a major concession to opponents of his bill by agreeing to limit damages in any lawsuit against a managed care company to the actual costs of the treatment that the company had denied and to prohibit claims for any pain and suffering and mental anguish that might have resulted from any delays.[169] The release of special prosecutor Kenneth Starr's report on the Monica Lewinsky scandal the next week, however, ensured that Congress would not consider complex substantive legislation for the remainder of the session.[170]

President Clinton decided to make managed health care reform his top legislative priority at the outset of the 106th Congress, and he featured the administration bill in his January 1999 State of the Union address.[171] Joined by thirty-two Democratic senators and representatives, the president went on an April "road tour" to promote the bill. Representative Norwood introduced a bill that was very similar to his previous bill except that it gave patients a right to seek immediate relief in court when a managed care provider denied doctor-recommended treatment. The House leadership again introduced a bill that lacked a right to sue HMOs. The Senate Health, Education, Labor, and Pensions Committee rejected Senator Kennedy's bill and approved a bill drafted by the Republican chairman of the committee, James M. Jeffords of Vermont, that lacked a provision allowing patients to sue. Undeterred, Senate Democrats forced the Republican leadership to agree to an open floor debate on the Kennedy bill in mid-July 1999 by stalling legislative action on an important agricultural appropriations bill.[172]

When Republican senators returned to their home states for the Fourth of July recess, they encountered a week-long barrage of television and radio advertisements financed by a $9 million war chest assembled by the Coalition for Affordable Quality Health Care. The American Association of Health Plans launched its own television ad campaign featuring an angry construction worker complaining that politicians were attempting to increase his health care costs.[173] Their backs apparently stiffened by the advertising and an intense lobbying campaign upon their return to Washington, D.C., Republican senators passed the Jeffords bill instead of the Kennedy bill by a 52–48 party-line vote after four days of intense debate. After President Clinton threatened to veto the Senate bill, the battle shifted to the House of Representatives where a group of Republican health care mavericks joined with House Democrats to pass a bill co-sponsored by Representative Norwood and the Democratic Michigan congressman John Dingell that allowed patients to sue managed care facilities in state or federal courts without any limitations on damages.[174]

As the House and Senate bills moved to conference committee in late 1999, Speaker of the House Dennis Hastert, a long-time opponent of the right to sue HMOs, appointed only one supporter of the Norwood/Dingell bill to the House's thirteen-member contingent, and that member was not Norwood or any of the other prominent backers of the bill.[175] Vice President Al Gore, by now the front-runner for the Democratic presidential nomination, then seized the initiative by supplementing his standard stump speech with a horror story about a six-month-old boy who needed constant medical attention but was forced to live at home after the family's HMO concluded that his medical needs could be met if one of his parents stopped working or they put him up for adoption to allow Medicaid to cover the expenses. In response, candidate George W. Bush made much of the fact that he had signed, albeit somewhat reluctantly, the stringent Texas patient protection act that the Supreme Court would later find to be preempted in the *Davila* case. In one of the 2000 presidential debates, Bush promised that if he were elected, "people will be able to take their HMO insurance company to court."[176] As the public's attention turned from health care to the heated political campaigns of the 2000 election season, the bills quietly died in the conference committee.

The prospects for a Patients' Bill of Rights improved in the newly elected Congress that convened in 2001 when Senator John McCain (R-Arizona) announced that he would join Democratic Senators Kennedy and Bob Graham of Florida in sponsoring a bill that would allow patients to sue HMOs in state court for compensatory and punitive damages.[177] Karl Rove, a presidential adviser and Republican strategist, however, talked Representative Norwood out of offering his bill in the House while the administration came up with its own bill. Soon thereafter, President Bush outlined several broad principles that he would like to see reflected in a patients' rights bill, including recognition of a patient's right to bring an action in federal court but only after exhausting administrative remedies. Echoing the position of the managed care industry, he insisted that "Americans want meaningful remedies, not a windfall for trial lawyers." He announced a month later that he would veto any bill that, like the Texas bill he had signed in 1997, allowed patients to sue in state court and did not otherwise strictly limit damage claims.[178]

The administration bill that appeared in mid-May required patients to appeal coverage denial decisions to an "independent" panel before they could sue in court for actual damages of not more than $500,000 with no punitive damages. This was the last straw for Norwood, who attacked the bill as one that "protects HMOs, not patients." He promised to "personally exhaust every effort to defeat it." Within a week, however, the politics of the issue changed when Senator Jeffords decided to leave the Republican Party and caucus with the Democrats. The new Senate Majority Leader, Tom Daschle (D-South Dakota), announced that the Senate's first order of business would be to enact an aggressive patients' rights bill. In the House, Representative Norwood introduced his own bill that closely resembled the McCain/Kennedy bill, and he convinced many Republicans to sign on as co-sponsors. The Republican leadership responded with a bill drafted by Representative Hastert that went further than the administration preferred in allowing some patients to sue in state court but stopped far short of the Norwood bill.[179]

When the Senate took up the McCain/Kennedy bill in mid-June, "everybody who is anybody in Washington was lobbying" for or against it. President Bush promised a veto if it was not amended to reflect his principles. The Senate nevertheless passed a slightly amended McCain/Kennedy bill by a vote of 59–36.[180] As attention shifted to the House, President Bush invited Norwood to the White House to negotiate a compromise bill. The eight other House sponsors of the Norwood/Dingell bill agreed to allow Norwood to play that role on the condition that he not reach agreement without first consulting with them.[181] After spending several minutes expressing his admiration for Norwood's ability to outmaneuver the White House on this important issue, Bush concluded with "Now that I've kissed your ass, what do I have to do to get a deal?" After that, it took less than fifteen minutes for Norwood to agree to the vague outlines of an agreement. Norwood said that he needed to consult with his co-authors before making the deal public, but the president persuaded Norwood to join him for an impromptu press conference at the White House pressroom before returning to Capitol Hill.[182]

At the press conference, it became clear that the "compromise" bill would allow beneficiaries to sue managed care providers in state court, but only after an independent review. State actions would be governed by federal law, and damages for pain and suffering would be capped at $1.5 million. Moreover, if the independent reviewer agreed with the provider, the plaintiff would have to rebut a presumption that the provider's decision was appropriate. Punitive damages would be available, but only if the company refused to abide by the decision of an independent reviewer. Finally, on close inspection, it became apparent that the managed care provider got to select the "independent" reviewer from among anyone who did not have a direct financial relationship with the company.[183]

When the evening network news featured Norwood touting his "compromise" bill in the White House press room, the bill's other sponsors were outraged that he had broken his promise to consult with them first. Norwood returned to the Hill to receive what one of his aides described as an "ass-whipping" from his colleagues, but it was too late for him to back out. Beyond providing an opportunity for his co-sponsors to express their anger, the meeting accomplished little, in part because Norwood had not worked out the details of the deal with the White House staff. That happened later that evening in an exceedingly contentious meeting to which White House domestic adviser Josh Bolton came prepared with detailed language for insertion into the bill as a floor amendment. Norwood's aides were surprised, for example, to discover express preemption provision language, not explicitly agreed to by Norwood, that would have preempted all state laws and regulations, as well as state lawsuits. One aide later complained that "Josh Bolton screwed us over" at that meeting.[184]

Despite angering his co-authors, Norwood was able to persuade enough moderate Republicans to support the "compromise" language that it passed the House on a 226–203 vote the next day. Unbeknown to Norwood, however, the House Ways and Means Committee had weakened the bill even further that morning when it changed the language requiring the plaintiff to prove that the managed care decision was "a" proximate cause of injury to "the" proximate cause of injury, thus arguably requiring the plaintiff to eliminate all other potentially negligent actors before he could win a lawsuit against a managed care provider. One of the House bill's co-sponsors suggested that the administration had insisted on a "compromise" bill that it knew supporters of strong patients' rights legislation could not support because its real agenda was "to create an impasse with the Senate, and leave us once again without managed care reform."[185]

The dimming prospects for enacting a compromise Patients' Bill of Rights Act fell to zero on September 11, 2001, as the public's attention shifted from health care and similar domestic priorities to national security and the threat of global terrorism. Divisive debates of the sort that would have been inevitable had the House and Senate leadership appointed a conference committee on the patients' rights bill were definitely not the order of the day at a time when national unity was an important priority.[186]

President Bush put the issue back on the table in early February 2002 in a speech calling on Congress to enact the House bill, and Senator Kennedy agreed to work with the White House to come up with a compromise bill.[187] The negotiations expanded to include Representative Norwood and Senators John Edwards (D-North Carolina) and McCain and continued through June, during which time Senate Majority Leader Daschle refrained from naming senators to the conference committee. By early August, the negotiators were very close to an agreement, and the senators asked for a meeting with President Bush himself to seek his "personal intervention to resolve the difficult issues dividing us." After President Bush declined to meet with them, the congressional sponsors of the Patients' Bill of Rights threw in the towel.[188]

The politics of managed care reform changed again when the 2002 election turned the Senate back over to the Republican Party, increased the Republican majority in the House of Representatives, and made it clear that President Bush could have his way on the issue.[189] He announced early on that he would not accept any legislation that did not include a $250,000 cap on pain and suffering. This was a showstopper for supporters, who knew that the cap would effectively preclude most lawsuits. The sponsors of the Patients' Bill of Rights introduced bills again in the 108th Congress, but the bills languished in the House and Senate committees to which they were assigned.[190] Managed care abuse moved back onto the public agenda in early 2003 when the Supreme Court agreed to hear the *Davila* case.[191] The Bush administration received some criticism when it filed an amicus curiae brief in that case arguing that the very statute that President Bush had boasted about signing during the 2000 presidential debates was in fact unconstitutional.[192] Despite Justice Ginsburg's plea for congressional action, the brief dose of publicity attending the Supreme Court's June 2004 decision holding that all of the state laws were in fact preempted by the ERIS Act failed to stimulate sufficient support for managed care reform to force the bills out of committee.[193]

One of the reasons that the Patients' Bill of Rights faded from public view after September 11, 2001, may have been the fact that the managed care industry implemented internal changes to render their decisions less arbitrary and more responsive to the desires of the medical community. To some extent, the changes that the industry implemented were voluntary responses to the public outcry that was generating pressure for reform.[194]

CONCLUSIONS

Judged by the amount of time and energy that Congress devoted to federal preemption of state common law claims during the late 1990s and early 2000s, the preemption war has been a matter of profound national importance. On more than one occasion, the petroleum industry and its allies in Congress were willing to derail an energy bill that was a high priority for the George W. Bush administration and congressional Republicans rather than sacrifice the preemptive liability shield that it supported. Strong support from a powerful House leader allowed the industry to have its way. Similarly, the Senate Majority Leader pulled a major Defense Appropriations Act off the Senate floor to ensure sufficient time to take up the gun shield law prior to an August recess, during which momentum might have dwindled. For the last two years of the Clinton administration and the first year of the George W. Bush administration, patients' rights legislation was at the top of the congressional agenda, and throughout that time, the most contentious issue by far was whether Congress should amend the ERIS Act to allow injured plaintiffs to sue managed care companies in state court. The arcane issue of federal preemption thus dominated the domestic agenda and even played a prominent role in the public debates preceding the pivotal 2000 presidential election. That election ultimately determined the outcome of the debate as the George W. Bush administration adopted the same pro-preemption position in the battles over ERIS Act reform that it had taken on numerous other fronts in the preemption war.

One reason that the preemption issue can generate so much political heat is that it generates powerful political arguments in both the vertical and the horizontal dimensions. Strong vertical arguments played a critical role in the battles over the MTBE liability waiver as California and several states from the northeast that were seriously affected by groundwater contamination consistently protected the rights of their municipalities to sue the petroleum industry for compensation by arguing that the liability waiver would shift tens of billions of dollars in cleanup costs from the oil industry to state taxpayers. A coalition of state attorneys general also emphasized the right of state common law courts to address the simple nuisance issues presented by leaking underground storage tanks. Opponents of the gun shield act also stressed the importance of allowing evolving state common law to determine the validity of claims by urban municipalities and the unfairness of saddling local governments with the expense of paying for the treatment of indigent victims of handgun violence. Advocates of the Patients' Bill of Rights stressed the wisdom of allowing the state laboratories to function as they should in a federal system, pointing to the successful statutory solutions that both the California and Texas legislatures had come up with before the Supreme Court declared them unconstitutional in the *Davila* case.

At the same time, horizontal politics played a visible and at times decisive role in the congressional debates over many of the preemption bills discussed here. Many of the debates focused directly on the relative institutional competence of agencies and courts. By framing the ongoing firearms litigation as attempts to impose "regulation through litigation," proponents of the gun shield law illustrated both the absence of any pressing need for protective justice (the industry was, after all, already regulated by the BATF) and the threat that "judicial activism" posed to the congressional prerogative to determine regulatory policy. The cities, public interest groups, and plaintiffs' attorneys who were busily pressing doctrinally ambitious public interest lawsuits against the firearms industry were in an especially weak position to defend those lawsuits from the "regulation through litigation" claim, because their lawsuits sought injunctive relief (in some cases exclusively) that clearly had no corrective justice function. Indeed, some of the more outspoken supporters of the lawsuits made it clear to the media that putting manufacturers of cheap and easily concealed "Saturday Night Special" handguns out of business was exactly what they had in mind.[195]

The debates also focused on the substantive merits of the lawsuits that would be preempted, raising in Congress issues like the responsibility of firearms manufacturers for gun violence, the legitimacy of allowing HMO nurses to override the judgment of medical doctors, and the need to clean up MTBE-contaminated groundwater. The horizontal "overdeterrence" argument had a special political salience in the context of the gun shield act, where the proponents of the law raised the specter of a beleaguered domestic firearms industry that was on the brink of throwing in the towel and leaving both the nation's armed forces and security-conscious citizens at the mercy of foreign gun suppliers. Although Congress did not debate the vaccine shield act, its supporters could defend its otherwise highly questionable pedigree on the "emergency" need to combat both bird flu and bioterrorism with vaccines that would not be developed and produced without the assurance against overdeterrence that only a liability shield could provide. Overdeterrence was also featured in the debates over the Patients' Bill of Rights as opponents argued that increased managed care rates resulting from lawsuits would deter employers from providing any medical care benefits to employees.

Horizontal corrective justice concerns played a role in all of the battles, but they played a prominent role in only one of them—the battle over HMO liability reform. The proponents of amending the ERIS Act strongly relied on corrective justice in the horror stories they employed, in the rhetoric they invoked, and even in the title ("Patients' Bill of Rights") of the bill they employed to accomplish the task. Corrective justice played a minor role in the debates over MTBE, because neither of the most prominent opponents of the liability shield, the plaintiffs' lawyers and municipal water utility districts, were politically attractive exemplars of the injustice of shielding the petroleum industry from liability. It played an equally modest role in the debates over the gun shield law because neither the public interest litigation, which sought primarily injunctive relief, nor the private interest litigation, which was not directed at the criminals who were the immediate cause of harm, had been directed primarily at achieving corrective justice. Corrective justice concerns had no role whatsoever to play in the congressional debates over the vaccine shield law, because there were no debates.

Finally, the preemption war in Congress demonstrates the difficulties that even very determined industries and public interest groups face in overcoming the inertia of the status quo in a legislative body where a determined opposition with the support of forty senators can stop most important legislation. The proponents of both the MTBE liability shield and the Patients' Bill of Rights failed to change the law after spending huge amounts of energy and money. The history of the gun shield law is less germane, because it did not bring about a change in the law with respect to public interest litigation, which was already failing to gain legal ground before Congress ever took up the issue. The very brief history of the vaccine shield law suggests that one strategy for avoiding congressional inertia is to pass the preemptive law in the dead of night as a rider to an essential appropriations bill. From the perspective of open government and deliberative governance, however, that law represents a failure of the legislative process, not a success. Moreover, the experience may be limited to topics that can be framed in a way that invokes powerful national security and/or public health interests.

The best way for Congress to ensure that a federal agency's output will or will not preempt state common law claims is to write a strong express preemption provision that clearly encompasses common law duties or a savings clause that clearly preserves common law actions. That approach also has the virtue of allowing Congress to engage in a serious debate about what is clearly an issue of great national importance. Since many of the modern health and consumer protection statutes are already on the books and unlikely to be overhauled in the near future, however, this is obviously a strategy of limited immediate utility, a point to which we shall return in Chapter 10.

Chapter 6 The Preemption War in the Federal Agencies

Sometimes Congress explicitly delegates the power to preempt state law to a federal agency. The Surface Mining Control and Reclamation Act, for example, specifically authorizes the implementing agency to preempt state laws and to specify which laws are preempted.[1] None of these statutes, however, explicitly authorizes a federal agency to preempt state *common law* claims. Even absent an express delegation of the power to preempt, agency determinations concerning the preemptive effect of their statutes are of considerable importance. The Supreme Court in the famous *Chevron* case held that when federal agencies mean for their interpretations of ambiguous statutory language to have the force of law (speaking through the procedural vehicles of notice-and-comment rulemaking or formal adjudication), the issue before a court that is asked to review the agency action is not whether the agency's interpretation of the statute is the "correct" one but whether it is a "reasonable" one.[2] For example, after the Animal and Plant Health Inspection Service (APHIS), which is empowered to regulate animal vaccines, promulgated a special preemption regulation, most courts relied on the regulations to hold that common law claims addressed to APHIS-approved animal vaccines were preempted.[3] We discuss the extent to which courts should defer to agency preemption rules in more detail in Chapter 10.

In cases in which the agency acts through less formal vehicles, such as policy statements, guidance documents, and amicus curiae briefs, that do not have the force of law, the courts generally afford somewhat less deference to the agency's interpretation, upholding it if the agency can persuade the court that its interpretation is correct.[4] In these less formal contexts, the positions of Executive Branch agencies have varied over time on the question whether their regulatory activities preempted state common law claims. Prior to *Cipollone,* the government rarely took the position that regulatory programs preempted state common law actions because common law preemption was never mentioned in express preemption provisions and it probably did not occur to them that words like "requirement" applied to the common law. During the George H. W. Bush administration, the Department of Transportation took a middle-of-the-road position in *Geier,* arguing that the Federal Motor Vehicle Safety Act did not expressly preempt state common law claims and that its regulations would not ordinarily impliedly preempt those claims. The government's amicus curiae brief argued only that the agency's regulations did preempt the plaintiff's particular airbags-only claim.[5] Late in the same administration, the Federal Railway Administration's (FRA) brief in *Easterwood* took a similar middle-of-the-road position with respect to the Federal Railway Safety Act, arguing that the agency's grade crossing regulations would preempt state common law claims only at federally funded intersections.[6]

President Clinton made his views on preemption clear in an executive order that remained in effect through both George W. Bush administrations. Executive Order 13,132, which established federalism principles and policies for regulatory agencies, instructed them to find that federal statutes preempt state law "only where the statute contains an express preemption provision or there is some other clear evidence that Congress intended preemption of State law, or where the exercise of State authority conflicts with the exercise of Federal authority under the Federal statute." Furthermore, "[a]ny regulatory preemption of State law shall be restricted to the minimum level necessary to achieve the objectives of the statute pursuant to which the regulations are promulgated."[7]

Regulatory agencies generally followed these directives as the preemption war broke out during the Clinton administration in the late 1990s. In *Shanklin,* the FRA adhered to its prior position that most collision cases at federally funded grade crossings were preempted but limited preemption to federally funded grade crossings where the states and the FRA made site-specific engineering judgments.[8] The Environmental Protection Agency (EPA) adhered to its traditional position that the federal pesticide act did not preempt common law claims.[9] The Clinton administration also favored overturning the ERIS Act's broad preemption of common law claims against managed care providers in its version of the Patients' Bill of Rights law. One exception was the government's amicus curiae brief in *Buckman* defending the "important federal interest in permitting the Food and Drug Administration (FDA) to decide for itself whether it has been defrauded, and, if so, what sanction is appropriate."[10] As in previous administrations, agencies did not write common law preemption into their regulations and guidance documents during the Clinton administration.

This all changed as the preemption war raged on during the George W. Bush administration. In the Supreme Court, the Bush administration usually took the position that common law claims were preempted. In *Davila,* it argued that the Texas statute that President Bush himself had signed as governor of Texas was preempted by the Employee Retirement Income Security Act, and, in *Bates,* it departed from previous administrations to urge the Court to find that common law claims regarding EPA-approved pesticide labels were preempted.[11] Similar amicus briefs in *Riegel* and *Kent* argued that the Food, Drug and Cosmetics Act preempted state common law claims involving fully approved medical devices and the fraud exception to a Michigan statute prohibiting claims against manufacturers of FDA-approved drugs.[12] One exception to this strong trend was the government's amicus brief in *Sprietsma,* filed early in the Bush administration, which agreed with the plaintiffs that the Coast Guard's failure to require propeller guards did not preempt common law claims.[13] While the Bush administration's amicus curiae briefs frequently mentioned the importance of federalism, they either failed to mention or belittled corrective justice concerns, even in cases where a statutory savings clause suggested that protecting corrective justice should be an agency goal.

This chapter describes the quiet effort by several federal agencies during the George W. Bush administration to preempt state common law litigation through aggressive administrative interpretations of federal regulatory laws in informal contexts largely out of public view. In most cases, this represented a dramatic shift from past agency practice. Perhaps for this reason, the agencies buried these new interpretations within lengthy preambles to regulations, sometimes without allowing an effective opportunity for public comment, in a process that Professors Sam Issacharoff and Catherine Sharkey have referred to as "backdoor federalization."[14] After taking a quick look at a short-lived attempt by the FRA to expand the range of its preemptive power during the second half of the Clinton administration, this chapter visits the three most prominent Bush administration initiatives in the contexts of food labeling regulations, automobile roof crush rules, and rules for mattress flammability.

SAFETY DEVICES AT GRADE CROSSINGS

The Federal Railroad Administration (FRA) in 1995 formally proposed a rule that would have preempted all state common law claims based upon a railroad's negligence in failing to provide an adequate warning at grade crossings, whether or not the grade crossing in question had been federally funded. The regulation would have greatly expanded the scope of federal preemption to include hundreds of thousands of unprotected grade crossings that did not have automatic gates or other active systems. The preamble to the proposal maintained that an "ad hoc system of grade crossing improvements, driven by tort law" would defeat the "goal of a uniform national program based on planning and prioritization." Moreover, tort awards would divert scarce railroad company dollars from investments in grade crossing warning devices to "compensating those killed or injured in accidents or their survivors," a result that reflected "sound public policy only when the railroad has breached a duty to them that is appropriate for the railroad to have."[15] The agency was apparently convinced that it was *never* appropriate for the railroad to have a duty to compensate the victims of poorly conceived or badly maintained grade crossings.

A broad coalition of interest groups, ranging from the Illinois Public Interest Research Group and the National Association of Attorneys General to the American Trucking Association, weighed in against the proposal.[16] Events also conspired against it. Less than twenty-four hours after the agency's June 1995 public hearing on the proposal, a family of seven migrant workers was killed at an Oregon grade crossing protected only by a crossbuck and a stop sign. In October, seven high school students in a school bus waiting for a green light in Fox River Grove, Illinois, were killed by a commuter train traveling fifty miles per hour.[17] After being accused in a nationally syndicated editorial of shielding railroads from their legal responsibilities, the agency withdrew the proposal "based on public comments and FRA's determination that railroad safety will not be best served by issuance of such a regulation at this time."[18] The agency has never resurrected the proposal, and grade crossing litigation has continued for crossings that are not federally funded.

PRESCRIPTION DRUG REGULATION

Tim Tobin and his wife, Deborah, and baby daughter, Alyssa, loved visiting Alyssa's doting grandparents Don and Rita Schell at the Schell residence in Gillette, Wyoming.[19] In 1998, when Alyssa was nine months old, Deb and Alyssa drove to Gillette for what turned out to be an extended two-week visit after Deb became ill. During much of this time, Don was feeling despondent because of the recent deaths of his brother and of Rita's father, who was also his favorite hunting and fishing buddy. Don had occasionally suffered bouts of depression in the past, usually when things were not going well at work. During these times, the rest of the family tried to be supportive, and Don appreciated their efforts to help him manage his way out of the depression. A doctor had once prescribed Prozac, an FDA-approved antidepressant, but Don became quite agitated while on that drug. His doctor had prescribed two different drugs to take the edge off of his jitteriness, but neither of them had worked. This time, Don consulted a different physician, who prescribed a new drug called Paxil and gave him some samples to use until he could get to a drugstore.

Two days after Don started taking Paxil, Tim drove to Gillette for a brief visit before returning home with Deb and Alyssa. When Tim arrived at the Schell house at around 4:00 P.M., no one answered the door. Assuming that they were out running errands, Tim headed into town to look for them. When he returned a couple of hours later, he discovered that all the cars were parked in the garage, and he noticed that a light was on upstairs. He and a neighbor then called the police. After they arrived, Tim broke out a back window, entered the house, and rushed upstairs. What he discovered there could not be forgotten in three lifetimes. Early that morning, Don had fired six bullets out of a .22 caliber pistol into his wife, his daughter, and his granddaughter. He then shot them at point blank range with a .357 magnum revolver before turning the gun on himself. All four of them lay dead in a single bloodstained room. Tim does not remember much about the rest of that day, but he had a very hard time adjusting to the loss. He could not begin to fathom how a loving husband and father and doting grandfather could have murdered the very people who meant the most to him, even if he was very depressed.

Dr. David Healy, an internationally prominent expert in diagnosing and treating depression, testified in a lawsuit that Tim Tobin later filed against GlaxoSmithKline Corporation that Don Schell's otherwise incomprehensible conduct was caused by Paxil. Like Prozac and other drugs in the same family of antidepressants, Paxil causes a small percentage of the patients taking it to become severely agitated to the point at which they pose a deadly risk to themselves and others.[20] Not everyone, however, agrees with Healy. Dr. Charles Preuss, another well-regarded specialist in depression, testified for GlaxoSmithKline that there is no reliable scientific evidence that Paxil causes either suicide or violent behavior in anyone who takes it. Preuss blamed Tim's terrible loss on Don Schell's state of depression, no more and no less. Moreover, Preuss and many other psychiatrists are firmly convinced that Paxil and its chemical cousins help many more people than they harm by reducing anxiety, depression, and aggression.[21] Tim Tobin doesn't buy that argument. As far as he is concerned, "[w]hether we are statistically significant or not, four people dead is too many."[22]

FDA Authority to Regulate Prescription Drugs

The Federal Food Drug and Cosmetic Act (FDC Act) requires manufacturers of all prescription medications to obtain FDA approval before marketing them in the United States. To secure that approval, the manufacturer must demonstrate to FDA that the drug will be "safe and effective" for the approved uses and that its labeling will not be "false or misleading."[23] The manufacturer's "New Drug Application" (NDA) is typically a very lengthy submission containing the results of animal testing, pharmacological studies, and "clinical" trials in which doctors administer the drug to human volunteers under controlled conditions. All of these studies are done under the supervision and control of the drug companies or their contractors.[24] In the early 1990s, however, Congress created an abbreviated "fast track" approval process for new drugs to "address unmet medical needs" for "serious or life-threatening condition[s]" that has greatly reduced the time that FDA takes to approve those drugs.[25] Congress has always carefully avoided granting FDA authority to regulate the practice of medicine, reserving that function to state regulation and common law. Thus, a physician is free to prescribe an approved drug for any use, whether or not FDA has approved it for that specific use. About 21 percent of the 725 million prescriptions that doctors wrote in 2001 were for such "off-label" uses.[26]

The premarket approval process does not address all of a drug's potential risks, because the testing protocols are incapable of detecting side effects that occur relatively rarely, have long latency periods, or adversely affect subpopulations (like children and the elderly) that were not represented in the premarket testing. Consequently, FDA approval of a drug is by no means a guarantee that the drug will not produce adverse side effects in those who use it according to its label, and it offers even less assurance to those who take it for unapproved uses. FDA has a postmarketing surveillance program for monitoring approved drugs for evidence of adverse side effects, but that program has been chronically starved for resources (as we shall see in Chapter 7), and it has not provided an adequate "backstop" to the premarket approval process.[27]

The primary function of a prescription drug label is to apprise prescribing physicians of the drug's risks and benefits. FDA regulations mandate the format and content of labels, describing in general terms the information that they must contain on proper uses and dosage, as well as the information that manufacturers must provide under the general topics of "contraindications," "warnings," "precautions," and "adverse reactions." The NDA includes draft label instructions and warnings, and the manufacturer and FDA officials typically discuss the contents of the proposed label in some detail during the approval process.[28]

FDA has the power to withdraw its approval at any time if it finds that "clinical or other experience, tests, or other scientific data show that such drug is unsafe for use" or if it concludes that "new information" renders the labeling false or misleading.[29] Under FDA regulations, a label must be revised to include a warning "as soon as there is reasonable evidence of an association of a serious hazard" with the drug, and "a causal relationship need not have been proved."[30] The manufacturer initiates changes to the labels of approved drugs by submitting a Supplemental New Drug Application, but prior FDA approval is not required for any changes designed to "add or strengthen" a "contraindication, warning, precaution, or adverse reaction," a "statement about drug abuse, dependence, psychological effect, or overdosage," or an instruction about "dosage and administration that is intended to increase the safe use of the drug product." The manufacturer may also "delete false, misleading, or unsupported indications for use or claims for effectiveness" without FDA approval. FDA may, but never does, disapprove these unilateral changes at a later time.[31]

FDA Regulation of SSRI Drugs

The Paxil that Don Shell was taking prior to murdering his family is one of a family of drugs called selective serotonin reuptake inhibitors (SSRIs) that can alleviate serious mental depression by maintaining levels of a protein called serotonin in the brain. The first widely used SSRI, a drug marketed in the United States under the trade name Luvox as a treatment for obsessive-compulsive disorder (OCD) in children, became a household word when the media reported that one of the adolescent murderers at Columbine High School had been taking that drug. The SSRI drugs filled a huge potential market as FDA approved a continuing stream of them in the late 1980s and early 1990s.[32] As with Vioxx, FDA learned much more about the side effects of SSRI drugs after they were in wide use throughout the country.

In the mid-1950s, scientists had identified a syndrome called "akathisia" that is characterized by "an inner sense of restlessness and an inability to stand still."[33] Although akathisia later became widely recognized as a suicide and homicide risk factor for some antipsychotic drugs, it was a poorly understood condition and was frequently dismissed as mere "agitation" in clinical trials. Scientists overseeing the clinical trials for the SSRI drug Prozac, for example, responded to reports of akathisia like that observed by Don Schell's first doctor by recommending that some of the patients be given an additional drug to reduce those symptoms. Since the labels for the approved SSRI drugs failed to reference akathisia, doctors prescribing them did not know to keep an eye out for signs of mental turmoil in their patients.[34]

The first scientific article indicating that SSRI drugs could cause patients to behave abnormally was published in February 1990 by the Harvard University researcher Dr. Martin Teicher. The article, which "prompted a firestorm of criticism" from the pharmaceutical industry, concluded that Prozac caused an elevated incidence of suicide in adult males. Eli Lilly's scientists responded with their own "meta-analysis" of data from the company's clinical trials, which found no evidence that patients taking Prozac became any more suicidal than those taking a non-SSRI antidepressant drug or a placebo. After an FDA-convened advisory panel concluded that "there was not clear evidence of an increased risk of suicidality in association with the use of Prozac," FDA decided to take no action. Although the agency had no legal authority to require Eli Lilly to conduct postapproval testing, the company, at FDA's suggestion, hired a prominent scientist to conduct a large "double-blind" clinical study with input from Teicher. The consultant met with Teicher, drew up the study protocols, approached prospective investigators, and prepared clinical trial materials, but the pressure to take action had died down by then, and the company shelved the study.[35]

The evidence that SSRI drugs caused akathisia and suicidal thoughts continued to mount during the early 1990s, but FDA took no action to limit their use or change their labels.[36] Instead, it continued to approve new SSRI drugs like Paxil.[37] Healy testified at Tim Tobin's trial that the data from the thirty-four clinical trials that GlaxoSmithKline submitted with its NDA to FDA strongly suggested that it produced akathisia in "a significant proportion" of the healthy volunteer adults and that it caused some patients to become suicidal or violent. Moreover, another significant proportion of the Paxil-administered patients had dropped out of the study because they could not tolerate the side effects, sometimes after only a single dose.[38]

Things began to go badly for manufacturers of SSRI drugs in May 2003 when the British equivalent of FDA reacted to a series of company-conducted clinical trials involving children and adolescents by requiring GlaxoSmithKline to place warnings on Paxil labels stating that it could cause young people under eighteen to kill or harm themselves.[39] FDA reacted to this development more than a year later by issuing a public health advisory recommending that "Paxil not be used in children and adolescents." In March 2004, FDA requested but did not demand that manufacturers of SSRI drugs change their labels to include "a Warning statement that recommends close observation of adult and pediatric patients treated with these agents for worsening depression or the emergence of suicidality." The agency still declined to require the company to change the label for Paxil to incorporate this warning.[40]

Things went from bad to worse in the summer of 2004 when GlaxoSmithKline settled a lawsuit brought by New York Attorney General Eliot Spitzer alleging that it had committed consumer fraud by failing to disclose all of the relevant information in its clinical studies for Paxil. Spitzer later explained that he filed the Paxil suit after discovering strong evidence of serious deception in the company's scientific reports. He took action on behalf of New York citizens, because "we were not seeing the type of behavior at the FDA that we wanted."[41] Based on a reevaluation of the scientific evidence, FDA required manufacturers to put the strongest warning available under FDA's regulations on *all* antidepressant drugs stating that "[a]ntidepressants increase the risk of suicidal thinking and behavior (suicidality) in children and adolescents with MDD [major depressive disorder] and other psychiatric disorders."[42] In June 2005, FDA issued a public health advisory bringing to the public's attention several recent scientific publications suggesting "the possibility of an increased risk for suicidal behavior in adults who are being treated with antidepressant medications."[43] This was, of course, far too late for Don Schell's family.

The widely publicized SSRI story was by no means the first time that flaws in the FDA new-drug approval process and postapproval surveillance system had received public attention, nor would it be the last.[44] The SSRI regulatory failures had only barely receded from public view when the Vioxx crisis described in Chapter 1 erupted. In light of these embarrassing failings, one might have expected the agency's political leadership to approach its public health protection responsibilities with a degree of humility about its capacity to detect and properly address chicanery on the part of drug companies, its ability to withstand and deflect company-generated pressures, and its power to take bold action when postmarketing information revealed that previously approved drugs were causing unanticipated side effects. Surely, the poorly funded agency would welcome all the help it could get from common law courts that, in lawsuits like those filed by Attorney General Spitzer and Tim Tobin, could reinforce or even supplement the agency's efforts to advance its mission of protecting the public health. Instead, FDA, in 2002, launched an aggressive campaign to preempt state common law actions that became a major battleground in the preemption war.

FDA Changes its Preemption Tune

Tim Tobin's lawyers convinced a Wyoming jury that Paxil was a defectively designed product and that GlaxoSmithKline had negligently failed to warn Don Schell's doctors of the risk that Paxil would make some people taking it suicidal and/or violent. The jury found Glaxo liable to Tim Tobin and to the estates of Deborah and Alyssa Tobin in the amount of slightly more than $6 million. After the court upheld the verdict, it became the first judgment rendered for a plaintiff in a lawsuit involving an SSRI drug.[45] It would not be the last.

A year and a half after the *Tobin* verdict, Lois Colacicco was diagnosed with breast cancer. When she complained to her doctor that her chemotherapy treatment was leaving her tired and depressed, he prescribed Paxil and a generic equivalent for the depression. She began to manifest signs of akathisia almost immediately, and her doctor sent her to a psychiatrist, who kept her on the drug after specifically noting that she was neither homicidal nor suicidal. Less that a week later, Colacicco met with a social worker at a local elementary school to discuss the possibility of volunteer work, and she seemed to be in good spirits. Upon returning home after the meeting, she drew a warm bath, eased into the tub, and sliced herself several times with a razor blade.[46]

Her husband's wrongful-death action against GlaxoSmithKline and the generic drug manufacturer alleged that the SSRI drug had caused her to commit suicide in roughly the same way that it had caused Don Schell to kill his family. It was a difficult case to make on the merits, and lawyers both before and after the *Tobin* verdict often failed to demonstrate a cause-effect relationship between Paxil and violent conduct.[47] Long before a jury heard a word of testimony, however, Colacicco's lawsuit was dismissed because the George W. Bush administration had adopted a radically new position on federal preemption of common law "failure-to-warn" claims against manufacturers of FDA-approved drugs. Dan Troy, the man President Bush appointed to be FDA's new chief counsel, had invited defense counsel to request amicus curiae briefs from the agency in pending cases, and FDA had responded to the resulting invitations with briefs strongly urging courts to find plaintiffs' claims preempted.[48]

FDA's position was of particular interest to many courts, because the FDC Act is silent on the preemption question in the context of drug regulation.[49] Prior to Troy's intervention, the courts in dozens of cases had uniformly concluded that the doctrine of implied preemption did not apply to common law defective design and failure-to-warn claims against FDA-approved drugs.[50] Most courts recognized that FDA approval was evidence of the fact that the drug or device was not defective for FDA-approved uses, but they still allowed juries to decide otherwise on the basis of testimony presented at the trials.[51] According to Professor George W. Conk, this reflected a judicial recognition that "FDA does not claim to review products for optimal design" but instead approves drugs "if they meet the agency's threshold standards for safety and efficacy."[52] As we learned in Chapter 2, the *Restatement (Third) of Products Liability* accepted that proposition for all federally regulated products and even favored drugs and devices with a special test for liability.[53]

Many of the courts that rejected preemption arguments relied on the FDA regulations allowing drug companies to strengthen their labels unilaterally, subject only to the possibility that FDA might subsequently disapprove the change.[54] One federal district court cited the preamble to the 1998 regulations stating that FDA's drug regulations "establish the minimal standards necessary, but were not intended to preclude the states from imposing additional labeling requirements."[55] Another referred to a 1994 preamble in which FDA recognized that "product liability plays an important role in consumer protection."[56] In short, before the preemption war broke out, in the late 1990s, the courts found it "rather difficult to believe that Congress or the FDA would, without comment, remove all means of judicial redress for those injured"[57] by drug company failures provide reasonable warnings to doctors.

Troy's efforts bore immediate fruit in Texas, where two different federal district courts in 2004 relied on an FDA amicus curiae brief to conclude that FDA's approval of the SSRI drug Zoloft preempted state common law failure-to-warn claims.[58] By that time, FDA was gradually shifting its position on the SSRI drugs to require more and more warnings of precisely the sort that the plaintiffs in the two Texas cases had suggested would be required to comply with the manufacturer's common law duty to warn. The tide quickly turned against FDA as several other district courts rejected the FDA briefs in cases involving Zoloft and other SSRI drugs.[59] One court relied on the affidavit of a former deputy director of FDA's Office of Enforcement in which he stated that he did not know "of any case where FDA has considered a product to be 'misbranded' because it had a stricter warning on the label than FDA had originally approved."[60]

The Labeling Regulations

It was time for the agency to try a new preemption strategy. As noted earlier, courts had frequently relied upon FDA statements made in preambles to regulations of its intent not to preempt state law. Prior to 2006, FDA had on four occasions stated an intent to preempt state *regulations* that were inconsistent with particular FDA requirements. But these had been special cases, like the regulations requiring tamper-resistant packaging and labeling for over-the-counter drugs in the wake of the 1982 Chicago Tylenol disaster, in which the agency specifically concluded that national uniformity was essential to protect public health.[61] None of these rare statements of preemptive intent, however, spoke to state common law claims, and FDA had otherwise "stayed on the sidelines" of preemption litigation throughout its 77-year history.[62] In early 2006, FDA revived a moribund Clinton administration rulemaking initiative aimed at establishing requirements for the "content and format" of labels for human prescription drugs and biological products. Although the Clinton administration's notice of proposed rulemaking stated that the regulations did "not preempt state law,"[63] the preamble to the Bush administration's final regulation purported to do exactly that.[64]

Responding to concerns expressed by some manufacturers that complying with the rules might make them more vulnerable to product liability claims, FDA assured the industry that "under existing preemption principles such product liability claims would be preempted," because "FDA approval of labeling under the act . . . preempts conflicting or contrary state law." In the agency's view, the dozens of prior judicial opinions to the contrary were based upon a "misunderstanding of the act," because the agency now interpreted the act to "establish both a 'floor' and a 'ceiling.'" The preamble stressed that FDA was the "expert Federal public health agency charged by Congress with ensuring that drugs are safe and effective, and that their labeling adequately informs users of the risks and benefits of the product and is truthful and not misleading." State common law actions, by contrast, "encourage, and in fact require, lay judges and juries to second-guess the assessment of benefits versus risks of a specific drug to the general public . . . sometimes on behalf of a single individual or group of individuals."

The preamble expressed the agency's concern that "[e]xaggeration of risk could discourage appropriate use of a beneficial drug," a phenomenon that the agency referred to as "overwarning." The preamble continued that "[o]verwarning, just like underwarning, can . . . have a negative effect on patient safety and public health." Attempts by states "to impose additional warnings can lead to labeling that does not accurately portray a product's risks, thereby potentially discouraging safe and effective use of approved products or encouraging inappropriate use and undermining the objectives of the act." FDA therefore concluded that six specific kinds of claims were preempted by the labeling regulations, and it announced that federal preemption "would include not only claims against manufacturers . . . , but also against health care practitioners [i.e., doctors] for claims related to dissemination of risk information to patients beyond what is included in the labeling."

Reactions to FDA's Change of Heart

The pharmaceutical industry was thrilled with the new regulations,[65] but they drew heavy criticism from Democratic leaders in both houses of Congress and from public interest groups. In a strongly worded letter to Secretary of Health and Human Services Michael Leavitt, Senators Edward M. Kennedy (D-Massachusetts) and Christopher J. Dodd (D-Connecticut) charged that, in light of "recent questions about FDA's ability to ensure the safety of prescription drugs," it was "a particularly inopportune time to remove the safety net that state consumer protection laws provide."[66] Although Congress clearly had the power to overturn the agency's interpretation by amending the FDC Act, the more immediate question was how the new assertion of preemptive authority would play out in the courts that were already entertaining hundreds of failure-to-warn cases involving FDA-approved prescription drugs like Paxil and Vioxx.

The new regulations had their hoped-for effect on some courts, one of which was still presiding over Colacicco's case. The court, in the *Colacicco v. Apotex, Inc.,* relied on both the regulations and an amicus curiae brief that the agency prepared specifically for that case.[67] Joseph Colacicco's loss was Dan Troy's gain, and it was a victory that he could proudly cite to his law partners when he returned to the private sector to represent the pharmaceutical industry.[68] Several courts reached the same outcome in the context of different drugs, including the SSRI drugs.[69] In an opinion written by Justice Stephen Breyer's brother Charles, one court stated that it was obliged to give deference to FDA's view on the preemption issue, because Congress had "delegated the responsibility for administering the FDCA to the FDA," and that "implie[d] the authority and expertise to determine which state laws conflict with its regulations."[70]

A large majority of the courts that considered the matter, however, was unwilling to defer so quickly to FDA's new position.[71] A federal district court in Nebraska, in a case involving both Zoloft and Effexor, noted that it "was inconsistent with the primary purpose of both the FDCA and the FDA's regulatory scheme," which was "to protect the public."[72] The court pointed out in a footnote that the agency had failed to comply with the applicable "federalism" executive order requiring agencies to communicate with the states and to allow them to participate in regulatory proceedings that may result in a preemption determination. Pointing to recent developments, including congressional hearings, a recommendation for a black box warning from an FDA scientific advisory committee, and the conclusion of numerous experts that there was a link between SSRI drugs and suicidality, a district court in Washington concluded that "it would be inconceivable to this Court to argue that an additional warning regarding suicidality would be false and misleading."[73]

The Supreme Court agreed to resolve the dispute in *Wyeth v. Levine,* a case in which the Vermont Supreme Court declined to defer to FDA's newly adopted position on preemption. The case arose when Diana Levine, a professional singer and guitarist, went to a Vermont health clinic complaining of one of her frequent migraine headaches and associated nausea.[74] The nurse at the clinic inadvertently administered the prescribed treatment, which included Wyeth's prescription drug Phenergan, with a syringe employing a method referred to in the medical community as an "IV push." There were two problems with this technique. First, the preferred method for intravenous injection of Phenergan was via the "drip" method through which the drug is mixed in a saline solution and allowed to flow into a vein slowly over a period of time. This drip method is much safer than the "IV push" method because it minimizes the risk that the doctors and nurses will mistakenly inject the drug into an artery, rather than a vein, and this is exactly what happened to Ms. Levine. Wyeth knew full well that if Phenergan was directly injected into an artery, it would rapidly destroy it, and necrosis and gangrene could follow soon thereafter. One of Wyeth's experts testified at the trial that he would hesitate to administer the drug through the IV push method for precisely that reason. Nevertheless, the label that Wyeth submitted and that FDA approved for Phenergan did not warn doctors and nurses not to use the IV push method. For seven weeks following the injection, Ms. Levine suffered excruciating physical pain as she watched her hand and then her lower arm slowly die. Two career-ending amputations caused her further physical pain and a great deal of emotional distress. After settling with the clinic for an undisclosed sum, Ms. Levine sued Wyeth in a Vermont state court and received a $6.8 million jury verdict.

On appeal, the Vermont court upheld the verdict, finding that there was no conflict between state common law and the federal statute. The Vermont court first rejected Wyeth's argument that FDA had rejected an adequate warning that it had submitted for inclusion on the label because it was too strong. Although FDA had rejected the proposal, the court held that the agency's terse explanation for that action did not indicate whether it had paid any attention at all to the question whether the IV push technique was appropriate for the drug. Nothing in that explanation remotely suggested that a stronger warning would be misleading. It was therefore not "impossible" for Wyeth to comply with its obligations under both Vermont and federal law. Concluding that the agency's assertion in the preamble did not deserve judical deference, the court stressed that the agency's unamended regulations allowed drug manufacturers to strengthen a warning without prior FDA approval. Unlike most other courts, however, the court relied on language in an uncodified provision of the 1962 amendments to the statute stating that "[n]othing in the amendments made by this Act . . . shall be construed as invalidating any provision of State law . . . unless there is a direct and positive conflict between such amendments and such provisions of State law." The court believed that this language limited the court's conflict preemption analysis to whether it was impossible for Wyeth to comply with both the federal statute and Vermont's common law. Having already determined that it would be possible for the company to comply with both obligations, the court upheld the jury verdict.[75]

Assuming that Congress does not intervene in the interim, the Supreme Court will resolve the issue before the end of June 2009. Because most products liability claims involving prescription drugs turn on the adequacy of the warnings on their labels, this case has enormous implications for all present and future drug litigation. Among other things, a Supreme Court ruling in favor of Wyeth would throw into question all of the pending litigation regarding the Vioxx-like COX-2 inhibiting pain killers and SSRI antidepressants. Although it is venturesome at this juncture to predict how the Court will come out, the following section of this chapter suggests some reasons why the Court should let the Vermont court's judgment stand.

FDA's New Position on the Merits

The content of a drug's label is substantially within the control of the manufacturer. The final wording "is typically the result of negotiations between regulators and the sponsor," and FDA does not have the authority to compel label changes unilaterally.[76] Under its 1965 regulations, drug companies may change drug labels without FDA approval to "add or strengthen a contraindication, warning, precaution, or adverse reaction."[77] Indeed, manufacturers have an affirmative duty under FDA regulations to revise a drug's labeling "as soon as" there is "reasonable evidence" of an "association" of "serious adverse reactions and potential safety hazards," a command that, in the view of Professor Richard Nagareda, "undercuts the possibility of conflicting state-law commands arising from tort liability."[78] FDA may, of course, disapprove the change, but it has not done so in practice, nor has it ever attempted to demonstrate that a drug was misbranded because it included a warning that FDA refused to require.[79] Thus, manufacturers are free to comply with their common law duty to make doctors aware of new information about a drug's hazardous side effects without coming into conflict with FDA regulatory requirements. The preamble to the labeling regulations dismissed this powerful argument with the unhelpful observation that "in practice manufacturers typically consult with FDA before [strengthening labels] to avoid implementing labeling changes with which the agency ultimately might disagree."[80] What manufacturers "typically" do, however, is not at all relevant to what they are legally required to do under the FDA regulations.

The agency's amicus curiae briefs and preamble incorrectly suggested that the scientific staff's reaction to a Supplemental NDA containing a label change is functionally equivalent to its reaction to an NDA containing the proposal for the original label. In the case of a new drug, any attempt to market the unapproved product should result in a swift enforcement action in court, and the only issue will be whether or not FDA has approved the drug. In the case of a label change to "strengthen" the warning, the agency review is often quite cursory in nature and does not result in a formal approval or disapproval; nearly all of the time, the change simply goes into effect. Even if the agency staff subsequently concludes that the new label is false or misleading, the company is free to market the drug under that label until such time as the Department of Justice files an enforcement action, in which the government has the burden of proving that the drug is "misbranded" because the label is false or misleading. Before any action is taken against the company, the lawyers must persuade a judge or (in the case of a criminal action) a jury that the label is in fact false or misleading.[81] Thus, at the end of the day, the ultimate decision maker on the question whether a label change is false or misleading is not the FDA staff but the same entity that decides whether a product is defective because of a failure to warn in a common law action—the jury. In both cases, the agency's expertise is relevant, but not determinative.

NHTSA ROOF CRUSH REGULATIONS

Patrick Parker and Penny Shipler didn't know what hit them. When Patrick Parker swerved to avoid colliding with a deer on a lonely stretch of Texas Panhandle highway, he could not have known that his instinctive reaction would leave him paralyzed from the neck down for the rest of his life. He was wearing his lap belt and shoulder harness, and he had every reason to expect that he would survive a collision with a deer. What he did not expect was that the abrupt avoidance maneuver would cause his Ford F-250 pickup truck to roll over. Penny Shipler, a waitress in Lincoln, Nebraska, had accepted a ride home with a co-worker after a long evening's work when her friend lost control of her Chevy Blazer and it rolled over several times. The police found Shipler hanging upside down by her shoulder harness, paralyzed from the neck down. What hit both Patrick Parker and Penny Shipler was the roofs of the vehicles they were riding in as they collapsed during the rollovers.[82]

Parker and Shipler were victims of a regulatory failure extending all the way back to the initial standard-setting exercise undertaken by the National Highway Traffic Safety Administration (NHTSA) soon after its creation, in 1966. NHTSA decided to put pickup trucks and vans in a separate category because they were not used very often for transporting passengers and because they would need to be extensively modified to meet the standards it was contemplating for passenger cars. The agency followed this conclusion with a hurried decision to include "multipurpose vehicles" in the truck/van category, even though they were clearly designed to be passenger vehicles. When auto manufacturers in the 1990s adapted the pickup chassis to a new kind of multipurpose vehicle called a "sport utility vehicle" (SUV), the new creations remained in the same class as pickup trucks.[83]

In 1991, NHTSA extended the roof strength requirements of its Standard 216 from automobiles to cover pickup trucks, SUVs, and some vans.[84] This patchwork solution, however, failed to take into account the much greater propensity of high-mounted pickup trucks and SUVs to suffer rollover accidents when drivers steered sharply to avoid unexpected obstacles. Worse, it failed to take advantage of the opportunity that the 1991 rulemaking presented to update the agency's aging mid-twentieth century standard to meet the expectations of twenty-first-century drivers. In 2001, about 6,900 people suffered some injury due to collapsing roofs during rollovers annually, and around 3,700 of those were wearing seat belts. Statistics like these and a highly publicized rash of accidents involving rollovers of Ford Explorer SUVs outfitted with Bridgestone/ Firestone tires (a story of its own that we will review in Chapter 9) inspired NHTSA, in 2005, to issue a notice of proposed rulemaking to upgrade Standard 216. Yet, while the regulations may one day protect future drivers from broken necks, they will also protect manufacturers from lawsuits by future victims like Parker and Shipler, both of whom were paid substantial sums for their devastating injuries.[85]

By 2005, the common law courts had entertained hundreds of claims like those of Parker and Shipler, many of which involved victims who were killed or paralyzed by collapsing roofs while their shoulder harnesses were securely fastened. In the litigation, the defendants took the same position that the industry maintained in the ongoing NHTSA rulemaking: that roof crush protections were wholly unnecessary because the damage was caused when people fell into the roof during a rollover and not when the roof collapsed on their heads. In both forums, manufacturers relied upon a study undertaken by a former General Motors accident investigator using unbelted dummies in Chevrolet Malibu passenger cars with and without protective networks of steel bars called "roll cages."[86] The plaintiffs' experts interpreted the data differently and also relied on the common-sense observation that a fall through the six to eight inches between a passenger's head and the roof of an upside-down car was not enough to cause the severe damage routinely observed in rollover crashes. They concluded that the serious damage that occurred in rollover cases resulted from the violent intrusion of the roof into the passenger space, a point that was especially clear in the case of belted passengers. Engineering experts pointed out that the industry could easily strengthen vehicle roofs with inexpensive "low-tech" improvements like the roll cages used to protect NASCAR drivers or steel reinforcement of existing roofs.[87]

The discovery conducted in connection with the common law litigation revealed the by-now familiar story of an industry driven more by marketing and cost considerations than by attention to consumer safety. For example, internal company documents showed that Ford Motor Company in 1999 actually reduced the strength of the front pillars of one of its pickups to bring the vehicle's "strength-to-weight" ratio closer to the minimum required by NHTSA's Standard 216. All of this had a predictable impact on juries throughout the country, which began to add significant punitive damage awards to the compensation they ordered the automakers to pay to injured plaintiffs.[88] A court of appeals compared Ford's use of a fiberglass roof on its Bronco SUVs to "involuntary manslaughter" in affirming a $4 million judgment and a $290 million punitive damages award that caused the entire industry to sit up and take notice.[89] At the same time, the common law courts were sending a message to NHTSA by rejecting several attempts by defendants to invoke compliance with Standard 216 as a defense, finding that its minimal requirements were archaic and wholly inadequate.[90]

The original Standard 216 employed a "static" test for roof strength requiring that the roof not collapse more than five inches when subjected to a pressure equal to 1.5 times the vehicle's weight (up to a maximum of five thousand pounds) from a horizontal steel plate pushed by a hydraulic ram. The static test was in fact developed by the automobile industry after discovering that the roofs could not pass a more accurate "dynamic" test in which the vehicles were dropped from a prescribed height to the ground. Indeed, the roofs could not even pass a test proposed by NHTSA's predecessor prior to 1966 that would have applied force directly to the pillars framing the front window that frequently must bear the brunt of the external forces during a rollover. Instead of designing stronger roofs, the industry decided to design a weaker test, and NHTSA obligingly adopted it in 1971 as a temporary measure that would do until it could come up with a better one. Subsequent testing over the years, however, repeatedly demonstrated that roofs that easily passed the 1971 test routinely collapsed during rollovers because the forces encountered frequently exceed 1.5 times the vehicle weight and because real-life rollovers involve multiple impacts and produce nonhorizontal forces.[91]

Consumer groups urged NHTSA to adopt one of the two available "dynamic" tests for roof strength that the industry had developed—the old "drop" test in which the vehicle was dropped from a predetermined height and the modern "dolly" test that produced an actual rollover.[92] The U.S. automakers strongly resisted dynamic testing, a position that was clearly at odds with that of their European subsidiaries. Ford's Volvo subsidiary argued in internal memos that increased roof strength did enhance safety and boasted that its vehicles routinely passed the dolly test. Ford's ham-handed response was to tell Volvo to stop emphasizing roof strength and get in line with the industry position.[93] DaimlerChrysler told the agency that passenger safety "is not likely to be enhanced as a result of additional roof crush requirements" at the same time that its Mercedes-Benz subsidiaries were touting in advertisements the fact that their roofs passed the dynamic test.[94] The industry position finally collapsed in late 2004 when a careful statistical analysis of rollover accidents undertaken by NHTSA engineers found a clear correlation between the extent of roof intrusion and the seriousness of occupant injuries.[95]

When NHTSA finally proposed its long-awaited regulations, in late 2005, safety activists were exceedingly disappointed. The proposed rules would retain the static test but would up the applied pressure from 1.5 to 2.5 times the weight of the vehicle and eliminate the five-thousand-pound maximum. At the same time, they would expand the allowable intrusion from 5 inches to 7.63 inches, thereby reducing the standard's stringency. The proposal would also extend the standard's applicability for the first time to large pickup trucks and SUVs weighing between five thousand and ten thousand pounds. All of these modest improvements would come at the minimal cost of less than $11.00 per vehicle, about one-third the price of a single tank of gas.[96] Pointing out that by the agency's own admission, almost 70 percent of current models already complied with the proposed rules, consumer activists argued that the agency had apparently once again acquiesced in the auto industry's reluctance to depart from the status quo.[97]

What did depart considerably from the status quo was an eight-paragraph section of the preamble entitled "Civil Justice Reform" that announced the agency's intention to preempt all future common law roof strength claims. No future plaintiff would be able to take the position in court that a vehicle complying with NHTSA's minimum standard was defectively designed, no matter how much evidence his or her lawyers could amass that the manufacture had shirked its duty to sell a reasonably safe vehicle and no matter how far roof strength technology evolved before the agency got around to amending the rule again. The Department of Transportation's general counsel, who had represented General Motors and the American Automobile Manufacturers Association before joining the government, explained that the agency thought that "it would be helpful to the courts to know if a rule has a preemptive effect or not."[98] The agency's exclusive preemption rationale was its fear that complying with common law obligations might upset the "balance between efforts to increase roof strength and reduce rollover propensity" by inducing manufacturers to install top-heavy roof protection technologies that would shift the center of gravity of pickups and SUVs upward, a problem that the European subsidiaries had somehow managed to avoid at a reasonable expense.[99]

The agency's brief analysis, however, betrayed a lack of familiarity with the common law's protective justice function. While the agency's concern for balance between roof strength and rollover propensity might have been germane to standards established by state agencies, it was of only marginal relevance to state common law claims, because common law damage judgments do not "require" manufacturers to employ any particular technology. It also ignored the fact that common law juries would also have to consider the tendency of any suggested roof crush resistance technology to add to rollover risks when they were determining whether a particular defendant's roof was defectively designed. Finally, it apparently overlooked the rather obvious fact that the common law incentives had thus far had no impact at all on the industry, despite its having settled hundreds of roof crush cases and having suffered numerous adverse judgments, including a punitive damage award that was so high that the Supreme Court sent it back to the lower court for reconsideration.[100] In that historical context, the argument that the fear of adverse jury awards would cause the automobile industry to implement imprudent roof protection technologies had an especially hollow ring.

Safety advocates bitterly complained that the preemption provision represented a thoroughly unjustified windfall for the auto industry at the expense of rollover crash victims. A group of attorneys general from twenty-six states maintained that the preemption provision would shift some of the medical expenses for roof crush victims from the auto industry to state Medicare and Medicaid funds. Their claim was supported by a report prepared for the National Conference of State Legislatures estimating that the preemption provision would cost states between $49 and $71 million per year.[101] Even many in the industry were surprised (though, in their cases, quite pleasantly) that the agency was going to relieve them of the burden of defending their roof designs in court.[102] At a cost of $11 per vehicle, this was cheap liability insurance, indeed.

CPSC MATTRESS REGULATIONS

The Flammable Fabrics Act (FF Act) was enacted in 1953 to empower the Secretary of Commerce to promulgate "flammability standards" protecting consumers and homeowners against the risk of fires.[103] One of the earliest targets of the "regulatory reform" movement, the statute was amended in 1981 in ways that made it much more difficult for the implementing agency, now the Consumer Product Safety Commission (CPSC), to promulgate regulations.[104] A flammability standard for a fabric, which may simply require a label, must be "stated in objective terms" and based on findings supported by "substantial evidence" that it "is needed to adequately protect the public against unreasonable risk" of fire and is "reasonable, technologically practicable, and appropriate."[105] The Commission must further find that the standard's benefits "bear a reasonable relationship to its costs" and that the regulation "imposes the least burdensome requirement which prevents or adequately reduces" the relevant fire risk.[106] If the regulatee suggests a voluntary standard, the Commission may not promulgate a legally binding standard absent a specific finding (supported by the record) that compliance with the voluntary standard is not likely to result in an "adequate reduction" of the risk or that it is unlikely that there will be "substantial compliance" with the voluntary standard.[107]

The original federal fabric flammability standard was adopted by Congress itself in the 1953 statute when it simply incorporated into the statute a voluntary standard that the fabrics industry had written during the early 1950s.[108] Prior to 2005, CPSC and its predecessors had promulgated only two other standards, one very controversial standard specifically addressing children's sleepwear and one governing carpets and rugs.[109] Otherwise, the original 1953 standard remained in effect for all clothing textiles.[110]

The statute contains an express preemption section, added in 1976, providing that once a federal standard has been promulgated, no state may establish or continue in effect a "flammability standard or other regulation" for the same product that is designed to protect against the same risk unless it is identical to the federal standard.[111] The Senate Report on the 1976 bill says that it was added to clarify that the flammability standards promulgated under the Act were not meant to be "merely minimum standards" but "uniform national requirements."[112] The statute does not contain a savings clause for common law actions, but it does allow for states and local governments to petition CPSC for an exemption from preemption for a particular regulation or other action.[113]

Prior to the *Cippolone* case, it apparently did not occur to litigants that the express preemption provision of the FF Act might apply to common law claims. The clothing flammability standard did come up frequently in litigation, usually as evidence in support of a defendant's contention that its product could not be defective because it complied with a federal standard, but not by way of a preemption claim in a motion to dismiss.[114] The first post-*Cippolone* case in a federal court of appeals was decided just after the Supreme Court decided the *Lohr* case and therefore had the benefit of both opinions. In that case, the sweatshirt and T-shirt that twelve-year-old Alisa DeBold was wearing ignited when she reached across a stove to turn off a whistling kettle and joined the 4,150 people each year who are either killed or hospitalized by clothing ignitions. The court held that the preemption provision's reference to a "standard or other regulation" implied that Congress was "addressing those standards that are contained in statutes or administrative directives," and not common-law duties.[115] All of the other courts that have addressed the issue and the Commission itself agreed that CPSC flammability standards did not preempt state common law claims.[116]

On March 15, 2006, CPSC promulgated the first new regulation under the FF Act in more than twenty-five years, a flammability standard for mattress sets.[117] Because a mattress contains "a substantial amount of flammable materials," the agency concluded that one that ignites in a bedroom fire "will burn rapidly, and will quickly reach dangerous flashover conditions within a few minutes," thereby rendering the room instantly uninhabitable. The standard prescribed performance tests for mattresses designed to "minimize or delay flashover when a mattress is ignited in a typical bedroom fire." It also prescribed informational labeling regarding such things as the month of manufacture, but it did not require safety-related information or demand any particular warning.

The preamble to the final rule stated that it would "preempt inconsistent state standards and requirements, whether in the form of positive enactments or court created requirements." The Commission's one-sentence policy justification for this conclusion expressed its belief that such standards, "no matter how well intentioned, have the potential to undercut the Commission's uniform national flammability standard, create impediments for manufacturers whose mattress products enter the stream of interstate commerce, establish requirements that make dual state and federal compliance physically impossible, and cause confusion among consumers seeking to understand differing state and federal mattress fire requirements." The agency provided no empirical data or analysis to support any of these predictions. Noticeably missing from the explanation, with the possible exception of the concern expressed for avoiding customer confusion, was any safety-related justification.

The Commission's legal analysis cited no judicial precedent for the agency's new position, no doubt because none existed, nor did it attempt to explain how the words "standard or other regulation" could be construed to include the indirect incentives provided by the threat of common law liability. Instead, the agency focused on the meaning of the word "requirement," which is not found in the statute at all, but did turn up at one point in the legislative history. Most of the legal analysis focused on the language in the FF Act requiring the agency to ensure that the benefits of its standards outweighed the costs imposed on manufacturers. Without explaining how this language was relevant to the statute's preemption section, which was added to the statute five years before the cited language, the Commission concluded that "[r]equiring mattress manufacturers to use specific materials or methodologies to reach the flammability standard's goals," a result that the common law would certainly not require but might indirectly induce, "could impose greater costs and interfere with the particular balance the Commission struck between competing public policy considerations." Although the common law had peacefully coexisted with CPSC's other flammability standards for more than fifty years, the threat of common law liability would now interfere with "the flexibility and business discretion" that manufacturers needed "to decide what combination of design and materials is appropriate to meet the federal flammability standard."

Unlike the mattress standard, the CPSC standard for the kind of flammable fabrics that Alisa DeBold was wearing when she made her fateful attempt to turn off a whistling teapot has not been amended in more than half a century. Expert testimony offered in several trials in the intervening years noted that a piece of newspaper easily passes that ancient standard.[118] Based on the staff's conclusion that "[n]umerous new technologies, products and modern equipment have been developed" in the fifty years since the original standard went into place, CPSC, in May 2002, issued an Advance Notice of Proposed Rulemaking stating its intention to update that standard if the industry does not come up with a voluntary standard instead.[119] So far, nothing has come of this initiative. At this pace, we might expect to see an update of the new mattress standard in 2060 or so. It is certainly possible that fire prevention technologies will have progressed to a considerable degree long before then, but the common law will provide no incentive to mattress manufacturers to incorporate those technologies if courts accept the CPSC's position on preemption. Since the standard clearly does preempt all nonidentical state and local regulations, the industry may have effectively won a fifty-year reprieve from any pressures to make its mattress products safer.

CONCLUSIONS

Although federal regulatory agencies have a great deal of expertise in the substantive areas covered by their statutory mandates, they have no special expertise in the law or policy of preemption. At best, they are in a good position to opine on the desirability of uniformity in how the companies subject to their requirements go about their business. They are not, however, in a better position than courts to predict the effect of ad hoc common law litigation on uniformity, and they have no expertise at all in the subtleties of preemption doctrine. Executive Branch agencies were therefore not active in the early stages of the preemption war. This began to change after the Supreme Court, in *Geier,* signaled that preemption doctrine was available to agencies inclined to expand their powers beyond their traditional regulatory boundaries to co-opt state tort law. The FRA during the second half of the Clinton administration launched an exploratory foray but quickly withdrew when two dramatic grade crossing accidents provided a very public demonstration of the importance of corrective justice to the innocent victims of grade crossing accidents.

The federal agencies became much more aggressive during the George W. Bush administration in extending their territorial reach. FDA fired the initial salvos of this battle with amicus curiae briefs asserting preemptive jurisdiction over approved drug labeling for the SSRI drugs. It then launched a full-scale attack under the cover of darkness when it inserted a broad preemptive provision applicable to all drugs into the preamble to a final labeling rule. These actions represented a unilateral act of aggression by FDA aimed at rearranging a longstanding and rather stable relationship between federal drug regulation and the common law, which has traditionally deferred to FDA regulation of pharmaceutical drugs but has not been willing to surrender its corrective justice role to the agency's promise of optimal protection.[120] The apparently unshakable conviction of the agency leadership in the inerrancy of the scientific judgments of its staff is mystifying, given the fact that FDA scientists are the first to acknowledge that assessing the efficacy and toxicological risks of drugs is an inexact science and that real-world experience often belies sanguine assessments based on laboratory and clinical studies.

Ironically, at the very moment that FDA's lawyers were claiming, in cases involving the SSRI antidepressant drugs, that any label other than the one negotiated between the company and the agency was unsupported by "science," several district courts were subjecting plaintiffs' claims that SSRI drugs caused violent and suicidal behavior to a "scientific" evaluation that easily exceeded the intensity of the agency's cursory postmarketing surveillance program. In *Miller v. Pfizer, Inc.,* for example, a federal district court independently commissioned two prominent experts on drug epidemiology and neuropsychopharmacology, one of whom had served on the original FDA advisory committee that had recommended Zoloft's approval, to review Dr. David Healy's testimony that

Zoloft caused the plaintiffs' thirteen-year-old son to commit suicide.[121] The panel reviewed Healy's testimony in great detail, read and summarized all of the published and unpublished studies cited in that testimony, and prepared a lengthy report. On the basis of that report, extensive briefing by both the plaintiff and defendant, and a two-day hearing in which lawyers for both sides questioned the panel members and presented additional evidence, the court concluded that Healy's testimony did not pass the tests of relevance and scientific reliability that the Supreme Court had established for expert testimony in the seminal case of *Daubert v. Merrell-Dow Pharmaceuticals, Inc.*[122] Common law courts have gone to similar lengths to evaluate the "scientific" reliability of expert testimony in other cases involving SSRI and other drugs.[123]

NHTSA and CPSC soon followed FDA's lead with attacks of their own. Both agencies had until then remained neutral in the battles that raged over their standards in the courts. NHTSA's amicus curiae brief in the *Myrick* litigation, a case in which the Supreme Court held that NHTSA's failure to require antilock brakes in large trucks did not preempt common law claims that manufacturers should have installed them anyway, noted that "Congress' chosen methods of increasing automotive safety include both the establishment of federal minimum standards and the preservation of common law tort liability on the part of even those manufacturers that comply with those standards."[124] In the *Geier* case, the government reaffirmed that position and recognized that "any tension" between its position on common law claims and its position on state-promulgated regulatory standards, which were preempted, "reflects a compromise between the interests in uniformity and in permitting States to compensate accident victims."[125] The agency's strong assertion of the preemptive scope of its roof crush regulation thus represented a "sea change" in the agency's attitude toward preemption.[126] A NHTSA employee who worked on that regulation before his retirement told the press that the preemption provision had been "dropped in from out of the blue" near the end of the internal agency decision-making process.[127] Unlike the government's brief in *Geier*, the roof strength preamble contained not a word about the corrective justice function of the common law.

Judicial reactions to the dramatic entry of a new institutional player into the preemption war have been mixed, but it is fair to say that the agencies had considerably more success in advancing the George W. Bush administration's overall tort reform goals than the White House had in persuading Congress to enact tort reform legislation. As Professor Nagareda notes, the reforms "go a fair way toward achieving nationwide, on a wholesale basis, a foreclosure of tort litigation previously thought possible only by more painstaking, retail means: the securing of reform legislation or judicial decisions on a state-by-state basis."[128] We now turn our attention to whether this has, on the whole, been a desirable development.

Chapter 7 Agencies, Juries, and the Public Interest

The decision to preempt requires Congress to balance a number of important considerations, not the least of which is the comparative institutional competence of federal regulatory agencies and state common law courts in providing protective justice and corrective justice while at the same time allowing the national economy to run efficiently. This chapter focuses exclusively on the question of institutional competence, and the two chapters that follow examine the other arguments for and against preemption. Among other things, this chapter explores arguments about comparative strengths and weaknesses of common law courts and federal regulatory agencies in providing technical expertise, policymaking expertise, relevant information, common-sense judgment, and responsiveness to changing information and policies as they arise.

TECHNICAL EXPERTISE

Perhaps the most vigorous argument for federal agency preemption of state common law claims is the "enormous comparative advantage" that federal agencies have over judges and juries in the expertise required to resolve highly technical questions of science, engineering, and economics that typically arise when federal regulatory requirements arguably come into conflict with common law duties.[1] Proponents of preemption argue that regulatory agencies are able to call on expert resources and information-gathering abilities "that dwarf those of any trial jury." By contrast, the common law allows "unsophisticated jurors" with "20-20 hindsight" to second-guess the considered judgment of the agencies.[2] They complain that jurors are technically illiterate and far too inclined to substitute various "heuristics" for clear rational thought on the complex questions that often arise in litigation regarding topics that are subject to federal regulation. In the eyes of preemption proponents, juries reach demonstrably wrong results in many cases.[3]

Federal regulatory agencies typically employ their own experts to gather information and prepare analyses of proposed agency actions. When specialized expertise is required, they can hire independent consultants. They can also call on more formal sources of expertise by empaneling scientific advisory committees or contracting with the National Academy of Sciences to study a particular scientific issue. Preemption proponents argue that, for all their faults, agencies "provide the best, reasonably unbiased, source of balanced expertise available in these matters."[4] Judges and juries, on the other hand, cannot be trusted to resolve the kinds of technical, medical, and scientific questions that tend to arise in litigation involving regulated products and activities. Because they lack any capacity to "internalize scientific data appropriately," their efforts amount to little more than intuitive assessments "of the credibility and demeanor of competing expert witnesses" that, as often as not, "yield outcomes in conflict with generally accepted scientific understandings." The bottom line is that courts "are simply not qualified to second-guess" regulatory agency decisions.[5]

Even the most serious critics of federal agency preemption do not seriously contest the proposition that regulatory agencies can draw on more technical resources than juries as a general matter. They question, however, whether the relevant federal agencies do in fact devote more resources to the particular technical issues in any given rulemaking or licensing exercise than the lawyers on both sides of litigation devote to the same issues with the aid of expert consultants in corresponding litigation.[6] They caution that "even the most well-intentioned agencies" cannot assess and manage risks "with anything close to the comprehensive rationality" that the proponents imply. Furthermore, what juries lack in scientific and technical expertise, they more than make up for in good sense and sound moral judgment, two qualities that are often sorely lacking in bureaucracies.[7] When academics claim that mock juries reach the "wrong" result, for example, the basis for the claim is usually that they departed from what the academics viewed as the "correct" result as determined by quantitative cost-benefit balancing analysis.[8] Yet, many scholars not wedded to the quantitative cost-benefit balancing paradigm as the sole measure of rationality strongly disagree with that facile assessment, arguing that values other than economic efficiency have a rightful role in a jury's assessment of a defendant's conduct.[9]

Critics of preemption further argue that the likelihood that juries will be hoodwinked by unscrupulous experts peddling "junk science" is quite small in the years since the Supreme Court, in the famous case of *Daubert v. Merrell-Dow Pharmaceuticals, Inc.,*[10] assigned a "gatekeeper" role to district court judges to ensure the relevance and reliability of expert testimony.[11] Far from being swayed by smooth-talking experts, experimental studies suggest, jurors are often quite skeptical of experts and focus carefully on their credentials and motives.[12] Proponents of preemption respond that the gatekeeping role played by judges "may ameliorate, but cannot eliminate, the inherent inconsistency between sound science and a system of paid and coached 'expert' witnesses."[13]

Despite its undeniable benefits, expertise does have its limits. The federal regulatory process is notoriously plagued by scientific uncertainties, some of which may be resolved with additional research or practical experience and many of which may never be fully resolved.[14] To avoid complete "paralysis by analysis," agencies administering product-licensing regimes must allow beneficial but potentially dangerous products to enter the marketplace, and standard-setting agencies must promulgate regulations governing potentially risky activities without knowing how the risks will play out in the future.[15] Furthermore, agency experts cannot possibly anticipate all the ways that an innovative regulatee might come up with to evade or circumnavigate the requirements that the agency writes into its regulations and permits.[16]

Expertise may have a very limited role to play in resolving many of the issues that both regulatory agencies and common law courts commonly encounter. It is not obvious, for example, that experts are any more competent than jurors to evaluate the adequacy of a warning to communicate risks to ordinary consumers. Likewise, expert opinion may be largely irrelevant to situations in which "consumer expectation" is the dominant decision-making criterion. Petite women have a reasonable expectation that a properly functioning seatbelt will adequately restrain them during a collision and not allow them to "submarine" into the dashboard, for example, even though the safety experts have concluded that the risk of submarining is extremely low for taller passengers.[17]

The continuing saga of automobile airbags regulation well illustrates the difficulties that federal agencies face in using their technical expertise to anticipate and respond to the adverse effects of regulated activities in a complex technological and political milieu. As automakers began to comply with NHTSA's passive restraint standard (described in detail in Chapter 4), consumers quickly became convinced that airbags really did save lives.[18] Congress responded, in 1991, by instructing NHTSA to promulgate regulations requiring both driver-side and passenger-side airbags in all cars and light-duty trucks, to become effective in 1997 and 1998, respectively.[19] Then something happened that consumers definitely did not expect. On April 21, 1993, six-year-old Diana Zhang was killed in a minor "fender bender" accident as she was riding unbelted in the passenger seat of her mother's 1993 Volvo. When the passenger-side airbag properly deployed, the bag and module cover struck Diana in the head and upper body and propelled her into the roof of the car. The impact of this airbag-caused collision killed Diana, and she became the first of many child fatalities caused by passenger-side airbags.[20]

The auto industry, the agency, and consumer groups were all well aware of the passenger-side airbags problem, but they had been arguing for twenty-five years over what to do about it. Automakers warned NHTSA in the 1970s that tests with dummies indicated that passenger-side airbags posed a threat to small children riding in the passenger seat.[21] A team of NHTSA experts concluded, however, that the risks to children could be "substantially reduced by careful design," and they recommended that manufacturers meet the standard by installing "dual-inflation" airbags that were capable of deploying at lower speeds in lower velocity crashes.[22] The 1984 "compromise" passive-restraint rule (discussed in Chapter 4) nevertheless retained high-speed airbags as an allowable option, a move that took the pressure off the industry to develop the nascent "dual-inflation" airbag technology.[23]

Reacting to Diana Zhang's death, NHTSA, in February 1994, issued a warning to all parents to keep their young children out of the passenger seat of vehicles with passenger-side airbags, and later that year it allowed manufacturers to install switches in vehicles without back seats to allow parents to turn the airbags off.[24] By late 1995, however, five more children had been killed by passenger-side airbags, and NHTSA knew that it had a problem that could not be solved by a general warning.[25] Everyone agreed that airbags saved more people than they killed, but something had to be done to reduce the risks that passenger-side airbags posed to kids. The public interest groups and airbag manufacturers pressed for either "dual-inflation" airbags or "smart" airbags with "passenger detection systems" that would detect the presence of a child or short adult in the passenger seat and inflate at a lower speed.[26] Instead, NHTSA, in August 1996, proposed a rule requiring fairly dramatic warnings to be posted at four different locations in autos with passenger-side airbags, and, in November 1996, the industry voluntarily sent letters to owners of twenty-two million vehicles with passenger-side airbags warning them not to allow children under thirteen to occupy the front passenger seat.[27]

If warnings did not work in 1994, however, it was unclear why they would work in 1997. One obvious next step was for NHTSA to promulgate regulations implementing a technological solution like dual-inflation or smart airbag technologies, some of which were already in place in upper-end vehicles. One industry executive warned, however, that "[w]e don't want to be in the position of making the same mistakes with smart bags that were made with their dumb predecessors."[28] It was a fair warning, and NHTSA seemed inclined to agree. Congress, however, thought otherwise and instructed NHTSA to require smart airbags on a phased basis through September 1, 2006.[29]

A senior fellow at the Brookings Institution concludes that NHTSA's airbag story is by no means unique. In his view, the challenges of new technologies and unanticipated failures of existing technologies "exist in every regulated industry that you look at."[30] Furthermore, as the head of the National Transportation Safety Board candidly observed, "[p]eople in Washington don't like to say anyone made a mistake."[31] The description of the regulatory history of Vioxx in Chapter 1 and of SSRI drugs in Chapter 6 shows a similar inability on the part of regulatory agencies to anticipate all of the adverse effects of their decisions and a reluctance to acknowledge and react to the failure of past predictions.

Common law courts, on the other hand, are not so constrained by the need to anticipate future developments and to react to past mistakes.[32] Because most common law claims are filed after the product or activity at issue has in fact caused harm, courts have the benefit of hindsight. A jury depends upon expert testimony from both sides to educate it on the technical and scientific aspects of the issues in individual cases. It therefore hears the good and the bad news about the safety technologies that the defendant employed and alternatives that it could have employed. It is not bound by the factual findings of any previous jury, and it ordinarily does not even learn about prior verdicts during the trial.

Even with the guidance of the very best experts, a jury is no more omniscient than a regulatory agency, but a jury will not allow its decision to be affected by its reluctance to acknowledge past mistakes.

POLICYMAKING EXPERTISE

A less obvious but nevertheless powerful reason to prefer federal regulation over common law litigation is that agencies can develop an expertise in policymaking quite apart from their purely technical expertise. Agency expertise in policymaking comes not only from hiring professionals with training in economics and the social sciences but also from the experience that agency staffs gain by dealing with the nitty-gritty of policymaking on a day-to-day basis through procedures that are designed to maximize the number of interests and the range of information that the agency considers. Attempts by plaintiffs to accomplish "regulation through litigation" in the courtroom are wholly lacking in this highly relevant policymaking expertise.[33]

We learned in Chapter 2 that agency actions typically undergo an extensive period of review and comment from other agencies within the administration, the affected industries, and the general public. Thus, agencies have a greater capacity than courts to elicit and consider the views of a broad range of interests.[34] This matters because most serious public policy issues are "polycentric" in nature in that their legitimate resolution requires the decision maker to weigh a number of different perspectives no one of which necessarily aligns with any of the others.[35] Soliciting input from the full range of affected interests will ordinarily make more useful information available to the decision maker.[36] Courts "only receive the information that the litigants choose, for their own self-interested reasons, to provide," and the adjudicatory model that they employ becomes rather unwieldy when the number of perspectives exceeds two. Thus, for example, juries may be overly inclined to find defendants liable because they do not hear from representatives of the people who might be deprived of useful products and services if defendants are discouraged from developing new products.[37]

Agencies also receive information about the intensity of the support or opposition of various political constituencies that is generally unavailable to courts because it is not relevant to the narrow legal disputes that arise between litigants.[38] Judicial procedures are designed to dispense corrective justice, a function that typically involves shifting loss from a single victim to one or more entities that caused the loss.[39] They are not well adapted to shifting health or safety risks from one segment of the population to another or to avoiding inadvertent shifts of this nature.[40] The fact that agency decisions reflect the input of politically relevant information from a broader range of interests generally lends greater legitimacy to decisions that have clear political dimensions.[41]

The advantage of agencies in the area of policymaking expertise is unquestionably relevant to public interest litigation, like the municipality firearms cases discussed in Chapter 5, where an important object of the litigation is to resolve an important issue of public policy. Indeed, one purpose of the litigation may be to force a regulated industry to take a particular action that an agency has specifically declined to require in the exercise of its regulatory responsibilities. In this context, the complaint that the plaintiffs are attempting to accomplish "regulation through litigation" has some salience, and preemption may be appropriate. The policymaking expertise of agencies, however, does not ordinarily support federal agency preemption of the far more typical "private interest litigation" brought by injured parties against one or two defendants seeking only compensation for damages caused by negligent conduct or defective products. In these cases, public policy plays a role in framing the antecedent common law rules that govern the trial, but the primary goal of corrective justice does not require input from multiple perspectives.

REGULATORY FAILURE

The argument that federal regulatory agency action should preempt state common law claims presumes that the agencies possessing comparative institutional advantages over courts will in fact employ their regulatory powers effectively to prevent harm to consumers in advance. Indeed, since preemption completely divests the courts of their corrective justice function, the implicit assumption must be that agencies will do their job so well that there will be no need for corrective justice because no one is likely to be wrongfully damaged by the regulated products or activities. To anyone at all familiar with the performance of federal regulatory agencies, this is a preposterous assumption. The Vioxx story recounted in Chapter 1 is just one of many recent accounts of serious regulatory failure that appear almost daily in the newspapers. Even strong proponents of preemption, like Professor W. Kip Viscusi, recognize that in many cases litigation "stems from a real or perceived failure by regulators to address potential harms to society."[42]

Students of federal regulation have identified several systemic causes of regulatory failure. Agencies over time become "captured" by the industries they are supposed to be regulating and become much less aggressive in implementing their statutory responsibilities. Conflict of interest pervades the decision-making process as high-level agency officials rotate in and out of the government through a "revolving door" that leads directly to the corporate offices or law firms of the regulated companies. Those agencies that avoid capture are easily manipulated by regulatees that exploit informational advantages and known agency weaknesses to their economic advantage. Agencies perennially lack sufficient resources to do their jobs in an age of "hollow government." Resource shortages and a general ossification of the regulatory process means that agencies move at a glacial pace that fails to keep up with evolving industry practices and improving safety technologies, a failing that is of particular relevance to the preemption war. In the following pages, we briefly examine each of these reasons for doubting the proposition that *ex ante* regulatory controls imposed by federal agencies are sufficiently robust that they warrant relieving the common law courts of both their protective justice and their corrective justice responsibilities.

Agency Capture

Observers of federal regulation, ranging from the Chicago School founder George Stigler to the consumer activist Ralph Nader, worry about the possibility that regulatory agencies over time become "captured" by the very entities that they are supposed to be regulating.[43] Classic capture theory posits that profit-seeking companies support the reelection efforts of key legislators in return for sympathetic legislation and legislative oversight. The bureaucrats charged with implementing the legislation, who look to Congress for their rewards and punishment, then run the regulatory program in a way that primarily benefits the regulatees. In an age of permanent campaigns in which political fundraising never ceases, high-level political appointees in the White House and the agencies subtly trade regulatory leniency for the implicit promise of generous campaign contributions, which in turn lead to re-election and additional political power. And so it goes in a vicious circle to the benefit of the regulatees and the detriment of the erstwhile beneficiaries of the regulatory programs.

A good deal of anecdotal evidence supports this "conspiratorial" version of the agency capture theory.[44] Almost from the inception of the modern consumer protection age, industry groups have had disproportionate access to the White House, either directly in the Oval Office or indirectly through the various "regulatory czars" located in the Office of Management and Budget.[45] We saw in Chapter 4 how Henry Ford and Lee Iacocca directly intervened with President Nixon to demand that NHTSA back off from its announced plans to require airbags in passenger automobiles. By the mid-1990s, the regulated industries also obtained unprecedented access to the committees in Congress in charge of agency oversight and appropriations. Lobbyists for regulated industries were invited to write the regulatory reform bills that grew out of an associated effort called "Project Relief," a coalition of more than three hundred business and lobby groups that met with the congressional leadership on a weekly basis to discuss ways to reduce the impact of federal regulation on the business community.[46]

Until the Vioxx scandal put it under the public microscope, the FDA's new drug approval process showed strong evidence of capture dating back to the Prescription Drug User Fee Act of 1992.[47] Enacted in response to loud complaints from the pharmaceutical industry and its allies about lengthy approval times for new drugs, the new law empowered FDA to charge "user fees" to offset agency expenses so long as FDA spending on new drug applications stayed above 1992 levels. The 1992 Act had a dramatic impact on FDA approval of new drugs for three primary reasons: (1) the user fees provided additional resources to the division in charge of new drug approval; (2) the performance goals that it also established (e.g., act on 90 percent of new drug applications within ten months) provided a strong incentive to get the drug approvals out the door on time; and (3) the annual reports that FDA had to prepare provided a convenient vehicle for White House and congressional supervision.[48] The corresponding risk, of course, was that the agency would push new drug approvals out the door before the scientific staff had adequately reviewed the evidence of their potential for devastating side effects. In a survey of one thousand FDA employees undertaken by the Inspector General of the Department of Health and Human Services, 18 percent of the respondents said they had been "pressured to approve or recommend approval for a [new drug application] despite reservations about the safety, or quality of the drug."[49] The raft of drug withdrawals that occurred in the wake of the Amendments suggests that this was a very real risk. Thirteen FDA-approved drugs were withdrawn in the four-year period between 1997 and 2001, whereas only ten withdrawals occurred in the twenty-year period between 1974 and 1993.[50] Congress changed the law somewhat in 2003 to allow FDA to devote user fees to postmarket surveillance of drugs for up to three years after approval.[51]

In less conspiratorial versions of the capture theory, agencies succumb to the sustained influence of one-sided information, blandishments, and threats from the regulated entities that are ever-present in agency hallways, on Capitol Hill, and in the media. An agency faced with limited resources and overwhelming responsibilities usually finds it very difficult to maintain a constantly vigilant posture with respect to all of the activities under its jurisdiction. The simple rule of bureaucratic life that "you can't go to the mat every time" limits the extent to which an agency can force a recalcitrant industry to conform to an ideal statutory conception of the public interest. The regulated industries know that, in the words of a former gun industry lobbyist, "[t]he closer relationship you have toward the regulator, the better off you are," and they are prepared to spend significant resources to obtain and maintain access to regulatory decision-makers.[52] The interests of the beneficiaries of the regulatory programs, on the other hand, are diffuse because the impacts of regulatory decisions on the daily lives of individual beneficiaries are ordinarily imperceptible. Even when individual beneficiaries are sufficiently affected by a regulatory decision to take notice, they generally "lack preexisting organizations through which their concerns can easily be channeled." The result is an "asymmetry between public and industry attentiveness" on the part of federal agencies.[53]

Single-industry regulatory agencies are especially susceptible to capture, because they depend so heavily upon the industry they regulate for the information they need and for political support in the appropriations process. Over time, informal arrangements evolve under which agency officials "jawbone" with representatives of regulatees about informational needs, technological alternatives, costs, and other regulatory issues relevant to individual products.[54] Reviewers in the Food and Drug Administration's Office of New Drugs, for example, perform "dual roles" as helpful adviser to new-drug applicants and regulatory reviewer of their applications, and they conduct more than a thousand meetings per year with drug companies to provide advice. These closed-door negotiating sessions provide regulatees invisible opportunities to persuade agency personnel that their views of the regulatory issues correspond to the public interest as reflected in the agency statutes.[55] Such informal arrangements can even blossom into cooperative research agreements in which agency personnel participate in industry-funded safety-related research.[56]

The Federal Railway Administration (FRA) provides an illuminating example of the capture phenomenon. Its regulatory programs focus on a single highly concentrated industry, and the beneficiaries consist of an extremely diffuse collection of hundreds of millions of citizens who live in the vicinity of railroad tracks or drive their vehicles over grade crossings. The industry is intensely aware of even modest regulatory impositions because the costs are multiplied over thousands of trains and tens of thousands of highway intersections. Individual members of the affected public, by contrast, have little reason to follow the agency's regulatory efforts because train derailments and grade crossing accidents rarely intrude into their lives.

Although the FRA has always been heavily influenced by the railroad industry, its politically appointed leadership, in the early 2000s, decided that the agency and the industry should become "partners" in a common enterprise. Under this new arrangement, the official enforcement policy was to cite instances of noncompliance but to encourage voluntary compliance in extensive negotiations before taking more forceful action. Whistleblowers and former company inspectors tell of demands from their superiors to "take some short cuts" if they want to keep their jobs and of being fired for "tagging" too many cars for repairs. When San Antonio FRA inspectors cracked down on the Union Pacific Railroad in 2004 for repeatedly failing to correct defective tracks that had caused five deadly train derailments in five months, they were quickly upbraided by the agency's deputy administrator, who demanded that they stop being "overly aggressive." The deputy administrator, it turned out, was a close friend of the chief lobbyist for Union Pacific, and they had in fact vacationed together several times on Nantucket since she took over in 2001. The agency's associate administrator for safety later complained that "[e]very time we did some significant enforcement, particularly on Union Pacific, I would be called in and asked why." The Department of Transportation's inspector general later concluded that FRA had too heavily emphasized its "partnership" aspirations to the detriment of its critical enforcement responsibilities.[57]

Proponents of preemption respond that the capture thesis is "supported by little more than anecdote and suspicion," and some even contend that the health and safety agencies "have become more beholden to groups that purport to represent the public interest."[58] In truth, little empirical evidence of capture is available to support either view, in part because it is very difficult to study empirically a process that is by its nature secretive. The theory, however, retains an appealing explanatory force, and it is fully consistent with a large and growing body of anecdotal evidence.

Another response to the capture theory is that a close relationship between agencies and regulatees is an entirely appropriate vehicle for ensuring that politically unaccountable agency officials weigh the interests of the regulated community in the "delicate balance" that defines the public interest. While this is undoubtedly true, it should still be of some concern that the beneficiaries of the regulatory programs, who also have a strong interest in keeping the agencies accountable, generally lack the same access to agency decision makers.

Because courts are designed not to be politically accountable, judicial proceedings are by and large insulated from the outside political pressures that can give rise to agency capture. Unlike single-industry agencies, common law courts entertain claims from hundreds of plaintiffs against hundreds of different defendants every year. Although industries that are perennial defendants in litigation, like the auto and drug industries, may press for tort reform in state legislatures and in Congress, they do not attempt to influence judges in the same direct way that they importune agency officials. Because the common law courts "have long provided a safer haven from the corruption that can accompany the making of statutes and regulations," explains Professor Anita Bernstein, they are more "likely to treat injured persons fairly."[59]

Agency Manipulation

Even if we reject the capture theory, the asymmetry in resources between the regulated industry on the one hand and agency staff and regulatory beneficiaries on the other provides ample opportunities for regulatees to manipulate the regulatory process to their advantage. Professor Carl Bogus observes that "[m]ost manufacturers may be responsible most of the time, but human nature is such that there will always be attempts to bluff regulators," and when that happens, "the advantage lies with the manufacturer."[60] Because federal agencies typically rely heavily upon regulated entities for the scientific, economic, and statistical information they need to support effective regulation, regulatees can manipulate agency assessments of their products and activities in at least three broad ways. They can withhold relevant information. They can misreport, mischaracterize, or otherwise present in a misleading way the information that they do provide to the agency. And they can attempt to "manufacture uncertainty" about the risks posed by their products and activities by "deconstructing" information that operates to their detriment.

When regulatees have an obligation to provide sufficient information to convince the federal agency that their products or activities meet the relevant statutory test for approval (e.g., that a drug is "safe and effective"), they may be tempted to "hide" data indicating that the product or activity does not meet the statutory test. The same temptation may affect compliance with statutory obligations to report information on the adverse consequences of their products once they have entered the marketplace.[61] We saw in Chapter 1, for example, how the manufacturer of Celebrex waited until four months after FDA had finished its review of the COX-2 drugs to submit the results of an unpublished clinical study showing a statistically significant increase in heart attacks among those taking the drug.

Regulatees can also manipulate the information that they do share with regulatory agencies. In this regard, the story recounted in Chapter 1 of Merck's manipulation of the scientific studies that it commissioned on the anti-inflammatory drug Vioxx is all too typical. When a company conducts its own scientific or economic studies or contracts with a private "contract research organization" to do the study, it can manipulate the study design to maximize the likelihood of favorable results and minimize the chance of unfavorable results.[62] Since there is usually a good deal of room for "interpretation" of the hard data, sponsors can influence the conclusions reached by the authors and the way that they report them in the scientific literature, a phenomenon that one scientist has referred to as "sponsor spin." Recall Merck's "interpretation" of data from a large clinical trial comparing Vioxx with naproxen to conclude that naproxen was a remarkably effective heart attack preventive. Worse still, reports abound of clinical trial reports being ghost written for the signature of prestigious academic researchers by companies hired by the drug manufacturers that sponsored the studies.[63] Observers of "regulatory science" report "[s]trong and consistent evidence" demonstrating that "industry-sponsored research tends to draw pro-industry conclusions."[64]

Finally, when independent scientists in academia or government conduct studies that have adverse implications for a regulated product or activity, the regulated entities can sponsor studies designed to rebut those implications. The hidden purpose of this "counterscience" is to "manufacture uncertainty" about the studies and thereby forestall governmental action pending "further research." Ideally, the company-funded studies will even "point the finger" in the direction of some other possible culprit. Failing that, companies can sponsor critiques of the studies in the academic literature and assemble blue ribbon panels of sympathetic scientists to cast doubt on the offending studies. If all else fails, companies can attack the messenger by threatening litigation or sponsoring scientific misconduct charges against the scientists who produce the unwelcome studies.[65]

The regulatory agencies themselves are ordinarily oblivious to the fact that they are being manipulated at the time it happens, and they rarely discover that they have been manipulated after the fact. Lawyers for injured plaintiffs, by contrast, have every incentive to uncover evidence of agency manipulation during the discovery process. We learned in Chapter 2 that defense counsel may rely on the fact that an expert regulatory agency has bestowed the seal of approval on their clients' products or activities to persuade the jury that their conduct was not negligent or the products not defective. The easiest and most effective way to undermine this powerful defense is to demonstrate that the defendant manipulated the regulatory process to its advantage. If the manipulative efforts were aggressive enough, they may even be used offensively by plaintiffs' lawyers to paint an ugly picture of a greedy defendant that will stop at nothing to increase the bottom line.[66]

This powerful tool for probing regulatee manipulation of federal regulatory programs, however, is rapidly losing its potency because of the broadening applicability of federal preemption doctrine to cases in which agency manipulation is an issue. To the extent that FDA has its way and failure-to-warn cases involving FDA-approved drugs are dismissed at the outset on preemption grounds, there will be no probing discovery of the drug approval process. Even if FDA's position does not ultimately prevail in the courts, we saw in Chapter 4 that the Supreme Court, in *Buckman,* held that persons injured by medical devices that received required federal approval through fraudulent manipulation of the regulatory process by a consultant for the manufacturer did not have a state common law claim against the consultant.[67] Several lower courts have expanded that holding to dismiss separate counts in lawsuits directed to wrongful manipulation of the regulatory process by the manufacturers themselves. It remains to be seen whether the lower courts will limit discovery into regulatee manipulation of FDA and other agencies for the purpose of meeting a defendant's expected "regulatory compliance" defense.

Conflict of Interest

Another important aspect of the asymmetry that exists between regulated industries and the beneficiaries of regulation is the potential for conflict of interest. Federal laws prohibit a regulatory official from having a significant economic stake in the outcome of a regulatory proceeding.[68] Although the incidence of direct financial conflict of interest on the part of regulatory agency officials is exceedingly small, the laws governing the more subtle conflict that results from the "revolving door" through which agency officials move back and forth between the regulated industry and regulatory agency are less stringent and less vigorously enforced. A former government employee cannot represent someone in the private sector in a matter that the employee handled "personally and substantially," and senior government employees are barred for a year from representing any entity before their former agency.[69] Neither of these modest requirements poses a serious barrier to former agency officials bent on profiting in the private sector from their public sector experience. The even less direct conflict of interest on the part of experts who serve as consultants to agencies and sit on agency scientific advisory committees is moderated almost exclusively by marginally enforceable agency-promulgated disclosure requirements.[70]

The primary concern with the revolving door is that officials will attempt to build "a store of goodwill with industry" if they know that a job awaits them at the end of their stints in the agencies.[71] While it is virtually impossible to prove that this has happened after the fact, cases raising serious suspicions of undue influence are not uncommon. For example, FRA's chief safety official in 2004 accepted a job offer worth $324,000 in salary, bonuses, and stock options from a railroad company several days after visiting its headquarters to discuss its continuing safety problems.[72] On the other side of the revolving door, the concern is that officials who are appointed to agencies from industry jobs will tend to share the worldviews of their recent employers.

Some of the agencies that have been the most active in the preemption war have also been the ones with the most rapidly spinning doors. No fewer than five former chief counsels left FDA to work for law firms that represent pharmaceutical companies, Dan Troy being merely a recent example.[73] The chairman of CPSC during much of the early 2000s had been a partner in an Albuquerque law firm that represented defendants in common law products liability cases. He left the agency in mid-2006 to join a large midwestern law firm where he planned "to advise manufacturers on product safety compliance, legislative and regulatory matters."[74] Four former administrators of NHTSA left the agency for jobs in the automobile industry.[75] When plaintiffs' attorneys complained to NHTSA that one former administrator was violating government ethics guidelines by testifying as an expert for auto manufacturers, two former NHTSA chief counsels who had since become private attorneys working for the auto industry came to his defense.[76] After the former administrator decided to end the controversy by avoiding cases involving vehicles he had worked on, his position as a defense witness was filled by a former NHTSA enforcement director and associate administrator.[77] Several midlevel civil service employees have also departed NHTSA for more lucrative jobs in the auto industry.[78]

Scientific advisory committees, composed of scientists from outside the federal government, play an important role in federal regulatory activities. The federal pesticide statute creates a special scientific advisory body called the Scientific Advisory Panel and requires EPA to seek the advice of that body before taking important regulatory actions regarding pesticides.[79] FDA also makes extensive use of advisory committees in deciding whether to approve new drugs and how to address existing drugs for which problems have arisen subsequent to FDA approval. And we saw in connection with the *Sprietsma* case in Chapter 4 that the Coast Guard relies heavily on a special advisory committee in regulating motor boats. According to the Federal Advisory Committee Act (FAC Act), advisory committees must be "fairly balanced in terms of the points of view represented," and the agency must ensure that they will "not be inappropriately influenced by the appointing authority or by any special interest."[80]

Unfortunately, the FAC Act's requirements are sufficiently malleable that they give agencies discretion to assemble committees that are "stacked" in the direction of a predetermined outcome. They also do an uneven job of screening out scientists with financial conflicts of interest to secure the proper balance.[81] For example, the Center for Science in the Public Interest in 2004 urged FDA to remove three of the eleven scientists appointed to an FDA advisory board evaluating the link between SSRI drugs and suicide in young people because they had been paid consultants for the companies that make the drugs that the panel was investigating.[82] Similarly, the advisory committee that the Coast Guard relied on in *Sprietsma* consisted of nine doctors and engineers, all but one of whom had testified as expert witnesses for either plaintiffs or defendants in litigation involving motorboat safety.[83]

Common law courts must, of course, deal with the obvious conflict of interest on the part of the expert witnesses who testify for pay for the parties. This conflict is clearly revealed to the judge and jury at the outset of the testimony, and any potential for biasing the outcome is greatly reduced by the fact that both sides pay for expert testimony. The decision makers themselves, however, are rarely conflicted. Although most judges were employed by law firms prior to assuming their positions and an occasional judge leaves the bench to practice with a law firm, strict rules policed by attorneys for the parties ensure that they do not hear cases involving their former colleagues. The juries that decide the facts and apply the relevant standard of care to those facts are carefully screened by lawyers for both sides to ensure that they do not have an economic stake in the outcome. Any offer of a future job to a juror while serving on the jury would be prosecuted as a serious crime.

Limited Agency Resources

Even in flush times, federal regulatory agencies rarely have sufficient resources to address adequately all of the risks that their expansive authorities bring within their regulatory purview.[84] And times have not been flush for regulatory agencies since the late 1970s. If a federal agency lacks sufficient resources to implement its preemptive decisions by monitoring regulatee compliance and punishing noncompliance, then the implicit promise that its regulatory requirements will eliminate the need for corrective justice is a tragically hollow one. Sadly, this appears to be the case for all of the agencies that have been active in the preemption war.

BATF Resources. BATF has become the poster child for perennially resource-starved agencies because it is intensely disliked by gun owners and the firearms industry, as well as by politically powerful organizations like the National Rifle Association. According to one former NRA official, a primary goal of that institution was "to keep [B]ATF small and poor because if it's small and poor, it can't be an effective law enforcement agency." BATF's 1,700 or so enforcement officials, only a few of whom are detailed to the agency's firearms unit, are able to conduct on-site inspections for only about 13,000 of the more than 100,000 federally licensed firearms dealers per year. Whistleblowers have reported that the gun industry is fully aware of these limitations and has conducted its marketing strategies accordingly.[85]

NHTSA Resources. All of the federal regulatory agencies suffered severe budget cuts, morale loss, and a brain drain during the early years of the Reagan administration, when Budget Director David Stockman implemented what he later referred to as a "Trojan horse" strategy for reducing the influence of federal agencies over the private sector by cutting taxes and starving the federal government. Unlike many of the others, however, NHTSA never recovered from the 50 percent budget cut that it took during those years. Even after it received a modest $9 million increase in its budget in 2000, NHTSA's inflation-adjusted budget remained 25 percent below its pre-Reagan level. The predictable consequence, according to a NHTSA consulting engineer, is a "continuous erosion of regulatory function." With fewer than one thousand employees and an extremely thin research budget, NHTSA is, in the words of Professor David Vladeck, "one 'David' facing many Goliaths."[86]

FRA Resources. The 421 inspectors working for the Federal Railroad Administration are responsible for 1.6 million rail cars operating on nearly 219,000 miles of track with 158,000 signals and switches. With such a small staff, FRA inspects only 0.2 percent of railroad operations per year. It rarely conducts full investigations of grade crossing accidents, much less penalizes a railroad that violated its regulations in connection with an accident. In 2003, for example, FRA fully investigated only four of the nearly three thousand grade crossing accidents that occurred, and it imposed fines for only about 2 percent of the violations that it uncovered in its partial investigations. The agency acknowledges that it investigates only "extraordinary or unusual circumstances," usually involving three or more deaths in a single accident. Even if FRA were inclined to investigate more grade crossing accidents, it often does not learn of them until as long as a month has passed, despite a regulation requiring railroads to report them within twenty-four hours.[87]

Because it lacks sufficient resources of its own, FRA relies heavily upon the railroads themselves to inspect rolling stock and track for compliance with FRA safety regulations.[88] This solution, of course, puts the fox firmly in charge of the henhouse, with predictable results. One large company's accident investigation manual advised its investigators to be careful about "the degree and extent to which obviously harmful and possibly inflammatory evidence is documented." In taking photos of the accident scene, for example, the manual instructed investigators that "[a] panoramic view taken at one point might show a possible view obstruction, while an unobstructed view may be demonstrated by moving slightly closer to or away from the crossing." On the other hand, the investigator was to go to great lengths to gather and document evidence of fault on the part of the motorist.[89] The fact that the large railroad companies have scaled back the number of inspectors in the wake of a wave of mergers in the late 1990s means that they are an even less adequate substitute for federal inspectors.[90]

FDA Resources. Outside observers have consistently expressed concern about the severe mismatch between the huge responsibilities that Congress has assigned to the FDA and the resources that it has provided to the agency to meet those responsibilities.[91] A 2006 report by the National Institute of Medicine concluded that FDA "lacks the resources needed to accomplish its large and complex mission today, let alone to position itself for an increasingly challenging future."[92] FDA scientists agree. In a 2006 survey of almost one thousand FDA scientists, 70 percent believed that FDA did not have sufficient resources to protect the public health and help the public obtain the accurate science-based information it needs for using medications. Even the industry recognizes that "FDA is drowning under the weight of its added responsibilities and its budget woes." Exacerbating the problem is the fact that FDA's appropriations, for historical reasons, originate not in the health-related appropriations subcommittees but in the agriculture-related subcommittees, whose priorities are not necessarily those of the agency or its constituencies. The White House has also repeatedly turned a deaf ear on FDA requests for additional funds in the administration's annual budget.[93]

Nowhere is the agency's chronic lack of resources more apparent than in its Office of Drug Safety (ODS), the entity charged with "postmarketing" surveillance of drugs that FDA has already approved. The agency has never devoted more than a small fraction of its available resources to the postmarketing surveillance program. Thus, while the Office of New Drugs (OND) employs more than one thousand scientists to review a few dozen new drug applications per year, ODS employs only 109 employees to evaluate the safety of thousands of drugs that are already on the market. When Congress reauthorized the user fee program in 2002, it allowed FDA to use the fees for postmarket surveillance during the first three years following a drug's approval. Even so, the surveillance program receives only about 7 percent of the agency's overall budget. The 2007 amendments to the Food, Drug and Cosmetics Act provided for an additional $25 million per year in user fees for existing drug safety programs, and its Senate sponsor predicted that Congress would appropriate an additional $25 million per year for that purpose. The impact of this significant new influx of resources remains to be seen. In the words of Dr. Bruce Psaty, a well-known heart specialist, this arrangement "is just what the industry desires—a powerful engine to approve drugs and a weak effort to investigate safety in the postmarketing setting." For some patients whose doctors continue to prescribe drugs while the information on the risks that they pose builds up in company and agency files, the results have been devastating.[94]

Similar resource shortages plague FDA's postmarketing surveillance efforts with respect to medical devices. According to a congressionally mandated report by the National Academy of Science's Institute of Medicine (IOM), FDA "recognizes that it has not done well in monitoring the status and fulfillment of studies that it has required in connection with the premarket approval of medical devices or subsequently." The report concluded that "[t]o the extent that significant questions related to device safety have been asked and then neglected by the agency, the result may be avoidable harm to patients and their families and a breach of public trust," strong words indeed for that cautious scientific body.[95] Similarly, FDA has few resources to monitor compliance with its adverse-effects reporting requirements or to analyze the reports when they do come in. Observers have long complained that the agency does not maintain an adequate data collection system for defective devices, and the agency itself in 2003 acknowledged that its postmarket surveillance program was "not working well."[96]

Another predictable consequence of limited resources is poor agency morale. Several surveys of FDA medical officers conducted in the early 2000s revealed a serious morale problem among the agency staff. In a 2006 survey of about one thousand agency scientists conducted by the Union of Concerned Scientists, 40 percent described morale at the agency as either "poor" or "extremely poor," and only 32 percent believed that the agency was "moving in the right direction." A recent survey of four hundred employees undertaken by the Inspector General of the Department of Health and Human Services found that 36 percent of the surveyed employees were only somewhat confident or not confident at all about the agency's safety decisions. When it came to monitoring previously approved drugs for safety, 47 percent were "somewhat confident" and 19 percent were "not confident at all" about the agency's ability to do an adequate job.[97]

Common Law Resources. Absent a nationwide regulatory catastrophe approaching the magnitude of the terrorist attacks of September 11, 2001, substantial increases in regulatory agency budgets are not a realistic possibility in an era in which tax cuts, foreign wars, national security, and disaster relief are competing budget priorities. Lawyers for the victims of accidents resulting from violations of agency regulations or fraudulent manipulation of federal regulatory processes can supplement scarce agency enforcement resources both by uncovering fraud and violations and by providing a strong additional incentive to comply with regulatory requirements.[98] Ironically, while agency enforcers are crying out for assistance, their lawyers are rapidly cutting off this potentially significant source of aid.

Addressing resource shortages in FDA's medical device surveillance and enforcement program, an agency spokesperson acknowledged, in mid-2005, that "[w]e can't do this whole job by ourselves." The government's lawyers in *Buckman,* however, argued that the agency's enforcers were perfectly capable of handling the frauds that were being perpetrated on the agency without any assistance from plaintiffs' attorneys by way of common law actions based on fraud on the agency. And in the *Riegel* case the government was so confident in the sufficiency of the resources that FDA could put into approving new devices, it argued that *all* common law claims involving fully approved devices should be preempted.[99]

The situation is even worse at the FRA, where the agency is so strapped for resources that it has delegated much of the responsibility for inspecting rolling stock to the regulated industry itself. Local police investigators typically investigate grade crossing accidents more thoroughly than either FRA or railroad investigators. A Brinkley, Arkansas, policeman reported that while he was investigating the scene of a grade crossing collision, railroad employees cut the vegetation that had been obstructing the view of the track from the road, backed up a second train that had also been obstructing the view, and removed the bulbs from the brake lights of the victim's vehicle. Local police, however, have no authority to demand critical information from the railroads. The attorneys for the victims of grade crossing crashes, by contrast, have a strong incentive to dig deeply into the evidence to uncover such shenanigans.[100] Since the Supreme Court's holding, in *Shanklin,* that most common law claims involving federally financed grade crossings are preempted, however, any added incentive to comply with FRA regulations provided by the threat of subsequent litigation is much diminished.

Limited Agency Responsiveness

Regulation is not an especially effective legal tool for addressing risks in areas where scientific understandings and protective technologies are rapidly changing, for the simple reason that bureaucracies react very slowly to changed circumstances.[101] Regulatory agencies are generally cautious about launching new regulatory initiatives for many very good reasons. Any new governmental intervention, however desirable from a public policy perspective, will necessarily generate opposition from the target industry. Before the agency can get started in earnest, it must first overcome any opposition in OMB or other agencies in the administration that may have an interest in the outcome. Worst of all, rulemaking at the federal level has become so "ossified" with extraneous procedures, burdensome analytical requirements, and the necessities of compiling an adequate rulemaking record for judicial review that agencies are reluctant to take on controversial issues unless forced to do so by political pressure or agency-forcing lawsuits. A vice president of the National Safety Council observed in 2002 that "[a] rule has to go through an extraordinarily complicated gauntlet before it can be issued," and the standard of acceptability appears to be "absolute perfection."[102]

When agencies do decide to forge ahead, they tend to assemble the available resources and expertise for a single massive regulatory initiative that they hope will resolve the relevant issues for the foreseeable future. Once it has completed this Herculean effort, an agency is understandably reluctant to revisit the regulation in response to new information or technological improvements, even when it is receiving constant feedback on the effectiveness of past rules through required reports of adverse outcomes in the real world. Thus, the federal regulatory requirements that defendants invoke to preempt state common law claims usually reflect not current information and technologies but the often-obsolete information and technologies that were available at time the agency completed the rulemaking exercise.[103]

NHTSA Responsiveness. Professor Jerry Mashaw's classic 1987 study of NHTSA rulemaking documents an agency so hampered by the analytical and informational requirements imposed by OMB and reviewing courts that thousands of people could die unnecessarily between the time that the agency takes up a rulemaking initiative and the time it successfully guides the final product through the tortuous process. Little has changed in the intervening years. As of 2002, the agency had substantially updated only four of the eighteen original standards that it promulgated in the late 1960s and early 1970s, despite dramatic changes in the passenger vehicle fleet. NHTSA did not update the original 1969 standard for head restraints until 2004, despite significant advances in antiwhiplash technology in the 1980s and 1990s. The original 1967 tire safety standards for bias-ply tires were not updated for steel-belted radial tires until 2003, in the wake of the Bridgestone/Firestone fiasco. The agency revised the original fuel system integrity standard in 1974 but did not revisit it again until 2003 in response to several catastrophic accidents involving Ford Crown Victoria police cars. Sometimes NHTSA abandons update initiatives after years of contemplating revisions and moves on to more pressing matters. One agency critic observes that "[t]he agency not only simmers for years, it simmers for decades and nothing happens."[104]

FDA Responsiveness. Although FDA dramatically accelerated the pace of its reviews of new drug applications after it began to receive user fees in 1992, its postmarketing surveillance and follow-up process had, until the Vioxx scandal, slowed down.[105] Before FDA may force a company to withdraw a drug, it has to provide the company notice of its reasons for doing so and an opportunity for a full adjudicatory hearing. Consequently, the agency nearly always attempts to negotiate withdrawals with the companies, rather than force them through legal action. When the company resists, the drug remains on the market while the proceedings drag on.[106]

CPSC Responsiveness. CPSC has not amended the original industry-derived standard for flammable fabrics for more than fifty years, despite the agency's own acknowledgment that "[n]umerous new technologies, products and modern equipment have been developed" in the interim.[107] In the years since 1972, when Congress granted CPSC authority to promulgate flammability standards for other products, it has promulgated exactly three, and it has never revisited any of them. It took thirty years for CPSC to revisit its mattress flammability standard, and when it finally did, the agency decided that the standard would so well withstand the test of time that it should preempt all subsequent common law claims.

EPA Responsiveness. When it amended the pesticide statute, in 1972, Congress told EPA to revisit and "reregister" all of the previously registered pesticides after requiring the registrants to conduct additional health and safety studies in accordance with modern toxicological testing requirements. EPA decided not to review and update pesticide labels until after the reregistration process was done. By 1986, not a single reregistration had been completed, and Congress amended the statute in 1988 to require that the agency complete the reregistration process by 2008. In the meantime, the only legally binding vehicle for updating pesticide labels as new toxicological information becomes available is the pesticide registrant's own continuing obligation to ensure that the pesticide is not misbranded.

FRA Responsiveness. The FRA is unique among the agencies studied here in that it must contend with an institutional prod that keeps it constantly aware of the need to revise its regulations. The National Transportation Safety Board (NTSB) is a nonregulatory federal agency that investigates the causes of fatal public transportation-related accidents and recommends how to avoid similar accidents in the future. The FRA, however, often ignores or rejects NTSB recommendations, and when it does accept NTSB advice for a regulatory initiative, the rulemakings go on for years, prompting one NTSB chairman to complain that "[t]hese items can't remain in rulemaking forever."

A good example is a longstanding NTSB recommendation that FRA require railroads to implement a nationwide "positive train separation" (PTS) and Advanced Train Control (ATC) system using modern computer technologies and global positioning systems to force two trains to slow down and/or stop automatically when the distance between them gets too small or when a train passes a change-of-speed signal post without complying (because a fatigued engineer is asleep or for some other reason). In NTSB's view, these systems "have the ability to eliminate almost all rail collisions." The railroads have fiercely resisted PTS systems on the ground that their estimated cost of $1 to $3 billion is unwarranted by the benefits in terms of lives saved and reduced property damage.

In the meantime, FRA's aging, 1970s-vintage rules, in which FRA establishes speed limits for various classes of track and railroads assign track to classes, remains in place, with its preemptive effect on common law claims. The head of the American Association of Railroads asked whether preventing seven fatalities per year by changing from the low-tech speed limits to high-tech PTS and ATC systems was "the most prudent use of our money."[108] So long as it can continue to avoid compensating the families of those "fatalities" by complying with the existing FRA rules, the industry's answer to that question will always be "No."

Common Law Responsiveness. The regulatory process suffers by comparison to the judicial process in its ability to respond to changes in information and technology.[109] Common law duties are broadly crafted and therefore easily adaptable to changes in understandings about the adverse consequences of business activities and to new developments in practices and technologies for reducing or eliminating those adverse consequences. Common law litigants can assemble a team of experts who are familiar with the latest scientific studies and safety technologies for one case and assemble a different team for the next one.[110] If the jury finds that a reasonable company would have changed its practices or adopted newer technologies, then the defendant should have adapted in the same or a similar way.

The notorious litigation over breast implant medical devices provides a good case in point. By the time that Congress gave FDA the authority to regulate medical devices, in 1976, thousands of women had already received silicone breast implants. FDA proposed to put the devices in the stringently regulated Class III category six years later, and it spent the next six years arguing with the industry over whether the implants really belonged in the less burdensome Class II category. Having finally prevailed, FDA then spent another three years promulgating a rule describing the kinds of studies that the companies would have to submit to obtain full approval. When the company-submitted data finally arrived, in July 1991, the agency staff concluded that they were not sufficient to support the safety of the devices and called for a moratorium on new sales until additional information from forthcoming epidemiological studies became available.[111] In the meantime, discovery in common law litigation was prying information from company files indicating that the companies knew that implants were leaking, that they had withheld the results of short-term animal studies from FDA, and that their scientists shared the FDA staff's concern that the implants could cause immune system and connective tissue disorders. The courts upheld several large jury awards against the manufacturers. After the epidemiological studies concluded that the implants did not cause the disorders, however, the courts reacted in the late 1990s by dismissing most of the pending claims. FDA finally got around to ending the moratorium in November 2006. By then, however, it was too late for the manufacturer, which had gone bankrupt. Professor Jodi Hersch concludes that "[h]ad FDA requested the information from the manufacturers in a more timely fashion, the risks, or lack thereof, would have been known, and the litigation crisis" that resulted in the bankruptcy of the major producer of the implants "would have been avoided."

Proponents of preemption point out that resolving issues of social policy through common law litigation can also be a frustratingly slow process. Most state and federal courts face very full dockets, and it often takes years before a products liability case can be tried before a jury. For example, Alexis Geier was injured seven years before the Supreme Court heard the appeal from the trial court's dismissal of her case on preemption grounds. Had she prevailed in the Supreme Court, it could have been several more years before a jury decided whether or not the 1987 vehicle in which she was riding should have been equipped with airbags.[112] The speed with which cases come to trial varies greatly from jurisdiction to jurisdiction, however, and some courts clear cases from their dockets quite expeditiously. During the time that it takes for an agency to promulgate a major rule, courts throughout the country can be deciding cases, even if some are held up by crowded dockets. Furthermore, the vast preponderance of lawsuits are settled, and injured plaintiffs receive compensation without a lengthy trial.[113]

Consequences

In a perfect world, federal agencies would ensure that regulatees do not expose the beneficiaries of regulatory programs to undue risks to their health and economic well-being, and there would be no need for common law litigation to redress harms due to past wrongdoing. But, as Professor Vladeck observes, "that would be a world where the [relevant agency] never lacks the information, personnel, technical data and other resources needed to deal immediately with emerging . . . hazards; where the agency acts as soon as it identifies a problem requiring a regulatory solution; where rules are updated swiftly to reflect needed design changes, technological advances or scientific knowledge; where companies quickly and candidly inform the [agency] about the problems they identify; and where regulatory decisions are made free from political considerations—without pressure from regulated industry, congressional committees and the White House and the Office of Management and Budget."[114] The world that we live in does not even remotely approximate perfection, and it is not likely to any time in the foreseeable future.[115] When the agency fails to deliver on its promise to protect, preemption deprives the beneficiaries of both the protective justice backstop that the common law courts can provide and the corrective justice to which deserving plaintiffs are entitled.

FERRETING OUT INFORMATION

According to Professor Peter Schuck, "[a] legal system's ability to mobilize high-quality policy-relevant facts . . . at a relatively low cost is perhaps the most important precondition for the effectiveness of its policies—and ultimately their legitimacy."[116] This is not strictly a matter of expertise. In comparing agencies to courts in this regard, the issue is which institution has the stronger incentive to bring relevant information to the attention of the decision maker. To the extent that regulatory agencies cannot generate the information they need for accurate decisionmaking, the advantage in technical expertise that they have over courts is largely lost.[117]

When a sound decision requires the kind of information that is typically generated by the social sciences about the impact of policies on affected communities, constituencies, and economies, the information-gathering capacity of agencies clearly exceeds that of courts.[118] Agencies may also have greater access to scientific and technical information, although that information is typically available to litigation experts, as well. Agencies tend to take both kinds of information at face value in the decision-making process.[119] When the relevant information comes from entities with an interest in the outcome of the regulatory proceeding, however, the assumption that it is free from bias may be inappropriate, and a deeper inquiry into its bona fides may be warranted. Yet, agencies have little incentive to do this. Agency staffers reap no particular rewards for uncovering evidence of bias and misrepresentation in information presented to the agency. Even if they were inclined to probe, agencies often lack the necessary investigational tools, like the power to demand underlying data or to compel testimony.[120]

State common law litigation, on the other hand, provides strong incentives to lawyers for private litigants to uncover information relevant to the hazards of the products and activities at issue. Furthermore, litigants have the wherewithal to obtain underlying data and get to the bottom of possible fraud and deception. Professor Wendy Wagner observes that "the courts provide litigants with direct access to industry files and personnel, which allows them to pry 'stubborn information' on the adverse effects of their products and activities out of the hands of companies that have no incentive at all to make it available to regulatory agencies or the general public."[121] As often as not, the information that agencies do obtain on underlying malfeasance by regulatees comes to them indirectly through tort litigation.[122]

The sordid history of the fungicide benlate provides a good example of how multiple lawsuits in many states can smoke out the truth in a way that an agency cannot match.[123] Benlate was the most widely used fungicide in the world until the 1980s, when commercial nurseries in Florida and Hawaii began to suffer mysterious damage to benlate-treated ornamental plants. The nurseries claimed that E. I. DuPont de Nemours and Company, the manufacturer, had allowed benlate to become contaminated with a potent herbicide called sulfonylurea (SU) that it manufactured and stored in the same warehouse. EPA was sufficiently concerned that on September 1, 1989, it issued "stop sale" orders preventing the sale of certain lots of benlate. While DuPont continued to maintain its innocence, discovery in pending cases revealed that DuPont had failed to disclose to the plaintiffs (and undoubtedly to EPA, as well) a series of contamination tests on affected properties that it had commissioned in 1993 that had demonstrated that many of the tested soils tested positive for SU herbicides. Rather than accept those results, DuPont had the tests "repeatedly redone and massaged" until they reached the right results. DuPont then produced misleading "summaries" of the results to the plaintiffs through an outside expert witness who was also not given all of the information.

The deception began to unravel in 1994 when a DuPont employee revealed in a deposition that DuPont possessed previously undisclosed documents containing the actual results of the contamination tests and that DuPont had prepared an eighty-four-page summary of contamination test results from 1987 to 1991 for benlate manufactured at the suspect plant. A court in Hawaii ordered DuPont to produce those documents and another six boxes of documents that it failed to produce in the Hawaii litigation but had produced in a Texas case. The whole story slowly came out as courts throughout the country ordered DuPont employees and lawyers to be deposed about the coverup. A Georgia court ordered DuPont to pay the plaintiffs $6.8 million in attorneys fees, and it further ordered DuPont to pay a whopping $100 million sanction or place a full-page ad confessing its malfeasance in *The Wall Street Journal,* a remedy that was later reversed on appeal as a thinly disguised criminal sanction.[124] Tellingly, EPA played no role whatsoever in revealing the truth about benlate, and it is inconceivable that it would have gone to the kind of effort undertaken by the plaintiffs' attorneys to get to the bottom of DuPont's deception.

The benlate case is by no means unique. Reports of catastrophic tire tread separations in Continental General GT52S tires led to a 1993 NHTSA preliminary investigation in which it asked the company to provide any documents relating to possible defects in the tires. After reviewing the company's submissions, the agency closed the investigation. Attorneys in several lawsuits brought on behalf of victims of crashes allegedly caused by GT52S tire failures, however, used their subpoena power to force the company to produce many damning documents that it had failed to disclose to the agency. By the time the new information came out, the five-year statute of limitations on NHTSA recalls had run, and the agency declined to pursue the matter.[125]

The informational advantages of litigation must, however, be discounted to the extent that information obtained in litigation never sees the light of day. Corporate defendants routinely stamp damning documents produced in litigation "Confidential" and insist that they be protected by judicial protective orders subjecting anyone who discloses that information to steep civil and even criminal penalties. The companies then demand that all of those documents be returned or destroyed as a precondition to settling the cases. Unless a case actually goes to trial and the documents are introduced as evidence, the public and the relevant federal agencies may never learn of their existence.[126]

According to Professors Daniel Gilvelber and Anthony Robbins, the latter a former head of the National Institute for Occupational Safety and Health, "[c]ivil litigation uncovers a great deal of otherwise unavailable information about practices and products which may cause disease and injury."[127] For example, General Motors Corporation over several years quietly settled more than two hundred lawsuits brought by badly burned victims of defective side-mounted gas tanks on pickup trucks before the public learned of the problem, in the early 1980s. Similarly, Eli Lilly and Company settled eight thousand cases involving the schizophrenia drug Zyprexa in a single settlement containing a secrecy agreement that protected documents indicating that the company knew that the medication caused huge weight gains in many patients and increased blood-sugar levels to dangerously high levels in some. The information came to light only after an attorney in an unrelated case stumbled across many of the documents and made them available to the *New York Times*.[128]

Plaintiffs' attorneys are licensed professionals and subject to certain ethical obligations to their clients and society that are typically managed by state supreme courts. One of the most profound of these is the lawyer's duty to represent his or her client diligently in litigation and negotiations.[129] This means that the lawyer is ethically obliged to place the interests of the client above those of the general society in most situations, including settlement negotiations. Only if the *client* is willing to risk leaving large monetary proposals on the settlement table is the lawyer permitted to insist on disclosure. If, as is usually the case, the client elects to take the money and sign the nondisclosure agreement, the lawyer is ethically obliged to limit disclosure, as well.

Congress and the agencies can ameliorate the problem of secrecy agreements to some extent. For example, the Transportation Recall Enhancement, Accountability, and Documentation (TREAD) Act of 2000 required auto and tire manufacturers to provide all claims, lawsuit complaints, and other data concerning deaths and injuries allegedly caused by their products to NHTSA, but the law also contained a provision prohibiting the agency from making information stamped "confidential" available to the public.[130] The CPSC promulgated a similar rule requiring manufacturers to report to the agency alleged product defects that were the subject of three judicial judgments or private settlements in any two-year period.[131] State legislatures and courts have likewise been reacting to the disclosure problem by changing the civil trial discovery rules to prohibit litigants from agreeing not to disclose information suggesting that a product or ongoing activity poses a substantial risk to public health or safety or to the environment.[132] These state laws are, or course, irrelevant to the extent that federal law preempts the underlying common law claims.

Despite the prevalence of defendant-imposed secrecy agreements, common law litigation indisputably yields a great deal of information about the risks of regulated products and activities that would otherwise not come to the attention of federal regulatory agencies. Professor Robert Rabin concludes that to the extent that lawsuits "provide the educational function of revealing massive cover-ups of health information by industries like asbestos, or occasional efforts to conceal risk information from regulatory agencies like the FDA, then it is undeniably the case that tort law is serving a positive function of some consequence."[133] Federal preemption of those common law claims would deprive agencies and the public of this valuable source of risk information.

JURY NULLIFICATION AND BIAS

Distrust of juries on the part of many proponents of preemption goes beyond their legitimate concern for jury competence in addressing complex technical questions to a rather strong conviction that juries are generally biased in favor of plaintiffs and are therefore inclined to disregard the judge's instructions and render favorable verdicts without regard to the legal principles that should be governing their decisions. Naturally sympathetic toward the plight of injured plaintiffs and understandably wanting to help them, jurors quickly figure out who has the deep pockets and realize that they are free to use the lawsuit as a vehicle for redistributing wealth regardless of the merits of the claims and defenses of the parties before it. Consequently, they are inclined to award excessive damages for "pain and suffering" and to stick corporate defendants with "blockbuster" punitive damage awards. At the same time, juries are insufficiently attuned to the benefits that the products and activities at issue provide to consumers and society as a whole.[134] Politically accountable federal agencies, by contrast, take a broader view of cumulative, systemic effects of government intervention and of the "inevitable tradeoffs" involved in designing products and disclosing risk information.[135] Critics, such as Peter Huber of the Manhattan Institute, are therefore troubled that "[t]welve jurors from off the street can . . . veto the positive safety choices of a regulatory agency at will."[136]

To defenders of the jury system, these empirical claims remain wholly unproved. Based almost exclusively on anecdotal evidence derived from headline-grabbing jury awards in cases involving questionable claims and large verdicts that are usually reversed by the courts, they are, in the words of Professor Thomas F. Burke, the handiwork of "a dedicated corps of image-makers, business interests that have conjured a litigation 'crisis' for their own political ends."[137] What empirical evidence does exist seems to tell a different story.[138] According to careful statistical analyses prepared by Professor Theodore Eisenberg of thirty years' worth of data from federal cases compiled by the Administrative Office of the United States Courts, juries are much less inclined to find for the plaintiff in products liability cases than judges, and they are inclined to award lower damages when they do. In judge-decided verdicts, plaintiffs win about 40 percent of the time, and in jury-decided cases, they win only about 30 percent of the time.[139] These numbers certainly do not suggest a strong bias on the part of either judges or juries against defendants. Another major study funded by the National Science Foundation concluded that jurors are not biased against corporations and are not swayed by the financial resources available to corporate defendants.[140]

Preemption critics point out that a jury does not get to decide a case until the judge first concludes that the plaintiff has offered sufficient evidence to support a claim under an accepted legal theory.[141] Some courts have also gone to great lengths to avoid jury bias on highly technical issues by appointing carefully selected panels of experts to advise them on the scientific reliability of studies relied upon by plaintiffs' experts.[142] Judges also retain the power to overturn "outlier" jury verdicts, and the available empirical evidence suggests that judges and the lawyers themselves in posttrial settlement negotiations "tend to very substantially alter the awards downward, particularly the larger awards."[143] Finally, the fact that many of the proponents of preemption are also opponents of protective federal regulation suggests to preemption critics a bias of their own in favor of a laissez faire approach that generally favors risk producers over their victims.[144]

LAWSUIT ABUSE

Preemption advocates argue that when agencies do take action, greedy trial lawyers "pile on" with frivolous lawsuits based upon conduct that was lawful at the time it took place or, if unlawful, does not warrant the severe punishment that successful lawsuits impose. In support of his agency's recent aggressive efforts to preempt common law suits against drug companies, former FDA commissioner Mark McClellan (grandson of one of the founders of modern tort law, Page Keeton) complained that plaintiffs' lawyers were "[u]sing information that they get from us" to "file a few suits for very sick patients in states and counties that are considered quite favorable to plaintiffs, while they build up big inventories of less seriously ill patients or even people who used the drug but are not even sick." Sounding a similar refrain, a prominent spokesperson for corporate defendants in the "tort reform" debates, the former law professor Victor E. Schwartz, argues that "[e]ntrepreneurial plaintiffs' lawyers and activist state judges are increasingly working to bypass elected lawmakers and impost their own public policy choices on Americans."[145]

As with the jury bias claim, little empirical evidence supports the charge that lawyers routinely parlay FDA actions into lucrative lawsuits. Nearly all of the significant regulatory actions that FDA took during McClellan's tenure, for example, were *preceded* by lawsuits against the relevant manufacturers. McClellan's complaint that trial lawyers tend to shop around for the most receptive forums for their lawsuits and cultivate stables of clients, some with more deserving claims than others, in the hope of achieving large global settlements has a much sounder basis in fact. But that is a larger problem of the common law system generally and will not be remedied by selective preemption of a few varieties of common law claims. The fact that both McClellan and Schwartz linked it to the preemption war suggests that broader "tort reform" is the real agenda of some preemption proponents.

The concern raised by preemption proponents regarding the adverse impact on the national economy of "public interest" lawsuits in which plaintiffs seek broad injunctive relief, rather than individual damages, is considerably more plausible. Cases like the firearms lawsuits filed by several municipalities and public interest groups and a similar group of lawsuits filed by individual plaintiffs seeking injunctions that would force manufacturers to recall allegedly defective tires have the potential to drive up litigation costs and ultimately to force defendants to take action beyond that required by the regulatory agencies that are charged with protecting public health while maintaining a strong economy. Referring to this alleged conspiracy as the "litigation industry," Michael S. Greve of the American Enterprise Institute urges "corporate America" to "serve as a public interest proxy in resisting rent seeking and redistribution through litigation."[146]

This criticism of "public interest" lawsuits is a valid one that bears serious public attention. Plaintiffs in this far-ranging species of tort litigation are not demanding corrective justice so much as they "seek to change the rules that govern industry-wide business practices." Their attorneys have admitted that the litigation is an attempt to achieve an "end run" around legislators and agencies that appear unwilling to resolve the relevant social issues in a way that is acceptable to their clients.[147] These actions are invariably polycentric in nature, and they require courts to craft "complex remedies and an administrative apparatus to execute it."[148] When a federal agency already exists and is charged with the same broad policymaking task, it may make sense to preempt the duplicative judicial action and allow the agency to go about its business unimpeded by a competing institution. As we have seen, regulatory agencies are far from perfect, and there are no doubt occasions in which the asymmetry between regulatee and beneficiary influence on regulatory outcomes justifies outside intervention. It is less clear, however, that the intervention should come by way of public interest lawsuits in common law courts.

Proponents of preemption argue that the common law is precisely the wrong way to go about fixing a broken regulatory process. When a court is obliged to supervise a broadly applicable injunctive remedy, it is performing an unfamiliar role for which a regulatory agency, however dysfunctional, is far better suited. Public interest common law litigation forces the courts out of the role that they are best adapted to playing—that of impartial dispensers of corrective justice. The proper remedy for regulatory failure may be in court, but it should come by way of judicial review of regulatory action or inaction. Finally, insofar as damages are at stake in public interest tort litigation, the plaintiffs are effectively asking courts to shift wealth not from negligent defendants to innocent plaintiffs but from innocent consumers of poorly regulated products to governmental entities and public interest advocates.[149] Even broadly construed, corrective justice does not demand gross redistributions of this nature.

The fate of the public interest gun control litigation will no doubt warn many plaintiffs' attorneys away from such litigation in the future. The cost of defending the lawsuits and of implementing any injunctive remedies were borne not by the criminals who were directly responsible for the damage but by gun manufacturers and purchasers of firearms.[150] The claims for injunctive relief were so suspect that the courts were very reluctant to entertain them, and some plaintiffs' lawyers abandoned the cases as it became clear that the courts would not be especially receptive to the broad claims. Congress ultimately put an end to most of them with the Protection of Lawful Commerce in Arms Act, but, at the same time, it preempted quite valid private interest claims seeking corrective justice from gun manufacturers and distributors that were taking a "see-no-evil" approach to the way their products were being marketed in violation of federal firearms laws.

CONCLUSIONS

The comparative institutional perspective offered in this chapter does not provide a firm basis for declaring either side in the preemption war the victor. Federal agencies have clear institutional advantages over common law courts and juries when it comes to some kinds of technical and policymaking expertise, but those advantages are not overwhelming, and they are irrelevant to many of the issues that arise in both regulation and litigation. It takes a hubris more commonly found in politically appointed officials than in the agency's technical experts to claim that a federal agency has so thoroughly considered the potential beneficial and adverse consequences of regulated products or activities that after-the-fact liability for any and all adverse consequences is wholly unwarranted. The very real possibility of regulatory failure suggests, at the very least, that Congress and the courts should be very cautious about presuming that agencies can adequately fill the corrective justice void that remains when a federal action preempts state common law claims.

Moreover, because the promise of protection that federal agencies offer is frequently a hollow one, for reasons of limited agency resources if nothing else, policymakers and courts should not dismiss out of hand the helping hand offered by common law litigation. Concerns about irrational jury verdicts and "blockbuster" damage awards have a very poor empirical foundation and therefore should be heavily discounted in the preemption debates. "Public interest" lawsuits seeking broad injunctive relief from judges, on the other hand, do raise serious concerns from the perspectives of both institutional competence and institutional accountability. Congress and the courts should therefore consider the nature of the relief requested, as well as the substantive context, in deciding whether to preempt. At the end of the day, the agencies have a legal and moral duty to the beneficiaries of their regulatory programs to ensure that their preemptive reach does not exceed their regulatory grasp.

Chapter 8 The Case for Preemption

Even the not-so-frequent fliers among us are quite familiar with the warnings that flight attendants must provide before takeoff, the "fasten seat belt" warning light that tells us to remain in our seats, and the passenger safety briefing cards in the seat pockets in front of us. And the words "Please remain seated while the flight attendant prepares for arrival and cross-check" are blazoned in the memories of frequent fliers anxious to make their connections. What most airline passengers may not know is that these warning rituals are prescribed by regulations and advisory circulars issued by the Federal Aviation Administration. Even frequent fliers who spend much of their lives on planes, however, have never seen or heard a warning to the effect that "Remaining seated while the seat belt sign is illuminated may cause you to contract deep vein thrombosis."

For some people, remaining seated for long periods of time in cramped quarters like the cabin of a commercial aircraft is a risk factor for deep vein thrombosis, a blood clot that develops in a vein (usually in the calf or thigh) and that may break off and travel to the lungs (in which case it is called a pulmonary embolism). Milton Witty III contracted deep vein thrombosis while traveling from Monroe, Louisiana, to Hartford, Connecticut, on a commercial airliner, and he sued Delta Air Lines alleging, among other things, that the company had a common law duty to warn him during the flight attendant's presentation, on the safety briefing card, or in some other conspicuous place of the risk of contracting deep vein thrombosis on a long trip. The court, in *Witty v. Delta Airlines,* held that Witty's claim was preempted by the FAA regulations and advisory circulars prescribing in great detail the content of the warnings that airlines must provide on domestic flights.[1]

The *Witty* example well illustrates the case for federal agency preemption of state common law claims. A victory for Witty would have sent a message to airlines that they should warn passengers of the risk of contracting deep vein thrombosis on long flights, but it would have been a message that they could not have heeded, because the FAA prescribed the preflight warnings in some detail. Furthermore, had the airline provided the warning, it might have encouraged passengers to violate FAA regulations governing conduct in flight. The airline could have complied with a common law duty to compensate Witty for its failure to warn him, but that hardly seems fair. A rule to that effect would essentially turn the airline into an insurer for the damages suffered by any passenger who could make a plausible case that he contracted deep vein thrombosis while on one of its flights. Compensation in such situations might implement a wise social policy in favor of redistributing wealth from airline passengers to victims of a disease associated with air travel, but it is not a policy that Congress has adopted. Finally, imposing on the airline a common law duty to compensate Witty despite its inability to warn him would send a perverse message to the airline industry to deny passage to persons who might be at high risk for deep vein thrombosis. This, too, might be a wise social policy, but it is not one that either the common law or Congress has adopted.

This chapter explores the arguments that advocates of federal preemption rely upon to support their position in the preemption war. In addition to considering the obvious need to avoid direct conflicts between federal regulations and common law obligations, we examine arguments based on the inefficiencies resulting from subjecting national markets to random after-the-fact changes in the rules in fifty different states, inefficiencies caused by uncertainty over the status of a product that has received government approval but is still subject to common law claims, reduced research incentives caused by the threat of expensive lawsuits, inefficiencies resulting from "overdeterrence," and administrative inefficiencies suffered by federal agencies as a result of common law–inspired incentives.

IMPOSSIBILITY

As suggested by the *Witty* case, the most powerful argument for allowing federal regulatory actions to preempt state common law claims is to avoid placing a defendant between the Scylla of a federal legal requirement and the Charybdis of a state common law obligation. When two legal requirements come into such direct conflict that complying with one requires noncompliance with the other, one of them should yield. The indisputable intent of express preemption clauses is to prevent such conflicts by eliminating the state law source of the conflict. The conflict argument, however, extends beyond statutes with express preemption clauses to any direct conflicts between federal regulatory requirements and state common law duties via the judge-created doctrine of "impossibility preemption," which exists whenever compliance with state law will cause the actor to violate federal law.

Opponents of preemption can still argue that the two legal regimes may peacefully coexist even in cases of such direct conflicts of legal obligations when the plaintiff seeks only monetary damages, because it is always possible to comply with the positive federal law and compensate the plaintiff.[2] While this is undoubtedly true, it usually represents a poor outcome from a policy perspective for the reasons discussed earlier. Using a legal system that to a large degree assesses liability on the basis of fault to turn a class of law-abiding corporate citizens into insurers will appear grossly unfair to most observers. Among other things, it is inconsistent with principles of corrective justice, because forcing the defendant to pay the plaintiff does not correct any legal wrong. Moreover, awarding damages in such cases can provide no protective justice role, because federal law prevents the defendant from reacting to the incentive by complying with the common law duty. Indeed, it may well send out perverse messages with unintended consequences.

In cases where the proponent of preemption can show a direct conflict between a common law duty and federal regulatory requirement, the preemption battle should therefore be over.[3] At the same time, decision makers should examine the preemption proponents' argument very carefully before concluding that such a conflict exists. Courts generally articulate common law duties in very broad terms like "reasonable person," "unreasonably dangerous," "reasonably safe," and "abnormally dangerous." An "impossibility conflict" exists only in situations where the plaintiff takes the position that the only way for the defendant to have complied with the common law duty was to have modified its product or activity in a way that would have necessarily caused it to violate a specific federal requirement. An example might be a case in which the plaintiff contends that the defendant's automobile was defectively designed because it failed to install an airbag that inflated to a pressure of no more than thirty pounds per square inch (psi) when the NHTSA standard for the airbag required it to inflate to a pressure of fifty psi. Such situations, however, are likely to arise only relatively rarely in the real world. Impossibility conflicts are more likely to arise in cases like *Witty* that involve warning defects where federal requirements specify precisely what language must be used and permit no other language.

UNIFORMITY

If agency expertise is the most frequently cited reason to favor federal agency preemption of state common law standards, then the need for uniformity in national markets runs a close second. The National Chamber of Commerce eloquently argues that, because "common-law decisionmaking is notoriously ill-suited to the establishment of nationwide standards that strike the proper balance among the multitude of societal interests at stake in a particular regulatory setting," the "general economic interests of the Nation are increasingly being sacrificed on the altar of the parochial interests of particular states, as declared by local state judges and juries." Federal agencies, by contrast, are "well suited to weigh competing interests and adopt appropriate and uniform national standards to govern particular aspects of the national economy."[4]

The uniformity theme plays well in the political arena, but it also echoes in the halls of academia. Proponents of preemption argue that common law "cannot ensure desirable consistency and coordination in legal requirements" that are "especially important for nationally marketed products."[5] "[E]xpert federal agencies, intimately familiar with the products and industries they regulate, are arguably far better suited [than common law courts] . . . to ascertain the degree of federal uniformity necessary to assure safety, efficacy and availability at a reasonable cost."[6] Since most products in the United States are "mass produced and mass distributed," allowing federal agencies to set "maximum standards" that common law duties cannot exceed "may allow the private sector to operate within a predictable and stable environment."[7] There may be less to this claim, however, than meets the eye.

National uniformity is an especially important consideration for product labeling. For example, FDA pays particular attention to prescription drug labels and warnings. Its regulations "permit warnings on the labels only when there is significant medical evidence of a possible health hazard," and they "preclude warning of a drug's unknown or theoretical adverse reactions."[8] Professor Richard Stewart argues that "juries in case-by-case litigation may focus on the particular accident in question and ask whether it could have been prevented by a warning that was not given or a different warning than the one given, without adequately considering the cumulative, systematic effects of many such case-specific decisions."[9] Companies have also taken the position that their customers have an interest in uniformity in labeling. The Product Liability Advisory Council, for example, argues that consumers "accustomed to standard labeling, with form and content approved by a single expert decision-maker," would prefer to avoid "discordant and inscrutable warnings derived from litigation, or fear of litigation, under the differing laws of 50 different jurisdictions."[10] Consumer groups do not, however, appear to share that concern.[11]

One variation of the uniformity argument focuses on interstate "spillovers" that may result from the application of differing common law rules to nationally marketed products. Proponents of preemption worry that diverse common law judgments may adversely affect citizens who by chance or design live in states with common law regimes that are less protective than those of most other states. To the extent that manufacturers react to common law judgments in one state by raising prices or modifying products or services sold in all states, the interests of consumers who choose to live in less protective states are negatively affected. Like interstate pollution, these spillover effects are, in the view of preemption proponents, undesirable in a federal system.[12]

Opponents of preemption do not deny that uniformity benefits national markets, but they dispute the degree to which state common law litigation contributes to nonuniformity in the legal requirements applicable to nationally marketed goods and services. The preemption proponents' frequent allusions to variation in common law duties from state to state rarely identify any particular nonuniform common law duty. In fact, the general contours of the common law are remarkably uniform across the states. State courts and legislatures are frequently persuaded by writers of uniform laws and restatements to apply consistent language in articulating common law liability rules. The universal test across the country for negligence is the "reasonable person" test. Likewise, the elements of a claim for intentional infliction of emotional distress and strict liability for unreasonably dangerous conduct vary imperceptibly from state to state. There is, as we saw in Chapter 2, some degree of variance among state supreme courts as to the finer points of products liability law on the degree to which a risk-utility test displaces consumer expectations as the primary focus. Professor Douglas A. Kysar demonstrates, however, that in the real world of the courtroom, the consumer expectation test readily morphs into the risk-utility test.[13] While there may be some interstate variance in the language that the courts use in instructing juries with respect to a particular common law claim, the basic concepts are the same throughout the country.

Preemption proponents respond that their complaint is not so much with variability in the content of law as it is with the uniformity of its application in similar cases by different juries. This problem, however, is not uniquely a problem of federalism. It is the problem of variation in the applicability of a single broad standard in any context. A manufacturer of a product faces this kind of variation even if its market is confined to a single jurisdiction, because jury awards can vary over time as well as from courtroom to courtroom within a single jurisdiction. The degree of variation does not increase when a state line separates the two courtrooms. The Supreme Court, in *Bates,* acknowledged that "properly instructed juries might on occasion reach contrary conclusions on a similar issue of misbranding," but it could see no reason to conclude that "such occurrences would be frequent or that they would result in difficulties beyond those regularly experienced by manufacturers of other products that everyday bear the risk of conflicting jury verdicts."[14] Upon close examination, the real complaint appears to be with a liability regime that depends so heavily on juries, a concern that we addressed in Chapter 7.

To the extent that the uniformity complaint goes to the inconsistent application of broad legal standards, it is an argument that applies with equal force to federal regulatory programs. We saw in Chapter 2 that most health and environmental standards are not specification standards that tell regulatees exactly how to go about their business but design or performance standards that give regulatees a fair degree of flexibility in achieving a required level of performance. Even in the context of product labeling, where federal requirements tend to be more specific, agencies typically exhibit a fair degree of flexibility in allowing regulatees to make safety-related changes without prior agency approval. In all of these cases, the regulatee must deal with the possibility that agency officials or, more realistically, the state officials who enforce the federal laws will not apply these broadly applicable federal regulatory requirements uniformly. To the extent that the regulatee presses the compliance issue by litigating it in an enforcement proceeding, the entity that will decide whether the regulatee complied with the broad requirement will be a judge or a jury. Hence, the potential for variance from jury to jury does not necessarily distinguish a federal regulatory program from state common law to any significant degree.

In the end, the uniformity argument may be an instance of proponents of preemption framing an argument in the vertical dimension to advance a less persuasive horizontal claim. In the vertical dimension, the proponents of preemption compare the supposedly uniform requirements of a federal regulatory program to the supposedly variable requirements of the common laws of different states. The horizontal reality behind the uniformity argument may be a desire to avoid common law obligations altogether. The result of uniformity-based preemption is a world in which manufacturers are forced to pay damages only for products or activities that violate the applicable federal requirements. Since most manufacturers are law abiding when it comes to such requirements (especially when they play a powerful role in determining what those requirements will be), uniformity-based preemption is effectively a liability shield.

UNCERTAINTY

Business people tend to crave predictability and eschew uncertainty in the legal requirements that apply to their products and activities. According to Professor Peter Schuck, companies want to know in advance with a high degree of accuracy how legal restrictions will apply in the circumstances they are likely to encounter and "make their long-term investments in technology and distribution networks accordingly." Predictable rules lead to greater efficiency by reducing the costs of ascertaining and applying the rules and by decreasing compliance and enforcement costs. The broad rules that determine liability in negligence and products liability litigation and the "black box" aspect of jury verdicts combine to make the common law system much less predictable than the regulatory process in many situations.[15] C. Boyden Gray, a former White House counsel, argues that common law liability "creates tremendous uncertainty for manufacturers," because the "wide differences in state laws, as well as the frequent changes in those laws, make it practically impossible for manufacturers of products sold throughout the United States to determine the standards of conduct to which they will be held."[16] Federal preemption of state common law claims reduces these uncertainties by subjecting all companies to an identical set of standards imposed by a single federal agency.

The advantage of federal regulation over state law in avoiding uncertainty, however, may not be as great as advertised. The federal regulatory process itself is highly uncertain. The automobile industry's experience with NHTSA's passive restraint requirements (discussed in Chapter 4) illustrates that the road from regulatory proposal to full compliance with a final rule is often full of unpredictable twists and turns that can take literally decades to negotiate. After watching NHTSA vacillate for a decade over whether to require airbags in cars, the primary U.S. manufacturers of the airbag technology got out of the business, in 1979. Two years later, General Motors announced that it was canceling its research program for a "second generation" of airbags because the advent of the Reagan administration's "regulatory relief" program made it clear that airbags would not be required in the near future after all.[17] These turned out to be wise decisions, because NHTSA did not mandate the use of airbags for another ten years.

Furthermore, the fact that Congress writes an express preemption provision into a regulatory statute does not automatically eliminate uncertainty. Indeed, to the extent that the prior law is settled against preemption, the congressional action will increase uncertainty while the meaning of the express preemption clause is parsed in litigation. If the Supreme Court does not resolve the matter fairly rapidly, the uncertainty can persist for decades as a "common law of preemption" develops in the lower courts. This is what has happened on the transportation deregulation battlefront, where neither the airlines nor the railroads know for sure whether particular actions will or will not be protected by the express preemption provisions in the relevant statutes.

If the concern is with uncertainty about the content of the relevant legal rules, it should largely be alleviated by the previously discussed fact that the relevant common law rules do not vary greatly from state to state. To the extent that the concern is with uncertainties in predicting how juries will make factual findings on highly uncertain causation issues or will apply the relevant legal rules to the facts of particular cases, these "are not issues of federalism in any meaningful sense" because those uncertainties would likewise plague a single uniform national liability regime.[18] Hence, like the uniformity argument, the vertical uncertainty argument may be masking a horizontal agenda. The only way to eliminate the business uncertainties inherent in common law liability is to eliminate that liability altogether, which is the horizontal solution that the companies making the uncertainty argument clearly prefer. But it relieves them of the uncertainties in the messages sent by common law by eliminating both the protective justice and the corrective justice functions of the common law.

Retaining the corrective justice function would require at least the creation of an alternative federal regime, which would give rise to many of the same uncertainties, especially with respect to the critical causation question.

From the consumer's horizontal perspective, the uncertainties created by a common law liability regime may in fact be a virtue. The greater responsiveness of the protective justice function of the common law (discussed in Chapter 7) ensures that as more information becomes available and safety technologies improve, more will be expected of the manufacturers of widely marketed products. As the Supreme Court noted in *Bates,* "the specter of damage actions may provide manufacturers with added dynamic incentives to continue to keep abreast of all possible injuries stemming from use of their product so as to forestall such actions through product improvement."[19] Not only will the potential for common law liability inspire manufacturers to keep their eyes open for new safety technologies, but it will also inspire innovative efforts by companies in the safety business to come up with technologies that manufacturers must adopt to meet the always-rising expectations of the common law.

In the end, the question for policymakers is how to strike the proper balance among the disincentives to invest in production and product technologies caused by the additional uncertainty that the common law provides over that already provided by the federal regulatory process, the incentive to invest in additional safety technologies that the same uncertainty provides, and the corrective justice that will be lost to the extent that uncertainties are reduced by reducing the availability of common law courts to injured plaintiffs. We will turn our attention to the policy balance in Chapter 10.

INNOVATION

For many years, advocates of "tort reform" have argued that the threat of common law liability adversely affects technological innovation.[20] Peter Huber, of the Manhattan Institute, argued in one of the earliest tort reform manifestos that "[j]urors can make reasonably sensible intuitive judgments about people —even about professionals—because we are all in the people-judging business every day of our lives," but jurors "are not experts about technology itself, and intuition here is a terrible guide." He concluded that "[t]he inexpert juror is predisposed at every turn to identify technologies that are novel, exotic, unfamiliar or adventuresome as unwelcome and fraught with danger."[21] Professor Richard Stewart agrees that a "dual track" of federal regulation and state common law liability "creates a combination of legal constraints, delays, and uncertainties that imposes disproportionate burdens on new products and processes."[22]

Framed in the horizontal dimension, the argument has special political salience when applied to innovation in the pharmaceutical industry. For example, the threat of future litigation may make insurance more expensive and thereby hamper new product entry into the pharmaceutical markets. A representative of Medtronic, Inc., the manufacturer of Lora Lohr's failed pacemaker and the catheter that exploded in Charles Riegel's vein, discussed in Chapter 4, noted that "[e]very dollar that we need to divert to pay for lawsuits takes money away from research and development." Mark McClellan, then Commissioner of FDA, made the point forcefully in the political arena when he expressed his concern "that our liability system is having some adverse effects on medical care, and is impeding affordable and timely access to innovative medical products."[23]

Preemption proponents rarely provide empirical support for their innovation claims. Peter Huber cited no empirical support at all for his assertion that jurors are psychologically biased against new technologies. We saw in Chapter 7 that there is in fact little, if any, empirical basis for such claims and a good deal of empirical evidence to the contrary. The relationship between liability and innovation is also an essentially empirical question for which there are few available data. After reviewing the existing information in 1994, Professor Teresa Schwartz agreed with the tort reformers that the common law might have "some adverse impact, although difficult to measure, on research and development with respect to some categories of [pharmaceutical] products," but she ultimately concluded that "no firm evaluation can be made of the impact of the liability system on the availability of prescription products."[24]

Opponents of preemption acknowledge the very real possibility that the threat of common law liability will cause manufacturers to draw back from developing innovative new products, but they argue that it is also possible that it will stimulate them to conduct additional safety testing on new products beyond the minimum required to obtain government approval. While this could lengthen the time it takes for valuable products to arrive on the market, consumers may appreciate the added assurance that these products are reasonably safe. Moreover, the strong incentives that the marketplace provides to be the first on the market with an innovative product or technology can easily overwhelm the modest disincentive attributable to the prospect of future liability.[25] Critics also point out that the impact of common law preemption on consumers is not limited to the increase in "affordable and timely access to innovative medical products" that would presumably result if manufacturers did in fact put "every dollar" saved through preemption into research and development, rather than advertising, profit margins, and executive compensation.[26] Preemption also deprives individuals like Susan Halvorsan, who have been damaged by products like Vioxx that entered markets too rapidly and were withdrawn too slowly, of any opportunity to petition the common law courts for the corrective justice that is their due.

OVERDETERRENCE

One argument for preempting state common law that resonates well in the public ear is the possibility that the threat of tort liability will stimulate companies to "overinvest" in defensive practices or insurance and raise prices to cover the added costs.[27] Framing the issue in the horizontal dimension again, McClellan stated unequivocally that "our liability system does significantly add to [drug] costs compared to other nations."[28] If one agrees with McClellan that the additional risk avoidance and insurance costs are attributable solely to the fear of baseless lawsuits and yield no social good, this unwarranted expense represents what economists call a "dead weight efficiency loss" for society. Beyond increasing prices for much-needed products, fear of baseless lawsuits may even inspire companies to pull perfectly good products from the shelves, all to the detriment of consumers. To the extent that federal preemption of state common law claims puts the minds of manufacturers at ease, then preemption can create a more efficient economy that makes better products available to consumers in greater quantities and at lower cost.[29]

The overdeterrence argument is especially persuasive in the context of product warnings. Few, if any, warnings are completely beyond criticism, and in hindsight a "factfinder can always find that a warning should have been more prominent or more specific." The prospect of tort liability therefore gives manufacturers an incentive to adopt a warnings strategy that "warns of nearly everything," and therefore conflicts with the federal agency's regulatory goals of "reliability and brevity."[30] Courts have cautioned that the "avalanche of information" inspired by fear of tort liability "is hardly conducive to informed decision-making" and that warnings "about dangers with less basis in science or fewer hazards could take attention away from those that present confirmed, higher risks."[31] This "information overload" confuses both consumers and their doctors and distracts the attention of both from the really important risks.[32] The objective of federal regulation, on the other hand, "is to provide just the right amount of warning—not too little certainly, but not too much either, for the risk on that side is to frighten users into less safe alternatives."[33] FDA featured this argument in its amicus curiae briefs and in the preamble to its drug labeling regulations, employing various framing words like "overwarning," "overdeterrence," and "underutilization" to capture the concept for public consumption.[34]

Preemption critics again complain that preemption advocates, including FDA, rarely provide empirical evidence to support their dire predictions that the mere threat of having to defend a lawsuit will produce steep price increases or drive important products from the market. In fact, Professors Clayton Gillette and James Krier suggest that cases involving mass exposures to broadly distributed "public risks" from mass-produced products and large industrial activities should pose little threat of overdeterrence, because that kind of litigation is already "structurally biased against victim access."[35] Because any given plaintiff is not at great risk and because of the great difficulties that plaintiffs in such cases face in proving that a particular defendant's products or activities caused any particular illness or injury, litigation by individual plaintiffs is seldom worth the considerable cost, however socially desirable it might be from the standpoint of protective justice. Consequently, this kind of litigation is probably "marked by too few claims and too little vigorous prosecution, with the likely consequence that too much public risk escapes the deterrent effects of liability."[36]

When used to support federal agency preemption of state common law claims, the overdeterrence argument assumes that the relevant federal statute is meant to provide "optimal" deterrence.[37] This is probably a fair assumption in the case of product licensing statutes, such as the FDC Act and the pesticide statute, that require the agencies to evaluate the costs and benefits of the regulated products. Even here, the overdeterrence argument still presumes that chronically resource-deprived federal agencies are capable of inducing the degree of deterrence that the statute demands. Safety statutes like the railroad act, the boating safety act, and the motor vehicle safety act are not intended to induce the "optimal" investment in protective technologies. To the contrary, these precautionary statutes generally require the agency to install the "best available technology" or to "err on the side of safety," approaches that have stimulated similar claims of "overregulation."[38] To the extent that the common law provides incentives to go beyond the requirements of aging regulations promulgated under such statutes, regulatees may perhaps complain of "uberoverdeterrence," but the outcome may be quite consistent with the policy underlying the preempting statute.

In the domain of FDA regulation of pharmaceutical labels, where the overdeterrence argument resonates most clearly, it fails to address two important realities. First, the argument that precautionary warnings will cause ill-informed consumers irrationally to "underutilize" drugs is debatable in an age in which, as one court observed, "pill-rolling apothecaries and the mortar and pestle" have been replaced "by drug manufacturers who urge the use of their drugs in mass-market print and television advertisements targeted directly at the public."[39] Second, the concern that doctors will be dissuaded by label warnings that do not comport precisely with FDA's assessment of the risks and benefits is wholly inconsistent with the agency's willingness to allow doctors to prescribe drugs for unapproved uses. Most doctors want to see more information about efficacy and potential adverse side effects on the labels of drugs. If the agency trusts doctors not to "overprescribe" drugs for unapproved uses, it seems odd that it would not likewise trust them not to be frightened by stronger warnings into "underprescribing" drugs for approved uses.[40]

ADMINISTRATIVE EFFICIENCY

Although rarely making an appearance in the preemption war, the claim that prosecution of common law claims in state court will seriously interfere with the ability of agencies to implement and enforce federal statutes is a strong argument for preemption. Such situations present a case of genuine conflict between state and federal legal regimes, and one or the other must yield. Under the Supremacy Clause, the law that must give way is state common law. A good example might be a situation in which a state court ordered a defendant to take an action that arguably violated a federal regulatory requirement, thereby calling on the agency to expend scarce enforcement resources prosecuting a violation that would not have occurred but for the common law action. The argument that common law claims merely have the potential to reduce the efficiency with which federal agencies go about their tasks, however, is another matter. Some small degree of inefficiency may be tolerable if the pursuit of state common remedies advances more important social goals.

The administrative efficiency argument played a powerful role in one small corner of the preemption war—the battle over common law "fraud on the agency" in the *Buckman* litigation, discussed in Chapter 4. In that case, the government strongly asserted an "important federal interest in permitting FDA to decide for itself whether it has been defrauded, and, if so, what sanction is appropriate."[41] Although the Court agreed with the plaintiff that his damage claim was not inconsistent with the agency's ability to regulate medical devices, it concluded that it would interfere with the "delicate balance of statutory objectives" that FDA had to strike in deciding whether or not to investigate and punish fraud. Furthermore, allowing the plaintiff's claim to go forward might precipitate a deluge of paper from medical device manufacturers that would interfere with the agency's other work.[42] Except for a rapidly diminishing number of fraud-on-the-agency cases, however, instances in which a court has held that the plaintiff's claim would hinder administrative efficiency are quite rare.

FDA's amicus curiae briefs and the preamble to its labeling regulations stressed the possibility that FDA's implementation of its regulatory responsibilities "would be disrupted and undermined if, driven in part by concerns about later state law tort liability, drug manufacturers were to engage in their own labeling determinations by adding warnings that, in FDA's judgment, were not based on reasonable scientific evidence of an association or causation."[43] The briefs and preamble did not, however, cite examples of jury verdicts that in the past had disrupted its programs or explain how the agency had managed to carry out its regulatory responsibilities for the thirty years during which it had acknowledged the fact that "product liability plays an important role in consumer protection."[44] The decision being challenged in a common law failure-to-warn claim is not the agency's decision to approve the product and its label but rather the company's decision to continue marketing the product as labeled instead of preparing a stronger label for FDA review. The threat that such a claim poses to the agency's implementation of its statutory responsibilities is not obvious.[45]

Since federal agencies are notoriously inefficient institutions to begin with, the modest impediment to administrative efficiency caused by common law litigation should not be an especially weighty consideration in any preemption analysis. It is, in any event, unlikely to come up in many cases. Nevertheless, Congress should pay attention to the impact of common law claims on the agency's ability to administer its statute in deciding whether to add express preemption clauses to statutes, and courts should continue to consider it in those rare cases in which it arises.

CONCLUSIONS

Like any general position on an important policy issue, some of the prominent arguments favoring federal agency preemption of state common law claims featured in this chapter are quite persuasive in some regulatory and factual contexts and less persuasive in others. Only the argument for avoiding direct conflicts that render it impossible for a defendant/regulatee lawfully to comply with both state common law and federal regulation is a sure winner in almost every conceivable context. The uniformity argument, which appears more frequently than the others in preemption battles, wilts upon close inspection in most regulatory/litigative contexts and should therefore be taken with a grain of salt and an eye out for the horizontal claim that it may be trying to disguise. Arguments for avoiding uncertainty and overdeterrence and for promoting innovation and administrative efficiency through preemption are plausible in most contexts and therefore have the potential to tip the balance that policymakers must strike in deciding whether or not to preempt in any given context. We will explore that balance in greater detail in Chapter 10.

Chapter 9 The Case Against Preemption

We begin our discussion of the case against preemption with the story of the disastrous marriage between the Ford Explorer and the Bridgestone/Firestone ATX tire. The story has its origins in a corporate marriage arranged by Henry Ford and Harvey S. Firestone in 1906 that was later solidified in the physical marriage of their grandchildren.[1] When the sport utility vehicle (SUV) became popular, in the late 1990s, Ford Motor Company engineers converted its successful Ford Ranger pickup truck into an SUV called the Ford Explorer.[2] The Rangers were already outfitted with Firestone tires. Ford engineers decided that a lower tire pressure would be desirable for the Explorer because its center of gravity would be much higher and because kid-carrying suburbanites would demand a smoother ride than drivers of dirt-hauling pickups. This, in turn, required Firestone to redesign the tires slightly to meet fuel economy requirements and to avoid catastrophic tire separation, which was more likely at low pressures. It also reduced the load-carrying capacity of the Explorer and increased the risk of tire failure due to vehicle overload. With tires filled at the pressure Ford needed, the maximum vehicle load was about the same as that for a large sedan, a fact that was not mentioned in the owner's manual or in Ford's advertising. Ford's solution also ignored the inability of the suburban consumer's untrained eye to detect underinflation, which reduced the weight-bearing capacity of the tire still further and increased the risk of tire failure on the road.

The other half of the ill-fated marriage was the faulty design and manufacture of the Bridgestone/Firestone ATX and Wilderness tires. In numerous accidents involving Firestone-equipped Explorers, the tread literally flew off the tires as they were spinning at high speeds.[3] Engineers later determined that tiny "fatigue cracks" had developed in the sidewalls and rapidly spread into the tire, causing it to lose its tread. The cracks could have been caused by faulty design of the tire sidewalls and tread, by poor manufacturing processes that allowed the rubber in the tires to dry out prior to tire construction, or by the presence of impurities in the rubber. The combination of bad tires and low carrying capacity turned the Explorer into a time bomb flying down the highway at seventy miles per hour. By late 2001, it had caused more than two hundred deaths and seven hundred injuries.

The problem was discovered not long after the first batch of Explorers hit the road by lawyers for victims of Ford Explorer rollovers and a private consultant named Sean Kane, who specialized in using NHTSA online data to uncover connections that eluded the agency.[4] Hoping to stimulate a recall, some victims filed complaints with NHTSA, but the agency never responded. In July 1998, a claims administrator at the State Farm Insurance Company e-mailed to NHTSA's investigations office documents showing that State Farm had received about twenty-one claims involving failures of Firestone ATX tires, at least fourteen of which were on Ford Explorers. Again, the agency took no action beyond adding the report to a bulging file containing twenty-six similar reports dating back to 1991, where it remained despite two more efforts by State Farm to call the agency's attention to the problem. At the time, NHTSA was preoccupied with responding to criticisms that it was over-regulating the auto industry from a Congress that was singlemindedly implementing the deregulatory promises of the "Contract with America."

Faced with a hostile Congress and a distracted federal agency, victims of the deadly Explorer/ATX tire combination had only one forum available to them: state common law courts. The lawsuits began in the south and the southwest, where higher temperatures exacerbated the tread separation problem. The initial litigation strategy of both Bridgestone/Firestone and Ford was to settle the mounting lawsuits before they went to trial and to insist that all documents produced during discovery be destroyed, returned, or placed under court seal.[5] This strategy succeeded until November 1999, when a thirty-six-year-old reporter working for a Houston television station heard about several tire separation cases from an attorney friend.[6] After meeting with a Houston woman who had lost both her legs and her husband when her Explorer rolled over after its Firestone ATX tires separated, the reporter soon identified more than thirty similar cases that were either pending in court or had been settled around the country. The reporter next located a former employee of a Bridgestone/Firestone plant in North Carolina who told her that plant managers frequently required the workers to use off-spec rubber in the ATX tires.

The nine-minute local news segment, which aired on February 7, 2000, prompted two responses. First, the station within days received a letter from Bridgestone/Firestone accusing it of airing "falsehoods and misrepresentations that improperly disparage Firestone and its product." Second, the segment generated hundreds of calls and e-mails from local viewers who had experienced similar accidents or knew someone who had. The station referred many of these inquiries to NHTSA, and the increased volume of complaints soon caught the attention of agency investigators. The agency opened a formal defect investigation on May 2, 2000. Later that month, a judge in Texas held that depositions and testimony taken in connection with an Explorer/ATX tire case were available for public inspection, and the story began to unravel as the plaintiffs' lawyers shared the documents with NHTSA and the press. The resulting publicity prompted an announcement by Firestone, on August 9, 2000, that it would be initiating the largest tire recall in U.S. history. At this point, NHTSA's investigation became moot, and more than one hundred victims of rollover crashes had filed lawsuits against Bridgestone/Firestone and Ford.

When the documents did begin to enter the public arena, they told a chilling story of deception and denial on the part of both companies.[7] Firestone had been tracking claims that its ATX tires were losing tread from 1994, when they accounted for 43 percent of the company's property damage and personal injury claims. After almost 10 percent of 229 tires from its Decatur, Illinois, production facility failed a high-speed durability test conducted in 1996 because of concerns about tire separation, the company modified the tires, in 1998, to widen the rubber strip between the two steel belts. By 1999, the company had received more than 1,100 accident claims, none of which had been shared with Ford or NHTSA at the time.

Internal Ford documents disclosed that Ford engineers had warned management in 1989, the year before the first Explorer hit the showrooms, that the engine was mounted so high that the prototype vehicle "demonstrated a rollover response . . . with a number of tire, tire-pressure [and] suspension configurations." They also knew that Explorer prototypes with the prototype Firestone ATX tires (called P235) had failed the rollover test developed by Consumer Reports. An internal memo written in 1989 by a Ford engineer reported that "management is aware of the potential risk with P235 tires and has accepted [that] risk." The engineers provided three fundamental options to management: mount the engine lower in the vehicle, widen the chassis by two feet, or lower the air pressure in the P235 tires and tighten the springs.[8] Management chose the third option. In early 1999, Ford switched to Goodyear tires for Explorers marketed in Saudi Arabia and neighboring countries because of the frequency of complaints of tread loss followed by rollovers in these locations, and it replaced the Firestone tires on more than fifty thousand vehicles in other countries. Yet, it did not share this information with NHTSA, and it did not ask Bridgestone/Firestone for its claims data until after the media had begun to generate pressure for a U.S. recall.

Both the Ford Explorer and the Bridgestone ATX tires fully complied with all relevant NHTSA standards.[9] Indeed, NHTSA's tests for tire safety, which were based on 1960 specifications that antedated steel-belted radial tire technology and assumed passenger car use, were not strictly applicable to the Explorer, which was classified as a light-duty truck.[10] An agency initiative to upgrade the standards during the Reagan administration was abandoned after the agency suffered severe budget cuts.[11] Had the courts held that compliance with NHTSA's standards preempted common law claims, as the companies and the George W. Bush administration have urged, an unexceptional agency failure to update archaic standards would have turned into a catastrophic failure of a nation to provide corrective justice to thousands of innocent victims of serious malfeasance on the part of two large corporations. Indeed, it is entirely possible that none of the information on company misconduct would have seen the light of day, and people might still be dying on the highways as a result.

This chapter explores the arguments that opponents of federal preemption rely upon to support their position in the preemption war, including the critical corrective justice function of tort compensation, the "backstop" role that common law courts can play by providing protective justice, the partnership role that state courts can play in the federal system, and the nonviolent alternative that tort liability offers to individuals and groups that believe that they are victims of corporate misconduct.

CORRECTIVE JUSTICE AND RISK SPREADING

The primary function of the common law is to dispense corrective justice by forcing those who have unlawfully damaged others to compensate their victims.[12] Since we examined this function in some detail in Chapter 2 and have touched on it at many points in the preceding pages, little more discussion is required here. Regulatory agencies can punish past wrongs resulting from violations of preexisting laws, but they are not in the business of shifting the loss from the victims to the wrongdoers. Federal agency preemption of state common law claims, in the words of Professor Robert Rabin, "leaves a compensation gap even in the best of all possible worlds where agencies are living up to the optimization ideal and regulated firms are adhering to the set standards."[13] By preventing state courts from performing their vital corrective justice function, preemption robs deserving victims of defective products and careless activities of their common law right to compensation.[14]

In some fairly uncommon situations, the common law can also play a risk-spreading role by ensuring that the beneficiaries of a widely used product or activity pay for the losses suffered by innocent victims. The risk-spreading function of the common law can have special relevance to federal regulation based on cost-benefit balancing. Agencies applying a cost-benefit decision rule may decide not to regulate a risky product or activity as stringently as they could because resulting risk reduction would not warrant the additional cost of a more stringent requirement. Those members of society who are later harmed by the product or activity do not suffer any less because they know that the failure to regulate did more good than harm to those who were not injured. It may be wise not to regulate when the winners win more than the losers lose, but it may also be wise to require the winners to compensate the losers indirectly by imposing liability on the manufacturer of the regulated product.

Preemption proponents note that more efficient mechanisms for spreading the risk from beneficiaries to victims are available, including first-party insurance and administrative no-fault reparations regimes.[15] When the only goal of the common law is to spread risk, these alternatives may well be preferable. To the extent, however, that corrective justice is a goal, they will not suffice because the compensation comes from either a pool of potential victims in the first instance or a pool of potential defendants in the latter. In neither case does the compensation come from the wrongdoer. In the case of first-party insurance, contributors to the pool might legitimately question why the payments they make into the insurance pool should subsidize a perfectly solvent entity whose wrongdoing caused the harm. The second option has the virtue of calling on the harm-producing industry to finance the compensation and thereby achieves a rough degree of corrective justice, and it is an option that should be open for consideration by Congress as it determines whether a regulatory regime should preempt common law liability.

LEGITIMACY

In a country like the United States that has historically maintained an open-eyed skepticism about the legitimacy of governmental intervention into private affairs, the civil justice system has, at least until the recent assaults by the tort reformers, retained a legitimacy that bureaucratic intervention through prescriptive rulemaking and permitting has never matched. Professor Jerry Mashaw concludes that the "most clearly legitimate form of coercive state intervention in our polity is remedial," because "[s]uch intervention attempts to correct past injury or injustice, usually in individual instances, and on the basis of widely-shared understandings of legal and moral responsibility."[16]

No one likes to be ordered around, especially if the entity doing the ordering is located in some far-off place and is not directly politically accountable to the people who are obliged to obey. Unlike federal bureaucrats, state judges are elected in many states, and where they are not elected, they are appointed and confirmed by state officials who are much more attuned to the political will of the people being affected by their decisions than are federal bureaucrats. Juries are not elected, but they are in a very real sense surrogates for "everyman" and in that sense are almost certainly better repositories of moral wisdom based upon shared values than is a federal bureaucracy. As Professor David Vladeck notes, "[w]hen a person sits in a jury room, his or her voice carries greater force than in any other setting or forum in our representative democracy."[17]

The Supreme Court has recognized that every state "has a body of tort law serving" the state's "compelling interest" in ensuring that victims of unlawful activities "are compensated by those who harm them" and that federal preemption of state common law remedies therefore represents a "serious intrusion into state sovereignty."[18] When federal bureaucrats conclude that their judgments about the risks and benefits of nationally marketed products and services should displace the judgment of local judges and jurors, the threat to local decision-making autonomy is palpable.[19] When, as is usually the case, that decision has the effect of protecting large national or multinational companies at the expense of injured local citizens, its legitimacy automatically becomes suspect in the minds of local citizens. When that decision is imposed *ipse dixit* or with only a brief explanation stressing the need for uniformity in national markets and the importance of avoiding overdeterrence, any remaining hint of legitimacy vanishes at the local level, and it begins to take on the acrid smell of oppression.

ACCOUNTABILITY

Federal regulations are designed to prevent future harm. Because violations of the regulations presumably have the potential to cause harm, companies are held accountable for those violations, whether or not the violations cause any harm, when the government forces then to pay civil or criminal penalties. State common law only rarely attempts to prevent future harm through injunctive relief, but it does hold companies accountable for past harm, whether or not they violate any state or federal regulations, by forcing them to compensate injured plaintiffs and occasionally to pay punitive damages. The El Dorado for a company bent on avoiding accountability is a world in which state common law is preempted by a federal regulatory regime that does not regulate. When the plaintiffs in the *Bates* pesticide labeling case stressed that EPA had abandoned any federal regulatory responsibility for ensuring that pesticides performed their intended functions as indicated on their labels, the Chamber of Commerce responded that the absence of regulatory accountability was irrelevant because the federal pesticide statutes' preemption provision did not "condition preemption on the existence of a counterpart federal regulation."[20] And, a 2006 advisory circular to products liability defense lawyers issued by the business-oriented Washington Legal Foundation stressed that the goal of the business community's overall preemption effort should be "to see that law students in 2016, when they hear about past pharmaceutical product liability cases, chuckle to themselves over this curious historical anomaly."[21]

Referring generally to manufacturers of pharmaceutical products, the jury forewoman in the Texas Vioxx trial recounted in Chapter 1 explained that "[w]e expect accountability; we expect them to be open with us; we expect them to be honest with us."[22] She was no doubt expressing the opinion of most Americans about the large and often impersonal companies that seem to be driven far more by the bottom-line demands of the marketplace than by concerns for the well-being of the families of their consumers. The Texas jury may have lacked FDA's expertise, but it expressed a moral outrage that was apparent only at the lowest levels of the FDA and was constantly squelched by upper-level agency officials until damning internal documents discovered by plaintiffs' lawyers appeared in the *New York Times* and the *Washington Post.* Unlike most Americans, however, the jury forewoman was in a position to hold the companies accountable for their actions, a function that FDA can perform only when the company violates a specific regulatory requirement.

When companies violate regulatory requirements, they are held accountable by the federal agencies only to the extent that those violations are detected and successfully prosecuted. The fact that the FRA, for example, conducts only four full investigations into the three thousand grade crossing accidents that occur annually tells the railroads that they are unlikely to be held accountable even for those accidents caused by violations of FRA requirements. If, as is currently the case, accidents at federally financed grade crossings are preempted, a plaintiff's attorney will have no incentive to take on the burden of representing a victim of an accident at such a crossing, and no one is likely to investigate whether the accident was or was not caused by a violation of FRA regulations. No one will dig deeply enough into the underlying facts to discover that the company changed the faulty signal device after the fact or trimmed the vegetation that had obscured the driver's line of vision.[23] No one, in short, will hold the company accountable for its past misconduct.

THE PROTECTIVE JUSTICE BACKSTOP

The common law's "protective justice" function is to provide a constant incentive to potential defendants to design and market their products and to conduct their activities in accordance with the relevant common law standards of care in order to avoid liability for damage caused by their failure to adhere to those standards. Indeed, in the minds of some torts scholars, this is such an important function that courts should craft the rules of tort law to focus that incentive on achieving an efficient allocation of resources. The protective justice function of the common law is relevant to the preemption war for three important reasons. First, it can provide backstop incentives to comply with federal regulatory requirements and to take action that is consistent with the precautionary policies that motivate most federal regulatory statutes when the agency has not yet implemented those policies. Second, it can provide incentives to take protective action beyond the minimum thresholds required by federal statutes and regulations that do not attempt to achieve an optimal degree of protection.

Finally, it is the protective justice function of the common law, not its corrective justice function, that causes it to run afoul of federal regulatory programs. When a company feels impelled by common law duties to act in a way that avoids liability, it may be motivated to take action that is inconsistent with a relevant federal regulatory requirement. For example, a federal specification standard might require regulatees to use one and only one technology that might not be as protective as other available technologies. To the extent that the common law provides an incentive to install a protective technology and to the extent that adopting the more protective technology violates the federal requirement, the common law and the federal law are in conflict. Such situations are quite rare, but common law incentives more frequently present a potential obstacle to the accomplishment of a federal policy that runs counter to safety or attempts to achieve safety in a particular way. Recall, for example, the *Geier* case, in which the Supreme Court held that common law claims based on the auto manufacturer's failure to install airbags presented an obstacle to achieving the policy underlying the NHTSA passive restraint regulation, which rejected an "airbags only requirement" in favor of giving companies the option of using either airbags or passive seatbelts or both.

Reinforcing Existing Requirements

The common law's least controversial protective justice function, from the perspective of the preemption war, is to provide additional incentives to regulatees to comply with federal regulatory requirements. We learned in Chapter 2 that the doctrine of negligence per se ensures that plaintiffs' attorneys will be looking carefully for aspects of a defendant's conduct that may have violated federal regulatory requirements to avail themselves of the procedural advantage that evidence of such a violation affords. The threat of being forced to compensate persons injured by violations of federal requirements can add considerably to the threat of being forced to pay statutory penalties for the same conduct. When statutory penalties are the only threat, companies can adopt "optimum" compliance strategies that discount the amount of the likely penalty by the probability that the agency will detect the violation, pursue it in an enforcement action, and bring that action to a successful completion. The unknown extent of common law liability makes strategic noncompliance much riskier. For this reason, the Supreme Court has over the years been especially reluctant to find that common law actions based on violations of federal regulatory requirements are preempted.[24]

Filling Anticipation Gaps

When they get around to it, regulatory agencies do a reasonably good job of reacting to existing problems by developing new requirements designed to prevent past harms from recurring. In such situations, they can analyze what caused the problem, identify techniques or technologies that are capable of fixing the problem, and impose forward-looking requirements designed to encourage regulatees to reduce the harms in the future. Agencies do a much less effective job of anticipating the adverse consequences of new risks posed by new or existing products.[25] Recall the failure of the warning requirement concerning the choking hazards of small balls in toys to anticipate the possibility that a seven-year-old autistic boy would choke while playing with a toy that is ordinarily used by much younger children. The common law provides an effective vehicle for filling the regulatory gaps that inevitably arise at the implementation stage because agencies can never anticipate and regulate every potentially socially undesirable aspect of an ongoing business and cannot possibly envision all of the possible ways that regulatees will react to regulatory programs.[26]

Agencies can also fail to anticipate how regulatees will react to regulatory requirements. Given access to sophisticated legal advice, companies can often change their products or activities in ways that comply with the regulations but still defeat the relevant statute's protective goals. Gun manufacturers, for example, have proven especially adept at finding ways around BATF regulations "without running afoul of the letter of the law." A good example is the mail order "firearms parts kit" that is not regulated as a gun but can easily be assembled into a gun with the parts provided in the kit.[27] The common law provides a continuing incentive to regulatees to avoid harming others, whether or not a regulatory agency anticipated that particular harm in promulgating its requirements.

Filling Response Time Gaps

Since agencies cannot possibly anticipate all of the undesirable effects of regulated products and activities at the time that they promulgate their regulations or issue their licenses, they must also be prepared to react to failures of their requirements to attain statutory goals when failures become apparent. FDA frankly acknowledges, for example, that "there is no way we can anticipate all possible effects of a drug from the clinical trials that precede approval."[28] Consequently, fully one-half of the adverse effects of newly marketed drugs are not discovered until after the drugs have been on the market for a while.[29] Agencies that carefully monitor the impact of their regulatory programs in the real world often discover that things did not go exactly as planned and realize that changes in the regulatory requirements are in order. In the time that it takes for the agency to recognize the problem and attempt to fix it, however, victims continue to incur damage, unless regulatees also have an incentive to detect and fix problems in the interim. The common law provides just the sort of incentive that can stimulate regulatees to act during the time it takes the agency to finalize regulatory action.[30]

The capacity of the common law to provide protection while agencies are responding to newly arising problems is especially useful in the case of a manufacturer's duty to warn consumers of product risks. The most important lesson that FDA took away from the Vioxx and SSRI drug incidents was that "the American public, both practitioners and patients, want to get clear, accurate information as early as possible."[31] In the case of pharmaceuticals, that desire is fortified by the right of patients to be fully informed of the risks and benefits of medical treatment before consenting to undergo treatment.[32] If the manufacturer knows that it may be held liable for failure to warn of the new hazard as soon as it becomes aware of the hazard, as many lower courts have held,[33] it will take steps to warn consumers without waiting until the relevant regulatory agency gets around to requiring an amendment to any previously required warning. If, however, common law claims are preempted, the manufacturer has no incentive to warn consumers, and it can devote its energies to attempting to convince the agency that the new information does not warrant any additional warnings.

When the incentive otherwise provided by the common law fails to stimulate action on the part of the regulatee, the common law's informational function may still help stimulate action by making information about the newly discovered risk available to the agency so that it can force the regulatee to act. Thus, the Supreme Court in the *Bates* pesticide case, for example, noted that state common law actions "may aid in the exposure of new dangers associated with" the relevant product or activity or inspire the relevant agency to "decide that revised labels are required in light of new information that has been brought to its attention."[34] Although their politically appointed superiors might deem such assistance unnecessary or inappropriate, resource-starved agency personnel are rarely inclined to turn away such help.

Easing Implementation

The added incentives that the common law provides through its protective justice function are also helpful in areas where the relevant agency's authority is difficult to exercise and the agency is therefore timid about using it.[35] For example, FDA can force the company to change a previously approved label only by initiating a formal enforcement action in federal court under the provisions of the law preventing companies from marketing "misbranded" drugs and devices in interstate commerce. The agency lacks the resources to invoke this option with any regularity, and to do so would in any event deprive patients of the product's benefits until the company made desired label changes. As a practical matter, the agency is therefore limited to cajoling the company into making the needed improvements. The company is free to decline and to take its chances that the agency will not pursue the matter. As often as not, this is a good bet.[36]

The common law has in the past played an important role in easing FDA's implementation of its statutory responsibility to ensure that drug labels provide adequate and up-to-date warnings. In the late 1960s, a growing body of scientific studies indicated that the powerful antibiotic chloromycetin caused aplastic anemia in some patients. FDA staff urged the manufacturer to amend the drug's warning to suggest that patients be hospitalized while doctors administered the drug, but the company declined to do so after concluding that hospitalization would be so expensive that doctors would just prescribe a different antibiotic. FDA took no further action to require the additional warning, but a federal court of appeals held that a jury could conclude that the company's common law duty to warn included a warning conforming to FDA's hospitalization suggestion.[37] Had this case been brought after FDA promulgated its 2005 labeling regulations, the company would no doubt have argued at the outset that the plaintiff's claims were preempted and relied on the regulations to support that proposition. If the courts accept FDA's new position, this powerful gap-filling function of the common law will be lost.

Beyond the Bare Minimum

When EPA learned, in 1977, that the pesticide benlate caused birth defects in laboratory animals, it deliberated for two years before even proposing to require the registrant to change the label to warn workers and other users that "[e]xposures to benlate during pregnancy should be avoided." More than three years after that, EPA issued a final determination requiring the registrant to provide a much less foreboding warning stating that benlate was "harmful if inhaled" and recommending that users "[w]ear a cloth or disposable paper dust mask during handling and mixing."[38] This modest change did not highlight the reproductive risk to pregnant women and did not distinguish benlate from a host of other pesticides. Benlate then became the most widely used fungicide in the world until a Florida jury, twenty years later, awarded a $4 million verdict to John Castillo, who, like the laboratory rats, was born without eyes after his mother was exposed to benlate near a "u-pick" strawberry field.[39] During the quarter century that benlate remained on the market after EPA first identified its reproductive risks, thousands of children were exposed to benlate in utero as their mothers inadvertently breathed it in the air near fields where it had been applied. Had the Florida court agreed with the American Chemistry Council's position that the federal pesticide act preempted all pesticide common law actions for damages (a position that the Supreme Court rejected in 2004 in the *Bates* case), benlate would no doubt still be on the market and still causing some children to be born blind.[40]

In the sometimes blinding rhetorical heat of the preemption war, some agencies and courts have apparently lost sight of the fact that Congress enacted the federal statutes giving rise to most of the preemption claims primarily to protect consumers and the environment against the perils of an unconstrained marketplace, not to protect companies from the risks of unconstrained juries. Professors Robert B. Leflar and Robert S. Adler point out that "[i]t would be an unusual logic that would readily interpret laws aimed at enhancing safety simultaneously to withdraw a chief incentive for achieving it."[41] Yet, as we have seen in Chapters 4 and 6, some agencies and lower courts have repeatedly applied this "unusual logic" to do exactly that, even in light of strong indications by Congress and the relevant Supreme Court precedent to the contrary.

Many torts scholars advocate a dual approach to product safety that employs both *ex ante* regulation and *ex post* common law liability regimes.[42] David Owen, the writer of a leading treatise on products liability law, observes that "[m]ost product safety statutes, and most product safety regulations promulgated thereunder, are designed to prohibit (and criminalize) only the clearest and most egregious hazards" and that "the limited budgets and other resources of safety agencies generally preclude them from being effective arbiters of optimal, rather than minimal safety." The common law's protective justice function provides additional incentives to reduce risks in a manner consistent with the protective goals of most regulatory statutes, beyond the level of risk reduction that agencies can effectively provide. While the dual approach is more burdensome to the regulated industries, "it normally works quite well to minimize government intrusion into product design and labeling decisions while protecting the basic safety rights of product consumers."[43]

Preemption proponents respond that the dual approach has its origins in old nineteenth-century cases involving railroad regulations and statutes that were limited in scope and admittedly not designed to prescribe optimum standards for the relevant industries. By contrast, Congress has adopted a risk-benefit balancing regulatory paradigm in many of the modern health and safety statutes, and agency decisions under these statutes *are* intended to achieve an "optimum" level of risk reduction.[44] Professor Lars Noah notes that tort law has evolved to encompass a far broader range of activities than the "context dependent collision cases" in which the "minimum standards" rationale was first employed.[45] According to Professor Richard Stewart, the risk now is that "jury nullification of regulatory risk-benefit balancing decisions can impose undue costs or otherwise restrict the use and development of socially beneficial products and processes.[46]

This response has considerable force in the context of product licensing statutes, like those that govern FDA drug and device approvals and EPA pesticide registrations, that employ a risk-benefit test for approving products.[47] In most other regulatory contexts, including transportation safety, environmental protection, food safety, and occupational safety and health, the federal statutes reject the cost-benefit balancing paradigm for feasibility-based approaches that are aimed at inducing regulatees to "do the best they can" or acceptable risk-based approaches designed to "protect public health" with an "adequate margin of safety." The additional incentive afforded by the threat of common law liability is entirely consistent with the goals underlying these statutes. Even in the context of cost-benefit balancing statutes, practical and political realities dictate a minimum threshold approach toward implementation. In the words of a former head of NHTSA, agencies tend to set standards at the level of the "20-yard field goal," because it is "easier to make than miss."[48]

Congress has on many occasions considered statutes that would shield federally regulated companies from common law liability, and it has on a few occasions enacted statutes like the gun shield act. When the primary purpose of the statute is to preempt common law claims, agencies and courts should not attempt to undermine that purpose by interpreting their reach narrowly or their exceptions broadly. For the most part, however, attempts to amend protective statutes to preempt state common law claims in Congress have failed, as we saw in the case of the MTBE liability shield.[49] Absent a clear congressional intent to protect regulated companies from liability for violating common law standards of care, the courts and the agencies should presume that Congress meant to allow common law actions that advance the precautionary policies underlying protective statutes to proceed in accordance with common law principles.

PARTNERSHIP

Before this country was a nation, it was a confederation of thirteen independent sovereignties, each of which had its own legislature, its own courts, and its own common law. In ratifying the Constitution, in 1789, the states surrendered a great deal of power to the newly created federal government to make laws governing commerce among the states. As the writers of the Federalist Papers were at pains to point out, however, they did not surrender their institutions of government, and the state courts continued to create and elaborate upon the common law that governed the day-to-day interactions of their citizens even as Congress over the next century created federal agencies and a separate federal judiciary to interpret and apply federal law. Although few doubt the wisdom of the founding fathers in creating a strong federal government, fewer still doubt that the states have a critical role to play in dealing with matters of local and regional importance. Judicial administration of the common law has for the most part been one of those functions that have traditionally been left to the states, and for good reasons having to do with the virtues of allowing local institutions to address local problems.[50] Leaving a domain of lawmaking discretion to local institutions also has advantages for the nation as a whole.

Bringing Combined Resources to Bear on Social Problems

Although the federal government has vastly greater resources than do most states to devote to issues of national importance, it is not capable of devising and implementing a solution to every social problem. The states, too, have resources to bring to bear on local problems as they arise. Local police investigators, for example, generally uncover a great deal more useful information about auto accidents, train crashes, and motor boat incidents than the FRA and the Coast Guard glean in their occasional investigations of those events. The common law courts can draw on the resources of motivated advocates who hire experts and dig deeply into the facts, sometimes uncovering evidence that regulatees have not disclosed to the relevant federal agency. The results of these intense investigations are usually available for the agency to use in crafting future regulatory protections. At the same time, state common law courts take advantage of the resources that federal agencies devote to establishing regulatory requirements by admitting evidence of compliance and noncompliance with federal agency regulations to prove that a defendant did or did not comply with the common law standard of care.[51]

The Advantages of Local Knowledge

Because state governments are closer to local problems, many observers believe that state governmental institutions are in a better position to understand the conditions that give rise to those problems and, consequently, to come up with more effective solutions to those problems than federal agencies. Professor Robert Rabin alludes to "a feedback dimension" of the law that appears to function much more effectively at the state level. When the states experiment with bold changes in tort law, either through judicial modifications of tort law doctrine or through legislative reforms, the impact of these reforms on real people is usually more apparent as the local media focus on the stories of individual plaintiffs and defendants who have been affected by the changes. Poorly conceived changes are more easily corrected through legislative action and judicial modifications of common law doctrine at the local level than are mistakes written into national legislation and regulations, where the advocates of change must compete with thousands of other proponents of hundreds of other legislative agendas.[52]

States as Laboratories for Innovation

The Texas law that Governor George W. Bush signed in 1997 allowing plaintiffs denied treatment to sue HMOs was by all accounts functioning smoothly. Texans were by and large happy with that state's law, and there was no evidence of any increase in health care or insurance costs as a result of the state's enactment of the moderate statute. During the law's four-year lifespan, only about 1,300 people out of millions of patients had requested review of a coverage denial by the independent panels established by the law, and only seventeen of those reviews had resulted in lawsuits at the completion of the panel process. A representative of the Texas Association of Business and Chambers of Commerce had concluded that the independent review mechanism that the law established as the prelude to any lawsuit had "worked well." A lawyer for HMOs suggested that few lawsuits were being filed because "[t]hese cases are extremely expensive to prosecute." These initial assessments indicated that the state had come up with a new model for achieving corrective justice in the context of managed health care that worked.[53] The Texas experiment came to an abrupt end, however, when the Supreme Court held that the statute was preempted by the ERIS Act in the *Davilla* case discussed in Chapter 5.

In cautioning his friends at the outset of the New Deal against the temptation to solve the problems of the Great Depression by creating huge federal agencies to take over the functions traditionally played by the states, Justice Louis Brandeis observed that the states may serve as governmental "laboratories" for conducting "economic experiments" to test new ideas and innovative approaches to governing that may be useful to other states or even the national government "without risk to the rest of the country."[54] A 2006 report prepared under the direction of the National Academy of Public Administration reaffirmed Justice Brandeis's wisdom in concluding that "[w]ith 50 laboratories of democracy in the states, and a strong central government designed to focus on needs that transcend state borders, without getting bogged down in local issues, this system has been able to find ways to meet new public service needs as they have emerged over the centuries to challenge old practices that no longer work as well as they once did.[55]

Proponents of preemption note that experimentation is also possible at the federal level.[56] Since most federal experiments must take place within the highly ossified procedural context of federal rulemaking, however, state-level experimentation through judicial decisions in multiple venues is no doubt easier, and the innovative advantages of having fifty laboratories over a single one is hard to deny. The United States Chamber of Commerce further cautions that experiments can fail. When they do, "the effects of even a small minority of states' unduly stringent liability standards come to be felt by consumers in all states," because "[t]hey must either pay higher prices or lose the option to buy products that have been withdrawn from the market because potential liability costs or litigation expenses are simply too high."[57] To the extent that the opponents of preemption respond to the threat of such "spillovers" with the argument that common law does not greatly vary from state to state, that argument is, of course, somewhat inconsistent with the argument that the states are laboratories of innovation.

CONCLUSIONS

In the absence of an alternative federally established compensation regime, federal preemption of state common law claims denies the victims of defective products and negligently conducted activities any opportunity to obtain corrective justice. When Congress does explicitly decide to preempt common law claims without providing an alternative route to compensation, as it did in enacting the gun shield statute, it must have concluded either that outstanding corrective justice claims are bogus (e.g., that gun manufacturers and dealers are not responsible for the consequences of crimes of violence committed by others) or that the impact of denying legitimate claims to justice is outweighed by more important policy considerations (e.g., the importance of easy availability of firearms to suburban consumers). This is, of course, a judgment that Congress is free to make under the Supremacy Clause, and it can be reversed by subsequent Congresses if the politics of the issue change. It remains true, however, that Congress is usually persuaded not to adopt this extreme approach to common law preemption explicitly, even when it is vigorously advocated, as in the case of the proposed MTBE liability shield.

When a regulatory agency decides that its decision so clearly achieves the optimal mix of regulatory costs and consumer benefits that no variance is permissible, even to provide corrective justice to deserving victims, the legitimacy of the determination is automatically suspect for many reasons, not the least of which is the very real possibility that the upper level officials responsible for the decision have been captured by the regulated industries that thereby escape accountability at common law for the socially undesirable consequences of their products and activities. When a court encounters a preemption issue, its primary focus must be on congressional intent, but when Congress has not spoken clearly to the issue of common law preemption, courts must also weigh the policy arguments pro and con. The loss of corrective justice will probably play strongly in that mix, along with the general virtues of federalism and the backstop function of the common law. How courts should go about balancing the policy arguments and the weight that they should give to agency declarations in that process are the subjects of the second half of the next chapter.

Chapter 10 Ending the Preemption War

The preemption war has been raging for almost two decades, and it shows no signs of coming to an end any time soon. In fact, it is altogether possible that the best solution for society as a whole is for the war to continue unabated. There will always be horizontal tension between advocates of a strong state common law with a weak regulatory compliance defense and advocates of strong preemption of common law claims by weak regulatory requirements. Perhaps a "war without end" is exactly what society needs to ensure that legal decision makers are always exposed to both points of view. The description of the ongoing battles in Chapters 4–6 and the analysis of the arguments for and against preemption in Chapters 7–9, however, provide many reasons for concluding that some degree of de-escalation is in order and that the inevitable tension should be consciously channeled toward more socially desirable goals.

It is no doubt presumptuous to believe that academic analysis can bring about a peaceful resolution to the conflict, but history teaches that thoughtful analysis often precedes careful deliberation over serious social problems. Besides, academic analysis is the primary resource that academics can contribute to solving social problems. In the hope that successful deliberation will preempt the civil disobedience that is likely if the preemption war continues unabated, we will spend the remainder of this book exploring how the one institution that is capable of ending the hostilities, Congress, might go about approaching the task of de-escalation and how, pending congressional intervention, the courts should go about encouraging de-escalation in individual cases.

WHY CONGRESS SHOULD END THE WAR

Congress is the only institution that can bring an end to the preemption war, for the simple reason that Congress is the only institution with the power to preempt. Congress is well aware of that power and of the need to exercise it wisely. The congressional debates over the bills that have become the foundation for the modern regulatory state turned on both horizontal issues concerning the proper degree of governmental intervention into private sector arrangements and vertical issues concerning the proper roles of state and federal government in implementing and enforcing those interventions. Unfortunately, those debates rarely, if ever, featured any discussion in either the horizontal or the vertical dimensions of the degree to which state common law should be affected by federal regulatory programs. Indeed, Congress only very rarely reacts to important Supreme Court preemption decisions one way or the other.[1] The preemption war has now escalated to the level at which Congress can no longer ignore this important aspect of the federalism question.

The Supreme Court in *Cipollone* and subsequent opinions extending *Cipollone's* reasoning across numerous regulatory programs have made Congress acutely aware of the propensity of courts to interpret words like "requirement" in preemption clauses to include state common law claims, whether or not Congress had the common law in mind when it wrote those words. Justice Scalia made the point explicit when he observed in *Riegel* that "Congress is entitled to know what meaning this Court will assign to terms regularly used in its enactments" and that "[a]bsent other indication, reference to a State's 'requirements' includes its common-law duties."[2] Cases like *Geier* that go a step further than *Cipollone* to interpret statutes with and without express preemption clauses to impliedly preempt state common law claims reinforce the Court's message to Congress that it should pay careful attention to the common law when it writes preemption provisions and associated savings clauses into statutes if it wants to preserve its power to decide that issue. The terrible muddle that the lower courts have made of the law of preemption under the Fair Credit Reporting Act is a good example of the kind of mischief that results when Congress fails to address common law preemption. Congress is now clearly on notice of its responsibility to balance the relevant policy considerations for and against common law preemption every time it enacts a new regulatory program or revisits an existing regulatory program.

Having failed to address common law preemption in the past, Congress has an obligation to take up the preemption issue proactively outside the normal process of revisiting and revising federal regulatory statutes. The asymmetries discussed in Chapter 7 that ensure that ongoing regulatory programs will, over time, grow moribund and even work to the advantage of the regulated industries likewise ensure that the preemption war will, over time, continue to favor regulated entities over regulatory beneficiaries. The regulated industries are often few in number and always intensely affected by regulatory programs in a way that gives them every incentive to band together to push back against every threatened regulatory intrusion. The threat of common law liability provides precisely the same incentive to pool their resources and spend them in large quantities to eliminate that threat through regulatory preemption. The beneficiaries of regulatory programs and state common law are diverse and diffusely spread throughout the economy. The benefits of regulatory programs remain hidden in the subconscious expectations of ordinary citizens that the government's regulatory authorities are doing their jobs and that courts are available in the unlikely event that they are injured by some company's malfeasance. For most citizens, those expectations are challenged only by the rare media exposé showing undue influence by an industry over its putative overseer or portraying gross injustice at the hands of an apparently impersonal legal system.

As a result of these asymmetries, potential defendants are far more likely to prevail in any given preemption battle that takes place in the regulatory agencies. Furthermore, agencies have an inherent conflict of interest that renders their judgments suspect when the issue is whether to expand or contract the domain over which they are permitted to exercise their regulatory powers. The asymmetries are not nearly as great in judicial preemption battles, because the beneficiaries of the common law have already been injured and are therefore well aware of the cost to them of preemption, and their attorneys have powerful incentives to bring resources to bear on the preemption issue. The debates in the courts, however, only rarely ascend to the meta-level where policies for and against preemption of common law claims are articulated and balanced.

The courts are therefore in no position to resolve the broad issues of national policy that common law preemption raises.

The asymmetries are certainly relevant to preemption battles in Congress, and they probably work in favor of the proponents of preemption. The battles in Congress over the gun shield law demonstrate the capacity of a coalition of a regulated industry and a politically powerful interest group to change the law in the context of an institution that is moved not by testimony refined through legal principles but by the need to finance future campaigns and the fear of political retribution. The MTBE experience, however, demonstrates that consumer groups and plaintiffs' attorneys can participate very effectively on the congressional battlefield, at least when it comes to playing defense. The fate of the Patient's Bill of Rights suggests that it is more difficult for that coalition to win an offensive battle. Still, the congressional battlefield offers the possibility on any given day of a fair fight. Thus, in another of the many ironies of the preemption war, any attempt by Congress to end the war will simply bring the war to Congress. But that is where the war ultimately belongs.

The question still remains whether this should be a high congressional priority. There are, of course, solid practical reasons to suggest that Congress should resolve the preemption problem sooner, rather than later. Because the law of preemption is cloudy but outcome-determinative, it behooves every defendant to raise the preemption defense in any case in which it plausibly applies. The war in the courts over ambiguous preemption clauses and implied preemption doctrine has therefore drained the limited resources of the civil justice system. It has also diverted the attention and the limited resources of the agencies to a matter of marginal relevance to their protective responsibilities, deprived them of the investigational resources of the plaintiffs' bar, and threatened the backstop that the common law's protective justice function provides for all-too-frequent occasions of regulatory failure.

The preemption war demands immediate congressional attention, however, for a much more powerful moral reason. Because the war has thus far gone very poorly for plaintiffs, it is taking a tremendous toll on the common law's capacity to provide corrective justice to the innocent victims of defective products, negligent activities, and fraudulent business practices that is only now becoming fully apparent. The undeniable injustice that has inadvertently resulted from piecemeal judicial resolution of the preemption issue and related corrective justice issues under the ERIS Act is just one of many reasons that congressional intervention is needed. That issue was once at the top of the congressional agenda and would no doubt have been resolved at that time if Congress had not been required to devote its exclusive attention to even more pressing matters in the aftermath of the September 11 attacks on the World Trade Center and the Pentagon. While a civil society can tolerate a certain degree of injustice, the civility begins to erode when the level of injustice exceeds the fuzzy threshold that causes the victims to abandon the civil justice system to pursue civil disobedience or even less civil alternatives. We have not yet crossed the fairly high threshold of tolerance for injustice that has traditionally existed in the United States, but we will arrive there at some point soon if the preemption war continues to trend in a consistently favorable direction for the business community. To avoid the social turmoil that will ensue when that happens, it behooves Congress to address the problem expeditiously.

Assuming that Congress will recognize its responsibility to bring about a reduction in hostilities, there remains the strategic question of whether Congress should go about addressing the preemption war all at once in an omnibus common law preemption bill or in a piecemeal fashion by taking up potentially preemptive programs one by one over some extended period of time. As desirable as it might be in theory, Congress cannot as a practical matter resolve the problem generically in one giant battle royal over an omnibus regulatory preemption bill. The MTBE and the Patients' Bill of Rights experiences demonstrate that it is easy enough for a determined opposition to derail a bill containing a controversial preemption provision even in the context of a single regulatory program. It is difficult to imagine that Congress could resolve the issue generically in a way that would command a sufficient degree of consensus to permit the enactment of an omnibus bill. More important, it is by no means clear that Congress *should* resolve the war generically by articulating an overall policy in favor of or against preemption in all cases because it is almost certainly the case that neither side is entitled to a complete victory.

WHY NEITHER SIDE SHOULD WIN THE WAR

In some regulatory contexts, preemption is clearly desirable. When Congress has created a regulatory agency to provide adequate *ex ante* protections and a compensation regime to provide a reasonable measure of corrective justice, it may be sensible to preempt attempts to circumvent the comprehensive federal program through state common law actions. Likewise, when a federal agency is providing adequate *ex ante* protection, public litigation by governmental entities and interest groups seeking broad injunctive relief rather than corrective justice for particular individuals may appropriately be preempted as an attempt to achieve "regulation through litigation." In both cases, the standard for "adequacy" of the *ex ante* protection afforded by federal agencies cannot be perfection, but it should demand considerably more than benign neglect.

In most cases, however, the question will be less clear-cut, and the answer will depend upon a careful balancing of several competing considerations.[3] Even programs that appear at first glance to be obvious candidates for preemption may appear less so on closer scrutiny. For example, the "adequacy" of the federal regulatory program in providing *ex ante* protection is, to a large degree, an empirical question that requires careful analysis and may have to be revisited periodically. Because the law of federal agency preemption is quite muddled, judicial resolution of the preemption question rarely reflects a careful balancing of relevant criteria. It is therefore incumbent on Congress to balance those criteria in the context of each important regulatory program.

We have seen in the preceding three chapters that both sides bring sound institutional and policy arguments to the debate. We may now draw on those policy arguments to articulate and elaborate briefly upon a set of generic criteria that Congress might apply in resolving the preemption issue in particular regulatory contexts. Since it is highly unlikely that even members of the relevant congressional committees will have the time to engage in heavily nuanced balancing of abstract criteria, we will also explore some "rules of thumb" to simplify the analysis in the context of individual programs.

CRITERIA FOR DECIDING WHEN TO PREEMPT

According to the National Academy of Public Administration (NAPA), the decision whether to preempt state law presents a challenge for Congress, because it "has little or no access to independent analysis of proposals to create new uniform national standards and the resulting adverse impacts that such standards may have on state and local governments." Consequently, "preemptions are being enacted more as a result of political pressures than as a result of balanced analyses of competing needs."[4] The preemption battle over firearms litigation, MTBE, and the Patients' Bill of Rights described in Chapter 5 vouch for the accuracy of NAPA's assessment. While much of the "independent analysis" that the NAPA report recommends must come on a case-by-case basis as Congress takes up individual bills, the criteria described here may provide some general guidance for Congress and the agencies as they contemplate the desirability of allowing federal regulatory requirements to preempt state common law claims.

Conflict Avoidance

The most powerful policy reason for preempting any state law is the potential for conflict between that law and federal law. In fact, this policy is so powerful that the Supreme Court long ago concluded that Congress could not possibly have ignored it and must, instead, have implicitly intended that it come into play in every situation with a potential for conflict.[5] The Supreme Court recognized that conflict comes in two varieties. First, two bodies of law may impose conflicting obligations on those who are subject to them. Thus, a state law that requires a person to take an action that violates a federal regulation presents a conflict that renders compliance with both impossible. A common law claim for damages would present such a direct and forceful conflict only in the difficult-to-imagine scenario in which a federal regulation prohibited a company from paying damages to an injured plaintiff. Common law injunctive relief, on the other hand, could easily bring about such a direct conflict.[6] Second, the two bodies of law may be at cross purposes, as when compliance with state law would present an obstacle to achieving an important policy underlying a federal regulation. We saw in Chapter 4 that lower courts have frequently concluded that compliance with common law duties that form the basis for tort claims would defeat an important federal policy, and we learned that those cases are often difficult to reconcile with one another. We also saw that conflict avoidance is an exceedingly difficult criterion to apply in a principled way.

The underlying message of the Supreme Court's conflict preemption cases is that policy conflict between the state and the federal systems is ordinarily an undesirable thing and should be avoided, all other things being equal. Since other things are rarely equal and since principled application of the conflict avoidance criterion is very difficult, it should not be the only, or even the dominant, consideration when Congress takes up preemption legislation. It should, however, command careful legislative attention.

- Congress should consider the extent to which state common law relief will conflict with federal regulatory requirements either because compliance with both will be impossible or because compliance with state common law duties will stand as an obstacle to the accomplishment of important federal objectives.

Corrective Justice

Because corrective justice is the primary function of the common law of torts, it is obviously an important consideration in the preemption policy balance.

When Congress decides to preempt common law without providing an alternative compensation vehicle, it is depriving the beneficiaries of the preempting regulatory program of something most American citizens highly value—access to a neutral judicial forum that has the power to shift the victim's loss to the tortfeasor who caused it. Before it deprives deserving citizens of their day in court, Congress should be very confident that the regulatory agency is performing its job exceedingly well, that the claims that it is preempting are exceedingly weak, or that allowing the claims to go forward will seriously impede the attainment of some other highly valuable federal policy.

The corrective justice consideration is, however, especially sensitive to the remedy sought. Corrective justice is not particularly well served by injunctive relief. Like agency regulations and permit requirements, the purpose of injunctive relief is to prevent future harm and thereby to avoid the need to compensate those who would be harmed in the absence of the relief. Like regulatory requirements, injunctive relief is typically not absolute in nature. In the regulatory arena, some potentially damaging activities are allowed to proceed because the risks they pose fall below some threshold of acceptability, because the regulatee has done the best that it can to reduce those risks, or because the benefits to society of the permitted activities outweigh their potential for harm. In the case of injunctive relief, the court is required to "balance the equities" in deciding whether to afford relief. Thus, corrective justice may to some extent be served by the *ex ante* protection afforded by injunctive relief, but it is rarely fully served by that relief. Compliance with injunctive relief, like compliance with regulatory requirements, may leave deserving victims uncompensated.

- Congress should consider the extent to which preemption will deprive persons harmed by the products or activities regulated by the federal program of compensation for their loss.

Institutional Competence

The primary advantage that regulatory agencies have over state common law is the expertise that they can bring to bear on the scientific and technical issues. Jurors can become confused or bored by complex presentations, and they may be more easily swayed than agency experts by irrelevant unscientific considerations. At the same time, agencies are far from omniscient, and the available empirical evidence suggests that juries are quite capable of comprehending complex scientific and technical issues objectively with the help of judge-screened experts. Moreover, for many issues that commonly arise before both agencies and courts, expertise is not really necessary or even especially helpful. A juror may be just as competent to judge whether a warning is likely to be heeded by an ordinary consumer as an agency expert. Agencies also develop a policymaking expertise that gives them a clear advantage over courts in addressing major issues of national policy of the sort that "public interest litigation" is aimed at resolving. That form of expertise is, however, less relevant to issues related to the risks of individual products and localized activities. Thus, the advantages of both technical and policymaking expertise are quite context-dependent.

Common law courts have institutional advantages over federal agencies that should also be weighed in the balance. Perhaps the strongest institutional advantage of common law litigation is its ability to squeeze information out of company files and to tease it out of company employees in depositions. That advantage, however, should be discounted to the extent that secrecy agreements are likely to keep such information out of the public domain. Courts are also better adapted than agencies to respond rapidly to developments in the real world as new information on the hazards of products and activities becomes available. Finally, courts are far less subject to capture, manipulation, and political pressure than federal agencies. Again, the institutional advantages of the common law are context-dependent.

- Congress should consider the extent to which regulatory agencies and court-managed juries have institutional advantages in resolving the particular substantive issues most frequently addressed by the relevant federal statute.

Institutional Capacity

The institutional advantages of either a court or an agency should be discounted to the extent that either one lacks the authority or the resources to use those advantages effectively. Congress ordinarily grants regulatory agencies rather broad-ranging authority within their regulatory domains, but occasionally agencies discover gaps in their authority or grey areas that are sufficiently worrisome that the agencies are reluctant to test it. Neither of these possibilities will discourage defendants (and even occasionally the agency itself) from claiming that agency requirements preempt state common law claims. Congress should be aware of this when it decides whether to write an express preemption provision into a statute and, when it does, in drafting the substantive provisions of the statute that will have preemptive force.

Since at least David Stockman's stint as head of the Office of Management and Budget during the Reagan administration, most federal regulatory agencies have been chronically starved for resources. As a practical matter, the promise that they offer to bring both technical and policymaking expertise to bear on issues that are also frequently litigated in common law courts may be a hollow one. At the same time, the parties to litigation can often bring considerable resources to bear on particular technical issues in high-stakes litigation where millions of dollars may change hands. The results of those efforts will often be available to the agencies as well as the courts.

- Congress should consider the extent to which the implementing agency has sufficient statutory authority and adequate resources to warrant displacing the capacity of common law litigation to bring resources effectively to bear on the relevant issues.

Agency Performance

The best measure of the likelihood that an agency will in fact take advantage of its institutional advantages is the agency's demonstrated ability to bring those advantages to bear on real-world problems in the past. Relevant considerations in this regard are the time it takes an agency to react to an identified problem and to implement a solution, evidence of agency captivity, and the general satisfaction (or lack thereof) on the part of the agency's beneficiaries with the agency's performance on the issues for which preemption is an option. Congress has created an institution to undertake just these sorts of evaluations. The Government Accountability Office (GAO) conducts hundreds of investigations into various aspects of agency performance every year, and GAO officials routinely bring their findings to the attention of congressional committees in testimony and in detailed reports.

The common law's protective justice function allows courts to play a valuable "backstop" role when agencies fail to provide the degree of protection envisioned by their authorizing statutes. The threat of common law liability provides incentives for regulatees to take protective action when evolving practices and technologies create unanticipated gaps in the coverage of regulations and permit requirements that are difficult for agencies to fill on a short-term basis. It also provides a disincentive to engage in artful schemes to avoid the reach of regulatory requirements. Finally, by providing a procedural advantage to plaintiffs who can show that their harm was caused by violations of regulatory requirements, common law litigation can assist agency enforcers in their compliance assurance efforts.

• Congress should consider the past regulatory performance of the relevant agency, the likelihood of poor regulatory performance in the future, and the extent to which the prospect of common law liability will advance the policies underlying the relevant federal statute.

Marketplace Efficiency and Technological Innovation

Inconsistency in legal requirements can result in inefficiency in production and marketing. For some businesses that operate in interstate commerce, complying with the requirements of a single regulatory agency, however stringent, is far more efficient than complying with requirements that vary from state to state. However, policymakers should be wary of unsupported claims based on the asserted need for uniformity when the preemption argument is directed to state common law, as opposed to state regulatory requirements. The uniformity argument has some salience in the context of labeling and similar areas where federal regulatory requirements are quite specific and inflexible. In most areas of federal regulation, where design and performance standards are far more common than specification standards, the uniformity argument should carry little weight unless supported by specific data and analysis.

The uncertainties caused by the inevitable variability of jury awards also detract from market efficiency, at least to the extent that they exceed the already existing uncertainties caused by the circuitous path that important regulations often take through the federal regulatory process and associated judicial review. The same uncertainties combine with the generally greater responsiveness of the common law to provide offsetting incentives to invest in safety technologies that should also weigh in the balance. The prospect of common law liability may cause regulatees to "overinvest" in safety to the detriment of useful products. To the extent that the amount invested in safety exceeds the value of the lives saved and damage caused discounted by the probability that damage will in fact occur, this "overdeterrence" is economically inefficient. This is of concern, however, only in regulatory contexts in which Congress has also decided to require the regulatory agency to employ a cost-benefit balancing approach in determining regulatory requirements. To the extent that Congress elects more precautionary approaches, like those based upon feasibility or margins of safety, the added deterrent function of the common law may, in fact, be more consistent with congressional policy than strict compliance with regulatory requirements.

- Congress should consider the extent to which potentially inconsistent or conflicting state common law rules will increase costs of production and deter beneficial economic activity without corresponding benefits to consumers and potential victims.

Federalism

The states have historically played the dominant role in protecting consumers and other victims of harmful business practices and activities. In some important areas, like environmental protection, that dominance has been displaced by that of federal agencies administering the landmark legislation of the 1960s and 1970s. Even in these areas, however, the states have retained a prominent role at the implementation phase. In other areas, like consumer protection generally, the states remain the dominant institutional actors. And state courts have traditionally been the dominant institutions for providing corrective justice and protective justice to American citizens. For issues in which local knowledge is important in crafting general rules and regulatory requirements, state courts and agencies may be the more desirable regulatory institutions, because they are closer to local problems. And, since "regulatory wisdom does not reside exclusively in federal agencies," the experiments with lawmaking that are constantly going on in the fifty states can benefit the nation as a whole.[7] In all of these areas, the combined resources of state courts and federal agencies can usually accomplish more than either one operating independently.

- Congress should consider the values underlying our federal system of government.

Administrative Efficiency

Although cooperation is a desirable norm, there will be occasions in which state courts and federal regulatory agencies may work at cross-purposes. When Congress identifies an area of federal regulation in which judicial resolution of common law claims will routinely and seriously interfere with the ability of agencies to implement and enforce federal statutes, it should consider preempting the state court litigation. At the same time, it should pay attention to how it can preserve the comparative advantages of the two institutions and the potential for mutual reinforcement by considering nuanced approaches like preempting only injunctive relief, which is more likely to interfere with federal agency implementation efforts.

- Congress should consider the extent to which potentially conflicting common law judgments will hamper the administration of important federal consumer protection programs.

Delegation to Agencies

One question that Congress has rarely answered when it has drafted preemption provisions is whether it should delegate the power to preempt to federal agencies along with the power to promulgate the substantive and procedural rules and regulations that are necessary to carry out federal regulatory programs. The power to preempt state common law involves two issues that have traditionally been of high political importance in this country—the allocation of power between the federal government and state governments and the allocation of power between the Executive Branch and the judiciary. The questions are ordinarily of sufficient importance that Congress should bear the exclusive responsibility for resolving them. Since the legitimacy of a federal bureaucracy's expanding its "turf" by denying state courts the power to dispense corrective justice will always be open to serious question, Congress should be very reluctant to delegate this important power to resolve these critical issues. And since agencies and courts may be inclined to assume that the power to preempt is implicit in general grants or rulemaking power, Congress should explicitly state in every regulatory statute whether or not it means to delegate the decision to preempt.

- Congress should rarely delegate the power to preempt to a federal regulatory agency. When Congress does intend to delegate that power, it should make that intention clear in the text of the statute.

RULES OF THUMB FOR THE BALANCING PROCESS

Congress should always pay attention to the preemption question when it writes federal regulatory statutes. Some of the older statutes, like the FDC Act, that were enacted prior to the advent of the modern administrative state, fail to mention preemption at all. Most of the modern consumer and environmental statutes do address preemption of state laws and regulations, but they were enacted before the Supreme Court's 1991 *Cipollone* opinion set off the preemption war and therefore fail to articulate congressional intent with respect to federal agency preemption of state common law claims. The result is a hodge-podge of lawmaking on this critical issue by courts and agencies as the preemption war rages on beneath the congressional radar. When it does claim congressional attention, the common law preemption issue tends to come up in the context of controversial substantive debates brought on by highly visible litigation, like the MTBE and firearms litigation or the Supreme Court's ERIS Act opinions.

Congress is the only institution that is capable of reducing the preemption war's current level of intensity, and it can do that only by revisiting previously enacted statutes one by one. Because the preemption issue itself lacks a high degree of political salience, persuading Congress to undertake this highly desirable task will not be easy. At both the horizontal and the vertical levels, the politics of preemption are inherently "wonkish" and therefore uninteresting to individual citizens who have not been directly affected by some aspect of the preemption war. Nevertheless, Congress has an obligation as the policymaker-in-chief on the preemption question to take it up every time a federal regulatory statute comes up for reauthorization or revision and, if necessary, to resolve it in individual bills addressed exclusively to common law preemption. Since it is nearly always easier to block legislation than to pass it, the legislative process is already structured to favor the status quo. Congress must overcome that de facto presumption in favor of current arrangements if it is to bring about a reduction in hostilities in the preemption war.

When Congress does take up the common law preemption question, it should engage in a careful balancing of the relevant criteria, including those identified in the previous section. It should carefully consider these criteria in the context of the relevant substantive aspects of the regulatory regime, the policies advanced by relevant common law claims, and the three primary forms of common law relief—injunctive relief to prevent future harm, compensation for past harm, and punitive damages. Because it is unrealistic to expect that any individual congressperson or relevant staff assistant will spend the time necessary to become intimately familiar with all of these relevant aspects of the preemption problem, the following rules of thumb may simplify the analysis. Like any guidelines, these rules of thumb are necessarily broad and thinly nuanced. They also reflect the criteria and analyses in this book and undoubtedly incorporate the author's own policy preferences to some degree. For that reason, the reader should take them with the appropriate grains of salt.

Congress should make its intent crystal clear.

Perhaps the clearest lesson of the preemption war in the courts is that when Congress means to preserve the corrective justice function of the common law, it must make that intention very clear. Although the "presumption against preemption" that the courts say they apply in addressing preemption claims should reduce the need for Congress to speak clearly to the question of common law preemption, it does not work out that way in the real world. The lower courts tend to honor that hortatory prescription in the breach as they become absorbed in the details of the regulatory program and the parties' predictions about how the indirect incentives provided by the common law's protective justice function may or may not interfere with the attainment of the program's overall goals. The highly confused state of the law governing preemption under the Fair Credit Reporting Act, for example, resulted from the fact that Congress inadvertently used the terms "requirement or prohibition" in the preemption provision that it added in 1996 to 1970 legislation that had already addressed preemption of common law claims. At the very least, Congress should not use words like "requirement" in express preemption provisions without making it crystal clear whether or not it means to preempt state common law claims. It can easily accomplish this by adding words like "or common law claim" when it intends to preempt such claims. When it does not mean to preempt such claims, it can make that intent crystal clear by adding an explicit common law proviso to the relevant preemption provision.

Congress should apply a presumption against preemption.

The National Academy of Public Administration's report on preemption concluded that "federal preemption should be used as seldom as possible, and only as a last resort."[8] Before allowing regulatory agencies to intrude so deeply into such an intensely local matter as the evolution of common law norms, depriving consumers of corrective justice and rejecting the resources that motivated attorneys can bring to factual investigations, Congress should be very confident that the agencies themselves have sufficient resources to keep up with the constant flow of information, adapt to changing circumstances, investigate abuse, and otherwise provide adequate protection.[9] And Congress should never avoid the due deliberation and debate that the preemption issue deserves by passing preemptive legislation in the dead of night as an appropriations rider, as it did with the PREP Act.

Congress should not allow federal minimum standards to preempt common law duties.

Most regulatory agencies are in the business of promulgating "minimum" across-the-board requirements that apply to all regulated entities in all anticipated situations, absent a demonstrated need for an exception or "variance." Such standards are frequently "feasibility-based" and intended merely to "bring the laggards up to speed." They do not generally represent the considered judgment of an expert agency on the optimal protective action that regulatees should take in individual situations. In this connection, Judge Richard Posner, a widely published proponent of the "Chicago School" of law and economics, observes that "minimum is not a synonym for optimum, or even adequate."[10] Common law courts typically allow defendants to present testimony that they have complied with minimum regulatory standards as evidence of reasonable care, but such evidence is never conclusive on the matter.

Congress should not take away a plaintiff's right to prove that the defendant's compliance with minimum federal requirements, which may have been promulgated decades ago by an agency that was "captured" by the regulated industry, did not necessarily satisfy the defendant's common law duties. For example, neither the minimum standard for train speeds in the *Easterwood* case nor the minimum standard requiring passive "crossbuck" signs at issue in *Shanklin* were designed to address every conceivable hazard that might arise at a railroad grade crossing. Even with virtually infinite resources at its disposal, the FRA could not possibly have envisioned every possible way that an automobile, bus, or truck might be put at risk at a grade crossing. Allocating responsibility for accidents of this irregular nature must be based upon a case-by-case assessment of the relevant risks and the technologies and avoidance measures available to reduce those risks. The protective justice function of the common law of torts provides an important incentive needed to ensure that the relevant actors do not shirk their responsibility to avoid such accidents. The Supreme Court in those cases held that the common law claims were preempted because they came within the meaning of the words "law, rule, regulation, order or standard" in the FRS Act's preemption provision.[11] Under the rule of thumb suggested here, Congress should revisit that provision to clarify that it was not intended to include state common law claims.

Congress should not preempt claims based upon fraud on the regulatory agency. The case against preemption is especially powerful when the plaintiff is prepared to prove that the regulatee manipulated the regulatory process to obtain a permit or product approval or to secure a more lenient regulatory requirement. In such cases, the regulatory process has demonstrably failed, and common law litigation can offer invaluable assistance to the agency staff in identifying the causes of that failure. Even some of the strongest proponents of preemption and the related "regulatory compliance" defense acknowledge the need for an exception for fraud on the agency.[12] The Supreme Court in *Buckman* nevertheless relied on the "delicate balance of statutory objectives" that the FDA had to strike in deciding whether or not to investigate and punish fraud to hold that the plaintiff's fraud on the agency claim was impliedly preempted.[13] Yet the remote possibility that a common law action might somehow interfere with the agency's prosecutorial discretion is rarely a good reason for preempting fraud on the agency claims. In many cases in which fraud on the agency is detected in common law litigation, the agency would not have known it had anything to prosecute but for the litigation. In any event, the common law claim is by no means a prosecution for the crime of fraud; it is merely an attempt by someone who has suffered foreseeable damage as a direct consequence of wrongdoing to obtain corrective justice from the wrongdoer. Because the lower courts have extended *Buckman* far beyond its limited facts, congressional intervention is much needed in this critical area.

Congress should generally not preempt state common law without substituting a federal corrective justice regime.

A federal regulatory regime is an adequate substitute for a common law regime only when the regulatory requirements are no less stringent than necessary to meet the social optimum, the requirements are perfectly enforced, and there are no sound reasons for spreading risk irrespective of fault. Only in such situations will the regulatory protections eliminate all future judicially recognizable damage claims. In any scenario in which these conditions do not hold, preemption will deprive deserving plaintiffs of legitimate demands for corrective justice. When Congress determines after due deliberation that the common law has become ineffective, inefficient, or otherwise counterproductive in a particular substantive area, preemption may be the only solution. But corrective justice is too important to a civilized society to be cast aside lightly in a hasty reaction to a perceived abuse of the common law process. Congress should therefore never preempt the common law without considering alternative vehicles for providing corrective justice to injured citizens. A number of models are available to provide corrective justice to deserving plaintiffs, including those provided by the Federal Employees Liability Act,[14] the National Childhood Vaccination Injury Act,[15] the Price-Anderson Act,[16] and the September 11 Victim Compensation Fund,[17] discussed in Chapter 3. Only when the preempted claims are not likely to achieve corrective justice at all (as, for example, in the case of the "public interest" firearms litigation) should Congress preempt state common law without providing any alternative forum.

RULES OF THUMB FOR JUDICIAL REVIEW OF AGENCY PREEMPTION

Although Congress must take the lead in ending the preemption war, the courts will also have an important role to play in interpreting past and future federal statutes establishing federal regulatory programs. The Supreme Court's primary responsibility must therefore be to articulate a clear set of principles to guide the lower courts in resolving individual cases and to communicate to

Congress how they will interpret future language aimed at resolving the preemption question in the context of state common law claims. Although the courts should not abandon the presumption against preemption in slavish adherence to regulatory agency assertions of preemptive power in amicus curiae briefs and preambles to regulations, they should do more that articulate hortatory phrases that can easily be circumvented by judges with their own policy agendas. At this point, it is fair to conclude that the Court has failed miserably in this regard.

With the Court's *Cipollone* holding that the word "requirement" could include state common law claims, corporate defendants launched a 15-year offensive aimed at sidestepping common law duties in favor of more lenient (or nonexistent) regulatory measures. It seemed for a very brief time that the Court's *Bates* opinion might be a clear signal to the lower courts to preserve the power of the states to provide corrective justice to their citizens. The Court, in *Bates,* recognized that the word "requirement" may include state common law claims but held that that does not end the inquiry. A court must still determine "whether the common law duties imposed by state law are sufficiently direct and prescriptive to constitute 'requirements,'" and the history of state tort law prior to the statute's enactment is relevant to this inquiry.[18] The *Bates* opinion suggested that lower courts had been misreading *Cipollone* to require a preemption finding every time a statute uses the word "requirement." The attitude toward preemption that pervades *that opinion* further counseled caution about expansive applications of implied preemption doctrine to state common law claims. But Justice Scalia's dicta in *Riegel* explicitly told Congress that when it uses the word "requirement" in an express preemption clause, the Court will interpret the clause to include state common law claims. And the opinion exudes a hostility to state common law that is fully consistent with aggressive use of implied preemption to preclude state common law claims. Given the erratic state of current Supreme Court jurisprudence in this critical area, the lower courts may be excused for feeling a bit whipsawed. For the same reason, the following suggested "rules of thumb" for the courts to employ in this analysis should be read more as recommendations than as restatements of the law with the same caveats as the rules of thumb previously suggested for Congress.

Claims based on violations of federal law are rarely preempted.

When the defendant's conduct violates a federal requirement in a statute or regulation, the plaintiff's claim based upon an alleged violation of a parallel common law duty complements federal law. State common law claims not only reach violations that government officials fail to detect but also pinpoint the violations that are arguably most deserving of prosecution because they have caused actual damage to protected citizens. Furthermore, the prospect of common law liability should provide additional encouragement to potential violators to comply with the federal requirements in the first place. The Supreme Court has on many occasions recognized the valuable reinforcing role that the common law plays in achieving compliance with federal regulatory requirements.[19]

Some plaintiffs' attorneys will, of course, attempt to take a free ride on the federal prosecution with parallel civil claims that rely upon the government to do all of the work, but such cases are not likely to impede the efficiency with which federal prosecutors go about their tasks, and they often produce additional information and evidence that the federal officials either overlooked or were not provided. Far more often, as we have seen, the common law action predates the federal prosecution, often by years, and it is the federal prosecutors who rely upon the prior work of the private attorneys. The only serious countervailing policy is the frequently overstated concern for "overdeterrence." The common law courts, however, can adequately address this concern through standard "negligence per se" doctrine, which allows a defendant to escape liability by demonstrating that it acted reasonably in the circumstances.

Only when an express preemption clause makes it very clear that Congress did not mean for any common law claims at all to survive should the courts dismiss on preemption grounds common law claims that allege violations of federal requirements.

Field preemption is ordinarily irrelevant to common law damage claims.

When Congress clearly expresses an intent to "occupy a given field, any state law falling within that field is pre-empted."[20] The doctrine of field preemption has appeared only rarely in the preceding pages, where we learned that the Supreme Court has thus far limited field preemption of common law claims to the fields of labor-management relations, employee benefits, and nuclear power regulation. The Court is "even more reluctant to infer [field] preemption from the comprehensiveness of regulations than from the comprehensiveness of statutes,"[21] and it specifically declined to do so in the context of motor boats in the *Sprietsma* case.[22] The doctrine of field preemption is therefore largely irrelevant to the issue of federal agency preemption of state common law damage claims for the simple reason that the "field" encompassed by regulation (protecting citizens from future harm) does not ordinarily include corrective justice. Even when Congress has provided an alternative route to corrective justice, the Supreme Court has been reluctant to conclude that it meant to preempt common law claims that go beyond the federal remedial program.[23] This rule of thumb merely recognizes that fact and cautions the courts against expanding the role of field preemption beyond its current narrow confines.

Do not presume that Congress meant to preempt when it did not say so.

Since congressional intent is the "touchstone" of preemption analysis, many legal scholars have recommended that the courts replace the judge-made doctrine of implied preemption with a "plain statement rule" for federal preemption of state statutes, regulations, and common law claims. Under this altogether sensible suggestion, no state common law claims would be preempted unless Congress unambiguously mandated preemption of such claims in an express preemption provision in the relevant statute.[24] A bright-line rule would prevent courts from engaging in a "freewheeling judicial inquiry" into statutory goals and agency implementation techniques in cases where Congress has given no indication in the language of the statute itself that it means for agency action to preempt state common law.[25] More important, it would discourage judges from insinuating their own policy preferences into the preemption inquiry. Finally, it would encourage Congress to speak more clearly to the issue of common law preemption when it really does mean to preempt.[26]

If the courts decline to adopt a plain-statement rule, they should abandon the "obstacle preemption" branch of implied preemption doctrine under which state law is preempted if it "stands as an obstacle to the accomplishment of the full purposes and objectives of Congress," at least in the context of state common law claims.[27] This ill-defined doctrine gives courts virtually boundless discretion to engage in an exercise of "imaginative reconstruction" in which they mine the hortatory statements of congressional purpose at the beginning of regulatory statutes for some indication of a congressional goal other than safety that might be impeded if common law claims are allowed to proceed.[28] Under the obstacle preemption doctrine, the courts are not limited to the statute's primary purpose, which is usually precautionary in nature, but can range even beyond the language of the statute to rely on concepts like the asserted need for agencies to strike a "delicate balance of statutory objectives."[29] Scholars across the political spectrum have criticized the flimsy theoretical basis for and the unconstrained reach of obstacle preemption doctrine.[30] The courts should abandon it altogether in cases where the issue is whether federal regulatory requirements preempt state common law claims.

Give effect to savings clauses.

At the very least, the courts should give effect to congressional intent by refraining from finding that a federal regulatory statute impliedly preempts state common law claims when Congress has gone to the trouble of enacting a savings clause providing that the statute does not expressly preempt such claims. The Supreme Court went astray in *Geier* when it held that common law claims could still be impliedly preempted under a statute that contained an express preemption provision for state and local laws and regulations and a savings clause for state common law claims. There is simply no reason, other than an uncritical devotion to the confusing and often inconsistent body of judge-made law on implied preemption, to consider what Congress *may* have intended to accomplish when a savings clause provides direct evidence of what Congress *did* in fact mean to accomplish.[31]

An agency failure to regulate should never preempt a common law claim.

Defendants have frequently urged courts to find implied preemption in cases in which an agency has considered but declined to impose regulatory restrictions on the product or activity that allegedly caused the plaintiff's harm, on the theory that the plaintiff's claim would stand as an obstacle to an implied congressional intent not to regulate that product or activity. This argument relies on an implication built upon an implication. First, the court must infer that Congress meant to delegate the decision whether to preempt to the agency. Second, the court must infer from the agency's failure to regulate that the agency concluded that the product or activity should not be constrained by government in any way. The first inference is always questionable, and especially dubious in the context of a statute containing a savings clause. The second inference is usually simply wrong. Indeed, it is so preposterous that even the preemption-friendly George W. Bush administration argued in an amicus curiae brief in the *Sprietsma* litigation that "the mere fact that the agency has made a considered decision to forgo federal regulation does not, in and of itself, give rise to an inference that all state law on the subject—including state tort law—is meant to be preempted."[32] The Court in that case agreed that the plaintiff's defective design claims were not preempted by the Coast Guard's decision not to require propeller protectors. The courts should continue to apply this sensible rule of thumb.

Minimum federal standards should not preempt state common law claims.

A feasibility- or risk-based federal health or environmental standard does not conflict with state claims based upon a common law standard of care that calls upon the defendant to rise above the minimum when a reasonable person in the defendant's position would do so. The rule of thumb that minimum federal standards do not preempt common law claims is a sensible one that recognizes the reality of regulatory failure while at the same time ensuring that regulatees provide the minimum amount of protection required by federal law.[33]

Specification standards are more preemptive than design or performance standards.

Although most federal regulatory requirements are design- or performance-based and therefore typically allow regulatees to choose from among a wide variety of compliance options, some fairly rare federally imposed restrictions are "specification" standards that give regulatees very little discretion at all. For the latter standards, the common law plaintiff's contention that the defendant should have behaved differently runs up against the reality that doing things differently would require the defendant to violate a federally imposed regulatory requirement. Not only would it be unfair for the court to order the defendant to pay damages, but it would also fail to advance corrective justice goals because a defendant that has no choice is ordinarily not viewed by the law as a wrongdoer. In applying this rule of thumb, however, the courts should understand that mere federal acquiescence in a particular practice or technology is not the same as a federal requirement.[34]

Failure-to-warn claims are more suspect than defective design and negligence claims.

When a federal regulatory program requires products to contain federally approved warnings on product labels, it is typically a violation of federal law for the label to vary from the federal requirement with respect to those warnings. Although the agencies generally give regulatees considerable leeway in amending previously approved labels, it remains the case that labeling requirements are often more like specification standards than performance standards. Unless the defendant can demonstrate that the agency would reject a more protective warning if it applied for a label change, a federally approved label should not automatically preempt common law failure to warn claims. When the agency has recently rejected a manufacturer's submission of a more stringent warning or the defendant clearly and convincingly demonstrates that the agency would reject it on the ground that it is inaccurate or unnecessary or would unduly deter the use of valuable products, the manufacturer does not have the legal option to adopt that warning, even if a jury subsequently finds it to be more effective under state common law.[35] Although such cases do not produce an absolute conflict between state and federal law, because the manufacturer has the option of complying with federal law and paying damages, it is nevertheless a situation in which preemption makes sense.

Damage claims are less suspect than claims for injunctive relief.

Most common law claims directed toward federally regulated products and activities are claims by injured plaintiffs for compensation for the losses that they have suffered. The Supreme Court has noted that "[t]he primarily private nature of claims for damages under state law . . . distinguishes them in a measure from the public nature of the regulation of future" activities.[36] Common law courts very rarely, if ever, order individual defendants to take any specific action other than to pay compensation to the victims of their defective products and unlawful activities.[37] When they do, the distinction between the common law and federal regulation begins to fade, because injunctive relief can look very much like a requirement imposed prospectively in a federal regulation or permit. And when plaintiffs seek broad injunctive relief against multiple defendants encompassing a significant portion of the relevant activity, the distinction disappears entirely. In such cases, the legitimacy of the judicial intervention in the face of an ongoing federal regulatory program is open to serious question.[38] Although the courts should still pay careful attention to the statutory language and to the overall purpose of the agency's statute, it should be easier for a defendant to rebut the presumption against preemption in cases raising claims for injunctive relief.

THE PROPER SCOPE OF JUDICIAL DEFERENCE TO AGENCY PREEMPTION DETERMINATIONS

The rules of thumb suggested here should guide the courts in the typical case where the agency has not expressed a view on the question whether its actions should preempt state common law claims. We saw in Chapter 6, however, that during the George W. Bush administration, agencies frequently took a formal position on the preemption question. This development raises the important but as yet unresolved theoretical question of the degree to which a court should defer to an agency's interpretation of the statute that Congress has charged it with administering on the question of whether that statute preempts state law.

In the seminal 1986 case of *Chevron USA v. Natural Resources Defense Council*,[39] the Supreme Court articulated a rule of thumb for the lower courts to apply in interpreting statutes administered by federal agencies that reads as follows:

> When a court reviews an agency's construction of the statute which it administers, it is confronted with two questions. First, always, is the question whether Congress has directly spoken to the precise question at issue. If the intent of Congress is clear, that is the end of the matter; for the court, as well as the agency, must give effect to the un-

> ambiguously expressed intent of Congress. If, however, the court determines Congress has not directly addressed the precise question at issue, the court does not simply impose its own construction on the statute, as would be necessary in the absence of an administrative interpretation. Rather, if the statute is silent or ambiguous with respect to the specific issue, the question for the court is whether the agency's answer is based on a permissible construction of the statute.[40]

In the ensuing years, *Chevron* has become one of the most widely cited cases in administrative law, and it has spawned a cottage industry of legal scholarship.[41] Although this is certainly not the place for an extended discussion of the *Chevron* doctrine, it is fair to say that, like the presumption against preemption, this easily articulated principle has proven difficult to apply in a consistent fashion in the real world.[42] The interesting theoretical question that arises in the preemption context is whether *Chevron* deference should trump the presumption against preemption, or vice versa.

The Supreme Court itself has remained curiously silent on this precise question. We saw in Chapter 4 that the plurality opinion in *Medtronic v. Lohr,* despite finding "ambiguities in the statute," declined to apply the *Chevron* deference analysis, noting instead that its interpretation was merely "substantially informed" by FDA's preemption regulations and concluding that "few, if any, common law duties have been pre-empted by this statute."[43] And the Court in *Geier* found that the agency's interpretation was entitled at most to "some weight."[44] In the 2007 case of *Waters v. Wachovia Bank,* which did not involve preemption of state common law claims, the Court once again declined to afford *Chevron* deference to an agency's interpretation of its statute to preempt state regulation of certain banking practices engaged in through bank subsidiaries. Having interpreted the language and purpose of the statute to preempt state laws, the Court put aside an argument that the agency's interpretation to that effect was not entitled to deference as "an academic question."[45]

Although the Supreme Court has not explicitly resolved the tension between the deference that federal courts traditionally afford agency interpretations of their own statutes and the presumption against preemption that they apply when the subject matter has traditionally been regulated by state law, there are many good reasons for resolving that question in most cases against preemption. First of all, the preemption question is ultimately a question of statutory interpretation, and courts are at least as adept as agency lawyers at ascertaining congressional intent on questions that are not directly within the agencies' expertise, *Chevron* to the contrary notwithstanding.

Second, the preemption question itself is only partially within an agency's expertise. As we explored in some detail in Chapter 7, agencies have expertise in technical matters, and even that expertise may be overrated when compared with that of the common law courts. Although an agency's technical expertise may on some occasions be relevant to one or more issues that arise in deciding whether or not to preempt, like the impact of nonuniformity on implementation of its statutory responsibilities, the agencies have no expertise at all on many of the other considerations, like federalism values and corrective justice.[46] Indeed, in some cases, it may not even be altogether clear that the agency has the authority to consider such concerns.[47]

Finally, the federal agency administering the potentially preempting federal program may not be the most objective entity to decide whether or not it is preemptive. Bureaucrats are not known for relinquishing their "turf" voluntarily to institutions that they do not necessarily trust. Furthermore, the regulated industries will almost certainly prefer federal regulation to state common law litigation and put pressure on the relevant agencies to find that their regulations are preemptive.[48] This was certainly true of the pharmaceutical industry, as we saw in Chapter 6, and it is most likely true for most other industries, as well, for reasons discussed in Chapter 2. To the extent that the regulated industries are able to influence the agencies, which, as we saw in Chapter 7, is often considerable, the preemption decision will not be as objective as a court's resolution of the matter. Indeed, a decision to defer to the regulatory agency may, in practice, be tantamount to a decision to defer it to the regulated industry.

The Supreme Court's apparent reluctance to defer to agency interpretations of federal regulatory statutes to preempt state law is therefore well founded. Not surprisingly, state courts are far less inclined to defer to federal agency preemption determinations than the lower federal courts.[49] The reasons that the courts have traditionally relied upon to justify deference to statutory interpretation by implementing agencies are not especially compelling in the context of preemption. At the end of a careful analysis of the issue, Professor Nina Mendelson concludes that "several factors . . . , taken together, weigh against *Chevron* deference to administrative interpretations of state law preemption."[50] The arguments against deferring to agency interpretations of their statutes to preempt state common law claims are sufficiently compelling that the courts should at most give agency interpretations "some deference" only some of the time.

CONCLUSIONS

Federal regulatory agencies play a vital protective role in our complex, interconnected, and often impersonal society. Congress created those agencies to provide much-needed protection to ordinary citizens from the health and safety hazards and the fraud that are the inevitable by-products of an unregulated marketplace. Agencies are often accused by business interests and their allies in Congress and think tanks of zealously imposing needless "command and control" requirements through "one-size-fits-all" regulatory requirements on the very companies that contribute the most to the country's economic well-being. It takes a special dedication to public service for a highly qualified professional to report for work every day to an institution that is so frequently the target of public approbation and ridicule and so seldom the recipient of public praise. These midlevel public servants are the real repositories of both technical and policymaking expertise in the agencies, not the upper-level political appointees who come and go with changes in career opportunities and administrations.

Career public servants soon accept the reality of limited resources that is an inevitable consequence of the constant drumbeat of criticism. They usually have the humility to know that their decisions are far from perfect and that implementing them in the real world is even more difficult. They freely admit that they can use all the help they can get. Their politically appointed superiors, however, are not always so self-effacing. Often entering and leaving through a lucrative revolving door, they are not necessarily as dedicated to the agencies' protective missions as their underlings, and they sometimes bring extrastatutory agendas with them. During the George W. Bush administration, one of those external agendas was tort reform.

Common law litigation has much to offer public servants in federal agencies. Professor Stephen Lubet observes that, "[j]ust as the profit motive can cause corporations to overlook potential safety hazards, it also inspires trial lawyers to uncover them."[51] The results of the combined efforts of plaintiffs' attorneys throughout the country can be made available to regulatory agencies to use in implementing their protective statutes. Because the doctrine of negligence per se usually gives plaintiffs a procedural advantage, those same lawyers will also pay careful attention to federal regulatory requirements that might have been applicable to the defendants at the time that their products and activities damaged the plaintiffs. The knowledge that the federal enforcement efforts may be supplemented by investigations led by highly motivated plaintiffs' attorneys can provide an added incentive to regulatees to comply with agency-imposed requirements.

Not every company that says it is in compliance with regulatory requirements really is. And even when a company does comply with federal standards, the bare minimum is not always socially acceptable, as anyone who has ever traveled far below the speed limit on a foggy day knows. The consideration that most frequently tips the balance in favor of allowing common law claims to proceed against defendants that comply with federal regulatory requirements is the corrective justice function that common law courts uniquely provide.

There are, of course, sound policy reasons on the other side of the battle lines. Fundamental fairness considerations argue strongly against forcing a defendant to pay damages for harm allegedly caused by conduct that a federal agency compels, and the efficiency of the national marketplace may demand the uniformity and certainty that companies need before they are willing to invest large sums in productive economic activity. In some cases, the added incentive that the threat of common law liability provides may be detrimental to innovation or induce an extreme conservativism in regulated companies that stifles economic growth.

The preceding three chapters have demonstrated that society will not be better off if either side wins the preemption war outright, because federal agency preemption of common law claims is not always right and not always wrong. This chapter has explored ways to achieve some degree of de-escalation of the preemption war by suggesting criteria and rules of thumb for deciding when preemption is and is not more likely to advance important public policies in the case of legislation and to comport with legislative intent in the case of litigation.

It should be apparent that the criteria and rules of thumb suggested here point more often in the direction of peaceful coexistence between the state common law and federal regulatory law than in the direction of federal dominance. This may, of course, merely reflect the author's views on the merits of the arguments for and against preemption, but it also reflects a realistic assessment of the institutional capacities of federal agencies and common law courts and the institutional asymmetry inherent in the fact that common law courts provide both *ex ante* incentives to protect and *ex post* corrective justice, while federal agencies provide only *ex ante* protection. It is also consistent with the "presumption against preemption" that the Supreme Court recognized long before the advent of the preemption war.

The question of federal preemption of state law has always been highly politicized, and it will remain so in the future.[52] The more limited question of federal preemption of state *common law* was born in controversy and has since become the focus of a major legal and political war. If the courts continue to be the primary battleground in the preemption war, they will become more deeply enmeshed in both the vertical and the horizontal politics of preemption than they already are. The war therefore poses a serious threat to the public's generally positive perception of the courts as neutral dispensers of justice. This is an unnecessary and therefore especially unfortunate development. Unlike controversial constitutional issues that the courts cannot avoid, they are involved in the preemption war only because the statutes they interpret so rarely speak directly to the question of common law preemption. Because that question is inherently political, it is the responsibility of that most political of all of the nation's political institutions, the Congress of the United States, to address it head-on in every relevant regulatory context.

Notes

CHAPTER 1. INTRODUCTION

1. *Questions Raised Over Michigan Law That Protects Drug Companies,* DETROIT FREE PRESS, January 2, 2005, at 1.
2. Laura Vozzella & Ivan Penn, *Lining Up Suits Against Painkillers,* BALTIMORE SUN, December 23, 2004, at A1.
3. *Questions Raised* (quoting Chuck Hadden, a lobbyist for the Michigan Manufacturers Association).
4. MICH. COMP. L. ANN. § 600.2946(5).
5. Taylor v. SmithKline Beecham Corp., 658 N.W.2d 127 (Mich. 2003).
6. Garcia v. Wyeth-Ayerst Laboratories, 385 F.3d 961 (6th Cir. 2004).
7. Food and Drug Administration, Requirements on Content and Format of Labeling for Human Prescription Drug and Biological Products, 71 Fed. Reg. 3922 (2006).
8. U.S. CONST., art. VI, Para 2.
9. Food and Drug Administration, Requirements on Content, 3934.
10. THOMAS F. BURKE, LAWYERS, LAWSUITS, AND LEGAL RIGHTS 6, 25 (2002).
11. LOU DUBOSE, JAN REID, & CARL M. CANNON, BOY GENIUS 103 (2003) (quote); *id.,* ch. 10.
12. BURKE, LAWYERS, 30.
13. Ralph Lindeman, *Agencies Move to Override State Law as Part of Federal Rulemaking Process,* 34 BNA PROD. SAFETY & LIABILITY REPT. 304 (2006); Stephen

Labaton, *'Silent Tort Reform' Is Overriding States' Powers,* New York Times, March 10, 2006, at C1; Myron Levin and Alan C. Miller, *Industries Get Quiet Protection From Lawsuits,* Los Angeles Times, February 19, 2006, at A1; Caroline E. Mayer, *Rules Would Limit Lawsuits,* Washington Post, February 16, 2006, at D1.

14. New State Ice Co. v. Liebmann, 285 U.S. 262, 311 (1932) (Brandeis, J., dissenting).
15. Gina Kolata, *Good Pill, Bad Pill: Science Makes It Hard to Decipher,* New York Times, December 22, 2004, at C1.
16. The history of the development of Celebrex and Vioxx is drawn primarily from Barry Meier, *Medicine Fueled by Marketing Intensified Trouble for Pain Pills,* New York Times, December 19, 2004, at 1.
17. 53 Fed. Reg. 41,516 (Oct. 21, 1988) (codified at 21 C.F.R. § 312.80–88).
18. Kolata, *Good Pill, Bad Pill;* Meier, *Medicine Fueled by Marketing;* Anna Wilde Mathews & Barbara Martinez, *Warning Signs: E-Mails Suggest Merck Knew Vioxx's Dangers at Early Stage,* Wall Street Journal, November 1, 2004, at A1.
19. Richard Stewart, *Doctor Is Questioned on Merck's Sales Tactics,* Houston Chronicle, July 20, 2005, at B3; Brooke A. Masters & Marc Kaufman, *Painful Withdrawal for Makers of Vioxx,* Washington Post, October 18, 2004, at A1; Bruce Japsen, *Merck's Case-by-Case Defense on Vioxx Aims to Cap Payouts,* Chicago Tribune, July 17, 2005, at C1.
20. Gardiner Harris, *F.D.A. Official Admits 'Lapses' on Vioxx,* New York Times, March 2, 2005, at A15; Mathews & Martinez, *Warning Signs;* Masters & Kaufman, *Painful Withdrawal.*
21. Kolata, *Good Pill, Bad Pill;* Meier, *Medicine Fueled by Marketing;* Masters & Kaufman, *Painful Withdrawal.*
22. National Institute of Medicine, National Academies of Sciences, The Future of Drug Safety 3–9 (2006).
23. Masters & Kaufman, *Painful Withdrawal;* Alex Berenson, Gardiner Harris, Barry Meier, & Andrew Pollack, *Dangerous Data,* New York Times, November 14, 2004, at A1.
24. Alex Berenson & Gardiner Harris, *Pfizer Says 1999 Trials Revealed Risks With Celebrex,* New York Times, February 1, 1999, at C1; Marc Kaufman, *Arthritis Drug Study in 2000 Found Risks,* Washington Post, Febuary 1, 2005, at A10; Tyler Marshall, *Pfizer Defends Painkiller Despite Federal Warning,* Los Angeles Times, December 20, 2004, at A23 (quote); Marc Kaufman, *Celebrex Trial Halted After Findings of Heart Risk,* Washington Post, December 18, 2004, at A1; Gardiner Harris, *Drug Trial Finds Big Health Risks in 2nd Painkiller,* New York Times, December 18, 2004, at A1.
25. Gardiner Harris & Alex Berenson, *F.D.A. Urges Doctors to Limit Prescriptions for Two Painkillers,* New York Times, December 24, 2004, at A17.
26. 21 C.F.R. § 314.80.
27. Masters & Kaufman, *Painful Withdrawal.*
28. Marc Kaufman, *New Study Criticizes Painkiller Marketing,* Washington Post, January 25, 2005, at A1; Amanda Spake, *A Sick Agency in Need of a Cure?* U.S. News & World Report, December 13, 2004, at 32 (censored quote); Rita Rubin, *Scientist Says FDA Called Journal to Block Vioxx Article,* USA Today, November 28, 2004, at A1; Masters & Kaufman, *Painful Withdrawal;* Mark Kaufman, *FDA Officer Suggests Strict Curbs on 5 Drugs,* Washington Post, November 19, 2004, at A1; Ricardo Alonso-Zaldivar, *Early*

Vioxx Alarms Alleged, Los Angeles Times, November 19, 2004, at A1; Gardiner Harris, *Drug-Safety Reviewer Says F.D.A. Delayed Vioxx Study,* New York Times, November 4, 2004, at A21 (scientific rumor quote); Marc Kaufman, *FDA Official Alleges Pressure to Suppress Vioxx Findings,* Washington Post, October 8, 2004, at A23 (be-prepared quote).

29. Gardiner Harris & Alex Berenson, *10 Voters on Panel Backing Pain Pills Had Industry Ties,* New York Times, February 25, 2005, at A1 (quote; Lanier confidence); Gardiner Harris, *F.D.A. Is Advised to Let Pain Pills Stay on Market,* New York Times, February 19, 2005, at A1 (committee vote); Alex Berenson & Barnaby Feder, *A Reminder That No Drug Is Risk-Free,* New York Times, February 19, 2005, at C1.
30. Marc Kaufman, *Painkiller Decision Suggests Shift in FDA's Risk-Benefit Equation,* Washington Post, April 11, 2005, at A3 (quote); Gardiner Harris, *F.D.A. Announces Strong Warnings for Painkillers,* New York Times, April 8, 2005, at A1.
31. Mathews & Martinez, *Warning Signs.*
32. Berenson, Harris, Meier, & Pollack, *Dangerous Data* (internal documents); Mathews & Martinez, *Warning Signs* (quotes).
33. Barry Meier, *Merck Canceled an Early Study of Vioxx,* New York Times, February 8, 2005, at C1.
34. Alex Berenson, *Evidence in Vioxx Suits Shows Intervention by Merck Officials,* New York Times, April 24, 2005, at A1.
35. Mathews & Martinez, *Warning Signs.*
36. Mathews & Martinez, *Warning Signs* (dodge quote); Barbara Martinez, *Vioxx Lawsuits May Focus on FDA Warning in 2001,* Wall Street Journal, October 5, 2004, at A1 (other quotes).
37. Alex Berenson, *Some Pointed Questioning at the Vioxx Trial in Texas,* New York Times, July 19, 2005, at C1; Alex Berenson, *First Vioxx Suit: Entryway Into a Legal Labyrinth?* New York Times, July 11, 2005, at A1 (100,000 lawsuits); Berenson, Harris, Meier, & Pollack, *Dangerous Data* ($10 billion).
38. Alex Berenson, *In First of Many Vioxx Cases, a Texas Widow Prepares to Take the Stand,* New York Times, July 13, 2005, at A1; Richard Stewart, *Widow's Suit Against Vioxx Maker to Set Tone for Rest,* Houston Chronicle, July 4, 2005, at A1 (Ernst quotes).
39. The description of the trial is drawn from Alex Berenson, *Jurors in the Vioxx Trial Hear Closing Arguments,* New York Times, August 18, 2005, at C1; Bruce Nichols, *Vioxx Trial Has Huge Implications for Merck,* Dallas Morning News, August 17, 2006, at A2; Richard Stewart, *Merck Employee Stands Firm on Vioxx Clinical Trials,* Houston Chronicle, August 12, 2005, at B3; Alex Berenson, *At Midpoint of Vioxx Trial, Merck Looks Battered,* New York Times, August 6, 2005, at C1; Richard Stewart, *Attorney Questions Drug Maker's Motives,* Houston Chronicle, August 6, 2005, at B1; Alex Berenson, *In Vioxx Trial, Battle Nears Over Coroner's Testimony,* New York Times, July 28, 2005, at C3; Richard Stewart, *Vioxx Trial Evidence Arrives by Truckload,* Houston Chronicle, July 27, 2005, at B1 (157 boxes); Alex Berenson, *At Vioxx Trial, a Discrepancy Appears to Undercut Merck's Defense,* New York Times, July 20, 2005, at C1; Richard Stewart, *Doctor Is Questioned on Merck Sales Tactics,* Houston Chronicle, July 20, 2005, at B3; Berenson, *Some Pointed Questioning;* Richard Stewart, *FDA Warning Focus*

in Day 1 of Vioxx Trial, HOUSTON CHRONICLE, July 19, 2005, at B1; Richard Stewart, *Sides Stake Positions as Vioxx Trial Opens,* HOUSTON CHRONICLE, July 15, 2005, at B1.

40. Richard Stewart, *Heart Center Official Says Vioxx Not to Blame in Death,* HOUSTON CHRONICLE, August 13, 2005, at B7; Richard Stewart, *Clogged Arteries Caused Death, Pathologist Says,* HOUSTON CHRONICLE, August 9, 2005, at B4; Richard Stewart, *Heart Attack Led to Fatal Arrhythmia,* HOUSTON CHRONICLE, August 2, 2005, at B6; Richard Stewart, *Surprise Witness OK'd in Vioxx Trial,* HOUSTON CHRONICLE, July 29, 2005, at B3.
41. Carrie Johnson, *Merck Agrees to Blanket Settlement on Vioxx,* WASHINGTON POST, November 10, 2007, at D1 ($4.85 billion settlement); Lisa Girion & Dana Calvo, *Merck Loses Vioxx Case,* LOS ANGELES TIMES, August 20, 2005, at A1 (jury statements); Alex Berenson, *Jury Calls Merck Liable in Death of Man on Vioxx,* NEW YORK TIMES, August 20, 2005, at A1 (jury foreman quote); Ruth Rendon & Richard Stewart, *Vioxx Jurors Talk About Verdict,* HOUSTON CHRONICLE, August 20, 2005, at A10 (source of punitive-damage amount); Richard Stewart, *Vioxx Jury Awards Widow $253 Million,* HOUSTON CHRONICLE, August 20, 2005, at A1; Bruce Japson, *Volleys on Vioxx Focused on Cause,* CHICAGO TRIBUNE, August 18, 2005, at C1 (closing argument).
42. Gardiner Harris, *A Firebrand on Drug Safety,* NEW YORK TIMES, November 20, 2004, at A16 (profound failure quote); Mark Kaufman, *FDA Officer Suggests Strict Curbs on 5 Drugs,* WASHINGTON POST, November 19, 2004, at A1 (FDA incapable quote); Masters & Kaufman, *Painful Withdrawal* (Grassley quote); Robert Cohen & Ed Silverman, *What's Next for Drug Regulation,* NEW JERSEY STAR-LEDGER, October 3, 2004, at A1 (Ray quotes).
43. Cohen & Silverman, *What's Next* (Nisson quote).
44. DAVID G. OWEN, PRODUCTS LIABILITY LAW (2005), 895.
45. Scott A. Smith & Duana Grage, *Federal Preemption of State Products Liability Actions,* 27 WILLIAM MITCHELL L. REV. 391, 392 (2000).
46. Garcia v. Wyeth-Ayerst Laboratories, 385 F.3d 961, 966–67 (6th Cir. 2004).

CHAPTER 2. REGULATION AND LIABILITY: TWO WELL-WORN ROUTES TO CONSUMER PROTECTION

1. RALPH NADER, UNSAFE AT ANY SPEED: THE DESIGNED-IN DANGERS OF THE AMERICAN AUTOMOBILE (1965).
2. JUSTIN MARTIN, NADER: CRUSADER, SPOILER, ICON ch. 4–5 (2002).
3. 80 Stat. 718 (1966), 15 U.S.C. § 1381, et seq.
4. *See* MICHAEL PERTSCHUK, REVOLT AGAINST REGULATION 5–45 (1982); SUSAN J. TOLCHIN & MARTIN TOLCHIN, DISMANTLING AMERICA 16–20 (1983); David Vogel, *The "New" Social Regulation in Historical and Comparative Perspective, in* REGULATION IN PERSPECTIVE 155–85 (Thomas K. McCraw ed., 1981).
5. MARTIN, NADER, ch. 16.
6. DAVID G. OWEN, PRODUCTS LIABILITY LAW 1–3 (2005).
7. *See* ROBERT E. CUSHMAN, THE INDEPENDENT REGULATORY COMMISSIONS (1941).
8. 29 U.S.C. § 151, et seq.

9. 34 Stat. 768 (1906).
10. *See* Stephen Breyer, *Analyzing Regulatory Failure: Mismatches, Less Restrictive Alternatives, and Reform,* 92 HARV. L. REV. 549 (1979).
11. *See,* e.g., 21 C.F.R. § 314.80 (drug adverse effects); 21 C.F.R. pt. 803 (medical device adverse effects).
12. 5 U.S.C. § 553.
13. 5 U.S.C. § 706.
14. *See* OFFICE OF TECHNOLOGY ASSESSMENT, UNITED STATES CONGRESS, ENVIRONMENTAL POLICY TOOLS 19 (1995).
15. *See* FREDERICK ANDERSON, ET AL., ENVIRONMENTAL IMPROVEMENTS THROUGH ECONOMIC INCENTIVES 14 (1977); Bruce A. Ackerman & Richard B. Stewart, *Comment: Reforming Environmental Law,* 37 STAN. L. REV. 1333, 1336–37 (1985).
16. Robert W. Hahn & Robert N. Stavins, *Incentive-Based Environmental Regulation: A New Era From an Old Idea?* 18 ECOLOGY L.Q. 1 (1991); Breyer, *Analyzing Regulatory Failure,* 581–82.
17. *See* OFFICE OF TECHNOLOGY ASSESSMENT, ENVIRONMENTAL POLICY TOOLS, 19; Thomas O. McGarity, *Media Quality, Technology, and Cost-Benefit Balancing Strategies for Health and Environmental Regulation,* 46 L. & CONTEMP. PROB. 159, 163–64 (1983).
18. *See* McGarity, *Media Quality,* 162–64.
19. *See* RICHARD J. PIERCE, JR., SIDNEY A. SHAPIRO, & PAUL R. VERKUIL, ADMINISTRATIVE LAW AND PROCESS 41 (2004).
20. *See* PIERCE, SHAPIRO, & VERKUIL, ADMINISTRATIVE LAW, 91–92; THOMAS O. MCGARITY, REINVENTING RATIONALITY: THE ROLE OF REGULATORY ANALYSIS IN THE FEDERAL BUREAUCRACY ch. 18 (1991); Oliver Houck, *President X and the New (Approved) Decisionmaking,* 36 AM. U. L. REV. 535 (1987); Eric Olson, *The Quiet Shift of Power: Office of Management and Budget Supervision of Environmental Protection Agency Rulemaking Under Executive Order 12291,* 4 VA. J. NAT. RES. L. 1 (1984).
21. Motor Vehicle Manufacturers Ass'n v. State Farm Mutual Auto Ins. Co., 463 U.S. 29, 42 (1983).
22. Thomas O. McGarity, *The Courts and the Ossification of Rulemaking: A Response to Professor Seidenfeld,* 75 TEX. L. REV. 525 (1997); Robert L. Rabin, *Federal Regulation in Historical Perspective,* 38 STAN. L. REV. 1189, 1295–1315 (1986).
23. ENVIRONMENTAL PROTECTION AGENCY, PRINCIPLES OF ENVIRONMENTAL ENFORCEMENT ch. 2 (Materials Prepared for Environmental Enforcement Training, 1992); Clifford Rechtschaffen, *Competing Visions: EPA and the States Battle for the Future of Environmental Enforcement,* 30 ENVT'L. L. REPT. 10803, 10804 (2000).
24. *See,* e.g., 7 U.S.C. § 136l(b) (FIFR Act); 21 U.S.C. § 333 (FDC Act); 49 U.S.C. § 30170 (FMVS Act).
25. *See,* e.g., 7 U.S.C. § 136d(b) (FIFR Act); 21 U.S.C. § 355(e) (FDC Act).
26. *See,* e.g., 33 U.S.C. § 1319(b) (Clean Water Act); 42 U.S.C. § 7413(b) (Clean Air Act).
27. *See,* e.g., 7 U.S.C. § 136l(a) (FIFR Act); 49 U.S.C. § 30165 (FMVS Act).
28. 42 U.S.C. § 7420. See David L. Markell, *The Role of Deterrence-Based Enforcement in a "Reinvented" State/Federal Relationship: The Divide Between Theory and Reality,* 24 HARV. ENV. L. REV. 1, 10 (2000).

29. *See,* e.g., 33 U.S.C. § 1365 (Clean Water Act); 42 U.S.C. § 7604(a) (Clean Air Act).
30. *See,* e.g., 33 U.S.C. § 1365(d) (Clean Water Act); 42 U.S.C. § 7604(d) (Clean Air Act).
31. *See,* e.g., 33 U.S.C. § 1365(b) (Clean Water Act); 42 U.S.C. § 7604(b)(1)(B) (Clean Air Act).
32. *See* 42 U.S.C. § 7604(a) (Clean Air Act).
33. 21 U.S.C. § 334.
34. 7 U.S.C. § 136k.
35. *See,* e.g., 15 U.S.C. § 2106 (CPS Act); 49 U.S.C. § 30118(b)(2) (FMVS Act).
36. 33 U.S.C. § 1319(a)(5)(A) (Clean Water Act); 42 U.S.C. § 7413(a)(4) (Clean Air Act).
37. *See* Office of the White House Press Secretary, Summary Fact Sheet, The President's Economic Recovery Program and Regulatory Relief (June 6, 1981), *reprinted in* Materials on President Reagan's Program of Regulatory Relief (undated).
38. Executive Order No. 12291, 3 C. F. R. § 127 (1982).
39. Exec. Order No. 12630, 53 Fed. Ref. 8859 (1988) (takings); Exec. Order No. 12606, 52 Fed. Reg. 34188 (1987) (family); Exec. Order No. 12,612, 52 Fed. Reg. 41685 (1987) (federalism); Exec. Order No. 12261, 46 Fed. Reg. 2023 (1981) (trade).
40. *See* Thomas O. McGarity, *The Expanded Debate Over the Future of the Regulatory State,* 63 U. Chi. L. Rev. 1463, 1477 (1996).
41. Contract With America: The Bold Plan by Rep. Newt Gingrich, Rep. Dick Armey, and the House Republicans to Change the Nation 128 (Ed Gillespie & Bob Schellhas eds., 1995); H.R. 9, 104th Cong., 1st Sess. (1995) (omnibus regulatory reform); H.R. 5, 104th Cong., 1st Sess. (1995) (unfunded mandates).
42. Dan Balz & Ronald Brownstein, Storming the Gates: Protest Politics and the Republican Revival (1996); Elizabeth Drew, Showdown (1996); David Maraniss & Michael Weisskopf, Tell Newt to Shut Up (1996).
43. Executive Order No. 13422, 72 Fed. Reg. 2763 (January 23, 2007).
44. Jean Macchiaroli Eggen & John G. Culhane, *Gun Torts: Defining a Cause of Action for Victims in Suits Against Gun Manufacturers,* 81 N. Car. L. Rev. 115, 177–78 (2002); Susan Reaker-Jordan, *The Pre-emption Presumption That Never Was: Pre-emption Doctrine Swallows the Rule,* 40 Ariz. L. Rev. 1379, 1423 (1998).
45. Christopher H. Schroeder, *Corrective Justice and Liability for Increasing Risks,* 37 UCLA L. Rev. 439 (1990); Gary T. Schwartz, *Mixed Theories of Tort Law: Affirming Both Deterrence and Corrective Justice,* 75 Tex. L. Rev. 1801 (1997); Catherine Pierce Wells, *Tort Law as Corrective Justice: A Pragmatic Justification for Jury Adjudication,* 88 Mich. L. Rev. 2348 (1990); Richard W. Wright, *Substantive Corrective Justice,* 77 Iowa L. Rev. 625 (1992).
46. Dan B. Dobbs, The Law of Torts 19–21 (2000); Schwartz, *Mixed Theories,* 1832.
47. Eggen & Culhane, *Gun Torts,* 177 n. 308; Wright, *Substantive Corrective Justice,* 692; Wells, *Tort Law as Corrective Justice,* 2355 (quote).
48. Schroeder, *Corrective Justice,* 450.
49. Escola v. Coca-Cola Bottling Co., 150 P.2d 436, 441 (Cal. 1941) (Traynor, J., concurring).
50. Schwartz, *Mixed Theories,* 1802–03.
51. W. Kip Viscusi, *Overview, in* Regulation Through Litigation 5 (W. Kip Viscusi ed., 2002); Schwartz, *Mixed Theories,* 1803–06.
52. Richard Nagareda, *FDA Preemption: When Tort Law Meets the Administrative State,* 1

J. TORT LAW 1, 9 (2006) (referring to the law and economics view as the "dominant scholarly account"); Schroeder, *Corrective Justice,* 444; Schwartz, *Mixed Theories,* 1809–10.

53. Nagareda, *FDA Preemption,* 37.
54. Schwartz, *Mixed Theories,* 1831. *See also* Michael D. Green, *Safety as an Element of Pharmaceutical Quality: The Respective Roles of Regulation and Tort Law,* 42 ST. LOUIS U. L. J. 163 (1998).
55. VICTOR E. SCHWARTZ, KATHRYN KELLY, & DAVID PARTLETT, TORTS 3–4 (11th ed., 2005).
56. DOBBS, LAW OF TORTS ch. 3 (2000).
57. RESTATEMENT (SECOND) OF TORTS § 46.
58. OWEN, PRODUCTS LIABILITY, 61–66; RESTATEMENT (SECOND) OF TORTS § 281.
59. RESTATEMENT (SECOND) OF TORTS §§ 283, 314, 319.
60. *Id.* § 302A.
61. Timothy D. Lytton, *Tort Claims Against Gun Manufacturers for Crime-Related Injuries: Defining a Suitable Role for the Tort System in Regulating the Firearms Industry,* 65 MO. L. REV. 1, 21–45 (2000).
62. RESTATEMENT (SECOND) OF TORTS § 283.
63. *Id.* §§ 286, 288A, 288B; DOBBS, LAW OF TORTS, 311–28; OWEN, PRODUCTS LIABILITY, 84–91.
64. RESTATEMENT (SECOND) OF TORTS § 288C. *See* OWEN, PRODUCTS LIABILITY, 93–94.
65. OWEN, PRODUCTS LIABILITY, 93 (quote); Robert L. Rabin, *Regulatory Compliance,* 88 GEO. L. J. 2049, 2051 (2000).
66. PETER W. HUBER, LIABILITY: THE LEGAL REVOLUTION AND ITS CONSEQUENCES 50 (1988).
67. OWEN, PRODUCTS LIABILITY, 886. *See also* Rabin, *Reassessing,* 2051–52; Richard B. Stewart, *Regulatory Compliance Preclusion of Tort Liability: Limiting the Duel-Track System,* 88 GEO. L. J. 2167, 2168 (2000).
68. OWEN, PRODUCTS LIABILITY, 887; Jerry J. Phillips, *Comments on the Reporters' Study of Enterprise Responsibility for Personal Injury,* 30 SAN DIEGO L. REV. 241 (1993).
69. RESTATEMENT (SECOND) OF TORTS § 821B.
70. *Id.* §§ 821D, F, 822.
71. Rylands v. Fletcher, L.R. 3 H.L. 330 (1868).
72. RESTATEMENT (SECOND) OF TORTS § 519.
73. *Id.* § 520.
74. OWEN, PRODUCTS LIABILITY, 17–20; MARK A. GEISTFELD, PRINCIPLES OF PRODUCTS LIABILITY 10–19 (2006); Douglas A. Kysar, *The Expectations of Consumers,* 103 COLUM. L. REV. 1700, 1709–14 (2003).
75. RESTATEMENT (SECOND) OF TORTS § 402A; GEISTFELD, PRINCIPLES, 10–19.
76. RESTATEMENT (SECOND) OF TORTS § 402A, comment g.
77. OWEN, PRODUCTS LIABILITY, 293–296; GEISTFELD, PRINCIPLES, 26; Jerry J. Phillips, *Consumer Expectations,* 53 S. CAROLINA L. REV. 1047 (2002).
78. RESTATEMENT (SECOND) OF TORTS § 402A, comment k.
79. OWEN, PRODUCTS LIABILITY, 561; George W. Conk, *Is There a Design Defect in the Re-*

statement (Third) of Torts: Products Liability? 109 YALE L. J. 1087, 1093 (2000); Margaret Gilhooley, *The Effect of Products Liability Litigation on Innovation: Innovative Drugs, Products Liability, Regulatory Compliance, and Patient Choice,* 24 SETON HALL L. REV. 1481, 1489 n. 29 (1994); Catherine T. Struve, *The FDA and the Tort System: Postmarketing Surveillance, Compensation, and the Role of Litigation,* 5 YALE J. POLICY & LEGAL ETHICS 587, 609–10 (2005).

80. JEAN STAPLETON, PRODUCT LIABILITY 5 (1994) (quote). *See also* Carl T. Bogus, *War on the Common Law: The Struggle at the Center of Products Liability,* 60 MO. L. REV. 1, 13–30 (1995); Kysar, *Expectations,* 1701–02. *See* OWEN, PRODUCTS LIABILITY, 303–07 (describing risk-utility test).
81. OWEN, PRODUCTS LIABILITY, 299–300; James A. Henderson & Aaron D. Twerski, *Achieving Consensus on Defective Product Design,* 83 CORNELL L. REV. 867, 878–79 (1998) (quote).
82. OWEN, PRODUCTS LIABILITY, 301; GEISTFELD, PRINCIPLES, 26; Bogus, *War on the Common Law,* 12 (quote); Kysar, *Expectations,* 1701–02; Conk, *Design Defect,* 1103–04.
83. GEISTFELD, PRINCIPLES, 26–27; Phillips, *Consumer Expectations,* 1047–48; Kysar, *Expectations,* 1718–22.
84. RESTATEMENT (THIRD) OF TORTS—PRODUCTS LIABILITY §§ 1, 2.
85. *Id.* § 6(c), (d).
86. *Id.* § 6, comment b.
87. *Id.* § 6, comment g.
88. OWEN, PRODUCTS LIABILITY, 33; GEISTFELD, PRINCIPLES, 26–27; Kysar, *Expectations,* 1703, 1726–28 (deeply suspicious quote). *See,* e.g., Potter v. Chicago Pneumatic Tool Co., 694 A.2d 1319 (Conn. 1997).
89. HUBER, LIABILITY, 53.
90. Conk, *Design Defect,* 1088–89, 1094 (without debate quote); Teresa M. Schwartz, *Regulatory Standards and Products Liability: Striking the Right Balance Between the Two,* 30 MICH. J. L. REFORM 431, 459 (1997) (supernegligence quote). *See also* Teresa M. Schwartz, *Prescription Products and the Proposed Restatement (Third),* 61 TENN. L. REV. 1357, 1378 (1994).
91. James A. Henderson, *Prescription Drug Design Liability Under the Proposed Restatement (Third) of Torts: A Reporter's Perspective,* 48 RUTGERS L. REV. 471, 481 (1996) (reporter's response quote).
92. RESTATEMENT (THIRD) OF TORTS—PRODUCTS LIABILITY § 4(a), (b).
93. Schwartz, *Regulatory Standards,* 433–34.
94. DOBBS, LAW OF TORTS, 1047–53.
95. OWEN, PRODUCTS LIABILITY, 47.
96. DAN B. DOBBS, LAW OF REMEDIES 5–6, 9 (1993); Douglas Laycock, *The Death of the Irreparable Injury Rule,* 103 HARV. L. REV. 687 (1990) (rule honored in the breach).
97. DOBBS, LAW OF TORTS, 48.
98. Philip Morris USA v. Williams, 127 S.Ct.1057 (2007); State Farm Mut. Automobile Ins. Co. v. Campbell, 538 U.S. 408 (2003); Cooper Industries, Inc. v. Leatherman Tool Group, Inc., 532 U.S. 424 (2001); Honda Motor Co. v. Oberg, 512 U.S. 56 (1994). *See* DOBBS, LAW OF TORTS, 1063–68, 1071–74; OWEN, PRODUCTS LIABILITY, 48.

99. HUBER, LIABILITY (advocating tort reform); OWEN, PRODUCTS LIABILITY, 24 (describing tort reform); Bogus, *War on the Common Law*, 2 (criticizing tort reform); THOMAS F. BURKE, LAWYERS, LAWSUITS, AND LEGAL RIGHTS 31 (2002) (Clinton veto).
100. David G. Owen, *Federal Preemption of Products Liability Claims*, 55 S. CAR. L. REV. 411, 412–13 (2003).
101. *See*, e.g., Viet Dinh, *Reassessing the Law of Preemption*, 88 GEO. L. J. 2085 (2000); M. Stuart Madden, *Federal Preemption of Inconsistent State Safety Obligations*, 21 PACE L. REV. 103, 104–05 (2000); Richard J. Pierce, *Regulation, Deregulation, Federalism, and Administrative Law: Agency Power to Preempt State Regulation*, 46 U. PITT. L. REV. 607, 629 (1985).

CHAPTER 3. THE LAW AND POLITICS OF PREEMPTION

1. U.S. CONST., art. VI, Para 2.
2. Hillsborough County v. Automated Medical Laboratories, Inc., 471 U.S. 707, 713 (1985).
3. JOSEPH F. ZIMMERMAN, CONGRESSIONAL PREEMPTION: REGULATORY FEDERALISM 1 (2005).
4. NATIONAL ACADEMY OF PUBLIC ADMINISTRATION, BEYOND PREEMPTION: INTERGOVERNMENTAL PARTNERSHIPS TO ENHANCE THE ECONOMY 1 (2006) (quote). *See also* ZIMMERMAN, CONGRESSIONAL PREEMPTION, 7 (preemption statistics).
5. Richard C. Ausness, *Preemption of State Tort Law by Federal Safety Statutes: Supreme Court Preemption Jurisprudence Since Cipollone*, 62 KY. L. J. 913, 920–21 (2003); Richard J. Pierce, *Regulation, Deregulation, Federalism, and Administrative Law: Agency Power to Preempt State Regulation*, 46 U. PITT. L. REV. 607, 636–37 (1985). *See*, e.g., 30 U.S.C. § 1254(g) (Surface Mine Control Act).
6. Robert L. Rabin, *Federalism and the Tort System*, 50 RUTGERS L. REV. 1, 28 (1997).
7. Erie Railroad Co. v. Tompkins, 304 U.S. 64 (1938).
8. *Id.*, 78.
9. Cipollone v. Liggett Group, Inc., 505 U.S. 504, 516 (1992).
10. Rice v. Santa Fe Elevator Corp. 331 U.S. 218, 230 (1947).
11. Bates v. Dow Agrosciences, LLC, 544 U.S. 431, 449 (2005) (quoting New York State Conference of Blue Cross & Blue Shield Plans v. Travelers Ins. Co., 514 U.S. 645, 655 (1995)); Hillsborough County v. Automated Medical Laboratories, Inc., 471 U.S. 707, 716 (1985).
12. English v. General Electric Co., 496 U.S. 72, 87–90 (1990); Silkwood v. Kerr-McGee Corp., 464 U.S. 238, 251 (1984). *See* CSX Transportation, Inc. v. Easterwood, 507 U.S. 658, 664 (1993).
13. Viet Dinh, *Reassessing the Law of Preemption*, 88 GEO. L. J. 2085, 2086 (2000) (quote). *See also* DAVID G. OWEN, PRODUCTS LIABILITY LAW 899 (2005); Mary J. Davis, *Unmasking the Presumption in Favor of Preemption*. 53 S. CAR. L. REV. 967, 968 (2002) (arguing that there is now a de facto presumption in favor of preemption).
14. Timothy D. Lytton, *The NRA, The Brady Campaign, & the Politics of Gun Litigation*, *in* SUING THE GUN INDUSTRY 152, 174 (Timothy D. Lytton, ed., 2005).

15. 45 U.S.C. §§ 51–60. *See* Dan B. Dobbs, The Law of Torts 40, 312 (2000); Rabin, *Federalism,* 26.
16. Rabin, *Federalism,* 26 (quote).
17. 42 U.S.C. § 300aa-11–15; Moss v. Merck & Co., 381 F.3d 501, 503 (5th Cir. 2004) (quote). *See* generally Thomas F. Burke, Lawyers, Lawsuits, and Legal Rights ch. 4 (2002).
18. Burke, Lawyers, 162–63; Division of Vaccine Injury Compensation, Department of Health and Human Services, National Vaccine Injury Compensation Program Strategic Plan 1 (2006) (providing statistics).
19. 42 U.S.C. § 300aa-21, 22. *See* Moss v. Merck & Co., 381 F.3d 501, 503 (5th Cir. 2004); Sykes v. Glaxo-SmithKline, 2007 WL 957337 (E.D. Pa. 2007); Blackmon v. American Home Products Corp., 328 F. Supp.2d 659, 665 (S.D. Tex. 2004); David R. Geiger & Mark D. Rosen, *Rationalizing Product Liability for Prescription Drugs: Implied Preemption, Federal Common Law, and Other Paths to Uniform Pharmaceutical Safety Standards,* 45 DePaul L. Rev. 395, 407 (1996).
20. 42 U.S.C. § 300aa-22(e).
21. 42 U.S.C. §§ 2001–2281.
22. 42 U.S.C. § 2014(hh); Duke Power Co. v. Carolina Environmental Study Group, 438 U.S. 59, 65–66 (1978).
23. In re TMI, 67 F.3d 1103 (3d Cir. 1995); O'Conner v. Commonwealth Edison Co., 13 F.3d 1090 (7th Cir. 1994); Wilcox v. Homestake Mining Co., 401 F. Supp.2d 1196, 1201 (D.N.M. 2005) (quote); McCafferty v. Centerior Service Co., 983 F. Supp. 715 (N.D. Ohio 1997).
24. Rabin, *Federalism,* 27.
25. 49 U.S.C. § 40101.
26. In re World Trade Center Disaster Site Litigation, 467 F. Supp.2d 372 (S.D.N.Y. 2006); Burke, Lawyers, 39–40.
27. Rabin, *Federalism,* 27 (preemption of common law rare).
28. Medtronic, Inc. v. Lohr, 518 U.S. 470, 485 (1996) (quoting Retail Clerks International Ass'n v. Schermerhorn, 375 U.S. 470, 485 (1996)) (quote); Pierce, *Regulation,* 629.
29. San Diego Building Trades Council v. Garmon, 359 U.S. 236, 246–47 (1959).
30. Cipollone v. Liggett Group, Inc., 505 U.S. 504 (1992).
31. Quoted in Cipollone v. Liggett Group, Inc., 505 U.S. 504, 513 (1992) (FTC quote) (1965 statute quote).
32. Quoted in *id.,* 515.
33. John A. Jenkins, The Litigators 118–29 (1989); Richard Kluger, Ashes to Ashes ch. 18 (1996).
34. Cipollone v. Liggett Group, Inc., 505 U.S. 504, 509–10 (1992).
35. *Id.,* 521 (quoting San Diego Building Trades Council v. Garmon, 359 U.S. 236, 247 (1959)).
36. *Id.,* 536 (Blackmun, J., concurring in part and dissenting in part).
37. In re Welding Fume Products Liability Litigation, 364 F. Supp.2d 669, 680–81 (N.D. Ohio 2005); Ausness, *Preemption,* 928 (quote).
38. The factual setting for the *Silkwood* case is taken from Silkwood v. Kerr-McGee Corp., 464 U.S. 238, 241–48 (1984).

39. The Court's description of the law of preemption is taken from *id.*, 248.
40. The description of the majority opinion is taken from *id.*, 250–57, 283.
41. Kenneth W. Starr, *Reflections on Hines v. Davidowitz: The Future of Obstacle Preemption,* 33 PEPPERDINE L. REV. 1 (2005).
42. *See* Samuel Issacharoff & Catherine M. Sharkey, *Backdoor Federalization,* 53 UCLA L. REV. 1353, 1356–57 (2006) (discussing the dimension of which law controls a dispute and the dimension of which forum should control the dispute).
43. Henry N. Butler & Jonathan R. Macey, *Externalities and the Matching Principle: The Case for Reallocating Environmental Regulatory Authority,* 14 YALE J. ON REG. 23 (1996); Richard B. Stewart, *Economics, Environment, and the Limits of Legal Control,* 9 HARV. ENVTL. L. REV. 1 (1985).

CHAPTER 4. THE PREEMPTION WAR IN THE COURTS

1. Richard C. Ausness, *Preemption of State Tort Law by Federal Safety Statutes: Supreme Court Preemption Jurisprudence Since Cipollone,* 62 KY. L. J. 913, 924–25 (2003); Jonathan V. O'Steen, *The FDA Defense: Vioxx and the Argument Against Federal Preemption,* 48 ARIZ. L. REV. 67, 71 (2006); David G. Owen, *Federal Preemption of Products Liability Claims,* 55 S. CAR. L. REV. 411, 422 (2003); David C. Vladeck, *Preemption and Regulatory Failure,* 33 PEPPERDINE L. REV. 95, 112 (2005).
2. Robert B. Leflar & Robert S. Adler, *The Preemption Pentad: Federal Preemption of Products Liability Claims After Medtronic,* 64 TENN. L. REV. 691, 698 (1997) (favored defense); Vladeck, *Preemption,* 99, 106 (quote); Davis, *Unmasking,* 1001; Susan Reaker-Jordan, *The Pre-emption Presumption That Never Was: Pre-emption Doctrine Swallows the Rule,* 40 ARIZ. L. REV. 1379, 1380 (1998).
3. Riegel v. Medtronics, Inc. 128 S.Ct. 999 (2008); Bates v. Dow Agrosciences, LLC, 544 U.S. 431 (2005) (pesticides).
4. Jerry L. Mashaw & David L. Harfst, *Regulation and Legal Culture: The Case of Motor Vehicle Safety,* 4 YALE J. REG. 257, 258 (1987).
5. 15 U.S.C. § 1381, now 49 U.S.C. § 30101, et seq.
6. 15 U.S.C. § 1392(d), now 49 U.S.C. § 30103(b)(1).
7. 15 U.S.C. § 1397(k), now 49 U.S.C. § 30103(e).
8. Larsen v. General Motors Corp., 391 F.2d 495 (8th Cir. 1968).
9. *Id.*, 501–02.
10. *Id.*, 506.
11. Timothy Wilson & Richard P. Campbell, *Effect of Federal Safety Regulations on Crashworthiness Litigation,* 22 TORT & INS. L. J. 554 (1987).
12. Geier v. American Honda Motor Co., 529 U.S. 861 (2000).
13. Department of Commerce, Initial Federal Motor Vehicle Standards, 32 Fed. Reg. 2408, 2415 (1967) (original standard); Jerry King, *For 30 Years, NHTSA Has Worked to Make Cars, Highways Safe,* CHICAGO TRIBUNE, July 27, 1997, at 5 (industry derivation).
14. Department of Transportation, Inflatable Occupant Restraint Systems, 34 Fed. Reg. 11,148 (1969); Donald D. Holt, *Why Eaton Got Out of the Air-Bag Business,* FORTUNE, March 12, 1979, at 116 (Ford quote); Robert J. Samuelson, *Auto Rules Test What Reagan*

Means by 'Getting Government off Our Backs,' 13 NAT. J. 136 (January 24, 1981) (only 10 percent of car passengers wear seat belts).

15. Motor Vehicle Mfgs. Ass'n v. State Farm Mut. Auto. Ins. Co., 463 U.S. 29, 34–35 (1983).
16. *Id.,* 35 (NHTSA allows interlock); Irvin Molotsky, *Transportation Department Rule on Air Bags May Come Thursday,* NEW YORK TIMES, April 9, 1984, at A20 (White House pressure); Holt, *Why Eaton,* at 116 (Ford lobbying).
17. Jerry L. Mashaw & David L. Harfst, *Inside the National Highway Traffic Safety Administration: Legal Determinants of Bureaucratic Organization and Performance,* 57 U. CHI. L. REV. 443 (1990); Larry Martz, *Detroit Fears Showdown at Credibility Gap,* NEWSWEEK, December 15, 1975, at 46.
18. Motor Vehicle and Schoolbus Safety Amendments of 1974, Pub. L. 93–492, 109, 88 Stat. 1482 (1974); Linda E. Demkovich, *The Nader Nadir?* 9 NAT. J. 1968 (December 17, 1977).
19. Motor Vehicle Mfgs. Ass'n v. State Farm Mut. Auto. Ins. Co., 463 U.S. 29, 37 (1983).
20. *Battle Likely Over Adam's Air Bags Order,* 9 NAT. J. 1089 (July 9, 1977).
21. Motor Vehicle Mfgs. Ass'n v. State Farm Mut. Auto. Ins. Co., 463 U.S. 29, 39 (1983) (agency explanation); Michael Wines, *Only Themselves to Blame,* 13 NAT. J. 2082 (November 21, 1981) (staff overridden); *Loosening the Rules on Auto Restraints,* BUSINESS WEEK, November 16, 1981, at 58 (proposal to rescind rule); Jonathan Rauch, *Fasten Your Seat Belts—There Is Turbulence Ahead on the Safety Front,* 13 NAT. J. 1158 (June 27, 1981) (agency explanation).
22. *Buckle Up, But Voluntarily, Says Safety Agency,* 13 NAT. J. 1958 (October 31, 1981); *You Will Go on a Long Journey, Seat Belt Fastened,* 14 NAT. J. 564 (March 27, 1982) (quoting testimony of NHTSA Administrator Raymond A. Peck).
23. Motor Vehicle Manufacturers Ass'n of the United States v. State Farm Mutual Automobile Ins. Co., 463 U.S. 443 (1983).
24. National Highway Traffic Safety Administration, Federal Motor Vehicle Safety Standard; Occupant Crash Protection, 49 Fed. Reg. 28962 (1984). *See* Nell Henderson, *U.S. Presses Seat Belt Laws,* WASHINGTON POST, July 12, 1984, at A1.
25. Ann Cooper, *Statehouses Pumped for Battle on Air Bags,* 17 NAT. J. 895 (April 27, 1985) (lobbying effort funded at $15 million per year); George B. Merry, *States Moving to Require Use of Auto Seat Belts,* CHRISTIAN SCIENCE MONITOR, November 29, 1984, at 6; Peter Grier, *New Auto Air-Bag Law Will Go Into Effect—Unless States Make Riders Buckle Up,* CHRISTIAN SCIENCE MONITOR, July 12, 1984, at 3.
26. Al Rothenberg, *Safety Activists Buckling Down,* CHICAGO TRIBUNE, May 31, 1992, at 1 (sabotage successful); Warren Brown, *Seat Belt Rules in California Hit Legal Snag,* WASHINGTON POST, August 30, 1984, at A21; Cooper, *Statehouses Pumped;* Nell Henderson, *U.S. Presses Seat Belt Laws,* WASHINGTON POST, July 12, 1984, at A1 (airbag proponents not pleased).
27. Geier v. American Honda Motor Co., 529 U.S. 861 (2000).
28. 15 U.S.C. § 1397(k). The description of the Court's opinion is taken from Geier v. American Honda Motor Co., 529 U.S. 861, 870–75, 879, 881–82 (2000).
29. Jack Keebler, *Passive Restraints: A Deadly Mistake,* ATLANTA JOURNAL & CONSTITUTION, August 16, 1991, at S1.

30. The description of the dissenting opinion is taken from Geier v. American Honda Motor Co., 529 U.S. 861 (2000), 891–92, 903–04 (Stevens, J., dissenting).
31. Harris v. Great Dane Trailers, Inc., 234 F.3d 398, 401 (8th Cir. 2000). See Mason A. Barney, *Note: Not as Bad as We Thought,* 70 Brooklyn L. Rev. 959, 984–88 (2005).
32. Griffith v. General Motors Corp., 303 F.3d 1276 (11th Cir. 2002).
33. *Id.,* 1282.
34. O'Hara v. General Motors Corp., 508 F.3d 753 (5th Cir. 2007) (Standard 205); Hurley v. Motor Coach Industries, Inc., 222 F.3d 377 (7th Cir. 2000) (Standard 208); O'Hara v. General Motors Corp., 2006 WL 1094427 (N.D. Tex. 2006) (Standard 207); Heinricher v. Volvo Car Corp., 809 N.E.2d 1094, 1098 (Mass. 2004) (Standard 208).
35. See James W. Ely, Jr., Railroads and American Law (2001); Gabriel Kolko, Railroads and Regulation 1–29 (1965); U.S. Government Accountability Office, The Federal Railroad Administration Is Taking Steps to Better Target Its Oversight, But Assessment of Results Is Needed to Determine Impact 6 (2007) (statistics).
36. Norfolk Southern Railway Co. v. Shanklin, Brief for the United States as Amicus Curiae, January 28, 2000, at 1 (citing Office of Inspector General, Department of Transportation, Audit Report: Rail-Highway Grade Crossing Safety i (1999)) (grade crossing statistics); Sara Kehaulani Goo, *Accidents Spur New Focus on Securing U.S. Rail Systems,* Washington Post, January 29, 2005, at A5 (derailment statistics).
37. Federal Railroad Administration, Selection and Installation of Grade Crossing Warning Systems; Notice of Proposed Rulemaking, 60 Fed. Reg. 11,649 (March 2, 1995).
38. See Grand Trunk Ry v. Ives, 344 U.S. 408 (1892); Continental Improvement Co. v. Stead, 95 U.S. 161 (1877).
39. Grand Trunk Railway Co. v. Ives, 144 U.S. 408, 420–21 (1892).
40. Nashville, Chattanooga & St. Louis Railway v. Walters, 294 U.S. 405, 422–23 (1935). See Franklin D. Roosevelt, "Fireside Chat on Reorganization of the Judiciary," March 9, 1937, *at* http:www.hpol.org/fdr/chat/.
41. U.S. Department of Transportation, Rail-Highway Crossings Study I-5 (1989), quoted in CSX Transportation, Inc. v. Easterwood, Brief for Petitioner, August 27, 1992, at 6.
42. Pub. L. No. 91–458, 84 Stat. 971 (1970), 45 U.S.C. § 20101, et seq.; H. Rept. No. 1194, 91st Cong., 2d Sess. (1970), 1970 U.S. Code, Cong. & Admin. News 4104, 4105 (1970) (quote).
43. 49 U.S.C. § 20101.
44. 49 U.S.C. § 20103.
45. 49 U.S.C. § 20106.
46. Highway Safety Act of 1973, Pub. L. No. 93–87, 97 Stat. 282 (1973) 130(a) (federal funding); 23 C.F.R. §§ 646, 655, 924, 1204 (grade crossing improvements); 49 C.F.R. § 213.9 (maximum train speeds).
47. 23 C.F.R. § 646.214(b) (grade crossing requirements); Federal Highway Administration, Manual on Uniform Traffic Control Devices for Streets and Highways 8B-1 (1988) (MUCTD); Norfolk Southern Railway Co. v. Shanklin, Brief for the United Transportation Union as Amicus Curiae, January 28, 2000, at 6–7 (citing National

TRANSPORTATION SAFETY BOARD, SAFETY STUDY: SAFETY AT PASSIVE GRADE CROSSINGS, VOL. 1: ANALYSIS vii, 5 (1998)) (cost of improvements); Norfolk Southern Railway Co. v. Shanklin, Brief Amicus Curiae of Kenneth W. Heathington, et al., January 28, 2000, at 22 (effectiveness of improvements). See CSX Transportation, Inc. v. Easterwood, 507 U.S. 658, 665–67 (1993) (describing the FRA regulations).

48. Letter from Stephen A. Trimble to All NARTC Members (March 26, 1990), *in* Norfolk Southern Railway Co. v. Shanklin, Brief of the Angels on the Tracks, et al., as Amicus Curiae, January 28, 2000, at Appendix 13.
49. CSX Transportation, Inc. v. Easterwood, Brief for Respondent, October 13, 1992, at 1–3.
50. CSX Transportation, Inc. v. Easterwood, 507 U.S. 658 (1993).
51. CSX Transportation, Inc. v. Easterwood, Brief for the United States as Amicus Curiae, August 27, 1992. The description of the Court's opinion is taken from CSX Transportation, Inc. v. Easterwood, 507 U.S. 658, 664, 667–73 (1993).
52. CSX Transportation, Inc. v. Easterwood, 507 U.S. 658, 674 n.14 (1993) (quoting U.S. DEPT. OF TRANSPORTATION, RAILROAD HIGHWAY SAFETY, PART I: A COMPREHENSIVE STATEMENT OF THE PROBLEM iv (1970)); Norfolk Southern Railway Co. v. Shanklin, Brief Amicus Curiae of Kenneth W. Heathington, et al., January 28, 2000, at 4 (stopping distance).
53. CSX Transportation, Inc. v. Easterwood, 507 U.S. 658, 675 n.15 (1993).
54. Norfolk Southern Railway Co. v. Shanklin, 529 U.S. 344 (2000).
55. Norfolk Southern Railway Co. v. Shanklin, Brief for the United States as Amicus Curiae, January 28, 2000, at 10. *See also* Norfolk Southern Railway Co. v. Shanklin, Brief Amicus Curiae of North Carolina, et. al, January 28, 2000, at 16 (quoting trial testimony).
56. Norfolk Southern Railway Co. v. Shanklin, 529 U.S. 344, 358 (2000).
57. Shanklin v. Norfolk Southern Railway, Co., 369 F.3d 978 (6th Cir. 2004).
58. Federal Railroad Administration, Track Safety Standards, 63 Fed. Reg. 33992, 33999 (June 22, 1998); Robert Pottroff, *Perilous Crossings,* TRIAL, April, 2006, at 60.
59. Lundeen v. Canadian Pacific Ry. Co., 447 F.3d 606 (8th Cir. 2006); Olberding v. Union Pacific R.R. Co., 454 F. Supp.2d 884 (W.D. Mo. 2006); Gillenwater v. Burlington Northern & Santa Fe Ry. Co., 435 F. Supp.2d 959 (E.D. Mo. 2006).
60. Shanklin v. Norfolk Southern Ry. Co. 369 F.3d 978 (2004) (on remand); Fuller v. BNSF Ry. Co., 472 F. Supp.2d 1088 (S.D. Ill. 2007); Kuntz v. Illinois Central R.R. Co., 469 F. Supp.2d 586 (S.D. Ill. 2007); Hodge v. Burlington Northern & Santa Fe Ry. Co., 461 F. Supp.2d 1044 (E.D. Mo. 2006); Petre v. Norfolk Southern Ry. Co. 458 F. Supp.2d 518 (N.D. Ohio 2006); Peters v. Union Pacific R.R. Co., 455 F. Supp.2d 998 (W.D. Mo. 2006); Kutilek v. Union Pacific R.R. Co., 454 F. Supp.2d 876 (E.D. Mo. 2006); Clark v. Illinois Central Railroad Co., 794 So.2d 191 (Miss. 2001).
61. MacFarlane v. Çanadian Pacific Railway Co., 278 F.3d 54 (2d Cir. 2002); Kiemele v. Soo Line Railroad Co., 93 F.3d 472 (8th Cir. 1996); Cox v. Norfolk & Western Railway Co., 998 F. Supp. 679 (S. D. W. Va. 1998); Boyd v. National Railroad Passenger Corp., 821 N.E.2d 95 (Mass. App. 2005); Clark v. Illinois Central Railroad Co., 794 So.2d 191 (Miss. 2001).
62. Fifth Third Bank v. CSX Corp., 415 F.3d 741 (7th Cir. 2005); Kalan Enterprises, LLC v. BNSF Railway Co., 415 F. Supp.2d 977, 981 (D. Minn. 2006) (quoting 49 U.S.C. § 20111(a)).

63. In re Derailment Cases, 416 F.3d 787, 794 (8th Cir. 2005); Julie Anderson, *Cleanup of Scottsbluff Spill Continues,* OMAHA WORLD HERALD, November 6, 2000, at 9.
64. Lundeen v. Canadian Pacific Railway Co., 507 F. Supp.2d 1006 (D. Minn. 2007); Mehl v. Canadian Pacific Railway Co., 417 F. Supp.2d 1104, 1110 (D. N. Dak. 2006) (regret quote); Jill Burcum, *Minot Residents Count Blessings After Derailment,* MINNEAPOLIS STAR TRIBUNE, January 20, 2002, at A20. See also Mayor & City of Baltimore v. CSX Transportation, Inc., 404 F. Supp.2d 869 (D. Md. 2003) (similar preemption analysis of Baltimore tunnel derailment); Marcia Myers & Heather Dewar, *Hazardous Materials Pass Daily—and No One Knows,* BALTIMORE SUN, July 20, 2001, at A1.
65. S. Rept. No. 248, 92d Cong., 1st Sess. 6, 10 (1971) (reports of deaths and injuries); John A. Tilley, *History of the U.S. Coast Guard Auxiliary* (January, 2001), *at http://www.uscg.mil/HQ/G-CP/HISTORY/Auxiliary%20History.html* (increase in recreational boating).
66. 46 U.S.C. §§ 4301–4311; Sprietsma v. Mercury Marine, 537 U.S. 51, 74 (2002) (quoting Pub. L. 92–75 2).
67. 46 U.S.C. §§ 4302, 4306, 4311, 13110.
68. Lewis v. Brunswick Corp., 107 F.3d 1494, 1499 (11th Cir. 1997) (agency acceptance of report); REPORT OF THE PROPELLER GUARD SUBCOMMITTEE OF THE NATIONAL BOATING SAFETY ADVISORY COUNCIL (November 7, 1989), *reprinted in* Sprietsma v. Mercury Marine, 537 U.S. 51 (2002), Joint Appendix, at 13, 34; David G. Savage, *High Court Rules Against Boating Industry in Propeller Case,* LOS ANGELES TIMES, December 4, 2002, at 3 (Johns Hopkins Report).
69. Elaine Dickinson, *Prop Guards Propelled to Supreme Court,* BOAT/U.S. MAGAZINE, September 1, 2002, at 19.
70. Sprietsma v. Mercury Marine, 537 U.S. 51 (2002). The description of the Court's holding is taken from *id.,* 64–70.
71. Sprietsma v. Mercury Marine, 537 U.S. 51, 65 (2002).
72. See ROBERT BURKHARDT, THE FEDERAL AVIATION ADMINISTRATION (1967); FRANK A. BURNHAM, CLEARED TO LAND! THE FAA STORY (1977).
73. Morales v. Trans World Airlines, Inc., 504 U.S. 374, 378 (1992).
74. 49 U.S.C. § 1305(a)(1).
75. 49 U.S.C. § 1506.
76. Hodges v. Delta Airlines, Inc., 44 F.3d 344, 336, 340 (5th Cir. 1995).
77. Koutsouradis v. Delta Airlines, Inc. 427 F.3d 1339 (11th Cir. 2003); Travel All Over the World, Inc. v. Kingdom of Saudi Arabia, 73 F.3d 1423 (7th Cir. 1996).
78. Charas v. Trans World Airlines, 160 F.3d 1259, 1261, 1265–66 (9th Cir. 1998). *See also* Taj Mahal Travel, Inc. v. Delta Airlines, Inc., 164 F.3d 186, 194 (3d Cir. 1998).
79. Smith v. Comair, Inc., 134 F.3d 254 (4th Cir. 1998); Kalantar v. Lurghansa German Airlines, 402 F. Supp.2d 130 (D.D.C. 2005); Chrissafis v. Continental Airlines, Inc., 940 F. Supp. 1292 (N.D. Ill. 1996); Rombom v. United Air Lines, Inc., 867 F. Supp. 214 (S.D.N.Y. 1994); Curley v. American Airlines, 846 F. Supp. 280 (S.D.N.Y. 1994).
80. Newman v. American Airlines, 176 F.3d 1128 (9th Cir. 1999). *But see* DeTerra v. America West Airlines, Inc., 226 F. Supp.2d 274 (D. Mass. 2002).
81. Smith v. America West Airlines, Inc., 44 F.3d 344 (5th Cir. 1995) (hijacker); Public Health Trust of Dade County Florida, v. Lake Aircraft, Inc., 992 F.2d 291 (11th Cir. 1993) (pas-

senger seats); Stone v. Frontier Airlines, 256 F. Supp.2d 28 (D. Mass. 2002) (defibrillator); Moore v. Northwest Airlines, Inc., 897 F. Supp. 313 (E.D. Tex. 1995) (disabled passenger); Rowley v. American Airlines, Inc., 875 F. Supp. 708 (D. Ore. 1995) (disabled passenger); Jamerson v. Atlantic Southeast Airlines, 860 F. Supp. 821 (M.D. Ala. 1994) (disabled passenger); In re Air Disaster, 819 F. Supp. 1352 (E.D. Mich. 1993) (training pilots).

82. Smith v. Comair, Inc., 134 F.3d 254 (4th Cir. 1998). *See also* Bennett v. Southwest Airlines Co., 2006 WL 1987821 (N.D. Ill. 2006) (claims of passengers and bystanders injured when airplane ran off runway preempted). *But see* Peterson v. Continental Airlines, Inc., 970 F. Supp. 246 (S.D.N.Y. 1997).

83. Travel All Over the World, Inc. v. Kingdom of Saudi Arabia, 73 F.3d 1423 (7th Cir. 1996) (baggage handling); Casas v. American Airlines, 304 F.3d 517 (5th Cir. 2002) (baggage handling); Lyn-Lea Travel Corp. v. American Airlines, 283 F.3d 282 (5th Cir. 2002) (tortious interference).

84. West v. Northwest Airlines, Inc., 995 F.2d 148 (9th Cir. 1993) (claim for punitive damages preempted); Taj Mahal Travel, Inc. v. Delta Airlines, Inc., 164 F.3d 186 (3d Cir. 1998) (claim for punitive damages not preempted).

85. Pub. L. 104–88, 109 Stat. 803 (1995).

86. 49 U.S.C. § 10501(b).

87. South Dakota v. Burlington Northern & Santa Fe Railway Co., 280 F. Supp.2d 919, 930–34 (D. S. Dak. 2003).

88. Pejepscot Industrial Park, Inc. v. Maine Central Railroad Co., 297 F. Supp.2d 326 (D. Maine 2003).

89. New England Central Railroad, Inc. v. Springfield Terminal Railway Co., 415 F. Supp.2d 20, 27 (D. Mass. 2006).

90. Suchon v. Wisconsin Central, Ltd., 2005 WL 568057, *4 (W.D. Wis. 2005); Cannon v. CSX Transportation, Inc., 2005 WL 77088, *4 (Ohio App. 2005); Guckenberg v. Wisconsin Central Ltd., 178 F. Supp.2d 954, 958 (E.D. Wis. 2001); Rushing v. Kansas City Southern Railway Co., 194 F. Supp.2d 493, 500–01 (S.D. Miss. 2001).

91. Emerson v. Kansas City Southern Railway Co., 503 F.3d 1126, 1131 (10th Cir. 2007). See also Rushing v. Kansas City Southern Railway Co., 194 F. Supp.2d 493, 501 (S.D. Miss. 2001) (construction of an earthen berm that caused rainwater to pool on the plaintiff's property was not preempted because it did not "directly relate to the manner in which" the railroad "conduct[ed] its . . . activities").

92. Maynard v. CSX Transportation, Inc., 360 F. Supp.2d 866, 872 (E.D. Ky. 2004); Friberg v. Kansas City Southern Railway Co., 267 F.3d 439, 443 (5th Cir. 2001).

93. New England Central Railroad, Inc. v. Springfield Terminal Railway Co., 415 F. Supp.2d 20, 27 (D. Mass. 2006).

94. The history of the Dalkon Shield is drawn from Richard B. Sobol, Bending the Law: The Story of the Dalkon Shield Bankruptcy (1991).

95. *Birth Control Case Nears End,* December 16, 1999, *at* file:///Volumes/Untitled/991216%20Birth%20Control%20Device%20Case%20Nears%20End.html

96. Medtronic, Inc. v. Lohr, 518 U.S. 470, 476 (1996).

97. 21 U.S.C. 360e(d)(2); Richard C. Ausness, *"After You, My Dear Alphonse!": Should the*

Courts Defer to the FDA's New Interpretation of 360k(A) of the Medical Device Amendments, 80 TULANE L. REV. 727, 731–33 (2006).

98. 21 U.S.C. § 360e(b)(1); Medtronic, Inc. v. Lohr, 518 U.S. 470, 478–79 (1996); Linda Greenhouse, *State Suits Allowed in Medical-Device Injuries,* NEW YORK TIMES, June 27, 1996, at B9.
99. 21 U.S.C. § 360k(a).
100. Robert S. Adler & Richard A. Mann, *Preemption and Medical Devices: The Courts Run Amok,* 59 MO. L. REV. 895, 917 (1995). *See also* Ausness, *"After You,"* at 741.
101. Lora Lohr's story is drawn from Medtronic, Inc. v. Lohr, 518 U.S. 470, 480–81 (1996); Sharon Schmickle, *Medtronic, Consumer Square Off,* MINNEAPOLIS STAR-TRIBUNE, April 24, 1996, at A5; Joan Biskupic, *Manufacturer Liability Is at Heart of Pacemaker Case,* WASHINGTON POST, April 22, 1996, at A4; June D. Bell, *Pacemaker Recipient Puts Heart Into Suit,* FLORIDA TIMES-UNION, April 21, 1996 (quote).
102. Medtronic, Inc. v. Lohr, 518 U.S. 470 (1996).
103. The description of the Court's opinion is taken from Medtronic, Inc. v. Lohr, 518 U.S. 470, 486–98 (1996).
104. Medtronic, Inc. v. Lohr, 518 U.S. 470, 508 (1996) (Breyer, J., concurring).
105. Medtronic, Inc. v. Lohr, 518 U.S. 470, 508 (1996) (O'Connor, J., concurring in part and dissenting in part).
106. See Barnaby J. Feder, *Medical Device Ruling Redraws Lines on Lawsuits,* NEW YORK TIMES, February 22, 2008, at C1.
107. Michael D. Green & William B. Schultz, *Tort Law Deference to FDA Regulation of Medical Devices,* 88 GEO. L. J. 2119, 2138 (2000); Robert B. Leflar & Robert S. Adler, *The Preemption Pentad: Federal Preemption of Products Liability Claims after Medtronic,* 64 TENN. L. REV. 691, 729 (1997); Vladeck, *Preemption,* 100–03, 120. The Supreme Court agreed to resolve the conflict among the courts of appeals in June 2007. Reigel v. Medtronic, Inc., 127 S.Ct. 3000 (2007).
108. Riegel v. Medtronics, Inc. 128 S.Ct. 999 (2008).
109. Except where otherwise indicated, the facts are taken from the Supreme Court's opinion.
110. U.S. Court to Hear Device Preemption Case, Pharmalot Blog, December 3, 2007, available at *http://www.pharmalot.com/2007/12/us-supreme-court-to-hear-device-preemption-case/* (quoting Riegel attorney Allison Zieve).
111. 128 S.Ct., at 1007.
112. Id., at 1008.
113. Id.
114. Id.
115. Id.
116. Id., 1011.
117. Adler & Mann, *Preemption and Medical Devices,* 945.
118. Vladeck, *Preemption,* 126.
119. See generally Catherine M. Sharkey, *Products Liability Preemption: An Institutional Approach,* 76 GEO. WASH. L. REV. 101 (2008).
120. The story of Harrikah Stanton is drawn from Stanton v. Astra Pharmaceutical Products, Inc., 718 F.2d 553, 556, 558–63 (3d Cir. 1983).

121. *See* THOMAS O. MCGARITY & WENDY E. WAGNER, BENDING SCIENCE (2008) (discussing techniques that affected parties such as pharmaceutical manufacturers employ to "bend" science in ways that advance their interests in regulatory decisionmaking).
122. Buckman Co. v. Plaintiffs' Legal Committee, Brief of Amicus Curiae United States, September 13, 2000, at 22–24, 28.
123. *Id.*, 13–20.
124. Buckman Co. v. Plaintiffs' Legal Committee, 531 U.S. 341 (2001). Except where otherwise noted, the facts and the Court's analysis are drawn from *id.*, 341, 346–51.
125. 21 U.S.C. § 360e(b)(1)(A), (B).
126. 21 C.F.R. § 807.87(k).
127. 21 U.S.C. § 360aaa (prohibition on marketing drugs for off-label uses).
128. Orthopedic Devises: Classification and Reclassification of Pedicle Screw Spinal Systems, 63 Fed. Reg. 40025, 40032 (July 27, 1998).
129 Buckman Co. v. Plaintiffs' Legal Committee, Brief Amicus Curiae of Public Citizen, October 23, 2000, at 2.
130. Buckman Co. v. Plaintiffs' Legal Committee, Brief Amicus Curiae of United States, September 13, 2000, at 10.
131. Pub. L. No. 94–295, 90 Stat. 539, 539 (1976) (preamble).
132. Sam D. Fine, *The Philosophy of Enforcement*, 31 FOOD DRUG COSM. L.J. 324, 328–29 (1976).
133. Woods v. Gliatech, Inc., 218 F. Supp.2d 802 (W.D. Va. 2002); Caraker v. Sandoz Pharmaceuticals Corp., 172 F. Supp.2d 1018, 1039–41 (S.D. Ill. 2001); Bryant v. Hoffmann-LaRoche, Inc., 585 S.E.2d 723 (Ga. Ct. App. 2003).
134. In re Medtronic, Inc., Implantable Defibrillators Litigation, 2006 WL 3478987 (D. Minn. 2006); In re St. Jude Medical, Inc. Silzone Heart Valves Products Liability Litigation, 2004 WL 45503 (D. Minn. 2004); Dawson v. Ciba-Geigy Corp., 145 F. Supp.2d 565 (D.N.J. 2001).
135. Morgan v. Brush Wellman, Inc., 165 F. Supp.2d 704 (E.D. Tenn. 2001).
136. *Id.*, 722. *See also* Nathan Kimmel, Inc. v. DowElanco, 275 F.3d 1199 (9th Cir. 2001) (claim for tortious interference with prospective business advantage preempted where plaintiff would be required to prove that defendant committed fraud on EPA in registering pesticide).
137. Bouchard v. American Home Products Corp., 213 F. Supp.2d 802, 812–13 (N.D. Ohio 2002). *See also* In re Baycol Products Litigation, 495 F. Supp.2d 977, 999-1000 (D. Minn. 2007) (same).
138. Desiano v Warner-Lambert & Co. 467 F.3d 85 (2d Cir. 2006). *But see* Garcia v. Wyeth-Ayerst Labs, 385 F.3d 961 (6h Cir. 2004) (contrary holding by sixth circuit).
139. Warner-Lambert Co. v. Kent, 128 S.Ct. 1168 (2008).
140. RACHEL CARSON, SILENT SPRING (1962); Randall Baker, *Rachel Carson's Silent Spring and the Beginning of the Environmental Movement in the United States, at* http://classwebs.spea.indiana.edu/bakerr/v600/rachel_carson_and_silent_spring.htmhttp://classwebs.spea.indiana.edu/bakerr/v600/rachel_carson_and_silent_spring.htm.
141. Federal Insecticide, Fungicide and Rodenticide Act of 1947, 61 Stat. 163 (1947).

142. U.S. Department of Health, Education and Welfare, Report of the Secretary's Commission on Pesticides and Their Relationship to Environmental Health 44–46 (1969).
143. Christopher J. Bosso, Pesticides and Politics: The Life Cycle of a Public Issue (1987); Donald T. Hornstein, *Lessons From Federal Pesticide Regulation on the Paradigms and Politics of Environmental Law Reform,* 10 Yale J. on Reg. 369 (1993); William H. Rodgers, Jr., *The Persistent Problem of Persistent Pesticides,* 70 Colum. L. J. 567, 570–74 (1970).
144. Pub. L. No. 104–170, 110 Stat. 1489 (1996); Pub. L. No. 94–140, 89 Stat. 751 (1975); Pub. L. No. 92–516, 86 Stat. 973 (1972).
145. 7 U.S.C. § 136a(c).
146. 7 U.S.C. § 136(q)(1).
147. 7 U.S.C. § 136j(a)(1)(E).
148. Bates v. Dow Agrosciences, LLC, Brief of Amici Curiae Natural Resources Defense Council, et al., September 13, 2004, at 10.
149. 7 U.S.C. § 136(q)(1)(A); 136a(f)(2).
150. Pub. L. No. 95–396, 22, 92 Stat. 819 (1978).
151. Bates v. Dow Agrosciences, LLC, 544 U.S. 431, 440 (2005) (citing Environmental Protection Agency, Pesticide Registration Notice 96–4, p. 5 (June 3, 1996)).
152. 7 U.S.C. § 136v(a).
153. 7 U.S.C. § 136v(b).
154. Bates v. Dow Agrosciences, LLC, 544 U.S. 431, 440–41 (2005). See Henderson v. Cominco America, Inc., 518 P.2d 873 (Idaho 1973); Ebers v. General Chemical Co., 17 N.W.2d 176 (Mich. 1945).
155. Bates v. Dow Agrosciences, LLC, Brief for Respondents, November 24, 2004, at 27, n. 17 (collecting cases). *See also* Betsy J. Grey, *Make Congress Speak Clearly: Federal Preemption of State Tort Remedies,* 77 B. U. L. Rev. 559, 588 (1997) (impact of *Cipollone* on pesticides litigation).
156. *See, e.g.,* Grenier v. Vermont Log Buildings, Inc., 96 F.3d 559 (1st Cir. 1996).
157. *See, e.g.,* Dow Agrisciences v. Bates, 332 F.3d 323 (5th Cir. 2003); Arkansas-Platte & Gulf Partnership v. Van Waters & Rogers, 981 F.2d 1177 (10th Cir. 1993); In re DuPont-Benlate Litigation, 859 F. Supp. 619 (D. Puerto Rico 1994).
158. Bates v. Dow Agrosciences, LLC, Brief for Petitioners, September 13, 2004, at 8–9.
159. *Id.,* 10–12.
160. Bates v. Dow Agrosciences, LLC, 544 U.S. 431 (2005).
161. *Id.,* 436. The description of the Court's opinion is drawn from *id.,* 443–51.
162. Bates v. Dow Agrosciences, LLC, Brief for American Chemistry Council as Amicus Curiae, November 23, 2004, at 2–3.
163. Letter from Lynn Goldman, Assistant Administrator for Pesticides, Toxic Substances, and Prevention, Environmental Protection Agency, to Patti A. Goldman (January 7, 1994), attachment to Bates v. Dow Agrosciences, LLC, Brief of Amici Curiae Natural Resources Defense Council, et al., September 13, 2004.
164. 29 U.S.C. § 151, et. seq.

165. 29 U.S.C. § 141, et. seq.
166. Linn v. United Plant Guard Workers of America, Local 114, 383 U.S. 53 (1966); San Diego Building Trades Council v. Garmon, 359 U.S. 236 (1959).
167. Robert A. Gorman, Basic Text on Labor Law (2004).
168. San Diego Building Trades Council v. Garmon, 359 U.S. 236 (1959).
169. *Id.*, 243.
170. Allis-Chalmers Corp. v. Lueck, 471 U.S. 202, 213 (1985).
171. Lingle v. Norge Division of Magic Chef, Inc., 486 U.S. 399, 410 (1988).
172. Restatement (Second) of Torts 46, comment d.
173. Farmer v. United Brotherhood of Carpenters and Joiners of America, Local 25, 430 U.S. 290 (1977).
174. *Id.*, 302.
175. Flibotte v. Pennsylvania Truck Lines, Inc., 131 F.3d 21 (1st Cir. 1997); Smith v. Houston Oilers, 87 F.3d 717 (5th Cir. 1996); Thomas v. LTV Corp., 39 F.3d 611 (5th Cir. 1994); Burgos v. Southwestern Bell Telephone Co., 20 F.3d 633 (5th Cir. 1994); Milne Employees Ass'n v. Sun Carriers, 960 F.2d 1401, 1413 (9th Cir. 1991); Harris v. Alumax Mill Products, Inc., 897 F.2d 400 (9th Cir. 1990); Brown v. Southwestern Bell Telephone Co., 901 F.2d 1250 (5th Cir. 1990); Johnson v. Anheuser Busch, Inc., 876 F.2d 620 (8th Cir. 1989); Chmiel v. Beverly Wilshire Hotel Co., 873 F.2d 1283 (9th Cir. 1989); Douglas v. American Information Technologies Corp., 877 F.2d 565 (7th Cir. 1989); Hyles v. Mensing, 849 F.2d 1213 (9th Cir. 1988).
176. Leucke v. Schnucks Markets, Inc., 85 F.3d 356 (8th Cir. 1996); Tellez v. Pacific Gas & Electric Co., 817 F.2d 536 (9th Cir. 1987); Blanchard v. Simpson Plainwell Paper Co., 925 F. Supp. 510 (W.D. Mich. 1995); Meier v. Hamilton Standard Electronic Systems, Inc., 748 F. Supp. 296 (E.D. Pa. 1990); Grimm v. US West Communications, Inc., 644 NW2d 8 (Iowa 2002); Commodore v. University Mechanical Contractors, Inc., 839 P.2d 314 (Wash. 1992).
177. Krashna v. Oliver Reality, Inc., 895 F.2d 111 (3d Cir. 1990).
178. Lightning v. Roadway Express, Inc., 60 F.3d 1551 (11th Cir. 1995) (mad-dogging); Jackson v. Kimel, 992 F.2d 1318 (4th Cir. 1993) (sex with supervisor); Survival Systems Division of Whittaker Corp. v. United States District Court for the Southern District of California, 825 F.2d 1416 (9th Cir. 1987) (sexual advances); Keehr v. Consolidated Freightways of Delaware, Inc., 825 F.2d 133 (7th Cir. 1987) (wife statements); Retherford v. AT & T Communications, 844 P.2d 949 (Utah 1992) (sexual advances). *See also* Sever v. Alaska Pulp Corp., 978 F.2d 1529 (9th Cir. 1992) (blackballing employee with other employers in retaliation for testifying before Congress); Galvez v. Kuhn, 933 F.2d 773 (9th Cir. 1991) (speeding up an assembly line in a successful attempt to cause injury to an assembly line worker); Knafel v. Pepsi-Cola Bottlers of Akron, Inc., 899 F.2d 1473 (6th Cir. 1990) (assigning employees receiving workplace injuries to tasks requiring heavy lifting contrary to the explicit instructions of company doctors).
179. Mattis v. Massman, 355 F.3d 902, 908 (6th Cir. 2004); Baker v. Farmers Electric Cooperative, Inc., 34 F.3d 274, 280 (5th Cir. 1994).
180. 29 U.S.C. § 651(b).
181. 29 U.S.C. § 655 (OSHA standards); 29 U.S.C. § 667(b) (state standards).

182. 29 U.S.C. § 667(c)(2).
183. 29 U.S.C. § 667(a).
184. In re Welding Fume Products Liability Litigation, 364 F. Supp.2d 669, 674 (N.D. Ohio 2005).
185. 29 U.S.C. § 653(b)(4).
186. Gade v. National Solid Wastes Management Ass'n, 505 U.S. 88 (1992).
187. Lindsey v. Caterpillar, Inc., 480 F.3d 202 (3d Cir. 2007); Pedraza v. Shell Oil Co., 942 F.2d 48 (1st Cir. 1991); In re Welding Fume Products Liability Litigation, 364 F. Supp.2d 669, 688 (N.D. Ohio 2005) (finding it "difficult to imagine a more explicit statement of Congressional intention to preserve and not pre-empt state common law"); Anderson v. Airco, Inc., 2003 WL 21842085 (D. Del. 2003); Fullen v. Philips Electronics North America Corp., 266 F. Supp.2d 471 (N.D. W.Va. 2002); Wickham v. American Tokyo Kasel, Inc., 927 F. Supp. 295 (N.D. Ill. 1996); Kilpatrick v. Delaware County Society for the Prevention of Cruelty to Animals, 632 F. Supp. 542 (E.D. Pa. 1986); Dukes v. Sirius Construction, Inc., 73 P.3d 781 (Mont. 2003).
188. One federal district court has, however, held that a state statute prohibiting employers from preventing employees from bringing handguns into workplace parking lots was preempted by OSHA's general duty clause. ConocoPhillips Co. v. Henry, 520 F. Supp.2d 1282 (N.D. Okl. 2007).
189. 49 U.S.C. § 31306. See Keaveney v. Town of Brookline, 937 F. Supp. 975, 980 (D. Mass. 1996).
190. Drake v. Laboratory Corp. of America Holdings, 458 F3d 48 (2d Cir. 2006).
191. Rector v. LaBone, Inc., 208 F. Supp.2d 987, 991–92 (E.D. Ark. 2002) (describing regulations).
192. 49 U.S.C. § 45106(a).
193. Ishikawa v. Delta Airlines, 343 F.3d 1129 (9th Cir. 2003).
194. *Id.,* 1132.
195. Drake v. Laboratory Corp. of America Holdings, 458 F3d 48 (2d Cir. 2006); Chapman v. Lab One, 390 F.3d 620 (8th Cir. 2004); Fife v. Cooksey, 405 F. Supp.2d 1131 (M.D. Fla. 2005); Glisson v. Occupational Health Centers of Arkansas, 2005 WL 1922574 (E.D. Ark. 2005); Burton v. Southwood Door Co., 305 F. Supp.2d 629 (S.D. Miss. 2003). *But see* Rector v. LaBone, Inc., 208 F. Supp.2d 987 (E.D. Ark. 2002).
196. Payne v. Western & Atlantic Railroad, 81 Tenn. 507, 518–19 (1884), overruled on other grounds, Hutton v. Waters, 179 S.W. 134, 138 (1915); Richard A. Epstein, *In Defense of the Contract at Will,* 51 U. Chi. L. Rev. 947, 947–48 (1984).
197. Novosel v. Nationwide Insurance Co., 721 F.2d 894 (3d Cir. 1983) (Pennsylvania law); Fragassi v. Neiburger, 646 N.E.2d 315, 318 (Ill. App. 1995); Boyle v. Vista Eyewear, Inc., 700 S.W.2d 859 (Mo. Ct. App. 1985).
198. 42 U.S.C. § 5851(a).
199. 29 U.S.C. § 660)(c)
200. 29 U.S.C. § 660)(c); 42 U.S.C. § 5851.
201. English v. General Electric Co., 496 U.S. 72 (1990).
202. *Id.,* 83.
203. Schweiss v. Chrysler Motors Corp., 922 F.2d 473 (8th Cir. 1990); Stansbury v. Sewell

Cadillac-Chevrolet, Inc., 2003 WL 260522 (E.D. La. 2003); Sorge v. Wright's Knitwear Corp., 832 F. Supp. 118 (E.D. Pa. 1993); Kilpatrick v. Delaware County Society for the Prevention of Cruelty to Animals, 632 F. Supp. 542 (E.D. Pa. 1986); Land v. Dow Chemical Co., 2000 WL 729401 (Tex. Civ. App. 2000); Sherman v. Kraft General Foods, Inc., 651 N.E.2d 708 (Ill. App. 1995); Fragassi v. Neiburger, 646 N.E.2d 315 (Ill. App. 1995); Shawcross v. Pyro Products, Inc., 916 S.W.2d 342 (Missouri App. 1995).

204. Knafel v. Pepsi-Cola Bottlers of Akron, Inc., 899 F.2d 1473 (6th Cir. 1990); Smolarek v. Chrysler Corp., 879 F.2d 1326 (6th Cir. 1989); Bettis v. Oscar Meyer Food Corp., 878 F.2d 192 (7th Cir. 1989); Hanks v. General Motors Corp., 859 F.2d 67 (8th Cir. 1988); Vincent v. Trend Western Technical Corp., 828 F.2d 563 (9th Cir. 1987). *But cf.* Klepsky v. United Parcel Service, 489 F.3d 264 (6th Cir. 2006) (claims for damages would not be preempted, but additional claim for reinstatement requires interpretation of CBA and therefore preempted).

205. Consumer Product Safety Act Amendments of 1981, Pub. L. No. 97–35, 1210, 95 Stat. 703 (1981). See R. David Pittle, *The Restricted Regulator,* 12 TRIAL 24–30 (May 1976); Teresa M. Schwartz, *The Consumer Product Safety Commission: A Flawed Product of the Consumer Decade,* 51 GEO. WASH. L. REV. 32 (1982); CPSC Announces Mattel is Recalling Another 8.5 Million Toys Made in China, 35 BNA PROD. SAFETY & LIABILITY REPT. 768 (Augusst 20, 2007); Nationwide Class Suit Over Mattel Toy Recall Seeks Medical Monitoring Due to Lead Paint, 35 BNA PROD. SAFETY & LIABILITY REPT. 780 (Augusst 27, 2007); CPSC, Chinese Agency Announce Agreement to Stop Use of Lead Paint in Children's Toys, 35 BNA PROD. SAFETY & LIABILITY REPT. 870 (September 17, 2007).

206. Pub. L. No. 92–573, 86 Stat. 1207 (1972); 15 U.S.C. § 2952.

207. 15 U.S.C. § 2056(a).

208. Aqua Slide 'N' Dive Corp. v. CPSC, 569 F.2d 831 (5th Cir. 1978). *See also* Southland Mower Co v. CPSC, 619 F.2d 499 (5th Cir. 1980).

209. 15 U.S.C. § 2075.

210. 15 U.S.C. § 2074(a).

211. 15 U.S.C. § 2072(c).

212. Moe v. MTD Products, Inc., 73 F.3d 179, 181 (8th Cir. 1995).

213. *Id.,* 182–83.

214. Leflar & Adler, *Preemption Pentad,* 744 (concluding that "the court's express preemption analysis was mistaken").

215. Cortez v. MTD Products, Inc., 927 F. Supp. 386, 390 (N.D. Cal. 1996).

216. Frazier v. Heckingers, 96 F. Supp.2d 486 (E.D. Pa. 2000); Ball v. BIC Corp., 2000 WL 33312192 (E.D. Mo. 2000); Cortez v. MTD Products, Inc., 927 F. Supp. 386, 390 (N.D. Cal. 1996).

217. Leipart v. Guardian Industries, Inc., 234 F.2d 1063 (9th Cir. 2000); Summerlin v. Scott Petroleum Corp., 324 F. Supp.2d 810 (S.D. Miss. 2004); Colon v. BIC USA, Inc., 136 F. Supp.2d 196 (S.D.N.Y. 2000).

218. Frith v. BIC Corp., 863 So.2d 960 (Miss. 2004).

219. 15 U.S.C. § 1261–62.

220. 15 U.S.C. § 1261(p)(1).

221. 15 U.S.C. § 1262(b).
222. 15 U.S.C. § 1278(a)–(c).
223. 15 U.S.C. § 1261n(b)(1)(A).
224. 15 U.S.C. § 1278.
225. 15 U.S.C. § 1261n(b)(3).
226. Mattis v. Carlon Electrical Products, 295 F.3d 856 (8th Cir. 2002); Milanese v. Rust-Oleum Corp., 244 F.3d 104 (2d Cir. 2001); Comeaux v. National Tea Co., 81 F.3d 42 (5th Cir. 1996); Moss v. Parks Corp., 985 F.2d 736 (4th Cir. 1993); Gougler v. Sirius Products, Inc. 370 F. Supp.2d 1185 (S.D. Ala. 2005); DeHaan v. Whink Products Co., 1994 WL 24322 (N.D. Ill. 1994); Busch v. Graphic Color Corp., 662 N.E.2d 397 (Ill. 1996); Jenkins v. James B. Day & Co., 634 N.E.2d 998 (Ohio 1994).
227. Brazier v. Hasbro, Inc., 2004 WL 515536 (S.D.N.Y. 2004).
228. *Id.,* *3.
229. *See* Anderson v. Stream, 295 N.W.2d 595 (Minn. 1980).
230. 15 U.S.C. § 1681.
231. TRW, Inc. v. Andrews, 534 U.S.19, 23 (2001). *See* S. Rept. No. 108–166, 108th Cong., 1st Sess. 5 (2003).
232. 15 U.S.C. 1681n, 1681o. *See* Safeco Insurance Co. of America v. Burr, 127 S.Ct. 2201 (2007).
233. 15 U.S.C. § 1681h(e).
234. S. Rept. No. 108–166, 108th Cong., 1st Sess. 5 (2003).
235. Michael E. Staten & Fred H. Cate, Does the Fair Credit Reporting Act Promote Accurate Credit Reporting? 14 (Harvard University Joint Center for Housing Studies Working Paper Series, 2004).
236. 15 U.S.C. § 1681s-2(a). *See* S. Rept. No. 108–166, 108th Cong., 1st Sess. 6 (2003); Karl F. Kaufmann, *Fair Credit Reporting Act Developments,* 59 Business Lawyer 1215 (2004).
237. 15 U.S.C. § 1681s-2(e).
238. 15 U.S.C. § 1681s-2(c). *See* Gordon v. Greenpoint Credit, 266 F. Supp.2d 1007, 1010 (S.D. Iowa 2003).
239. 15 U.S.C. § 1681s(2)(a)(6); Kaufmann, *Fair Credit Reporting,* 1219–20; Jeffrey Taft & Christine Poulon, *The FACT Act: The Latest Attempt at Overhauling the Fair Credit Reporting Act and the Fairness and Accuracy of Consumer Reports,* 121 Banking L. J. 194, 206–08 (2004).
240. 15 U.S.C. § 1681t(b).
241. Vasquez-Garcia v. Trans Union de Puerto Rico, 222 F. Supp.2d 150 (D. P. R. 2002).
242. Tracy Bateman Farrell, *Preemption of State Law by Fair Credit Reporting Act,* 8 ALR Fed.2d 233 (2006), at 6.
243. Roybal v. Equifax, 405 F. Supp.2d 1177 (E.D. Cal. 2005); Pirouzian v. SLM Corp., 396 F. Supp.2d 1125 (S.D. Cal. 2005); Riley v. General Motors Acceptance Corp., 226 F. Supp.2d 1316 (S.D. Ala. 2002); Hasvold v. First USA Bank, 194 F. Supp.2d 1228 (D. Wyo. 2002); Davis v. Maryland Bank, 2002 WL 32713429 (N.D. Cal. 2002); Jaramillo v. Experian Information Solutions, Inc., 155 F. Supp.2d 356 (E.D. Pa. 2001); Farrell, *Preemption of State Law,* 3.
244. Ryder v. Washington Mutual Bank, 371 F. Supp.2d 152 (D. Conn. 2005); Woltersdorf v.

Pentagon Federal Credit Union, 320 F. Supp.2d 1222 (N.D. Ala. 2004); Bank One v. Colley, 294 F. Supp.2d 864 (M.D. La. 2003); Stafford v. Cross Country Bank, 262 F. Supp.2d 776 (W.D. Ky. 2003); Vasquez-Garcia v. Trans Union de Puerto Rico, 222 F. Supp.2d 150 (D. P. R. 2002); Aklagi v. Nationscredit Financial, 196 F. Supp.2d 1186 (D. Kan. 2002); Farrell, *Preemption of State Law,* 4.

245. Vasquez-Garcia v. Trans Union de Puerto Rico, 222 F. Supp.2d 150, 161–63 (D. P. R. 2002).
246. Allis-Chalmers Corp. v. Lueck, 471 U.S. 202, 213 (1985).

CHAPTER 5. THE PREEMPTION WAR IN CONGRESS

1. Thomas F. Burke, Lawyers, Lawsuits, and Legal Rights 29 (2002).
2. Contract with America: The Bold Plan by Rep. Newt Gingrich, Rep. Dick Armey, and the House Republicans to Change the Nation 143 (1994). *See* Burke, Lawyers, 25.
3. Robert L. Rabin, *Federalism and the Tort System,* 50 Rutgers L. Rev. 1, 4 (1997).
4. The description of the TEC-DC9 and TEC-9 guns is taken from Jean Macchiaroli Eggen & John G. Culhane, *Gun Torts: Defining a Cause of Action for Victims in Suits Against Gun Manufacturers,* 81 N. Car. L. Rev. 115, 125–26 (2002), and Merrill v. Navegar, Inc., 28 P.2d 116, 119 (Cal. 2001).
5. The description of the Ferri rampage is taken from Merrill v. Navegar, Inc., 28 P.2d 116, 120 (Cal. 2001).
6. Eggen & Culhane, *Gun Torts,* 126–27; Tony Mowry, *The Protection of [Unlawful] Commerce in Arms Act—Does Congress Have the Power to Pass Special Legislation,* 14 Temple Pol. & Civ. Rights L. Rev. 225, 229 (2004) (fifty people a day).
7. Brian Siebel, *Gun Industry Immunity: Why the Gun Industry's "Dirty Little Secret" Does Not Deserve Congressional Protection,* 75 UMKC L. Rev. 911, 938 (2005); Daniel Feldman, *Legislating or Litigating Public Policy Change: Gunmaker Tort Liability,* 12 Va. J. Soc. Pol. & L. 140, 153 (2004).
8. Elizabeth T. Crouse, *Note, Arming the Gun Industry: A Critique of Proposed Legislation Shielding the Gun Industry From Liability,* 88 Minn. L. Rev. 1346 (2004).
9. James L. Daniels, *Violating the Inviolable: Firearm Industry Retroactive Exemptions and the Need for a New Test for Overreeaching Federal Prohibitions,* 38 James Marshall L. Rev. 955 (2005) (fortunate son quote); Scott Medlock, *NRA—No Rational Argument? How the National Rifle Association Exploits Public Irrationality,* 11 Tex. J. Civil Liberties & Civil Rights 39, 41–44, 52 (2005) (Bush resignation); Allen Rostron, *Lawyers, Guns & Money: The Rise and Fall of Tort Litigation Against the Firearms Industry,* 46 Santa Clara L. Rev. 481, 497–98 (2006) (mixed blessing); Ryan VanGrack, *The Protection of Lawful Commerce in Arms Act,* 41 Harv. J. Leg. 541, 549–50 (2004).
10. Bureau of Alcohol, Tobacco, and Firearms, Following the Gun: Enforcing Federal Laws Against Firearms Traffickers 5 (June 2000) (no prohibition on diversion); Hamilton v. Beretta U.S.A. Corp., 750 N.E.2d 1055, 1066, n.9 (N.Y. 2001) (detailed description of federal gun regulatory regime); Timothy D. Lytton, *The Com-*

plementary Role of Tort Litigation in Regulating the Gun Industry, in SUING THE GUN INDUSTRY 250, 255–55 (Timothy D. Lytton, ed., 2005); Peter H. Schuck, *Why Regulating Guns Through Litigation Won't Work, in id.,* 225, 231; Wendy Wagner, *Stubborn Information Problems & the Regulatory Benefits of Gun Litigation, in id.,* 271, 280; Eggen & Culhane, *Gun Torts,* 81 N.CAR. L. REV. 115, 119, 128–31 (2002).

11. Phillip J. Cook & Jens Ludwig, *Litigation as Regulation: Firearms, in* REGULATION THROUGH LITIGATION 67, 73 (W. Kip Viscusi, ed., 2002) (single inspection limit); Daniels, *Violating the Inviolable,* 958 (far too few resources quote, single inspection); Wagner, *Stubborn Information,* 271, 281 (10 percent inspected); Laura Sullivan, *Success of Shift in Guns Policy Is Debatable,* BALTIMORE SUN, October 27, 2004, at A1 (4.5 percent inspected in 2002).
12. Sullivan, *Success of Shift* (most prosecutions by local officials). *See also* Eric Lichtblau, *Justice Dept. Plans to Step Up Gun-Crime Prosecutions,* NEW YORK TIMES, May 14, 2003, at A18 (fewer than 1,600 prosecutions out of 420,000 reported stolen firearms).
13. Fox Butterfield, *Limits on Power and Zeal Hamper Firearms Agency,* NEW YORK TIMES, July 22, 1999, at A1.
14. Sullivan, *Success of Shift.*
15. Daniels, *Violating the Inviolable* (five years to complete); Cook & Ludwig, *Litigation as Regulation,* 67, 71 (quote); Wagner, *Stubborn Information,* 271, 281 (enforcement not a threat); Amit R. Paley, *Gun Seller's Case Reveals Hurdles of Enforcement,* WASHINGTON POST, July 23, 2006, at A1 (Baltimore example).
16. *See* Deborah R. Hensler, *The New Social Policy Torts: Litigation as a Legislative Strategy—Some Preliminary Thoughts on a New Research Project,* 51 DEPAUL L. REV. 493 (2001) (referring to the litigation as "social policy tort litigation"); Schuck, *Regulating Guns Through Litigation,* 225, 225; Wagner, *Stubborn Information,* 271, 272 (referring to the litigation as "regulatory litigation").
17. Timothy D. Lytton, *Introduction, in* SUING THE GUN INDUSTRY, 1; Timothy D. Lytton, *Lawsuits Against the Gun Industry: A Comparative Institutional Analysis,* 32 CONN. L. REV. 1247, 1255 (2000); Timothy D. Lytton, *Tort Claims Against Gun Manufacturers for Crime-Related Injuries: Defining a Suitable Role for the Tort System in Regulating the Firearms Industry,* 65 MO. L. REV. 1, 6 (2000).
18. Carl T. Bogus, *War on the Common Law: The Struggle at the Center of Products Liability,* 60 MO. L. REV. 1, 60 (1995); Crouse, *Arming the Gun Industry,* 1351; Eggen & Culhane, *Gun Torts,* 136, 138–41; Lytton, *Tort Claims Against Gun Manufacturers,* 11–14.
19. Lytton, *Introduction,* 1, 7–8; VanGrack, *Protection,* 557. *See* Melvin Claxton, *Defective Firearms Go Unchecked,* DETROIT NEWS, December 14, 2003, at A1 (describing many defectively designed and manufactured firearms).
20. Eggen & Culhane, *Gun Torts,* 150–54 (quote); Lytton, *Tort Claims,* 8–9.
21. Eggen & Culhane, *Gun Torts,* 142–45; Lytton, *Tort Claims,* 26–42.
22. Lytton, *Tort Claims,* 32, 36–42 (complex statistics); Fox Butterfield, *Gun Industry Ex-Official Describes Bond of Silence,* NEW YORK TIMES, February 4, 2003, at A14 (quotes).
23. Hamilton v. Beretta U.S.A. Corp., 750 N.E.2d 1055, 1061 (N.Y. 2001); Lytton, *Introduction,* 1, 8–9; Eggen & Culhane, *Gun Torts,* 148; Lytton, *Tort Claims,* 22.

24. Restatement (Second) of Torts § 390.
25. Timothy D. Lytton, *Halberstam v. Daniel and the Uncertain Future of Negligent Marketing Claims Against Firearms Manufacturers,* 64 Brooklyn L. Rev. 681, 688–89 (1998).
26. Hamilton v. Beretta U.S.A. Corp., 750 N.E.2d 1055, 1062–65 (N.Y. 2001) (quote); Lytton, *Tort Claims,* 45; Lytton, *Halberstam v. Daniel,* 704–05.
27. Crouse, *Arming the Gun Industry,* 1351 (a few have survived); Lytton, *Introduction,* 23–25 (clear attempts to circumvent); Siebel, *Gun Industry Immunity,* 914 n.14 (cases allowed to go to trial); Fox Butterfield, *Sniper Victims in Settlement With Gun Maker and Dealer,* New York Times, September 16, 2004, at A14 (Washington, D.C., sniper settlement).
28. Cook & Ludwig, *Litigation as Regulation,* 67; Lytton, *Introduction,* 1, 3 (quote); VanGrack, *Protection,* 544–45.
29. Lytton, *Introduction,* 1, 1–2; Richard C. Ausness, *Public Tort Litigation: Public Benefit or Public Nuisance,* 77 Temple L. Rev. 825, 826–27 (2004).
30. Hensler, *New Social Policy Torts,* 500.
31. Ausness, *Public Tort Litigation,* 840; Howard M. Erichson, *Private Lawyers, Public Lawsuits: Plaintiffs' Attorneys in Municipal Gun Litigation, in* Suing the Gun Industry, 129; Matt Labash, *Lawyers, Guns and Money,* The Weekly Standard, February 1, 1999, at 25.
32. Ausness, *Public Tort Litigation,* 856; Crouse, *Arming the Gun Industry,* 1354; Daniels, *Violating the Inviolable,* 962; VanGrack, *Protection,* 542.
33. *See,* e.g., Camden County Bd. of Chosen Freeholders v. Beretta, U.S.A., Corp., 273 F.3d 536, 539 (3d Cir. 2001).
34. Ausness, *Public Tort Litigation,* 841; Susan Finch, *N.O. Gun Suit Shot Down,* New Orleans Times-Picayune, April 4, 2001, at A1.
35. Lytton, *Introduction,* 843–53.
36. City of Cincinnati v. Baretta U.S.A. Corp., 768 N.E.2d 1136 (Ohio 2002); Crouse, *Arming the Gun Industry,* 1354–55 n. 52.
37. City of Gary v. Smith & Wesson Corp., 801 N.E.2d 1222, 1234–35 (Ind. 2003).
38. Daniels, *Violating the Inviolable,* 962–63.
39. City of Chicago v. Baretta U.S.A. Corp., 821 N.E.2d 1099, 1107–08 (Ill. 2004); Carl T. Bogus, *Guns in the Courtroom,* The Nation, March 31, 2003, at 36; Erichson, *Private Lawyers, Public Lawsuits,* 129, 134; Lytton, *Tort Claims,* 47.
40. City of Chicago v. Baretta U.S.A. Corp., 821 N.E.2d 1099, 1122–23, 1126 (Ill. 2004). *See* Lytton, *Complementary Role,* 250, 257.
41. The description of the NAACP case is drawn from National Association for the Advancement of Colored People v. Acusport, Inc., 271 F. Supp.2d 435, 446–50 (E.D.N.Y. 2003).
42. Robert F. Worth, *Gun Makers Not Liable for Violence, Jury Says,* New York Times, May 15, 2003, at B1.
43. Jim VandeHei, *Gun Firms on Verge of Winning New Shield,* Washington Post, May 5, 2003, at A1.
44. Feldman, *Legislating or Litigating,* 156 (deep pocket municipalities); Timothy D. Lytton, *The NRA, the Brady Campaign, and the Politics of Gun Litigation, in* Suing the Gun Industry, 152; Crouse, *Arming the Gun Industry,* 1363–64; Fox Butterfield, *Bill to Bar Suits Against Gun Industry Stuns Crime Victims,* New York Times, April 21, 2003, at A17 (quoting Lawrence G. Keane, General Counsel, National Shooting Sports Foundation).

45. Rostron, *Lawyers, Guns & Money,* 510; Richard B. Schmitt, *House Backs Bill to Limit Suits by Gun Victims Against Makers,* Los Angeles Times, April 10, 2003, at A34 (quoting Rep. Candice S. Miller (R-Mich.).
46. *See* Ausness, *Public Tort Litigation,* 899–900; Crouse, *Arming the Gun Industry,* 1364 (slippery slope); Lytton, *The NRA,* 152, 160; Frank Vandall, *A Preliminary Consideration of Issues Raised in the Firearms Sellers Immunity Bill,* 38 Akron L. Rev. 113 (2005), at 123–24; VanGrack, *Protection of Lawful Commerce in Arms Act,* 543.
47. Lytton, *The NRA,* 153 (political muscle quote).
48. Ausness, *Public Tort Litigation,* 897; Eggen & Culhane, *Gun Torts,* 180–81, 183–84.
49. Ausness, *Public Tort Litigation,* 897; Crouse, *Arming the Gun Industry,* 1364–65; VanGrack, *Protection of Lawful Commerce in Arms Act,* 547; Butterfield, *Bill to Bar Suits* (quoting David Lemongello) (innocent victim quoted).
50. Edward M. Kennedy, *Statement,* 151 Cong. Rec. S9380, 109th Cong., 1st Sess. (July 29, 2005) (only fifty-seven lawsuits had been filed against the gun industry out of an estimated ten million total torts suits filed from 1995 to 2005); Feldman, *Legislating or Litigating,* 157; Lytton, *The NRA,* 152, 167; VanGrack, *Protection of Lawful Commerce in Arms Act,* 547, 549–52.
51. VanGrack, *Protection of Lawful Commerce in Arms Act,* 545–46; Bill McAllister, *Gun Lawsuit Bill on Hold in House,* Denver Post, October 17, 2002, at A22 (House bill tabled); Deirdre Shesgreen, *Gun Control Advocates Turn Efforts From National to Local Government,* St. Louis Post-Dispatch, March 30, 2001, at A6 (NRA top priority).
52. Daniels, *Violating the Inviolable,* 967; Lytton, *The NRA,* 152, 169; Butterfield, *Bill to Bar Suits.*
53. Daniels, *Violating the Inviolable,* 967–68; Patricia Foster, *Good Guns (and Good Business Practices) Provide All the Protection They Need: Why Legislation to Immunize the Gun Industry From Civil Liability Is Unconstitutional,* 72 U. Cincinnati L. Rev. 1739, 1748 (2004).
54. Schmitt, *House Backs Bill;* John Tierney, *House Votes to Limit Lawsuits Against Gun Manufacturers,* New York Times, April 10, 2003, at A22.
55. Sheryl Gay Stolberg, *A Swing to the Middle on Gun Control,* New York Times, March 7, 2004, at D4 (LaPierre quote); Helen Dewar, *Gun Bill Dies After Sponsors Drop Support,* Washington Post, March 3, 2004, at A4; Edward Epstein, *Gun-Liability Bill Dies in Senate,* San Francisco Chronicle, March 3, 2004, at A16; Richard Simon, *Gun Lobby Outflanked in Senate Maneuvers,* New Orleans Times-Picayune, March 3, 2004, at A1; Sheryl Gay Stolberg, *Senate Leaders Scuttle Gun Bill Over Changes,* New York Times, March 3, 2004, at A1 (Finestein quote); James Gordon Meek, *High Noon Over Bill to Shield Gunmakers,* New York Daily News, April 27, 2003, at 24 (filibuster promised).
56. Julia Malone, *Bush Starts Tort Reform Fight in Judicial Hot Spot,* Atlanta Journal-Constitution, January 5, 2005, at A1.
57. *A Gift to the Gun Industry,* Washington Post, June 2, 2005, at A22; Jennifer A. Dlouhy, *Gunmakers Ask Congress for Immunity From Lawsuits,* Houston Chronicle, March 16, 2005, at A9.
58. Mary Curtius, *Bill Shielding Gun Makers From Suits Gains Support,* Los Angeles Times, July 27, 2005, at A15 (White House quote); Sheryl Gay Stolberg, *As August Recess Looms, Congress Finds High Gear,* New York Times, July 27, 2005, at A18; *Senators Pause to Aid*

Gun Lobby, San Francisco Chronicle, July 27, 2005, at B6; *No Gun Dealer Bailout,* Washington Post, July 26, 2005, at A18.

59. Shailagh Murray, *Senate Passes Bill Barring Gun Suits,* Washington Post, July 30, 2005, at A8; Craig Gilbert, *Senate OKs Kohl's Plan for Gun Safety Locks,* Milwaukee Journal Sentinel, July 29, 2005, at A8.
60. Amy Goldstein, *House Passes Ban on Gun Industry Lawsuits,* Washington Post, October 21, 2005, at A7; Ann McFeatters, *Gun Industry Wins Liability Protection,* Pittsburgh Post-Gazette, October 21, 2005, at A1.
61. Public Law. No. 109–92, 108th Cong. 1st. Sess. (2005); *Bush Signs Legislation Prohibiting Tort Suits Against Gun Makers for Misuse by Others,* 33 BNA Prod. Safety & Liability Rept. 1069 (October 31, 2005).
62. The description of the PLCA Act is drawn from Crouse, *Arming the Gun Industry,* 1367–72.
63. Crouse, *Arming the Gun Industry,* 1367–68.
64. *See* Thomas O. McGarity, Douglas A. Kysar, & Karen Sokol, The Truth About Torts: Lawyers, Guns, and Money 8 (Center for Progressive Reform White Paper #603, 2006).
65. Schuck, *Regulating Guns Through Litigation,* 225, 225; Wagner, *Stubborn Information,* 225, 226.
66. Lytton, *Introduction,* 1, 24.
67. Siebel, G*un Industry Immunity,* 930–36.
68. Cook & Ludwig, *Litigation as Regulation,* 67, 69; Lytton, *Introduction,* 1, 3; Crouse, *Arming the Gun Industry,* 1351.
69. City of New York v. Beretta U.S.A. Corp., 401 F. Supp.2d 244, 270-71 (E.D.N.Y. 2005).
70. Ileto v. Glock, Inc., 421 F. Supp.2d 1274, 1284-98 (C.D. Cal. 2006).
71. 21 U.S.C. § 151–59. *See* Jennie Clarke, *Comment, Federal Preemption: A Vaccine Manufacturer's Defense,* 56 U.M.K.C. L. Rev. 515, 525–29 (1988).
72. 42 U.S.C. § 262(a).
73. 21 C.F.R. § 601. *See* Blackmon v. American Home Products Corp., 328 F. Supp.2d 659, 665 (S.D. Tex. 2004); Clarke, *Federal Preemption,* 528–29.
74. Mazur v. Merck & Co., 742 F. Supp. 239, 246 n. 7 (E.D. Pa. 1990) (collecting cases). *See also* Morris v. Parke, Davis & Co., 667 F. Supp. 1322 (C.D. Cal. 1987).
75. 42 U.S.C. § 300aa-11–15, 22(e).
76. Division of Vaccine Injury Compensation, Department of Health and Human Services, National Vaccine Injury Compensation Program Strategic Plan 7 (2006).
77. Rebecca Adams, *Vaccine Makers Seek Inoculation From Suits,* CQ Weekly, December 5, 2005, at 3248; *Senate Funding Panel Told Rx Industry Needs Additional Help With Liability Issues,* 33 BNA Prod. Liability Rept. 484 (2005); United States General Accounting Office, Flu Vaccine: Recent Supply Shortages Underscore Ongoing Challenges (November 2004) (Statement of Janet Heinrich, Director, Health Care—Public Health Issues, Government Accountability Office).
78. Public Law No. 109–148, Div. C (2005).
79. Bill Theobold, *Vaccine Makers Helped Write Frist-Backed Shield Law,* The Tennessean,

May 8, 2006, at A1; PUBLIC CITIZEN CONGRESS WATCH, WILLFUL MISCONDUCT: HOW BILL FRIST AND THE DRUG LOBBY COVERTLY BAGGED A LIABILITY SHIELD 6 (2006) (citing a November 18, 2005, e-mail from Dave W. Boyer, Director of Federal Government Relations for the Biotechnology Industry Organization).

80. 109 CONG. REC. H13181 (December 22, 2005) (statement of Rep. Richard Obey); Adams, *Vaccine Makers Seek Inoculation,* 3248; *Kennedy, Dodd Object to "Backroom" Effort to Grant Drug Makers Broad Liability Shield,* 33 BNA PROD. LIABILITY REPT. 1145 (November 21, 2005).
81. PUBLIC CITIZEN CONGRESS WATCH, WILLFUL MISCONDUCT, 8; DIVISION OF VACCINE INJURY COMPENSATION, STRATEGIC PLAN, 1 (president signs bill); Marilyn Werber Serafini, *The Vaccine Crisis,* 38 NAT. J. 28 (2006); Catherine Hollingsworth, *Liability Shield Law for Vaccine Makers Signed by Bush, Seen as Far-Reaching* 34 BNA PROD. LIABILITY REPT. 7 (January 9, 2006).
82. 42 U.S.C. § 247d-6d(a)(1).
83. 42 U.S.C. § 247d-6d(d).
84. 42 U.S.C. § 247d-6d(c)(5).
85. DIVISION OF VACCINE INJURY COMPENSATION, STRATEGIC PLAN, 4, n.6.
86. 42 U.S.C. § 247d-6d(i)(2).
87. 42 U.S.C. § 247d-6d(i)(1), (7).
88. Scott Gold, *Gasoline Leak Poisons Wrightsboro Wells,* WILMINGTON MORNING STAR, June 28, 1995, at A1; Jeff Selingo, *Wrightsboro/Meeting Held on Gasoline Station Leak,* WILMINGTON MORNING STAR, September 15, 1995, at B2 (probably MTBE).
89. June 29, 2001, in Ft. Worth Texas; Jeff Selingo, *Residents File Lawsuit Over Conoco Leak,* WILMINGTON MORNING STAR, March 11, 1996, at A1.
90. Interview with Scott Summy, June 29, 2001, in Ft. Worth, Texas.
91. Cory Reiss, *Jury Rules Gas Firm Must Pay Millions,* WILMINGTON MORNING STAR, August 26, 1997, at A1; Cory Reiss, *Manager Says He Reported Gasoline Leak,* WILMINGTON MORNING STAR, August 5, 1997, at A1; Cory Reiss, *Judge Gives Tentative OK to Conoco Settlement,* WILMINGTON MORNING STAR, August 28, 1997, at A1.
92. Interview with Scott Summy, June 29, 2001, in Ft. Worth, Texas.
93. Environmental Protection Agency, Methyl Tertiary Butyl Ether (MTBE); Advance Notice of Intent to Initiate Rulemaking Under the Toxic Substances Control Act to Eliminate or Limit the Use of MTBE as a Fuel Additive in Gasoline, 65 Fed. Reg. 16094, 16096–97 (2000).
94. Michael Arndt, *Shell Starts Selling a Cleaner Gas Here,* CHICAGO TRIBUNE, April 12, 1990, at 1 (EPA employee quote); *Dramatic Gains for MTBE,* CHEMICAL WEEK, March 14, 1990, at 50 (quoting energy consultant DeWitt & Co) (fastest growing quote); Amy Stevens, *Arco to Sell Substitute for Leaded Gas,* WASHINGTON POST, August 16, 1989, at A2.
95. Environmental Protection Agency, Advance Notice, 16096–97. *See* Thomas O. McGarity, *MTBE: A Precautionary Tale,* 28 HARV. ENV. L. REV. 281 (2004).
96. Environmental Protection Agency, Advance Notice, 16097 ("turpentine-like"); ENVIRONMENTAL PROTECTION AGENCY, ACHIEVING CLEAN AIR AND CLEAN WATER: THE REPORT OF THE BLUE RIBBON PANEL ON OXYGENATES IN GASOLINE 76 (1999) (MTBE car-

cinogenic in animals); Arturo Keller, et al., Health & Environmental Assessment of MTBE: Report to the Governor and Legislature of the State of California as Sponsored by SB 521 20 (1998) ("objectionable," "bitter," "solvent-like," and "nauseating").

97. Environmental Protection Agency, Advance Notice, 16102 (quote); Environmental Protection Agency, Achieving Clean Air and Clean Water, 1, 17, 42 (MTBE characteristics, LUST description, MTBE used in one-third of U.S. gasoline).
98. The description of the *Communities for a Better Environment* and *South Lake Tahoe* litigation is drawn from Richard O. Faulk & John S. Gray, *Reunion in Salem: Updating the MTBE Controversy,* 36 Env. L. Rept. 10667, 10675–76 (2006).
99. Faulk & Gray, *Reunion in Salem,* 10676.
100. The description of the court's preemption holding is taken from In re: Methyl Tertiary Butyl Ether (MTBE) Products Liability Litigation, 175 F. Supp.2d 593, 612–14 (S.D.N.Y. 2001). See also 42 U.S.C. § 7545(c)(4)(A) (relevant Clean Air Act preemption provision).
101. In re: Methyl Tertiary Butyl Ether (MTBE) Products Liability Litigation, 457 F. Supp. 324 (S.D.N.Y. 2006).
102. National Energy Policy Development Group, Reliable, Affordable, and Environmentally Sound Energy for America's Future, Report of the National Energy Policy Development Group, Appendix 1 (May 2001) (Cheney Energy Task Force Report); Carolyn Loehhead, *House Passes Energy Bill—Drilling OKd,* San Francisco Chronicle, August 2, 2001, at A1 (House progress).
103. Elizabeth Shogren & Richard Simon, *Democrats Delay Senate Vote on Energy Bill,* Los Angeles Times, November 28, 2001, at A16.
104. Zachary Coile, *Senate OK's Ethanol-Rich Energy Bill,* San Francisco Chronicle, April 26, 2002, at A1 (ethanol shield); Richard Simon, *Plans Sputter to Strip Ethanol Rules From Senate Energy Bill,* Los Angeles Times, April 24, 2002, at A18 (bill easily approved); Dan Morgan, *In Energy Bill, A Daschle Nod to Key Farm States,* Washington Post, February 19, 2002, at A4 (Daschle Bill); Zachary Coile, *Senators Rap Ethanol Mandate,* San Francisco Chronicle, April 12, 2002, at A4 (California opposition); Douglas Holt, *EPA Decision Likely to Drive Ethanol Use,* Chicago Tribune, June 13, 2001, at A1 ($1 billion shift); George Raine, *The Ethanol Debate,* San Francisco Chronicle, June 9, 2001, at E1 (increased ethanol demand).
105. David Ivanovich, *National Energy Measure Running on Fumes,* Houston Chronicle, October 17, 2002, at A1 (MTBE shield demand); *Lawmakers Seek Liability Relief for MTBE,* Chemical Week, September 25, 2002, at 7 (MTBE shield demand); *Energy Bill on the Agenda Again,* National Petroleum News, January 1, 2003, at 12; *Energy Bill All But Dead,* National Petroleum News, December 1, 2002, at 8.
106. Don Fagin, *Fuel Additive Focus of Ban, Exemption,* Newsday, May 13, 2003, at A16 (quoting petroleum industry attorney Scott Segal); Richard Simon, *Energy Bill Seen as a Gusher of Industry Breaks,* Los Angeles Times, April 10, 2003, at A32.
107. McGarity, MTBE, 305–09.
108. Bill Walsh, *Energy Bill Boon to La. Firms,* New Orleans Times-Picayune, November 18, 2003, at A4 (DeLay priority); David Ivanovich, *Energy Bill on Its Way,* Houston

Chronicle, November 15, 2003, at A1 (DeLay priority); Richard Simon, *Republicans Agree on Sweeping Energy Bill,* Los Angeles Times, November 15, 2003, at A1 (Waxman report); Jane Kay, *GOP Backs Firms' Liability Relief From MTBE Lawsuits,* San Francisco Chronicle, October 8, 2003, at A2 (attorney general opposition); Laura Parker, *Energy Bill Provision May Stop Suits Over Water Polluted by Gas Additive,* USA Today, September 30, 2003, at A3 (water district attorney quote); Carl Hulse, *Energy Bill Is Likely to Have Protection on Gasoline Additives,* New York Times, September 26, 2003, at A18 (safe harbor quote); David Ivanovich, *Senators Reuse Bill on Energy,* Houston Chronicle, August 1, 2003, at B1 (previous bill passed).

109. Richard Simon, *Energy Measure Would Limit Liability of MTBE Producers,* Los Angeles Times, November 16, 2003, at A24 (rush to courthouse quote); Peter Behr & Dan Morgan, *Republicans Detail Aid for Energy Producers,* Washington Post, November 16, 2003, at A10 (Republican agreement); Carl Hulse, *Accord Reached By Republicans for Energy Bill,* New York Times, November 15, 2003, at A1 (Republican agreement); David Ivanovich, *Debate Over Energy Bill Driven by Gas Additive,* Houston Chronicle, October 14, 2003, at A1 (senators letter); Richard Simon, *Additive Rises to Top of Energy Debate,* Los Angeles Times, October 11, 2003, at A14 (senators letter).

110. Megh Duwadi & David Ivanovich, *Energy Bill Hits Senate Roadblock,* Houston Chronicle, November 22, 2003, at A1 (DeLay scapegoat quote); Zachary Coile, *GOP Brass Can't Pass Pork-Filled Energy Bill,* San Francisco Chronicle, November 22, 2003, at A1 (Daschle blames House Republicans); Richard Simon, *Senate Blocks Bush-Backed Energy Bill,* Los Angeles Times, November 22, 2003, at A1 (Senate vote); Michael Davis & Megh Duwadi, *Energy Bill's Fate May Hinge on MTBE Battle,* Houston Chronicle, November 21, 2003, at A1 (DeLay trial lawyers quote); Zachary Coile, *Fat Energy Bill Seen as Laden with Pork,* San Francisco Chronicle, November 21, 2003, at A2 (Hooters quote); Julie Hirschfield Davis, *Sweeping Energy Bill Stalls in Senate,* Baltimore Sun, November 20, 2003, at A3 (bill stalls in Senate); Richard Simon, *House OKs New Energy Policy,* Los Angeles Times, November 19, 2003, at A20 (House passes bill).

111. Gebe Martinez, *Bush Meets With GOP Allies in Push for Energy Bill,* Houston Chronicle, May 21, 2004, at A12 (DeLay quotes); David Ivanovich, *Republicans Won't Budge on MTBE,* Houston Chronicle, March 5, 2004, at A2; Carl Hulse, *Senators Try to Squeeze Slimmer Energy Bill Through Congress After Defeat Last Year,* New York Times, February 11, 2004, at A26.

112. Carl Hulse, *Water-Cleanup Measure Stalls Energy Bill,* New York Times, July 23, 2005, at A10 (House compromise fails); Carl Hulse, *Senate Bill Strives to Balance Oil and Alternatives,* New York Times, June 29, 2005, at A19 (Senate passes bill); Carl Hulse, *House Votes to Approve Broad Energy Legislation,* New York Times, April 22, 2005, at A14 (House passes bill); David Ivanovich, *DeLay's Issues Ensnarl Energy Bill,* Houston Chronicle, April 14, 2005, at B1 (House committee vote); Jeff Nesmith, *Big Energy Changes Afoot,* Atlanta Journal-Constitution, January 16, 2005, at D1 (better prospects).

113. Environmental Protection Agency, Regulation of Fuels and Fuel Additives: Removal of Reformulated Gasoline Oxygen Content Requirement and Revision of Commingling

Prohibition to Address Non-Oxygenated Reformulated Gasoline, 71 Fed. Reg. 8973 (February 22, 2006) (EPA announcement); Timothy B. Wheeler, *Refiners to Phase Out Use of MTBE,* BALTIMORE SUN, February 17, 2006, at B1 (EPA announcement); Faulk & Gray, *Reunion in Salem,* at 10672 (Bush signs bill); Mark A. Stein, *Congress Passes an Energy Bill in Time for the Drive Home,* NEW YORK TIMES, July 30, 2005, at C3 (conference committee action); Richard Simon & James Peltz, *Lawmakers Reach Deal on Energy Overhaul,* LOS ANGELES TIMES, July 27, 2005, at A22 (House drops MTBE provision).

114. Kuhl v. Lincoln National Health Plan of Kansas City, Inc., 999 F.2d 298 (8th Cir. 1993).
115. 29 U.S.C. § 1001(b). Aetna Health, Inc. v. Davila, Brief of United Policyholders as Amicus Curiae, January 22, 2004, at *24-*29; Donald T. Bogan, *Protecting Patient Rights Despite ERISA: Will the Supreme Court Allow States to Regulate Managed Care?* 74 TULANE L. REV. 951, 996 (2000); Stacy Roberts Sharp, *Note, ERISA Preemption and MCO Liability: The Court's Search in Aetna Health, Inc. v. Davila for Congress's Elusive Intent,* 84 TEX. L. REV. 1347, 1351 (2006).
116. 29 U.S.C. § 1002(1). *See* Pilot Life Insurance Co. v. Dedeaux, 481 U.S. 41, 44 (1987); John H. Langbein, *What ERISA Means by "Equitable": The Supreme Court's Trail of Error in Russell, Mertens, and Great-West,* 103 COLUM. L. REV. 1317, 1325 n. 52 (2003).
117. 29 U.S.C. § 1144(a) (preemption clause); 29 U.S.C. § 1144(b)(2)(A) (savings clause); 29 U.S.C. § 1144(b)(2)(B) (deemer clause).
118. 29 U.S.C. § 1132(a)(1)-(3).
119. Bogan, *Protecting Patient Rights,* 956.
120. Pilot Life Insurance Co. v. Dedeaux, 481 U.S. 41 (1987).
121. *Id.,* 56, 58.
122. Metropolitan Life Insurance Co. v. Massachusetts, 471 U.S. 724, 739 (1985); *See also* Ingersoll-Rand Corp. v. McClendon, 498 U.S. 133 (1990) (holding that ERISA preempted state common law claims); Catherine L. Fisk, *The Last Article About the Language of ERISA Preemption? A Case Study of the Failure of Textualism,* 33 HARV. J. LEGIS. 35, 60–66 (1996).
123. Shaw v. Delta Airlines, Inc., 463 U.S. 85, 97 (1983); District of Columbia v. Greater Washington Board of Trade, 506 U.S. 125, 129 (1992) (quoting Black's Law Dictionary 1288 (6th ed., 1990)). See Bogan, *Protecting Patient Rights,* 986; Fisk, *Last Article,* 64.
124. Aetna Health, Inc. v. Davila, Brief of United Policyholders as Amicus Curiae, January 22, 2004, at *14; Bogan, *Protecting Patient Rights,* 964–72, 974, 976–77.
125. Aetna Health, Inc. v. Davila, Brief for the United States as Amicus Curiae, December 18, 2003, at *25–*26; Aetna Health, Inc. v. Davila, Brief for the Chamber of Commerce of the United States as Amicus Curiae, December 18, 2003, at *13, *25–*26.
126. See Bogan, *Protecting Patient Rights,* 958; Fisk, *Last Article,* 39.
127. Great-West Life and Annuity Insurance Co. v. Knudson, 534 U.S. 204 (2002); Mertens v. Hewitt Associates, 508 U.S. 248 (1993); Massachusetts Mutual Life Insurance Co. v. Russell, 473 U.S. 134 (1985).

126. See Bogan, *Protecting Patient Rights,* 958; Fisk, *Last Article,* 39.
127. Great-West Life and Annuity Insurance Co. v. Knudson, 534 U.S. 204 (2002); Mertens

v. Hewitt Associates, 508 U.S. 248 (1993); Massachusetts Mutual Life Insurance Co. v. Russell, 473 U.S. 134 (1985).

128. Great-West Life and Annuity Insurance Co. v. Knudson, 534 U.S. 204 (2002); Mertens v. Hewitt Associates, 508 U.S. 248, 255 (1993).

129. Langbein, *What ERISA Means by "Equitable."*

130. Bogan, *Protecting Patient Rights,* 998.

131. Pegram v. Herdrich, 530 U.S. 211, 220 (2000).

132. Jonathan J. Frankel, *Note, Medical Malpractice Law and Health Care Cost Containment: Lessons for Reformers From the Clash of Cultures,* 103 YALE L. J. 1297, 1303 (1994).

133. Corcoran v. United Healthcare, 965 F.2d 1321, 1332 (5th Cir. 1992). (quote). *See* Sharp, *ERISA Preemption and MCO Liability,* 1354–56.

134. Nancy Mansfield, Joan T. A. Gabel, & Laurie B. Jablow, *Evolving Tension Between HMO Liability Precedent and Legislation,* 36 TORT & INS. L. J. 949, 951 (2001).

135. DiFelice v. Aetna U.S. Healthcare, 346 F.3d 442, 454 (3d Cir. 2003) (Becker, J. concurring).

136. *Id.;* Aetna Health, Inc. v. Davila, Brief Amicus Curiae of California Consumer Health Care Council, Congress of California Seniors and California Coalition for Ethical Mental Health Care, January 22, 2004, at *29.

137. Jane Bryant Quinn, *Health Insurance Firms Shielded Against Most Suits,* FLORIDA Sun-Sentinel, November 24, 1998, at D3; *Patients' Right to Sue Needed Check on Health Care Industry,* USA TODAY, October 19, 1998, at A26.

138. Aetna Health, Inc. v. Davila, Brief Amicus Curiae of the American College of Legal Medicine, January 20, 2004, at *9–*11; Aetna Health, Inc. v. Davila, Brief of the Council of State Governments, National Conference of State Legislatures, National Association of Counties, and International City/County Management Association as Amicus Curiae, January 22, 2004, at *11.

139. Bast v. Prudential Insurance Co., 150 F.3d 1003 (9th Cir. 1998).

140. Lind v. Aetna Health, Inc., 466 F.3d 1193 (2006).

141. Danca v. Private Health Care Systems, Inc., 185 F.3d 1 (1st Cir. 1999).

142. Jass v. Prudential Health Care Plan, Inc., 88 F.3d 1482 (7th Cir. 1996).

143. Aetna Health, Inc. v. Davila, 542 U.S. 200 (2004).

144. Aetna Health, Inc. v. Davila, Brief Amicus Curiae of California Consumer Health Care Council, Congress of California Seniors and California Coalition for Ethical Mental Health Care, January 22, 2004, at *6–*7.

145. Aetna Health, Inc. v. Davila, Brief of United Policyholders as Amicus Curiae, January 22, 2004; Aetna Health, Inc. v. Davila, Brief for Amicus Curiae Senators Edward M. Kennedy, John McCain, Bob Graham, and Representatives John D. Dingell, Charlie Norwood, George Miller, and Charles B. Rangel, January 22, 2004; Aetna Health, Inc. v. Davila, Brief of Amicus Curiae Health Administration Responsibility Project, January 22, 2004; Aetna Health, Inc. v. Davila, Brief Amicus Curiae of the American College of Legal Medicine, January 20, 2004; Aetna Health, Inc. v. Davila, Brief Amicus Curiae of California Consumer Health Care Council, Congress of California Seniors and California Coalition for Ethical Mental Health Care, January 22, 2004; Aetna

Health, Inc. v. Davila, Brief of the Council of State Governments, National Conference of State Legislatures, National Association of Counties, and International City/County Management Association as Amicus Curiae, January 22, 2004; Aetna Health, Inc. v. Davila, Brief of Texas, California, Connecticut, Delaware, Illinois, Kansas, Louisiana, Maryland, Minnesota, Missouri, Montana, Nevada, New Mexico, New York, Ohio, Oklahoma, Oregon, Puerto Rico, Utah, Vermont, Washington as Amicus Curiae, January 22, 2004.

146. Aetna Health, Inc. v. Davila, Brief for the United States as Amicus Curiae, December 18, 2003.

147. Aetna Health, Inc. v. Davila, 542 U.S. 200, 215 (2004); Aetna Health, Inc. v. Davila, Brief for the United States as Amicus Curiae, December 18, 2003, at *9, *25–*26.

148. Aetna Health, Inc. v. Davila, Brief for the United States as Amicus Curiae, December 18, 2003, at *16–17.

149. Aetna Health, Inc. v. Davila, 542 U.S. 200, 211–12 (2004).

150. *See* Andrews-Clarke v. Travelers Ins. Co., 984 F. Supp. 49, 59 (D. Mass. 1997).

151. Sharp, *ERISA Preemption,* 1376; Aetna Health, Inc. v. Davila, Brief of the Council of State Governments, National Conference of State Legislatures, National Association of Counties, and International City/County Management Association as Amicus Curiae, January 22, 2004, at *3.

152. *Under Fire,* St. Louis Post-Dispatch, August 30, 1998, at A1.

153. Aetna Health, Inc. v. Davila, 542 U.S. 200, 222 (2004) (Ginsburg, J., concurring) (quoting DiFelice v. Aetna U.S. Healthcare, 346 F.3d 442, 453 (3d Cir. 2003)).

154. Stephen Blakely, *The Backlash Against Managed Care,* Nation's Business, July, 1998, at 16; Robert Dreyfus, *Which Doctors?* New Republic, June 22, 1998, at 27; Susan Brink & Nancy Shute, *Are HMOs the Right Prescription?* U.S. News & World Report, October 13, 1997, at 60; George J. Church, *Backlash Against HMOs,* Time, April 14, 1997, at 32.

155. Frank Reeves, *House OKs HMO Rights,* Pittsburgh Post-Gazette, April 28, 1998, at B1; Peter T. Kilborn, *For Managed Care, Dial the Keepers of the Cures,* New York Times, November 3, 1997, at A14; Church, *Backlash,* 32.

156. S. 1890, 105th Cong., 1st Sess. (1997); H.R. 3605, 105th Cong., 1st Sess. (1997). *See* Eric Weissenstein & Jonathan Gardner, *Clinton Sets Agenda: Patient Protection Legislation Tops Democratic List,* Modern Healthcare, January 19, 1998, at 6 (House Bill); Amy Goldstein, *Clinton Backs "Bill of Rights" for Patients,* Washington Post, November 20, 1997, at A1 (Clinton bill); Church, *Backlash,* 32 (Kennedy bill).

157. Eric Weissenstein & Jonathan Gardner, *Clinton Sets Agendas* (leadership quote); Marilyn Chase, *Work in Progress; New Bill of Rights Makes a Modest Start at Protecting Patients,* Pittsburgh Post-Gazette, December 2, 1997, at E4; George Rodriguez, *Panel Calls for HMO Changes,* Dallas Morning News, November 20, 1997, at A1 (Lott quote).

158. Jonathan Cohn, *Congress Looks at the Managed Care Mess,* Baltimore Sun, February 27, 1998, at A19; Eric Weissenstein, *The Next Reform Fight,* Modern Healthcare, January 26, 1998, at 6; Janet Gemignani, *Maelstrom Over Patients Rights,* 12 Business & Health 10 (December, 1997) (Chamber of Commerce support).

159. Bill Walsh, *HMOs Gearing Up to Battle Push for Patients Rights,* New Orleans Times-Picayune, March 18, 1998, at A1; Mike McNamee & Richard S. Dunham, *Patient's Bill of Rights: Business Gets Out the Scalpel,* Business Week, March 9, 1998, at 47; Jonathan Cohn, *Congress Looks;* Alissa J. Rubin, *Democrats Push Tough Health Care Standards,* Los Angeles Times, February 17, 1998, at A1.
160. Peter T. Kilborn, *Bills Regulating Managed Care Benefit Doctors,* New York Times, February 16, 1998, at A1.
161. George J. Church, *Backlash Against HMOs,* Time, April 14, 1997, at 32.
162. Robert A. Jordan, *Kennedy Takes Aim at Managed Care,* Boston Globe, June 2, 1998, at C4 (manifesto); Alissa J. Rubin, *Democrats Push Tough Health Care Standards,* Los Angeles Times, February 17, 1998, at A1; Peter T. Kilborn, *Bills Regulating Managed Care Benefit Doctors,* New York Times, February 16, 1998, at A1.
163. *Costing Out Health Plan Lawsuits,* 9 Business & Health 11 (September 1, 1998); *Are HMOs Crying Wolf?* Business Week, August 3, 1998, at 83; Charles Ornstein, *Congress Divided on HMO Bill,* Dallas Morning News, July 22, 1998, at D1.
164. Howard Kurtz, *Managed Care Debate Heats Up the Airwaves,* Washington Post, July 28, 1998, at A2; Jim Drinkard, *Ads Carry Scent of Tobacco War,* USA Today, July 17, 1998, at A3 (ad quote); Terry M. Neal, *Health Insurers Launch TV Ad Blitz to Stop Bills,* Washington Post, June 27, 1998, at A1; Amy Goldstein, *Health Care Uproar Has Hill Scrambling,* Washington Post, May 31, 1998, at A1 (blew past quote).
165. Jeffrey Birnbaum, *Capitol Clout: A Buyer's Guide,* Fortune, October 26, 1998, at 177.
166. John A. MacDonald, *Health-Insurance Group Launching Advertising Blitz,* Hartford Courant, September 4, 1998, at A10.
167. Eliza Newlin Carney, *Bitter Medicine,* 30 Nat. J. 1554 (July 4, 1998) (task force bill); Amy Goldstein, *House GOP Plans Health Care Rights Bill,* Washington Post, June 25, 1998, at A1 (Norwood abandons bill); Robert Pear, *G.O.P. Unveils a Bill to Define Patients' Rights,* New York Times, June 25, 1998, at A1 (task force bill); Goldstein, *Health Care Uproar,* at A1 (unsure of Gingrich desires); Elaine S. Povich, *Battles Brew on Patient Rights,* Newsday, March 27, 1998, at A4 (bolder quote).
168. *Clinton Vows to Veto Republicans' Health Care "Bill of Rights,"* St. Louis Post-Dispatch, August 11, 1998, at A6; Alissa J. Rubin, *GOP Managed Care Bill Passes in House,* Los Angeles Times, July 25, 1998, at A13; Robert Pear, *White House Says Veto of "Patient Protection" Bill is Likely,* New York Times, July 24, 1998, at A18.
169. Bill Walsh, *Health Reform Dying on Vine,* New Orleans Times-Picayune, September 5, 1998, at A1.
170. Wayne J. Guglielmo, *How Monica Mania Stalled HMO Reform,* 75 Medical Economics 22 (December 28, 1998); Amy Goldstein, *Senate Kills "Patients' Rights" Bill,* Washington Post, October 11, 1998, at A1; Robert Pear, S*enators Reject Bill to Regulate Care by H.M.O.'s,* New York Times, October 10, 1998, at A1; *Patients' Rights—DOA,* The Oregonian, September 14, 1998, at B8.
171. Robert F. Howe, *The People vs. HMOs,* Time, February 1, 1999, at 46; Alissa J. Rubin, *Health Care Reform Top Issue in New Congress,* Los Angeles Times, November 30, 1998, at A1; Helen Dewar, *Democrats to Revive Health Measure,* Washington Post, November 6, 1998, at A4.

172. Alissa J. Rubin, *Attempt to Force Health Care Debate Shuts Down Senate,* Los Angeles Times, June 24, 1999, at A5 (Senate Democrats force vote); Michael Grunwald & Eric Pianin, *Senate Democrats Stall Spending Bills With HMO, Gun Amendments,* Washington Post, June 22, 1999, at A6; Alison Mitchell, *House G.O.P. Pushes Bills to Increase Patient's Rights But Keep Curbs on Suing H.M.O.'s,* New York Times, June 10, 1999, at A26 (House leadership bill); Edwin Chen & Nancy Trejos, *Clinton Pushes Patients' Bill of Rights,* Los Angeles Times, April 10, 1999, at A14 (road tour); Robert Pear, *A G.O.P. Bill on the Rights of Patients Advances,* New York Times, March 19, 1999, at A14 (Kennedy bill rejected); Robert F. Howe, *The People vs. HMOs,* Time, February 1, 1999, at 46 (Norwood bill).

173. Owen Ullman, *HMOs Spending for a Better Image,* USA Today, July 9, 1999, at A6 (CAQHC ad blitz); Dan Morgan, *Health Care Lobby Targets GOP Senators on Air,* Washington Post, July 5, 1999, at A3 (AAHP ad blitz).

174. Robert Pear, *House Passes Bill to Expand Rights on Medical Care,* New York Times, October 8, 1999, at A1; Amy Goldstein & Juliet Eilperin, *House Votes to Increase Rights of HMO Patients,* Washington Post, October 8, 1999, at A1 (Norwood/Dingell bill passed); Alison Mitchell, *Senate Approves Republican Plan for Health Care,* New York Times, July 16, 1999, at A1 (Senate vote, Clinton veto).

175. David Hess, *House Speaker Stacks Panel to Dodge Managed-Care Bill,* New Orleans Times-Picayune, November 4, 1999, at A12; William Neikirk, *Hastert Shuns Backers of Patients-Rights Bill,* Chicago Tribune, November 4, 1999, at 8.

176. Robert Pear, *Bush to Back State's Laws on Rights for Patients,* New York Times, January, 12, 2001, at A30 (Bush promise); Richard A. Oppel, Jr. & Jim Yardley, *Bush Calls Himself Reformer; The Record Shows the Label May Be a Stretch,* New York Times, March 20, 2000, at A16 (Bush reality); George Lardner, Jr., *Fact Check: On HMOs, a Reluctant Reformer,* Washington Post, February 1, 2000, at A10 (Bush response, Bush reality); Edwin Chen & Matea Gold, *Gore Singles Out a Family With a Health-Care Crisis,* Los Angeles Times, February 28, 2000, at A12 (Gore stump speech); *Gore Takes on Insurer as Policy Hits Home,* Newsday, February 28, 2000, at A16 (Gore stump speech).

177. Alissa Rubin, *McCain to Side With Democrats on Patients' Rights Bill,* Los Angeles Times, February 6, 2001, at A18; Robert Pear, *McCain Joining Democrats to Offer Health Rights Bill,* New York Times, February 6, 2001, at A17.

178. Anne E. Kornblut, *Bush Threatens to Veto Health Bill,* Boston Globe, March 22, 2001, at A2 (Bush veto promise); Edwin Chen & Alissa J. Rubin, *Bush Vows to Veto Patients' Rights Bill,* Los Angeles Times, March 22, 2001, at A1 (Bush veto promise); George W. Bush, *"Courage in a Time of Blessing,"* Washington Post, February 28, 2001, at A10 (Bush quote); Robert Pear, *Bush Outlines His Principles for Protecting Patient Rights,* New York Times, February 8, 2001, at 26 (Bush principles); Alissa J. Rubin, *Bush Tells of Goals in Patients' Rights Bill,* Los Angeles Times, February 8, 2001, at A1 (Bush principles); Bennett Roth & Karen Masterson, *Coalition Unveils Managed-Care Bill,* Houston Chronicle, February 7, 2001, at A1 (Rove action); Amy Goldstein & Helen Dewar, *Bush Urges Limited Patients' Rights,* Washington Post, February 7, 2001, at A4 (Rove action).

179. Robert Pear, *House G.O.P. Drafts Bill Expanding Patients' Right to Sue,* New York

Times, June 21, 2001, at A16 (Republican leadership response); Julia Malone, *Norwood Rejoins Fight for His Health Care Bill,* Atlanta Journal-Constitution, June 14, 2001, at A3 (Norwood bill introduced); Karen Tumulty, *A One-Man Earthquake,* Time, June 4, 2001, at 30 (Daschle announcement); Stephen Labaton, *Senate Switch Alters Outlook for Business,* New York Times, May 25, 2001, at C1 (Jeffords change); *Norwood Rips Bush's Patient' Rights Bill,* Atlanta Journal-Constitution, May 16, 2001, at A3 (Norwood quote); *Patients' Rights Bill Cues Showdown on HMO Suits,* Los Angeles Times, May 15, 2001, at A12 (administration bill).

180. Robert Pear, *Bill Establishing Patients' Rights Passes in Senate,* New York Times, June 30, 2001, at A1 (Senate vote); Susan Milligan, *Senate Approves Patients' Rights Bill,* Boston Globe, June 30, 2001, at A1 (Senate vote); Jill Zuckman, *Bush Pointedly Says He'll Veto Senate's Medical Bill,* Chicago Tribune, June 22, 2001, at 8 (Bush veto promise); Amy Goldstein, *Patients' Rights a Prescription for Lobbyists,* Washington Post, June 23, 2001, at A6 (lobbying quote, quoting Holly Bailey of the Center for Responsive Politics); James Kuhnenn, *HMO Bills See Heavy Lobbying in Senate,* Detroit Free Press, June 19, 2001, at A1 (heavy lobbying); Jim Drinkard, *Lobbyists Face Off on Patients' Rights,* USA Today, June 18, 2001, at A1 (heavy lobbying).

181. Marion Berry, *How Patients' Rights Became a Fight,* New York Times, September 1, 2001, at A15.

182. Dana Milbank & Juliet Eilperin, *On Patients' Rights Deal, Bush Scored With a Full-Court Press,* Washington Post, August 3, 2001, at A9 (Bush quote).

183. Charles Ornstein, *Official Sees Peril to HMO Reforms,* Los Angeles Times, August 6, 2001, at B7; Robert Pear, *Deal Is Reached on a Bill to Set Patients' Rights,* New York Times, August 2, 2001, at A1.

184. Marion Berry, *How Patients' Rights Became a Fight,* New York Times, September 1, 2001, at A15; Ryan Lizza, *Bolten the Door,* New Republic, August 20, 2001, at 12 (Norwood aide quotes); Susan Milligan, *Bush Says He Has Deal on Rights of Patients,* Boston Globe, August 2, 2001, at A1 (other sponsors outraged); Patty Reinert & Karen Masterson, *Patients Rights Bill Faces Vote in House,* Houston Chronicle, August 2, 2001, at A1 (other sponsors outraged).

185. Berry, *Patients' Rights* (co-sponsor quote); Robert Pear, *Matters of Law, and Semantics, in Health Bill,* New York Times, August 4, 2001, at A1 (Ways and Means Committee change); Greg Miller, *House OK's Patients' Rights Bill,* Los Angeles Times, August 3, 2001, at A1 (House vote); Robert Pear, *Measure Defining Patients' Rights Passes in House,* New York Times, August 3, 2001, at A1 (House vote).

186. Rob Hotakainen & Sarah McKenzie, *Domestic Agenda Is All But Dead,* Minneapolis Star-Tribune, September 30, 2001, at A1; David S. Broder, *Some Action on Hill Delayed to Avoid Divisive Debates,* Washington Post, September 24, 2001, at A1; Ronald Brownstein, *After the Attack; Rethinking Policy,* Los Angeles Times, September 18, 2001, at A1; Susan Milligan, *Threat of Terrorism Puts Domestic Agenda on Hold,* Boston Globe, September 17, 2001, at A12; Dana Milbank, *White House Staff Switches Gears,* Washington Post, September 17, 2001, at A25.

187. Karen Tumulty, *Health Care Has a Relapse,* Time, March 11, 2002, at 42; James A. Barnes, *Action Versus Inaction,* 34 Nat. J. 10 (March 9, 2002) (Kennedy agreement); Ed-

win Chen, *Bush's Prescription for Medical Reform,* Los Angeles Times, February 12, 2002, at A1 (Bush action); Dana Milbank, *Bush Outlines Health Plan, Raises Funds,* Washington Post, February 12, 2002, at A2 (Bush action).

188. Robert Pear, *White House and Senate Hit Impasse on Patients' Rights,* New York Times, August 2, 2002, at A1 (negotiations fail; quote); Janet Hook, *Negotiations Fail on Bill of Rights for HMO Patients,* Los Angeles Times, August 2, 2002, at A20 (negotiations fail); Susan Milligan, *Prognosis Bleak on Health Care,* Boston Globe, June 19, 2002, at A3 (negotiations continue); Robert Pear, *Bush Is Said to Be Set to Back Patients' Bill,* New York Times, June 7, 2002, at A16 (negotiations expand).
189. Jim VandeHei and Jonathan Weisman, *Republicans Poised to Enact Agenda,* Washington Post, November 7, 2002, at A1 (2002 election results).
190. Melanie Eversley, *Norwood Revives Patients' Rights Bill,* Atlanta Journal-Constitution, March 9, 2002, at A4 (bills introduced).
191. Aetna Health, Inc. v. Davila, 542 U.S. 200 (2004). *See* David G. Savage, *Patients' Right to Sue Before High Court,* Los Angeles Times, March 24, 2003, at A12; Patty Reinert, *Patients' Right to Sue, Sparked by Local Case, Goes to High Court,* Houston Chronicle, March 23, 2003, at A1; Charles Lane, *Court to Hear Insurance Case,* Washington Post, November 4, 2003, at A3.
192. M. Gregg Bloche, *Bush Turns His Back on Fight for Patients' Rights,* Los Angeles Times, March 21, 2004, at M3 (criticizing Bush administration for amicus brief).
193. Judy Holland, *Ruling for HMOs Spurs Push for Patients Rights,* Orlando Sentinel, June 27, 2004, at A9; John A. MacDonald, *Democrats and Bush Spar Over Suing HMOs,* Hartford Courant, June 25, 2004, at A11; David Savage, *High Court Limits Right to Sue HMOs,* Los Angeles Times, June 22, 2004, at A1; William M. Welch, *Democrats Renew Push for Patient Bill of Rights,* USA Today, June 22, 2004, at B7; Raymund Flandez, *HMOs Welcome Court Ruling,* Washington Post, June 22, 2004, at E1.
194. Melanie Eversley, *Norwood Revives Patients' Rights Bill,* Atlanta Journal-Constitution, March 9, 2002, at A4 (quoting Karen Ignani of the American Association of Health Plans); Sara Fritz, *Could HMOs Have Healed Themselves,* St. Petersburg Times, August 5, 2001, at A1.
195. Peter Franceschina, *Lawyer Determined to Penalize Gunmakers,* Florida Sun-Sentinel, November 10, 2002, at B1.

CHAPTER 6. THE PREEMPTION WAR IN THE FEDERAL AGENCIES

1. 30 U.S.C. § 1254(g)
2. Chevron USA, Inc. v. Natural Resources Defense Council, Inc., 467 U.S. 837, 843 (1984). In the fairly rare cases in which Congress expressly delegates responsibility for defining statutory terms to an Executive Branch agency, the question before the reviewing court is whether the agency's interpretation is "arbitrary and capricious." *Id.*
3. 21 U.S.C. § 159 (statute); 57 Fed. Reg. 38,758, 38,758–59 (1992) (preemption regulations); Symens v. Smithkline Beecham Corp., 2001 WL 263058 (8th Cir. 2001); Lynnbrook Farms v. Smithkline Beecham Corp., 79 F.3d 620 (7th Cir. 1996); Behrens v. United Vaccines, Inc., 189 F. Supp.2d 945 (D. Minn. 2002); Murphy v. Smithkline Beecham

Corp., 898 F. Supp. 811 (D. Kan. 1995); Brandt v. Marshall Animal Clinic, 540 N.W.2d 870 (Minn. Ct. App. 1996). See Scott A. Smith & Duana Grage, *Federal Preemption of State Products Liability Actions,* 27 William Mitchell L. Rev. 391, 406–07 (2000).

4. United States v. Mead Corporation 533 U.S. 218 (2001); Christensen v. Harris County, 529 U.S. 576 (2000); Skidmore v. Swift & Co., 323 U.S. 134 (1944); Thomas W. Merrill & Kristin E. Hickman, *Chevron's Domain,* 89 Geo. L. J. 833, 855–56 (2001).
5. Geier v. American Honda Motor Co., 529 U.S. 861, 881 (2000).
6. CSX Transportation, Inc. v. Easterwood, Brief for the United States as Amicus Curiae, August 27, 1992.
7. Executive Order 13,132, 64 Fed. Reg. 43255 (August 4, 1999), at §§ 2(a), 4(a)4(c).
8. Norfolk Southern Railway Co. v. Shanklin, Brief for the United States as Amicus Curiae, January 28, 2000, at 10.
9. Bates v. Dow Agrosciences, LLC, 544 U.S. 431, 437 n. 7 (2005).
10. Buckman Co. v. Plaintiffs' Legal Committee, Brief of Amicus Curiae United States, September 13, 2000, at 10.
11. Bates v. Dow Agrosciences, LLC, 544 U.S. 431, 437 n. 7 (2005); Aetna Health, Inc. v. Davila, 542 U.S. 200, 215 (2004).
12. Warner-Lambert Co. v. Kent, Brief for the United States as Amicus Curiae, November 28, 2007; Riegel v. Medtronic Inc., Brief for the United States as Amicus Curiae, October 19, 2007.
13. Sprietsma v. Mercury Marine, 537 U.S. 51, 68 (2002).
14. Samuel Issacharoff & Catherine M. Sharkey, *Backdoor Federalization,* 53 UCLA L. Rev. 1353 (2006).
15. Federal Railroad Administration, Selection and Installation of Grade Crossing Warning Systems; Notice of Proposed Rulemaking, 60 Fed. Reg. 11,649, 11651 (March 2, 1995).
16. Adrienne Drell & Lynn Sweet, *Proposal Would Limit Rail Accident Damages,* Chicago Sun-Times, November 8, 1995, at 8.
17. Stevenson Swanson, *Juggling Act at Railroad Crossings,* Chicago Tribune, November 1, 1995, at 1; Don Terry, *5 Killed as Commuter Train Hits School Bus,* New York Times, October 26, 1995, at A16.
18. Federal Railroad Administration, Selection and Installation of Grade Crossing Warning Systems; Termination of Rulemaking, 62 Fed. Reg. 42,733 (August 8, 1997); Coleman McCarthy, *Safety Program Doesn't Make the Grade,* Washington Post, June 27, 1995, at C9 (accusation).
19. The description of Tim Tobin's experience is drawn from Tobin v. Smith-Kline Beecham Pharmaceuticals, Trial Transcript, May 21, 2001, at 15–18; Sarah Boseley, *Health: "Four People Dead Is Four Too Many,"* The Guardian, August 9, 2001, at 8; Sarah Boseley, *Drug Firm Ordered to Pay Pounds 4.7M for Texas "Bloodbath,"* The Guardian, June 8, 2001, at 16.
20. Tobin v. Smith-Kline Beecham Pharmaceuticals, Trial Transcript, May 22, 2001, at 30.
21. Tobin v. Smith-Kline Beecham Pharmaceuticals, Trial Transcript, May 21, 2001, at 33, 47; Boseley, *Health.*
22. Boseley, *Health.*
23. 21 U.S.C. §§ 355(d), 393(b)(2)(B).

24. Marcia Angell, The Truth About the Drug Companies 27–29 (2005); Jerome P. Kassirer, On the Take 81–82 (2005); National Institute of Medicine, The Future of Drug Safety 2–2 through 2–5 (2006); David A. Kessler & David C. Vladeck, *A Critical Examination of the FDA's Efforts to Preempt Failure-to-Warn Claims,* 96 Geo. L. J. 461, 470–75 (2008) (general Description of FDA drug approval process).
25. Catherine T. Struve, *The FDA and the Tort System: Postmarketing Surveillance, Compensation, and the Role of Litigation,* 5 Yale J. Policy & Legal Ethics, 587, 595–97 (2005).
26. Angell, Truth, 32; National Institute of Medicine, Future, 2-7 (statistics).
27. National Institute of Medicine, Future, 2–6; *Risk and Responsibility: The Roles of FDA and Pharmaceutical Companies in Ensuring the Safety of Approved Drugs, Like Vioxx, Hearings Before the House Comm. on Government Reform,* 109th Cong., 1st Sess. (2005), at 23 (testimony of Steven Galston, Acting Director, Center for Drug Evaluation and Research, FDA); Michael D. Green & William B. Schultz, *Tort Law Deference to FDA Regulation of Medical Devices,* 88 Geo. L. J. 2119, 2132–33 (2000); Kessler & Vladeck, *FDA's Efforts,* 467–69, 483–91 (explaining that while 2007 Amendments to the Food, Drug and Cosmetics Act have expanded FDA's authority and resources regarding post-marketing surveillance, "only time will tell whether increased resources will result in better performance by the agency"); Catherine T. Struve, *FDA and the Tort System,* 5 Yale J. Policy & Legal Ethics 587, 598–606 (2005).
28. Letter from Patrick Ronan, Assistant Commissioner, FDA, to Hon. Mike Enzi, reprinted in *FDA's Drug Approval Process: Up to the Challenge?, Hearings Before the Senate Committee on Health, Education, Labor and Pensions,* 109th Cong., 1st Sess. 75, 79 (2005). See also Cartwright v. Pfizer, Inc., 369 F. Supp.2d 876, 879 (E.D. Tex. 2005); David G. Owen, Products Liability Law 607 (2005).
29. 21 U.S.C. § 355(e).
30. 21 C.F.R. § 201.57(e). *See* Kallas v. Pfizer, Inc., Amicus Curiae Brief for the United States, September 15, 2005, at 7.
31. 21 C.F.R. § 314.70(c)(6)(iii). See Mary J. Davis, *The Battle Over Implied Preemption: Products Liability and the FDA,* 48 B.C.L. Rev. 1089, 1105-06 (2007); Kessler & Vladeck, *FDA's Efforts,* 475–83.
32. David Healy, Let Them Eat Prozac 24 (2004) (Luvox/Columbine connection); Jennifer Couzin, *Volatile Chemistry: Children and Antidepressants,* 305 Science 468 (July 23, 2004). *See* Blanchard v. Eli Lilly & Co., 207 F. Supp.2d 308, 312 (D. Vermont 2002).
33. Blanchard v. Eli Lilly & Co., 207 F. Supp.2d 308, 311 (D. Vermont 2002) (citing Roger M. Lane, *SSRI-Induced Extrapyramidal Side-effects and Akathisia: Implications for Treatment,* 12 J. Psychopharmacology 192, 193 (1998)).
34. Healy, Prozac, 14–15; Sarah Boseley, *Journal Sent Prozac Papers That Disappeared During Murder Case,* The Guardian, December 31, 2004, at 9 (Prozac clinical trials).
35. Blanchard v. Eli Lilly & Co., 207 F. Supp.2d 308, 312 (D. Vermont 2002); Memorandum from Thomas P. Laughren to Members of PDAC and Peds AC re: Background Comments for February 2, 2004 Meeting of Psychopharmacological Drugs Advisory Committee (PDAC) and Pediatric Subcommittee of the Anti-Infective Drugs Advisory Committee (Peds AC), dated January 5, 2004, at 3 (advisory committee quote); David Healy, Let Them Eat Prozac 42, 45, 61 (2004) (firestorm quote).

36. Healy, Prozac, 50–53, 63, 79; Sarah Boseley, *Happy Drug Prozac Can Bring on Impulses to Suicide, Study Says,* The Guardian, May 22, 2000, at 8.
37. Laughren Memorandum, 1.
38. Tobin v. SmithKline Beecham Pharmaceuticals, Trial Transcript, May 22, 2001, at 41–42, 55.
39. Sarah Boseley, *Mood Drug Seroxat Banned for Under-18s,* The Guardian, June 11, 2003, at 9; Sarah Boseley, *Seroxat Warning Over Risk to Young,* The Guardian, June 10, 2003, at 6.
40. Food and Drug Administration, FDA Public Health Advisory: Worsening Depression and Suicidality in Patients Being Treated With Antidepressant Medications (March 22, 2004); Laughren Memorandum, 8.
41. Toni Clarke & Ransdel Pierson, *Spitzer Takes Aim at Health Regulators,* Reuters, November 12, 2004 (Spitzer quote); Barry Meier, *Two Studies, Two Results, and a Debate Over a Drug,* New York Times, June 3, 2004, at C1.
42. Food and Drug Administration, FDA Public Health Advisory: Suicidality in Children and Adolescents Being Treated With Antidepressant Medications (October 15, 2004).
43. Food and Drug Administration, FDA Public Health Advisory: Suicidality in Adults Being Treated With Antidepressant Medications (June 30, 2005).
44. *See* Philip J. Hilts, Protecting America's Health ch. 12 (2003).
45. Tobin v. Smith-Kline Beecham Pharmaceuticals, 164 F. Supp.2d 1278, 1280 (D. Wyo. 2001).
46. Colacicco v. Apotex, Inc., Complaint, 2005 WL 3134892 (E.D. Pa. 2005).
47. Miller v. Pfizer, 356 F.3d 1326 (10th Cir. 2004) (Zoloft); Cloud v. Pfizer, Inc., 198 F. Supp.2d 1118 (D. Ariz. 2001) (Zoloft); Smith v. Pfizer, Inc., 2001 WL 968369 (D. Kan. 2001) (Zoloft); Potter v. Eli Lilly & Co., 926 S.W.2d 449 (Ky. 1996) (Prozac).
48. Daniel E. Troy, *FDA Involvement in Product Liability Lawsuits,* Update, Jan.-Feb. 2003, at 4, 7–8 (article based on speech "originally delivered at FDLI's annual Advertising and Promotion Conference, September 11–12, 2002"); Dusek v. Pfizer, Inc., Affidavit of Jessica R. Dart, March 1, 2004, at 2. *See also* Margaret H. Clune, Stealth Tort Reform: How the Bush Administration's Aggressive Use of the Preemption Doctrine Hurts Consumers 2–3 (Center for Progressive Regulation White Paper No. 403 October 2004); Robert Pear, *In a Shift, Bush Moves to Block Medical Suits,* New York Times, July 25, 2004, at A1.
49. Cartwright v. Pfizer, Inc., 369 F. Supp.2d 876, 885 (E.D. Tex. 2005); Owen, Products Liability Law, 908.
50. Motus v. Pfizer, Inc., Brief of Amicus Curiae Public Citizen, April 21, 2003, at 12 (noting that no reported decision prior to 2003 had held that the FDCA preempts state common law damages actions with respect to drugs); Eve v. Sandoz Pharmaceutical Corp., 2002 U.S. Dist. LEXIS 23965 (S.D. Ind. 2002); Caraker v. Sandoz Pharmaceuticals Corp., 172 F. Supp.2d 1018 (S.D. Ill. 2001); Tobin v. Astra Pharmaceutical Products, Inc., 993 F.2d 528 (6th Cir. 1993); Feldman v. Lederle Laboratories, 592 A.2d 1176 (N.J. 1991); Hurley v. Lederle Laboratories, 863 F.2d 1173 (5th Cir. 1989); In re Tetracycline Cases, 747 F. Supp. 543 (W.D.Mo. 1989) (citing dozens of cases); Wells v. Ortho Pharmaceutical Corp., 788 F.2d 741 (11th Cir. 1986); MacDonald v. Ortho Pharmaceutical Corp., 475 N.E.2d 65

(Mass. 1985); Brochu v. Ortho Pharmaceutical Corp., 642 F.2d 652 (1st Cir. 1981). *But see* Grundberg v. Upjohn Co., 813 P.2d 89 (Utah 1991) (FDA-approved drug not defective under state law).

51. Mark D. Shifton, *The Restatement (Third) of Torts: Products Liability: The ALI's Cure For Prescription Design Liability,* 29 FORDHAM URBAN L. J. 2343, 2370 (2002).
52. George W. Conk, *Is There a Design Defect in the Restatement (Third) of Torts: Products Liability?* 109 YALE L. J. 1087, 1128 (2000).
53. RESTATEMENT (THIRD) OF TORTS—PRODUCTS LIABILITY § 6(d).
54. 21 C.F.R. § 314.70(c)(6)(iii). *See* Bell v. Lollar, 791 N.E.2d 849 (Ind. App. 2003); Caraker v. Sandoz Pharmaceuticals Corp., 172 F. Supp.2d 1018, 1033–34 (S.D. Ill. 2001); Feldman v. Lederle Laboratories, 592 A.2d 1176, 1193–94 (N.J. 1991).
55. Ohler v. Purdue Pharma, 2002 U.S. Dist. LEXIS 2368 *46–*49 (E.D. La. 2002) (citing Food and Drug Administration, Prescription Drug Labeling; Medication Guide Requirements, 63 Fed. Reg. 66378, 66,382–83 (December 1, 1998)).
56. Caraker v. Sandoz Pharmaceuticals Corp., 172 F. Supp.2d 1018, 1036 (S.D. Ill. 2001) (quoting 59 Fed. Reg. 3944, 3948 (1994)).
57. *Id.,* 1038.
58. Dusek v. Pfizer, Inc., 2004 WL 2191804 (S.D. Tex. 2004); Needleman v. Pfizer, Inc., 2004 WL 1773697 (N.D. Tex. 2004).
59. Zikis v. Pfizer, Inc., 2005 WL 3019409 (N.D. Ill. 2005); McNellis v. Pfizer, 2005 WL 3752269 (D.N.J. 2005); Witczak v. Pfizer, Inc., 377 F. Supp.2d 726 (D. Minn. 2005); Cartwright v. Pfizer, Inc., 369 F. Supp.2d 876 (E.D. Tex. 2005); Zikis v. Pfizer, Inc., Civ. No. 04C8104, Slip Opinion 7 (E.D. Ill. 2005).
60. McNellis v. Pfizer, 2005 WL 3752269 *9 (D.N.J. 2005).
61. Food and Drug Administration, Tamper-Resistant Packaging Requirements for Certain Over-the-Counter Human Drug and Cosmetic Products, 47 Fed. Reg. 50442 (November 5, 1982). *See also* Food and Drug Administration, Protecting the Identities of Reporters of Adverse Events and Patients; Preemption of Disclosure Rules, 59 Fed. Reg. 3944 (January 27, 1994) (protecting patient privacy from disclosure of adverse-event information); Food and Drug Administration, Labeling for Oral and Rectal Over-the-Counter Aspirin and Aspirin-Containing Drug Products, 51 Fed. Reg. 8180 (March 7, 1986) (requiring specific warnings about the potential for aspirin to cause Reyes syndrome when given to children and teenagers for flu and chicken pox); Food and Drug Administration, Pregnant or Nursing Women; Delegations of Authority and Organization; Amendment of Labeling Requirements for Over-the-Counter Human Drugs, 47 Fed. Reg. 54750 (December 3, 1982) (warning that pregnant or nursing women should consult a physician prior to taking drugs intended for systematic use).
62. Davis, *Battle Over Implied Preemption,* 1090 (2007); Kessler & Vladeck, *FDA's Efforts,* 462 (sidelines quote); Allison M. Zieve & Brian Wolfman, *The FDA's Argument for Eradicating State Tort Law: Why It Is Wrong and Warrants No Deference,* 34 BNA PROD. SAFETY & LIABILITY REPT. 308, 315 (March 27, 2006).
63. Food and Drug Administration, Requirements on Content and Format of Labeling for Human Prescription Drugs and Biological Products, 65 Fed. Reg. 81082, 81103 (December 22, 2000).

64. The description of the preamble is taken from Food and Drug Administration, Requirements on Content and Format of Labeling for Human Prescription Drugs and Biological Products, 71 Fed. Reg. 3922, 3934–36 (January 24, 2006).
65. David R. Singh, *Preamble to New FDA Prescription Drug Regulations Strengthens Manufacturers' Preemption Argument,* 34 BNA PROD. SAFETY & LIABILITY REPT. 184, 184 (2006).
66. Letter from Edward M. Kennedy and Christopher J. Dodd to Michael O. Leavitt (February 23, 2006). *See also* Letter from Henry A. Waxman and John D. Dingell to Michael O. Leavitt (February 23, 2006); Zieve & Wolfman, *The FDA's Argument,* 308.
67. Colacicco v. Apotex, Inc., 432 F. Supp. 2d. 514, 527–35 (E.D. Pa. 2006).
68. *Former FDA Chief Counsel Dan Troy and Special Assistant Coleen Klasmeier to Join Sidley Austin Brown & Wood LLP,* Press Release, dated January 6, 2005, *at* http://www.sidley.com/news/pub.asp?PubID=151356162005.
69. Ackermann v. Wyeth Pharmaceuticals, 2006 WL 2591078 (E.D. Tex. 2006); Abramowitz v. Cephalon, Inc., 2006 WL 560639 (N.J. Super. L. 2006).
70. In re Bextra and Celebrex Marketing Sales Practices and Product Liability Litigation, 2006 WL 2374742 *7 (N.D. Cal. 2006).
71. Prohias v. Pfizer, Inc., 490 F. Supp.2d 1228 (S.D. Fla. 2007); In re Vioxx Products Liability Litigation, 2007 WL 1952964 (E.D. La. 2007) (collecting cases); In re Zyprexa Products Liability Litigation, 489 F. Supp.2d 230 (E.D.N.Y. 2007); Weiss v. Fujisawa Pharmaceutical Co., 464 F.Supp.2d 666 (E.D. Ky. 2007); Perry v. Novartis Pharmaceutical Corp., 456 F. Supp.2d 678 (E.D. Pa. 2006); Laisure-Radke v. PAR Pharmaceutical, Inc., 2006 WL 901657 (W.D. Wash. 2006); Jackson v. Pfizer, Inc., 432 F. Supp.2d 964 (D. Neb. 2006); Weiss v. Fujisawa Pharmaceutical Co., 464 F. Supp.2d 666 (E.D. Ky. 2006); Levine v. Wyeth Laboratories, 2006 WL 3041078 (Vt. 2006). *See also* Barnhill v. Teva Pharmaceuticals USA, Inc., No. 06–0280-CB-M (S.D. Ala. filed April 24, 2007); Peters v. Astrazeneca, 417 F. Supp.2d 1051 (W.D. Wis. 2006) (finding a failure to warn claim involving an over-the-counter drug not preempted but not citing the FDA labeling regulations). *See* Davis, *Battle Over Implied Preemption.*
72. Jackson v. Pfizer, Inc., 432 F. Supp.2d 964, 967 (D. Neb. 2006) (quoting Witczak v. Pfizer, Inc., 377 F. Supp.2d 726, 732 (D. Minn. 2005).
73. Laisure-Radke v. PAR Pharmaceutical, Inc., 2006 WL 901657 *6 (W.D. Wash. 2006).
74. The factual setting for Wyeth v. Levine is drawn from Wyeth v. Levine, No. 06-1249, Respondent's Brief in Opposition, April 2007 and Mark H. Anderson, *Justices to Hear Cigarette Case,* WALL STREET J., January 19, 2008, at A6.
75. Levine v. Wyeth Laboratories, 2006 WL 3041078 (Vt. 2006).
76. NATIONAL INSTITUTE OF MEDICINE, FUTURE, 2-16 through 5-6; Margaret Gilhooley, *Addressing Potential Drug Risks: The Limits of Testing, Risk Signals, Preemption, and the Drug Reform Legislation,* 59 S. CAR. L. REV. 347, 383–84 (2008).
77. 21 C.F.R. § 314.70(c)(6)(iii); Food and Drug Administration, Requirements on Content, 3934.
78. 21 C.F.R. § 314.126(b); Richard Nagareda, *FDA Preemption: When Tort Law Meets the Administrative State,* 1 J. TORT LAW 1, 20 (2006) (quote); Jonathan V. O'Steen, *The FDA Defense: Vioxx and the Argument Against Federal Preemption,* 48 ARIZ. L. REV. 67, 82 (2006).

79. Motus v. Pfizer, Inc., Amicus Brief for the United States, September 3, 2002, at 7 (FDA may disapprove); Feldman v. Lederle Laboratories, 592 A.2d 1176, 1193 (N.J. 1991) (court could find no instance in which FDA disapproved); Nagareda, *FDA Preemption,* 32 (misbranding).
80. Food and Drug Administration, Requirements on Content, 3934.
81. 21 U.S.C. §§ 332, 333(a); In re Paxil Litigation, Brief of the United States of America, September 5, 2002, at 3. *See* Kessler & Vladeck, *FDA's Efforts,* 477-78; Zieve & Wolfman, 311.
82. Myron Levin and Alan C. Miller, *Industries Get Quiet Protection From Lawsuits,* Los Angeles Times, February 19, 2006, at A1 (Patrick Parker story); Bill Vlasic & Jeff Plungis, *Couple Wage Web Fight for New Roof Test,* Detroit News, April 13, 2004, at A9; Jeff Plungis & Bill Vlasic, *European Vehicles Exceed Standard for U.S. Car Roofs,* Detroit News, April 12, 2004, at A9 (Penny Shipler story).
83. Joseph Szczesny, *Safety Regulations Catch Up to Car Standards,* Chicago Tribune, April 29, 2001, at 3 (new standards for SUVs); Edward M. Ricci & Scott C. Murray, *Sport Utility Vehicles: Orphans of Auto Safety,* Trial, November 1, 1994, at 28 (no standards for multipurpose vehicles); Tom Lankard, *Closing the Loopholes,* AutoWeek, January 16, 1989, at 16 (multipurpose vehicles).
84. National Highway Traffic Safety Administration, Federal Motor Vehicle Safety Standards; Roof Crush Resistance, Notice of Proposed Rulemaking, 70 Fed. Reg. 49223, 49225 (August 23, 2005).
85. *Id.* (NHTSA notice of proposed rulemaking); Plungis & Vlasic, *European Vehicles Exceed Standard* (settlements); Christopher Jensen, *Regulators Considering Making Car Roofs Safer,* Cleveland Plain Dealer, November 8, 2001, at F1 (statistics).
86. Jeff Plungis & Bill Vlasic, *Ex-GM Executive Turns Courtroom Crusader,* Detroit News, April 11, 2004, at A9 (industry position); Myron Levin, *A Lonely Quest for Safer Cars,* Los Angeles Times, February 12, 2002, at A1 (General Motors study).
87. Lambert v. General Motors Co., 2003 WL 116173 (Cal. App. 4th Dist. 2003); Plungis & Vlasic, *European Vehicles Exceed Standard* (engineering experts); Levin, *A Lonely Quest* (plaintiffs' experts' different interpretation).
88. Levin and Miller, *Industries Get Quiet Protection* (punitive damages added); Jeff Plungis & Bill Vlasic, *Thousands Killed, Hurt as Auto Roofs Collapse,* Detroit News, April 11, 2004, at A9 (internal documents).
89. Romo v. Ford Motor Co., 122 Cal. Rptr.2d 139 (Cal. App. 2002).
90. Shipp v. General Motors Corp., 750 F.2d 418 (5th Cir. 1985); Garcia v. Brown, 889 So.2d 359 (La. App. 2d Cir. 2004); Gass v. NSK, Ltd, 2002 WL 31546998 (Cal. App. 2d Dist. 2002).
91. 49 C.F.R. § 571.216 (2006) (static test); Jeff Plungis & Bill Vlasic, *Safety Test Ignores Real-Life Conditions,* Detroit News, April 11, 2004, at A9 (pre-1966 test, subsequent testing); *Levin, A Lonely Quest* (industry developed static test that NHTSA adopted, subsequent testing).
92. Plungis & Vlasic, *Safety Test Ignores.*
93. Cindy Skrzycki, *NHTSA in for a Fight Over "Roof-Crush Rule,"* Washington Post, December 6, 2005, at D1 (Ford instruction to Volvo); Jeff Plungis, *Ford Pushes to Seal Memos*

on Vehicle Roof Strength, DETROIT NEWS, May 10, 2005, at A1; Plungis & Vlasic, *European Vehicles Exceed Standard;* Plungis & Vlasic, *Safety Test Ignores.*

94. Plungis & Vlasic, *Feds, Big Three Gird* (quote); Plungis & Vlasic, *Safety Test Ignores.*
95. Jeff Plungis, *Feds Link Injuries to Weak Roofs,* DETROIT NEWS, August 16, 2004, at A1.
96. National Highway Traffic Safety Administration, Roof Crush Resistance, 49225.
97. Skrzycki, *NHTSA in for a Fight;* Carrie Johnson, *Rules Proposed for Large-Vehicle Roof Strength,* WASHINGTON POST, August 20, 2005, at D1 (quoting Joan Claybrook of Public Citizen).
98. Cindy Skrzycki, *Agencies' Rules Quietly Enable Tort Reform,* WASHINGTON POST, September 27, 2005, at D1.
99. National Highway Traffic Safety Administration, Roof Crush Resistance, 49245.
100. State Farm Mutual Automotive Insurance Co. v. Campbell, 538 U.S. 408 (2003). *See* Jeff Plungis, *New Roof Rules Limit Carmaker Liability,* DETROIT NEWS, September 7, 2005, at A1.
101. TED R. MILLER & EDUARD ZALOSHNJA, ROOF-CRUSH STANDARDS: COSTS TO STATES OF NHTSA PROPOSED RULE (National Conference of State Legislatures, 2006); Levin & Miller, *Industries Get Quiet Protection* (Attorneys General); Carrie Johnson, *Rules Proposed for Large-Vehicle Roof Strength,* WASHINGTON POST, August 20, 2005, at D1 (safety advocates).
102. Levin & Miller, *Industries Get Quiet Protection* (quoting Barry Felrice of DaimlerChrysler); Plungis, *New Roof Rules.*
103. Public L. 83–88, 67 Stat. 111 (1953).
104. Consumer Product Safety Amendments of 1981, Public L. 97–35, title 12, subtitle A, 95 Stat. 703 (1981).
105. 15 U.S.C. § 1192(b).
106. 15 U.S.C. § 1192(b), (j)(2)(B), (C).
107. 15 U.S.C. § 1192(j)(2)(A).
108. Text of the Flammable Fabrics Act of 1953, as Amended in 1954, Prior to 1967 Amendment and Revision, 16 C.F.R. § 1609.1 (2005).
109. 16 C.F.R. § 1610–32 (2005).
110. Wilson v. Bradlees of New England, Inc., 96 F.3d 552, 555 (1st Cir. 1996); O'Donnell v. Big Yank, Inc., 696 A.2d 846, 853 (Pa. Super. 1997).
111. 15 U.S.C. § 1203.
112. S. Rept. No. 251, 94th Cong. 2d Sess. 12 (1975).
113. 15 U.S.C. § 1203(c).
114. Simien v. S.S. Kresge Co. 566 F.2d 551 (5th Cir. 1978); Brech v. J. C. Penney Co. 532 F. Supp. 916 (D. South Dakota 1982). *But see* Gryc v. Dayton-Hudson Corp., 297 N.W.2d 727 (Minn. 1980) (plaintiff's punitive damages claim not preempted)
115. Wilson v. Bradlees of New England, Inc., 96 F.3d 552, 553–56 (1st Cir. 1996); Directorate for Engineering Sciences, CPSC, Briefing Package, Standard for the Flammability of Clothing Textiles, ANPR to Amend and Update (2002), at 6 (burn statistics).
116. Perez v. Mini-Max Stores, Inc., 661 N.Y. Supp.2d 659 (Sup. Ct. 1997); O'Donnell v. Big Yank, Inc., 696 A.2d 846 (Pa. Super. 1997); Askenazi v. Hymil Manufacturing Co., 648

N.Y. Supp.2d 8895 (Sup. Ct. 1996); Consumer Product Safety Commission, Application for Exemption from Preemption, Final Rule, 56 Fed. Reg. 3414, 3415 (1991).

117. The description of the mattress standard is taken from Consumer Product Safety Commission, Standard for the Flammability (Open Flame) of Mattress Sets; Final Rule, 71 Fed. Reg. 13472, 13476, 13496–97 (2006).

118. O'Donnell v. Big Yank, Inc., 696 A.2d 846, 853 (Pa. Super. 1997) (standard not amended in fifty years); Gryc v. Dayton-Hudson Corp., 297 N.W.2d 727, 734 (Minn. 1980) (expert testimony).

119. Consumer Product Safety Commission, Standard for the Flammability of Clothing Textiles.

120. Restatement (Third) of Torts—Products Liability § 6(c) (emphasis added); Shifton, *The Restatement (Third) of Torts,* 2370.

121. Miller v. Pfizer, 196 F. Supp.2d 1062, 1065 (D. Kan. 2002), aff'd, 356 F.3d 1326 (10th Cir. 2004).

122. *Id.,* 1066–92; Daubert v. Merrell-Dow Pharmaceuticals, Inc., 509 U.S. 579 (1993).

123. Cartwright v. Pfizer, Inc., 369 F. Supp.2d 876, 886 (E.D. Tex. 2005); Moffett v. Smithkline Beecham Corp., 2005 WL 1595664 (S.D. Miss. 2005); Blanchard v. Eli Lilly & Co., 207 F. Supp.2d 308, 317–21 (D. Vermont 2002) (Prozac); Cloud v. Pfizer, Inc., 198 F. Supp.2d 1118, 1122–28 (D. Ariz. 2001) (Zoloft).

124. Freightliner Corp. v. Myrick, No. 94–286, Brief for the United States, Amicus Curiae, December 13, 1994, at 24–25.

125. Geier v. American Honda Motor Co., Brief for the United States as Amicus Curiae, November 8, 1999, at 9.

126. Catherine M. Sharkey, *Preemption by Preamble: Federal Agencies and the Federalization of Tort Reform,* 56 DePaul L. Rev. 227, 234 (2006).

127. Levin and Miller, *Industries Get Quiet Protection.*

128. Nagareda, *FDA Preemption,* 3.

CHAPTER 7. AGENCIES, JURIES, AND THE PUBLIC INTEREST

1. Richard J. Pierce, *Regulation, Deregulation, Federalism, and Administrative Law: Agency Power to Preempt State Regulation,* 46 U. Pittsburgh L. Rev. 607, 654–55 (1985) (quote); W. Kip Viscusi, *Overview, in* Regulation Through Litigation 2 (W. Kip Viscusi, ed., 2002).

2. Lars Noah, *Rewarding Regulatory Compliance: The Pursuit of Symmetry in Products Liability,* 88 Geo. L. J. 2147, 2150–51 (2000) (unsophisticated jurors); W. Kip Viscusi, et al., *Deterring Inefficient Pharmaceutical Litigation: An Economic Rationale for the FDA Regulatory Compliance Defense,* 24 Seton Hall L. Rev. 1437, 1467–68 (1994) (20-20 hindsight); Geier v. American Honda Motor Co., Brief of Washington Legal Foundation as Amicus Curiae, November 19, 1999, at 17 (dwarf quote).

3. W. Kip Viscusi, *Jurors, Judges, and the Mistreatment of Risk by the Courts,* 30 J. Legal Studies 107 (2001).

4. Richard A. Epstein, Overdose 201 (2006); Peter W. Huber, Liability: The Legal Revolution and Its Consequences 214 (1988) (reasonably unbiased quote); Steven P.

Croley & William F. Funk, *The Federal Advisory Committee Act and Good Government,* 14 YALE J. REG. 451 (1997) (advisory committees).

5. *Note, A Question of Competence: The Judicial Role in the Regulation of Pharmaceuticals,* 103 HARV. L. REV. 773, 780 (1990) (internalize data quote); Peter Huber, *Safety and the Second Best: The Hazards of Public Risk Management in the Courts,* 85 COLUM. L. REV. 277, 235 (1985) (courts not qualified quote). *See also* Robert L. Rabin, *Reassessing Regulatory Compliance,* 88 GEO. L. J. 2049, 2052 (2000); Richard B. Stewart, *Regulatory Compliance Preclusion of Tort Liability: Limiting the Dual-Track System,* 88 GEO. L. J. 2167, 2169 (2000); Catherine T. Struve, *The FDA and the Tort System: Postmarketing Surveillance, Compensation, and the Role of Litigation,* 5 YALE J. POLICY & LEGAL ETHICS, 587, 588 (2005) (describing the position of preemption proponents).
6. Timothy D. Lytton, *Tort Claims Against Gun Manufacturers for Crime-Related Injuries: Defining a Suitable Role for the Tort System in Regulating the Firearms Industry,* 65 MO. L. REV. 1, 53 (2000) (agency resources questioned).
7. David C. Vladeck, *Defending Courts: A Brief Rejoinder to Professors Fried and Rosenberg,* 31 SETON HALL L. REV. 631, 641 (2001) (good sense of jurors); Clayton P. Gillette & James E. Krier, *Risk, Courts, and Agencies,* 138 U. PA. L. REV. 1027, 1064 (1990) (comprehensive rationality quote); Mary L. Lyndon, *Tort Law and Technology,* 12 YALE J. REG. 137, 153–54, 157–58 (1995) (making both points).
8. *See, e.g.,* W. Kip Viscusi, *Jurors, Judges, and the Mistreatment of Risk by the Courts,* 30 J. LEGAL STUDIES 107 (2001); Reid Hastie & W. Kip Viscusi, *What Juries Can't Do Well: The Jury's Performance as a Risk Manager,* 40 ARIZ. L. REV. 901, 913 (1998).
9. David A. Hoffman, *How Relevant Is Jury Rationality?* 2003 U. ILL. L. REV. 507, 526–28 (2003); Gregory Mitchell, *Taking Behavioralism Too Seriously? The Unwarranted Pessimism of the New Behavioral Analysis of Law,* 43 WM. & MARY L. REV. 1907 (2002).
10. Daubert v. Merrell-Dow Pharmaceuticals, Inc., 509 U.S. 579 (1993).
11. Michael D. Green & William B. Schultz, *Tort Law Deference to FDA Regulation of Medical Devices,* 88 GEO. L. J. 2119, 2139 (2000); Thomas O. McGarity, *Our Science Is Sound Science and Their Science Is Junk Science: Science-Based Strategies for Avoiding Accountability and Responsibility for Risk-Producing Products and Activities,* 52 KAN. L. REV. 897 (2004); Rabin, *Reassessing,* 2063–65.
12. Neil Vidmar, *The Performance of the American Civil Jury: An Empirical Perspective,* 40 ARIZ. L. REV. 849, 863–64 (1998).
13. Stewart, *Regulatory Compliance,* 2177.
14. Thomas O. McGarity, *Substantive and Procedural Discretion in Administrative Resolution of Science Policy Questions: Regulating Carcinogens in EPA and OSHA,* 67 GEO. LAW JOURNAL 729, 810 (1979); Wendy E. Wagner, *The Science Charade in Toxic Risk Regulation,* 95 COLUM. L. REV. 1613 (1995).
15. DAVID G. OWEN, PRODUCTS LIABILITY LAW 887 (2005); Peter H. Schuck, *Why Regulating Guns Through Litigation Won't Work, in* SUING THE GUN INDUSTRY 225, 232 (Timothy D. Lytton, ed., 2005); Geier v. American Honda Motor Co., Brief of the National Conference of State Legislatures, Council of State Governments, National Association of Counties, National League of Cities, International City/County Management Association and U.S. Conference of Mayors as Amicus Curiae, October 22, 1999, at 12.

16. Lytton, *Tort Claims,* 51–52.
17. *See* General Motors Corp. v. Farnsworth, 965 P.2d 1209, 1220 (Alaska 1998) (allowing claim based on defective seatbelt design based on consumer expectation test).
18. Warren Brown, *Front-Seat Air Bags Will Be Standard by 1994,* WASHINGTON POST, July 10, 1991, at A1; Micheline Maynard, *Saved by the Bag,* USA TODAY, April 26, 1991, at A1; Jennifer Toth, *Air Bags, Seat Belts Required in Vans, Trucks,* LOS ANGELES TIMES, March 22, 1991, at D2.
19. Intermodal Surface Transportation Efficiency Act of 1991, Pub. L. 102–240, 105 Stat. 1914 (1991).
20. Hisrich v. Volvo Cars of North America, Inc., 226 F.3d 445, 448 (6th Cir. 2000) (collision killed Zhang); Leigh Anenson, *Great Expectations: The Role of the Consumer in Determining Defective Air Bag Design,* 38 TORT & INS. L. J. 963, 964 (2003).
21. Marcia Stepanek & Dan Freedman, *Accusations Fly in Dispute of Air-Bag Safety,* CLEVELAND PLAIN DEALER, November 17, 1996, at H4 (Chrysler and Ford warnings); James R. Healy & Jayne O'Donnell, *Deadly Air Bags: How a Government Prescription for Safety Became a Threat to Children,* USA TODAY, July 8, 1996, at B1 (General Motors warning).
22. Joan Claybrook, *The Safest Air Bags of All,* WASHINGTON POST, August 12, 1997, at A19 (op-ed); Joan Claybrook, *The Auto Industry, the Air Bag,* WASHINGTON POST, December 1, 1996, at C7 (op-ed); Warren Brown & Cindy Skrzycki, *U.S. Doubts on Air Bags Date to '69,* WASHINGTON POST, November 21, 1996, at A1.
23. Claybrook, *The Auto Industry.*
24. Warren Brown, *The Switch Is On,* WASHINGTON POST, August 25, 1995, at B1; *Switch Would Turn Off Airbag,* ORLANDO SENTINEL, October 13, 1994, at 13; Frank Swoboda, *U.S. Calls Air Bags Risk to Tots,* WASHINGTON POST, February 19, 1994, at A1.
25. *Air-Bag-Associated Fatal Injuries to Infants and Children Riding in Front Passenger Seats—United States,* 44 MORBIDITY AND MORTALITY WEEKLY REPORT 845 (1995) (reporting details of eight deaths); Michael Clements, *Child Deaths Prompt Study of Air-Bag Use,* USA TODAY, November 6, 1995, at B1; *Air Bags May Harm Children, Agency Warns,* LOS ANGELES TIMES, October 28, 1995, at A5.
26. Brown & Skrzycki, *U.S. Doubts on Air Bags Date to '69;* Donald W. Nauss, *Rules Proposed to Encourage Use of 'Smart' Air Bag Systems,* LOS ANGELES TIMES, August 2, 1996, at D1 (quoting Joan Claybrook, Public Citizen); Healy & O'Donnell, *Deadly Air Bags* (everyone agreed); Paul Leinert & Anita Leinert, *Chip Off the Old Block,* CHICAGO TRIBUNE, April 23, 1996, at E24 (quoting Clarence Ditlow, Center for Auto Safety).
27. Janet L. Fix, *Big 3 to Warn About Air Bags Letters, Labels to Focus on Kinds,* DETROIT FREE PRESS, November 2, 1996, at A1 (industry letters); Janet L. Fix, *NHTSA Calls for Air Bag Warning,* DETROIT FREE PRESS, August 2, 1996, at E1 (NHTSA proposed rule).
28. Warren Brown & David B. Ottaway, *Small Victims of a Flawed Safety Device,* WASHINGTON POST, June 2, 1997, at A1.
29. Transportation Equity Act for the 21st Century, Pub. L. No. 105–178, 112 Stat. 107 (1998).
30. Ben Wildavsky, *Deflating Air Bags,* 29 NAT. J. 322 (1997).
31. Stepanek & Freedman, *Accusations Fly.*
32. Timothy D. Lytton, *The Complementary Role of Tort Litigation in Regulating the Gun In-*

dustry, in SUING THE GUN INDUSTRY 250, 263 (Timothy D. Lytton, ed., 2005) (quote); Edward T. Schroeder, *A Tort by Any Other Name? In Search of the Distinction Between Regulation Through Litigation and Conventional Tort Law,* 83 TEX. L. REV. 897, 899 (2005); Vladeck, *Defending Courts,* 640.

33. Viscusi, *Overview,* 1. *See also* HUBER, LIABILITY, 83.
34. Viscusi, *Overview,* 1; Noah, *Rewarding Regulatory Compliance,* 2149–50; Schroeder, *A Tort by Any Other Name,* 922–23; Schuck, *Regulating Guns.*
35. James A. Henderson & Aaron D. Twerski, *Achieving Consensus on Defective Product Design,* 83 CORNELL L. REV. 867, 884–85 (1998); Richard B. Stewart, *The Reformation of American Administrative Law,* 88 HARV. L. REV. 1667, 1693–97 (1975).
36. Victor Schwartz & Leah Lorber, *State Farm v. Avery: State Court Regulation Through Litigation Has Gone Too Far,* 33 CONN. L. REV. 1215, 1220 (2001).
37. Schuck, *Regulating Guns,* 225, 234 (quote); Stewart, *Regulatory Compliance,* 88 GEO. L. J. 2167, 2174 (2000).
38. Schuck, *Regulating Guns,* 225, 236.
39. Daniel Feldman, *Legislating or Litigating Public Policy Change: Gunmaker Tort Liability,* 12 VA. J. SOC. POLICY & LAW 140, 159 (2004); Schwartz & Lorber, *State Farm v. Avery,* 1220.
40. HUBER, LIABILITY, 186; Schuck, *Regulating Guns,* 225, 234; Stewart, *Regulatory Compliance,* 2174.
41. Schroeder, *A Tort by Any Other Name,* 923–25.
42. Viscusi, *Overview,* 10.
43. CHARLES MCCARRY, CITIZEN NADER 217 (1972); George Stigler, *The Theory of Economic Regulation,* 2 BELL J. ECON. & MGMT. SCI. 335 (1971). *See also* PAUL J. QUIRK, INDUSTRY INFLUENCE IN FEDERAL REGULATORY AGENCIES 4–21 (1981); Jerry L. Mashaw & David L. Harfst, *Regulation and Legal Culture: The Case of Motor Vehicle Safety,* 4 YALE J. REG. 257, 270 (1987) (permanent campaigns); Cass R. Sunstein, *Constitutionalism After the New Deal,* 101 HARV. L. REV. 421, 448–49 (1987). *But see* David B. Spence, *The Shadow of the Rational Polluter: Rethinking the Role of Rational Actor Models in Environmental Law,* 89 CAL. L. REV. 917 (2001) (criticizing the capture theory as outdated and unsupported by the evidence).
44. Carl T. Bogus, *War on the Common Law: The Struggle at the Center of Products Liability,* 60 MO. L. REV. 1, 76–82 (1995) (providing examples of NHTSA failure to regulate the Ford Pinto and GM pickup side-saddle trucks).
45. JONATHAN LASH, KATHERINE GILLMAN, & DAVID SHERIDAN, A SEASON OF SPOILS 18–29 (1984); SUSAN J. TOLCHIN & MARTIN TOLCHIN, DISMANTLING AMERICA ch.2 (1983); Teresa M. Schwartz, *Regulatory Standards and Products Liability: Striking the Right Balance Between the Two,* 30 MICH. J. L. REFORM 431, 447–48 (1997); Vladeck, *Defending Courts,* 639.
46. ELIZABETH DREW, SHOWDOWN 114–17 (1996); DAVID MARANISS & MICHAEL WEISKOPF, TELL NEWT TO SHUT UP ch. 9 (1996).
47. Pub. L. No. 102–571, 106 Stat. 4491 (1992).
48. NATIONAL INSTITUTE OF MEDICINE, THE FUTURE OF DRUG SAFETY 1-2, 3-7, and Boxes

1.1, 2.1 (2006); RENA STEINZOR & MARGARET CLUNE, THE HIDDEN LESSON OF THE VIOXX FIASCO: REVIVING A HOLLOW FDA 13–14, 17 (Center for Progressive Reform White Paper No. 514, October 2005).

49. Marc Kaufman, *Many FDA Scientists Had Drug Concerns, 2002 Survey Shows,* WASHINGTON POST, December 16, 2004, at A1.

50. Steinzor & Clune, HIDDEN LESSON, 17.

51. NATIONAL INSTITUTE OF MEDICINE, FUTURE, 7–2.

52. QUIRK, INDUSTRY INFLUENCE, 13; Gillette & Krier, *Risk,* 1065–69 (1990); Howard Latin, *Ideal Versus Real Regulatory Efficiency: Implementation of Uniform Standards and 'Fine-Tuning' Regulatory Reforms,* 37 STAN. L. REV. 1267, 1331 (1985); Mashaw & Harfst, *Regulation and Legal Culture;* Stewart, *Reformation;* Laura Sullivan, *Success of Shift in Guns Policy Is Debatable,* BALTIMORE SUN, October 27, 2004, at A1 (lobbyist quote).

53. QUIRK, INDUSTRY INFLUENCE, 13 (quotes); Gillette & Krier, *Risk,* 1067–69.

54. QUIRK, INDUSTRY INFLUENCE, 5, 12 (single industry agencies susceptible); MICHAEL D. GREEN, BENDECTIN AND BIRTH DEFECTS (1996) (FDA drug approval); Thomas O. McGarity, *Politics by Other Means: Law, Science, and Policy in EPA's Implementation of the Food Quality Protection Act,* 53 AD. L. REV. 103, 203 (2001) (process for approving and amending pesticides tolerances); Lars Noah & Richard Merrill, *Starting From Scratch? Reinventing the Food Additive Approval Process,* 78 BOSTON U. L. REV. 329, 364 (1998) (process for affirming that food additives are "generally recognized as safe" at FDA); Schwartz, *Regulatory Standards,* 445 (CPSC product regulation).

55. OFFICE OF THE INSPECTOR GENERAL, DEPARTMENT OF HEALTH AND HUMAN SERVICES, FDA'S REVIEW PROCESS FOR NEW DRUG APPLICATIONS: A MANAGEMENT REVIEW iv (March 2003) (dual role quote).

56. DAN FAGIN & MARIANNE LAVELLE, TOXIC DECEPTION 46 (1996) (formaldehyde research agreement); GEORGE LOUIS CARLO & MARTIN SCHRAM, CELL PHONES: INVISIBLE HAZARDS IN THE WIRELESS AGE: AN INSIDER'S ALARMING DISCOVERIES ABOUT CANCER AND GENETIC DAMAGE 222 (2001) (cell phone health effects research agreement).

57. U.S. GOVERNMENT ACCOUNTABILITY OFFICE, RAIL SAFETY: THE FEDERAL RAILROAD ADMINISTRATION IS TAKING STEPS TO BETTER TARGET ITS OVERSIGHT, BUT ASSESSMENT OF RESULTS IS NEEDED TO DETERMINE IMPACT 12–13 (2007) (official enforcement policy); Walt Bogdanich, *U.S. Audit Criticizes Federal Regulators Over Methods of Railroad Safety Oversight,* NEW YORK TIMES, February 10, 2005, at A1 (Inspector General conclusion); Walt Bogdanich, *For Railroads and the Safety Overseer, Close Ties,* NEW YORK TIMES, November 7, 2004, at A1 (partners quote, Deputy Administrator quote, Associate Administrator quote); Scott Huddleston & Rima Shah, *Train Wreck Spews Deadly Fog,* SAN ANTONIO EXPRESS-NEWS, June 29, 2004, at A1 (Deputy Administrator upbraid); Penny Loeb, *Running Off the Rails,* U.S. NEWS & WORLD REPORT, May 27, 1996, at 40 (short cuts quote); .

58. Noah, *Rewarding Regulatory Compliance,* 2154 (beholden quote).

59. Anita Bernstein, *Products Liability in the Unites States Supreme Court: A Venture in Memory of Gary Schwartz,* 53 S. CAR. L. REV. 1193, 1219 (2002).

60. Bogus, *War on the Common Law,* 75. *See also* Jean Macchiaroli Eggen & John G. Culhane, *Gun Torts: Defining a Cause of Action for Victims in Suits Against Gun Manufactur-*

ers, 81 N. CAR. L. REV. 115, 186 (2002); William M. Sage, *Note, Drug Product Liability and Health Care Delivery Systems,* 40 STAN. L. REV. 989, 1019–20 (1988).

61. THOMAS O. MCGARITY AND WENDY E. WAGNER, BENDING SCIENCE ch.5 (2008); Michael D. Green, *Safety as an Element of Pharmaceutical Quality: The Respective Roles of Regulation and Tort Law,* 42 ST. LOUIS L. J. 163, 182 (1998); Sheldon Krimsky, *Publication Bias, Data Ownership and the Funding Effect in Science: Threats to the Integrity of Biomedical Research, in* RESCUING SCIENCE FROM POLITICS: REGULATION AND THE DISTORTION OF SCIENTIFIC RESEARCH (Wendy E. Wagner & Rena Steinzor, eds., 2005); Bogus, *War on the Common Law,* 74.
62. MCGARITY AND WAGNER, BENDING SCIENCE, ch. 4; MARCIA ANGELL, THE TRUTH ABOUT THE DRUG COMPANIES 108 (2005).
63. DAVID HEALY, LET THEM EAT PROZAC 112 (2004) (ghost writing); JEROME P. KASSIRER, ON THE TAKE 31 (2005) (ghost writing); SHELDON KRIMSKY, SCIENCE IN THE PRIVATE INTEREST 144 (2003); Thomas Bodenheimer, *Uneasy Alliance: Clinical Investigators and the Pharmaceutical Industry,* 342 NEW ENGLAND J. MED. 1539 (2000); *FDA's Drug Approval Process: Up to the Challenge? Hearings Before the Senate Committee on Health, Education, Labor and Pensions,* 109th Cong., 1st Sess. 68 (2005), (testimony of Dr. Thomas R. Fleming, University of Washington) (sponsor spin quote); Melody Petersen, *Madison Ave. Has Growing Role in the Business of Drug Research,* NEW YORK TIMES, November 22, 2002, at A1.
64. Justin E. Bekelman, Yan Li, & Cary P. Gross, *Scope and Impact of Financial Conflicts of Interest in Biomedical Research,* 289 J. AM. MED. ASS'N 454 (2003). *See also* Joel Lexchin, et al., *Pharmaceutical Industry Sponsorship and Research Outcome and Quality: Systematic Review,* 326 BRIT. MED. J. 1167 (2003).
65. MCGARITY AND WAGNER, BENDING SCIENCE, ch. 4, 7; KRIMSKY, SCIENCE IN THE PRIVATE INTEREST, 191; Jonathan Gabe & Michael Bury, *Anxious Times: The Benzodiazepine Controversy and the Fracturing of Expert Authority, in* CONTESTED GROUND 42, 48 (Peter Davis, ed., 1996); Clare Dyer, *Upjohn Sues for Libel,* 304 BRIT. MED. J. 273 (1992) (halcyon researcher sued in British court); Thomas O. McGarity, *Resisting Regulation With Blue Ribbon Panels,* 33 FORDHAM URBAN L. J. 1157 (2006) (blue ribbon panels).
66. See Teresa Curtin & Ellen Relkin, *Preamble Preemption and the Challenged Role of Failure to Warn and Defective Design Pharmaceutical Cases in Revealing Scientific Fraud, Marketing Mischief, and Conflicts of Interest,* 35 HOFSTRA L. REV. 1773 (2007).
67. Buckman Co. v. Plaintiffs' Legal Committee, 531 U.S. 341, 348 (2001).
68. 18 U.S.C. § 208.
69. 18 U.S.C. § 207.
70. MCGARITY AND WAGNER, BENDING SCIENCE, ch. 8.
71. QUIRK, INDUSTRY INFLUENCE, 19.
72. Bogdanich, *For Railroads and the Safety Overseer, Close Ties.*
73. MARGARET H. CLUNE, STEALTH TORT REFORM: HOW THE BUSH ADMINISTRATION'S AGGRESSIVE USE OF THE PREEMPTION DOCTRINE HURTS CONSUMERS 12 n. 27 (Center for Progressive Regulation White Paper No. 403, October 2004).
74. *Senate Confirms Stratton Nomination to Head CPSC by Unanimous Consent,* 30 BNA

PROD. SAFETY REPT. 655 (July 29, 2002); *Dykema Adds Hal Stratton in Washington,* Press Release, (July 17, 2006) (quote).

75. Jeff Plungis, *Agency's Work Hindered by Faulty Data,* DETROIT NEWS, March 4, 2002, at A4 (Sue Bailey, Dianne Steed, Jerry Curry); Jennifer Dixon, *Ford Hires Insider to Review Tires,* DETROIT FREE PRESS, July 3, 2001, at C1; Judy Sarasohn, *Special Interests; Ex-NHTSA Officials Take Industry's Side,* WASHINGTON POST, October 5, 2000, at A33 (Marion Blakey).
76. Sarasohn, *Special Interests;* Myron Levin, *Who's Watching Out for Safety?* LOS ANGELES TIMES, January 5, 2000, at G1.
77. Levin, *Who's Watching Out.*
78. Jayne O'Donnell, *Auto-Regulation Official Will Take Industry Job,* USA TODAY, August 16, 1996 (Barry Felrice, George Parker); Michael Clements, *Child Deaths Prompt Study of Air-Bag Use,* USA TODAY, November 6, 1995, at B1 (Barry Felrice).
79. 7 U.S.C. §§ 136d(b)(2), 136w(d).
80. 5 U.S.C. App. II § 5(c); 41 C.F.R. § 101–6.100(b)(2)(iii).
81. UNITED STATES GENERAL ACCOUNTING OFFICE, EPA'S SCIENCE ADVISORY BOARD PANELS: IMPROVED POLICIES AND PROCEDURES NEEDED TO ENSURE INDEPENDENCE AND BALANCE (June 2001); UNITED STATES GENERAL ACCOUNTING OFFICE, FEDERAL ADVISORY COMMITTEES, ADDITIONAL GUIDANCE COULD HELP AGENCIES BETTER ENSURE INDEPENDENCE AND BALANCE (April 2004).
82. *CSPI Urges Removal of FDA Panelists on SSRIs,* Press Release, (February 1, 2004).
83. REPORT OF THE PROPELLER GUARD SUBCOMMITTEE OF THE NATIONAL BOATING SAFETY ADVISORY COUNCIL, (November 7, 1989), *reprinted in* Sprietsma v. Mercury Marine, Joint Appendix, at 13, 15–16.
84. Schwartz, *Regulatory Standards,* 445–46.
85. Lytton, *Tort Claims,* 52 (thirteen thousand site inspections); Laura Sullivan, *Success of Shift in Guns Policy Is Debatable,* BALTIMORE SUN, October 27, 2004, at A1 (small and poor quote, quoting former NRA General Counsel Robert Ricker); Fox Butterfield, *Limits on Power and Zeal Hamper Firearms Agency,* NEW YORK TIMES, July 22, 1999, at A1 (1700 agents); Fox Butterfield, *Gun Industry Ex-Official Describes Bond of Silence,* NEW YORK TIMES, February 4, 2003, at A14 (industry aware of limitations).
86. DAVID A. STOCKMAN, THE TRIUMPH OF POLITICS ch. 4 (1986) (Trojan horse budget); Vladeck, *Defending Courts,* 639 (Vladeck quote); Jeff Plungis, *Money, Clout Key to Fixing NHTSA,* DETROIT NEWS, March 6, 2002, at A1 (modest increase); Myron Levin, *Upgrades on Auto Safety Standards Languish,* LOS ANGELES TIMES, September 18, 2000, at A1 (NHTSA engineer quote); Cindy Skrzycki, *NHTSA Will Share Hearing Spotlight,* WASHINGTON POST, September 5, 2000, at E1 (never recovered).
87. U.S. GOVERNMENT ACCOUNTABILITY OFFICE, RAIL SAFETY: THE FEDERAL RAILROAD ADMINISTRATION IS TAKING STEPS TO BETTER TARGET ITS OVERSIGHT, BUT ASSESSMENT OF RESULTS IS NEEDED TO DETERMINE IMPACT 14–15 (2007) (statistics); Elizabeth Williamson, *Railroad Firms Bringing Aboard Lawmakers' Lobbyist Relatives,* WASHINGTON POST, February 8, 2007, at A1 (quoting Rep. Corrine Brown); Bogdanich, *For Railroads and the Safety Overseer, Close Ties* (2003 investigations); Walt Bogdanich, *In Deaths*

at Rail Crossings, Missing Evidence and Silence, New York Times, July 11, 2004, at A1 (unusual circumstances quote, time lag).

88. U.S. Government Accountability Office, Rail Safety, 29; Williamson, *Railroad Firms Bringing Aboard Lawmakers' Lobbyist Relatives* (quoting Rep. Corrine Brown); Dan Weikel, *Over the Long Haul, Fatigue Kills,* Los Angeles Times, April 24, 2005, at A1; Nurith Aizenman, *The Case for More Regulation: Lax Federal Trucking and Railroad Safety Oversight,* Washington Monthly, October, 1997, at 16.
89. Bogdanich, *Deaths at Rail Crossings.*
90. *Railroad Safety, Hearings Before the Subcommittee on Surface Transportation and Merchant Marine of the Senate Committee on Commerce, Science and Transportation,* 107th Cong., 2d Sess. 60 (2002) 60 (testimony of Don M. Hahs, International President, Brotherhood of Locomotive Engineers).
91. Green, *Safety as an Element,* 174 ("FDA is woefully underfunded for its mandate"); Teresa M. Schwartz, *Prescription Products and the Proposed Restatement (Third),* 61 Tenn. L. Rev. 1357, 1387–88 (1994); Struve, *FDA and the Tort System,* 604–05.
92. National Institute of Medicine, Future, 7–1.
93. Union of Concerned Scientists, Voices of Scientists at FDA: Protecting Public Health Depends on Independent Science 2 (July 2006) (scientist survey); *FDA's Drug Approval Process: Up to the Challenge? Hearings,* 57 (testimony of Abbey S. Meyers, National Organization for Rare Disorders) (origin of FDA appropriations); Diedra Henderson, *Drug Makers Lobby U.S. to Hike FDA Funds,* Boston Globe, July 13, 2006, at A1 (industry quote, White House deaf ear).
94. National Institute of Medicine, Future, 7–1; David A. Kessler & David C. Vladeck, *A Critical Examination of the FDA's Efforts to Preempt Failure-to-Warn Claims,* 96 Geo. L. J. 461, 484 (2008) (2007 amendments); *Risk and Responsibility: The Roles of FDA and Pharmaceutical Companies in Ensuring the Safety of Approved Drugs, Like Vioxx, Hearings Before the House Committee on Government Reform,* 109th Cong., 1st Sess. 23 (2005) (testimony of Steven Galston, Acting Director, Center for Drug Evaluation and Research, FDA) (lack of resources for postmarket surveillance); *Ensuring Drug Safety: Where Do We Go From Here? Hearings Before the Senate Committee on Health, Education, Labor and Pensions,* 109th Cong., 1st Sess. 42 (2005) (testimony of Bruce M. Psaty, University of Washington) (statistics, industry desires quote); Steinzor & Clune, Hidden Lesson (2002 reauthorization, 7 percent). *But see* Epstein, Overdose, 127–28 (calling the concern "overblown").
95. National Institute of Medicine, Safe Medical Devices for Children 183, 190 (2005).
96. *Id.,* 152, 163 (not working well quote, quoting FDA report); Green & Schultz, *Tort Law Deference,* 2142 (few resources to analyze reports); Barry Meier, *Implants With Flaws: Disclosure and Delay,* New York Times, June 14, 2005, at A1 (no adequate data collection system).
97. National Institute of Medicine, Future, 3–2 (general assessment of poor FDA staff morale); Union of Concerned Scientists, Voices of Scientists, 3 (UCS survey); Marc Kaufman, *Many FDA Scientists Had Drug Concerns, 2002 Survey Shows,* Washington Post, December 16, 2004, at A1 (Inspector General survey).

98. Lytton, *Introduction,* 1, 29; Schwartz, *Prescription Products,* 1405; Struve, *FDA and the Tort System,* 591.
99. Riegel v. Medtronic Inc. 128 S.Ct. 999 (2008); Maura Lerner, *Hunting Down Dangers to the Heart,* MINNEAPOLIS STAR TRIBUNE, July 24, 2005, at A1 (can't do this quote).
100. Bogdanich, *Deaths at Rail Crossings.*
101. OWEN, PRODUCTS LIABILITY at 887; Mary L. Lyndon, *Tort Law and Technology,* 12 YALE J. REG. 137, 174 (1995); Schwartz, *Regulatory Standards,* 444–45.
102. Thomas O. McGarity, *Some Thoughts on Deossifying the Rulemaking Process,* 41 DUKE L. J. 1385 (1992); Plungis, *Money, Clout Key to Fixing NHTSA* (National Safety Council quote).
103. Robert B. Leflar & Robert S. Adler, *The Preemption Pentad: Federal Preemption of Products Liability Claims after Medtronic,* 64 TENN. L. REV. 691, 712 (1997); Schwartz, *Regulatory Standards,* 445.
104. Jerry L. Mashaw & David L. Harfst, *Inside the National Highway Traffic Safety Administration: Legal Determinants of Bureaucratic Organization and Performance,* 57 U. CHI. L. REV. 443 (1990) (Mashaw study); Jeff Plungis & Bill Vlasic, *Feds, Big Three Gird for Showdown,* DETROIT NEWS, April 13, 2004, at A1 (simmer quote, quoting Gerald Donaldson, Senior Research Director, Advocates for Health and Safety); Jennifer Dixon, *Ford Insists Cars Safe, But Cops Keep Dying,* DETROIT FREE PRESS, December 8, 2003, at A1 (fuel system standard); Jeff Plungis, *Tougher Fuel Tanks Ordered,* DETROIT NEWS, November 26, 2003, at D1 (fuel system standard); Jeff Plungis, *Vehicle Safety Standards Outdated,* DETROIT NEWS, March 3, 2002, at A1 (2002 statistics); Levin, *Upgrades on Auto Safety Standards Languish* (head restraints update, NHTSA abandons other update initiatives); Judy Pasternak, *Safety Agency Takes Heat Over Firestone Tire Recall,* LOS ANGELES TIMES, August 19, 2000, at A1 (tire standards).
105. OFFICE OF THE INSPECTOR GENERAL, DEPARTMENT OF HEALTH AND HUMAN SERVICES, FDA'S REVIEW PROCESS FOR NEW DRUG APPLICATIONS: A MANAGEMENT REVIEW ii (March 2003); Green, *Safety as an Element,* 179; *FDA's Drug Approval Process: Up to the Challenge? Hearings,* 18 (testimony of Sandra L. Kweder, FDA).
106. 212 U.S.C. § 355(e); NATIONAL INSTITUTE OF MEDICINE, FUTURE, 5–5, 5–11; GOVERNMENT ACCOUNTABILITY OFFICE, DRUG SAFETY: IMPROVEMENT NEEDED IN FDA'S POSTMARKET DECISION-MAKING AND OVERSIGHT PROCESS 10 (March 2006).
107. Consumer Product Safety Commission, Standard for the Flammability of Clothing Textiles; Advance Notice of Proposed Rulemaking, 67 Fed. Reg. 57771 (2002); DIRECTORATE FOR ENGINEERING SCIENCES, CPSC, BRIEFING PACKAGE, STANDARD FOR THE FLAMMABILITY OF CLOTHING TEXTILES, ANPR TO AMEND AND UPDATE (2002).
108. *Railroad Safety Hearings,* 10 (testimony of Marion C. Blakey, Chairman, NTSB) (NTSB ability quote); Charles Roisseau, *Fatigue Puts Rail Workers on a Dangerous Track,* HOUSTON CHRONICLE, January 4, 1998, at A1; Aizenman, *Case for More Regulation,* 16; Railroad Safety Hearings, 49 (testimony of Edward Hamburger, President, Association of American Railroads) (fierce resistance); Penny Loeb, *Running Off the Rails,* U.S. NEWS & WORLD REPORT, May 27, 1996, at 40 (NTSB forever quote, AAR prudent use quote).

109. Green, *Safety as an Element,* 179–81.
110. Leflar & Adler, *Preemption Pentad,* 712; Lyndon, *Tort Law and Technology,* 163–64.
111. The description of the breast implant litigation is drawn from Jodi Hersch, *Breast Implants: Regulation, Litigation, and Science,* in REGULATION THROUGH LITIGATION 142, 163–66, 177 (W. Kip Viscusi, ed., 2002) (quote); Rebecca Dresser, Wendy Wagner, and Paul Giannelli, *Breast Implants Revisited: Beyond Science on Trial,* 1997 WIS. L. REV. 705 (1997); David Brown & Christopher Lee, *FDA Ends Ban on Silicone Implants,* WASHINGTON POST, November 18, 2006, at A1.
112. Geier v. American Honda Motor Co., Brief of Washington Legal Foundation as Amicus Curiae, November 19, 1999, at 16.
113. *See* Marc Galanter, *Real World Torts: An Antidote to Anecdote,* 55 MD. L. REV. 1093, 1100 (1996).
114. David C. Vladeck, *Preemption and Regulatory Failure,* 33 PEPPERDINE L. REV. 95, 132 (2005).
115. OWEN, PRODUCTS LIABILITY, 893.
116. Schuck, *Regulating Guns,* 231.
117. Wendy Wagner, *Stubborn Information Problems and the Regulatory Benefits of Gun Litigation, in* SUING THE GUN INDUSTRY 225, 231, 271, 273–74 (Timothy D. Lytton, ed., 2005). *See also* Richard Nagareda, *FDA Preemption: When Tort Law Meets the Administrative State,* 1 J. TORT LAW 1, 17 (2006) (referring to the ability of the common law to provide "information updating").
118. Noah, *Rewarding Regulatory Compliance,* 2161.
119. Rabin, *Reassessing Regulatory Compliance,* 2069.
120. Vladeck, *Defending Courts,* 633–34.
121. Wagner, *Stubborn Information,* 274. *See also* Daniel J. Gilveber & Anthony Robbins, *Public Health Versus Court-Sponsored Secrecy,* 69 L. & CONTEMP. PROB. 132 (2006); Kessler & Vladeck, FDA's Efforts, 492-95; Vladeck, *Defending Courts,* 632; Wendy Wagner, *When All Else Fails: Regulating Risky Products Through Tort Litigation,* 95 GEO. L. J. 693 (2007).
122. Aaron S. Kesselheim & Jerry Avorn, The Role of Litigation in Defining Drug Risks, 297 J. Am. Med. Ass'n 308 (2007). See also Bogus, *War on the Common Law,* 4; Schwartz, *Prescription Products,* 1386; Vladeck, *Defending Courts,* 633–34.
123. The Benlate story is drawn from In re E. I. DuPont de Nemours & Co.-Benlate Litigation, 918 F. Supp. 1524, 1528–35 (M.D. Ga. 1995); Kawamata Farms v. United Agri Products, 948 P.2d 1055, 1064–66 (Hawaii 1997); Jan Hollingsworth, *DuPont to End Sales of Benlate,* TAMPA TRIBUNE, April 20, 2001, at 1. *See also* Living Designs, Inc. v. E. I. DuPont de Nemours & Co., 431 F.3d 353, 357 (9th Cir. 2005).
124. In re E. I. DuPont de Nemours & Co.-Benlate Litigation, 99 F.3d 363 (11th Cir. 1996); In re E. I. DuPont de Nemours & Co.-Benlate Litigation, 918 F. Supp. 1524, 1557 (M.D. Ga. 1995). *See also DuPont, Plaintiffs Plan to Appeal After $113 Million Award to Fern Growers,* 34 BNA PROD. SAFETY LIABILITY REPT. 572 (2006) (jury award of $113 million to 27 Costa Rican growers reduced to $60 million because of growers' comparative negligence).

125. Myron Levin, *General Tire Accused of Deceiving U.S. in Probe,* Los Angeles Times, November 20, 2000, at A1; Mark Skertic, *Court Records Reveal More Tire Troubles,* Chicago Sun-Times, October 3, 2000, at 1.
126. Laurie Kratky Dore, *Public Courts Versus Private Justice: It's Time to Let Some Sun Shine in on Alternative Dispute Resolution,* 81 Chi.-Kent L. Rev. 463 (2006); Andrew D. Goldstein, *Sealing and Revealing: Rethinking the Rules Governing Public Access to Information Generated Through Litigation,* 81 Chi.-Kent L. Rev. 375, 378 (2006) (arguing that current judicial nondisclosure rules "give too much weight to the interests of privacy and expediency at the expense of promoting judicial accountability, democratic engagement, and public confidence in the judicial system").
127. Gilveber & Robbins, *Public Health,* 132.
128. Richard Zitrin, *Secrecy's Dangerous Side Effects,* Los Angeles Times, February 8, 2007, at A21 (Eli Lilly settlements); Davan Maharaj, *Tire Recall Fuels Drive to Bar Secret Settlements,* Los Angeles Times, September 10, 2000, at A1 (General Motors settlements).
129. American Bar Association, Center for Professional Responsibility, Model Rules of Professional Conduct, Rule 1.3, comment 1 (2007) (providing that "[a] lawyer must also act with commitment and dedication to the interests of the client and with zeal in advocacy upon the client's behalf").
130. Public Law No. 106–414, 114 Stat. 1800 (2000). See Shawn Zeller, *Blowout,* 33 Nat. J. 17 (April 28, 2001); Mark Skertic, *Critics Assail Auto-Safety Bill,* Chicago Sun-Times, October 30, 2000, at 24; Janet L. Fix, *Groups Deride Auto Safety Bill,* Detroit Free Press, October 24, 2000, at D1; Cindy Skrzycki, *High-Speed Legislation; Auto Safety Bill Reflects Industry's Interests,* Washington Post, October 24, 2000, at E1.
131. 16 C.F.R. pt. 1116. See 15 U.S.C. § 2084.
132. John O'Dell, *Tire Recall Has Brought Many Changes in the Name of Secrecy,* Los Angeles Times, August 9, 2001, at 1.
133. Rabin, *Reassessing Regulatory Compliance,* 2069. *See also* Lytton, *Introduction,* 1, 31; Struve, *FDA and the Tort System,* 613; Bogus, *War on the Common Law,* 85.
134. Epstein, Overdose, 201; Huber, Liability, 186–87; Viscusi, *Overview,* 2; Charles Fried & David Rosenberg, *Redressing Harm: Who Decides?* 31 Seton Hall L. Rev. 625, 627 (2001); Noah, *Rewarding Regulatory Compliance,* 2163.
135. Noah, *Rewarding Regulatory Compliance,* 2163 (quote); Stewart, *Regulatory Compliance,* 2175.
136. Huber, Liability, 214.
137. Thomas F. Burke, Lawyers, Lawsuits, and Legal Rights 3 (2002) (quote); Galanter, *Real World Torts,* 1098; Richard Lempert, *Why Do Juries Get a Bum Rap? Reflections of the Work of Valerie Hans,* 48 DePaul L. Rev. 453 (1998).
138. Galanter, *Real World Torts,* 1110–11; Vidmar, *Performance of the American Civil Jury.*
139. Theodore Eisenberg, *Judicial Decisionmaking in Federal Products Liability Cases, 1978–1997,* 49 DePaul L. Rev. 323 (1999). *See also* Theodore Eisenberg, et al., *Juries, Judges, and Punitive Damages: An Empirical Study,* 87 Cornell L. Rev. 743, 779 (2002) (similar results for punitive damage awards).

140. Valerie P. Hans, *The Contested Role of the Civil Jury in Business Litigation,* 79 JUDICATURE 242 (1996).
141. Vladeck, *Defending Courts,* 641.
142. Rabin, *Reassessing Regulatory Compliance,* 2065–68.
143. Vidmar, *Performance of the American Civil Jury,* 898.
144. Gillette & Krier, *Risk,* 1086.
145. Mark B. McClellan, *FDA: Protecting and Advancing America's Health,* 14 HEALTH MATRIX 357, 363–64 (2004) (McClellan quote); Schwartz & Lorber, *State Farm v. Avery* (Schwartz quote).
146. Michael S. Greve, *States' Rights on Steroids,* AMERICAN ENTERPRISE FEDERALIST OUTLOOK, September/October, 2002, *at* http//:www.aei.org/fo/fo14441.htm (quote); Kevin M. McDonald, *Federal Preemption of Automotive Recalls: A Case of Too Many Backseat Drivers?* 71 TENN. L. REV. 471 (2004) (describing recall lawsuits).
147. Deborah R. Hensler, *The New Social Policy Torts: Litigation as a Legislative Strategy—Some Preliminary Thoughts on a New Research Project,* 51 DEPAUL L. REV. 493, 498 (2001).
148. Lytton, *Complementary Role,* 260.
149. *See* Viscusi, *Overview,* 3 (arguing that the tobacco litigation effectively constituted a tax on cigarette consumers).
150. Feldman, *Legislating or Litigating Public Policy Change.*

CHAPTER 8. THE CASE FOR PREEMPTION

1. Witty v. Delta Airlines, 366 F.3d 380 (5th Cir. 2004). See also Montalvo v. Spirit Airlines, 508 F.3d 464 (9th Cir. 2007) (same).
2. *See* Feldman v. Lederle Laboratories, 592 A.2d 1176, 1195 (N.J. 1991).
3. Richard Nagareda, *FDA Preemption: When Tort Law Meets the Administrative State,* 1 J. TORT LAW 1, 16 (2006); Caleb Nelson, *Preemption,* 86 VA. L. REV. 225, 231 (2002).
4. Geier v. American Honda Motor Co., Brief for the Chamber of Commerce of the United States of America as Amicus Curiae, November 19, 1999, at 20, 24 (quotes). *See also* Sprietsma v. Mercury Marine, Brief of the Product Liability Advisory Council, Inc. as Amicus Curiae, May 20, 2002, at 5; Ralph Lindeman, *Agencies Move to Override State Law as Part of Federal Rulemaking Process,* 34 BNA PROD. SAFETY & LIABILITY REPT. 304 (2006), (quoting David Price, Washington Legal Foundation).
5. Richard B. Stewart, *Regulatory Compliance Preclusion of Tort Liability: Limiting the Duel-Track System,* 88 GEO. L. J. 2167, 2169 (2000).
6. Scott A. Smith & Duana Grage, *Federal Preemption of State Products Liability Actions,* 27 WILLIAM MITCHELL L. REV. 391, 416 (2000). *See also* David R. Geiger & Mark D. Rosen, *Rationalizing Product Liability for Prescription Drugs: Implied Preemption, Federal Common Law, and Other Paths to Uniform Pharmaceutical Safety Standards,* 45 DEPAUL L. REV. 395, 396 (1996); Charles Fried & David Rosenberg, *Redressing Harm: Who Decides?* 31 SETON HALL L. REV. 625, 628–29 (2001).
7. Samuel Issacharoff & Catherine M. Sharkey, *Backdoor Federalization,* 53 UCLA L. Rev. 1353, 1371, 1385 (2006).

8. W. Kip Viscusi, et al., *Deterring Inefficient Pharmaceutical Litigation: An Economic Rationale for the FDA Regulatory Compliance Defense,* 24 Seton Hall L. Rev. 1437, 1445–46 (1994).
9. Stewart, *Regulatory Compliance,* 2175. *See also* Richard A. Epstein, Overdose 206 (2006); Viscusi, et al., *Deterring Inefficient Pharmaceutical Litigation,* 1440
10. Bates v. Dow Agrosciences, LLC, Brief for the Product Liability Advisory Council, Inc., as Amicus Curiae, November 24, 2004, at 18.
11. Bates v. Dow Agrosciences, LLC, Brief of Amici Curiae Natural Resources Defense Council, et al., September 13, 2004.
12. Issacharoff & Sharkey, *Backdoor Federalization* 1353, 1370, 1386–89; Catherine M. Sharkey, *Preemption by Preamble: Federal Agencies and the Federalization of Tort Reform,* 56 DePaul L. Rev. 227, 239 (2006) (addressing only diverse state regulatory requirements); Sprietsma v. Mercury Marine, Brief for the Chamber of Commerce of the United States of America as Amicus Curiae, May 20, 2002, at 24–25; Bates v. Dow Agrosciences, LLC, Brief of Croplife America and National Pest Management Association as Amicus Curiae, November 24, 2004, at 18; Geier v. American Honda Motor Co., Brief for the Chamber of Commerce of the United States of America as Amicus Curiae, November 19, 1999, at 20.
13. Douglas A. Kysar, *The Expectations of Consumers,* 103 Colum. L. Rev. 1700, 1715–25 (2003).
14. Bates v. Dow Agrosciences, LLC, 544 U.S. 431, 452 (2005).
15. Peter H. Schuck, *Why Regulating Guns Through Litigation Won't Work, in* Suing the Gun Industry 225, 242–43 (Timothy D. Lytton, ed., 2005).
16. C. Boyden Gray, *Regulation and Federalism,* 1 Yale J. Reg. 93, 97 (1983).
17. *At a Glance: A Weekly Checklist of Major Issues,* 13 Nat. J. 851 (May 9, 1981) (General Motors announcement); Donald D. Holt, *Why Eaton Got Out of the Air-Bag Business,* Fortune, March 12, 1979, at 116 (airbag dealer).
18. Robert L. Rabin, *Federalism and the Tort System,* 50 Rutgers L. Rev. 1, 12 (1997).
19. Bates v. Dow Agrosciences, LLC, 544 U.S. 431, 451 (2005) (quoting Ferebee v. Chevron Chemical Co. 736 F.2d 1529, 1541–42 (D.C. Cir. 1984).
20. Rabin, *Reassessing Regulatory Compliance,* 2061.
21. Peter W. Huber, Liability: The Legal Revolution and Its Consequences 157 (1988).
22. Stewart, *Regulatory Compliance,* 2169.
23. Mark B. McClellan, *FDA: Protecting and Advancing America's Health,* 14 Health Matrix 357, 362 (2004) (McClellan quote); Joan Biskupic, *Manufacturer Liability Is at Heart of Pacemaker Case,* Washington Post, April 22, 1996, at A4 (Medtronic quote); *Note, A Question of Competence: The Judicial Role in the Regulation of Pharmaceuticals,* 103 Harv. L. Rev. 773, 782 (1990) (insurance consequences).
24. Teresa M. Schwartz, *Prescription Products and the Proposed Restatement (Third),* 61 Tenn. L. Rev. 1357, 1404–05 (1994).
25. Mary L. Lyndon, *Tort Law and Technology,* 12 Yale J. Reg. 137, 155, 166–67 (1995).
26. Geiger & Rosen, *Rationalizing Product Liability,* 428.

27. Stewart, *Regulatory Compliance,* 2170; Geiger & Rosen, *Rationalizing Product Liability,* 428.
28. McClellan, *FDA,* 361. *See also Note, A Question of Competence: The Judicial Role in the Regulation of Pharmaceuticals.*
29. Huber, Liability, 2170; Viscusi, et al., *Deterring Inefficient Pharmaceutical Litigation,* 1461. *See also* Geiger & Rosen, *Rationalizing Product Liability,* 428; Schwartz, *Prescription Products,* 1360.
30. Viscusi, et al., *Deterring Inefficient Pharmaceutical Litigation,* 1468 (quotes). *See* Epstein, Overdose, 204–07; Huber, Liability, 53–57; Nagareda, *FDA Preemption,* 35 ("hindsight bias" of common law courts).
31. TSC Industries v. Northway, Inc., 426 U.S. 438, 448–49 (1976) (avalanche of information quote); Brooks v. Howmedica, Inc., 272 F.3d 785, 796 (8th Cir. 2001) (attention quote).
32. Margaret Gilhooley, *The Effect of Products Liability Litigation on Innovation: Innovative Drugs, Products Liability, Regulatory Compliance, and Patient Choice,* 24 Seton Hall L. Rev. 1481, 1487, 1501 (1994).
33. Huber, Liability, 213.
34. Food and Drug Administration, Requirements on Content and Format of Labeling for Human Prescription Drugs and Biological Products, 71 Fed. Reg. 3922, 3935 (2006); Motus v. Pfizer, Inc., Amicus Brief for the United States, September 3, 2002, at 23. *See also Note, A Question of Competence,* 783; *Risk and Responsibility: The Roles of FDA and Pharmaceutical Companies in Ensuring the Safety of Approved Drugs, Like Vioxx, Hearings Before the House Committee on Government Reform,* 109th Cong., 1st Sess. 82 (2005) (testimony of John E. Calfee, American Enterprise Institute).
35. Clayton P. Gillette & James E. Krier, *Risk, Courts, and Agencies,* 138 U. Pa. L. Rev. 1027, 1050 (1990).
36. Gillette & Krier, *Risk,* 1054. *See also* Lyndon, *Tort Law and Technology,* 168.
37. Nagareda, *FDA Preemption,* 37.
38. John M. Mendeloff, The Dilemma of Toxic Substance Regulation ch. 3 (1988).
39. Witczak v. Pfizer, Inc., 377 F. Supp.2d 726, 732 (D. Minn. 2005). See also David A. Kessler & David C. Vladeck, *A Critical Examination of the FDA's Efforts to Preempt Failure-to-Warn Claims,* 96 Geo. L. J. 461, 486–88 (2008).
40. See Mary J. Davis, *The Battle Over Implied Preemption: Products Liability and the FDA,* 48 B.C.L. Rev. 1140-41 (2007) (doctors want more information); Jonathan V. O'Steen, *The FDA Defense: Vioxx and the Argument Against Federal Preemption,* 48 Ariz. L. Rev. 67, 93–94 (2006).
41. Buckman Co. v. Plaintiffs' Legal Committee, Brief of Amicus Curiae United States, September 13, 2000, at 10.
42. Buckman Co. v. Plaintiffs' Legal Committee 531 U.S. 341, 351 (2001).
43. Kallas v. Pfizer, Inc., Amicus Brief for the United States, September 15, 2005, at 37.
44. Caraker v. Sandoz Pharmaceuticals Corp., 172 F. Supp.2d 1018, 1036 (S.D. Ill. 2001) (quoting 59 Fed. Reg. 3944, 3948 (1994)). See Allison M. Zieve & Brian Wolfman, *The FDA's Argument for Eradicating State Tort Law: Why It Is Wrong and Warrants No Deference,* 34 BNA Prod. Safety & Liability Rept. 308, 310 (March 27, 2006).
45. Zieve & Wolfman, *FDA's Argument,* 310–12.

CHAPTER 9. THE CASE AGAINST PREEMPTION

1. Terril Yue Jones, *Ford Plans to Replace More SUV, Truck Tires,* Los Angeles Times, May 22, 2001, at A1; Bill Vlasic, *Tire Recalls, Tragedies Tax Ford, Pirestone and Public,* Detroit News, September 3, 2000, at A1 (original purchases); John Greenwald, *Tired of Each Other,* Time, June 4, 2001, at 50 (wedding photograph).
2. The Ford Explorer description is drawn from Keith Bradsher, High and Mighty 323–24 (2002); Davan Maharaj & Myron Levin, *Consumer Group Says Ford Ordered Less Weight on Tires,* Los Angeles Times, January 5, 2001, at C1; Greenwald, *Tired of Each Other.*
3. The Bridgestone/Firestone tire story is drawn from John O'Dell, *Tire Recall Has Brought Many Changes in the Name of Secrecy,* Los Angeles Times, August 9, 2001, at 1; Ricardo Alonso-Zaldivar, *Firestone, Ford Bid to Cut Probe Short,* Los Angeles Times, December 20, 2000, at C3; Lauren Comander, *Firestone Cites Design Flaw, Process at Decatur,* Chicago Tribune, December 20, 2000, at 1; Terril Yue Jones, *Cause of Tire Failures Still a Matter of Dispute,* Los Angeles Times, October 22, 2000, at C1; Mark Truby, *Firestone Finds Tire Flaws,* Detroit News, October 18, 2000, at A1; Tamara Audi & Jennifer Dixon, *Documents Show Ford Was Warned About Tire Tread,* Detroit Free Press, October 6, 2000, at A1.
4. The story of NHTSA's inattention to the problem is drawn from Bradsher, High and Mighty, 307–09; James R. Healey, *Firestone Leaves an Indelible Mark,* USA Today, December 26, 2000, at B1; Alicia C. Shepard, *Local Heroes,* American Journalism Review, December, 2000, at 42; Ricardo Alonso-Zaldivar, *Errors, Short Staffing Led to Missed Tire Warnings,* Los Angeles Times, November 10, 2000, at A1; Tom Incantalupo, *Agency in Hot Seat,* Newsday, September 13, 2000, at A7; Cindy Skrzycki, *Agency Missed Early Tire Warnings,* Washington Post, September 12, 2000, at E1; Cindy Skrzycki, *NHTSA Will Share Hearing Spotlight,* Washington Post, September 5, 2000, at E1; Edmund Sanders, Judy Pasternak. & John O'Dell, *State Farm Says It Alerted Firestone to Problem in '97,* Los Angeles Times, August 16, 2000, at C1.
5. Bradsher, High and Mighty, 310; James R. Healey, *What You Don't Know About Your Tires,* USA Today, August 11, 2000, at B1 (documents from all known settlements sealed).
6. The story of the Houston television station and the Bridgestone recall is drawn from Shepard, *Local Heroes;* Healey, *Firestone Leaves an Indelible Mark;* Daniel Eisenberg, *Anatomy of a Recall,* Time, September 11, 2000, at 28; Vlasic, *Tire Recalls;* Cindy Skrzycki, *6.5 Million Tires Are Target of Recall,* Washington Post, August 10, 2000, at A1; James V. Grimaldi, *Second Firestone Plant Faulted,* Washington Post, August 18, 2000, at E1.
7. The information contained in the Ford and Firestone internal documents is drawn from Greenwald, *Tired;* Healey, *Firestone Leaves an Indelible Mark;* James V. Grimaldi & Cindy Skrzycki, *Firestone Redesigned Tires in 1998,* Washington Post, September 21, 2000, at E1; Cindy Skrzycki, *U.S. Seeks New Test for Tires,* Washington Post, August 12, 2000, at A1; Healey, *What You Don't Know.*
8. Greenwald, *Tired.*

9. Caroline E. Mayer, *New Car Safety Rules Weighed,* Washington Post, August 25, 2000, at E1 (quoting Ford Vice President for Environmental and Safety Engineering).
10. Judy Pasternak, *Safety Agency Takes Heat Over Firestone Tire Recall,* Los Angeles Times, August 19, 2000, at A1 (1960 specifications); Skrzycki, *U.S. Seeks New Test* (passenger car use).
11. Richard A. Ryan, *Safety Agency Wants More Clout,* Detroit News, September 7, 2000, at A1 (quoting NHTSA Administrator Sue Bailey).
12. W. Page Keeton, et al., Prosser & Keeton on Torts 6 (5th ed. 1984).
13. Robert L. Rabin, *Reassessing Regulatory Compliance,* 88 Geo. L. J. 2049, 2073 (2000).
14. Mary L. Lyndon, *Tort Law and Technology,* 12 Yale J. Reg. 137, 172 (1995); Catherine T. Struve, *The FDA and the Tort System: Postmarketing Surveillance, Compensation, and the Role of Litigation,* 5 Yale J. Policy & Legal Ethics, 587, 591 (2005).
15. Richard B. Stewart, *Regulatory Compliance Preclusion of Tort Liability: Limiting the Dual-Track System,* 88 Geo. L. J. 2167, 2181 (2000).
16. Jerry L. Mashaw & David L. Harfst, *Regulation and Legal Culture: The Case of Motor Vehicle Safety,* 4 Yale J. Reg. 257, 272 (1987).
17. David C. Vladeck, *Defending Courts: A Brief Rejoinder to Professors Fried and Rosenberg,* 31 Seton Hall L. Rev. 631, 641 (2001).
18. Medtronic, Inc. v. Lohr, 518 U.S. 470, 488 (1996) (serious intrusion quote); Simon & Shuster, Inc. v. New York Crime Victims Bd., 502 U.S. 105, 118 (1991) (compelling interest quote).
19. Nina A. Mendelson, *Chevron and Preemption,* 102 Mich. L. Rev. 737, 738 (2004).
20. Bates v. Dow Agrosciences, LLC, Brief of the Chamber of Commerce of the United States as Amicus Curiae, November 24, 2004, at 25.
21. Ralph Lindeman, *Agencies Move to Override State Law as Part of Federal Rulemaking Process,* 34 BNA Prod. Safety & Liability Rept. 304 (2006).
22. Alex Berenson, *Jury Calls Merck Liable in Death of Man on Vioxx,* New York Times, August 20, 2005, at A1.
23. Walt Bogdanich, *In Deaths at Rail Crossings, Missing Evidence and Silence,* New York Times, July 11, 2004, at A1.
24. Bates v. Dow Agrosciences, LLC, Brief for Petitioners, September 13, 2004, at 44, 47; Medtronic, Inc. v. Lohr, 518 U.S. 470, 495 (1996).
25. David G. Owen, Products Liability Law 887 (2005); Peter H. Schuck, *Why Regulating Guns Through Litigation Won't Work, in* Suing the Gun Industry 225, 232 (Timothy D. Lytton, ed., 2005); Timothy D. Lytton, *Tort Claims Against Gun Manufacturers for Crime-Related Injuries: Defining a Suitable Role for the Tort System in Regulating the Firearms Industry,* 65 Mo. L. Rev. 1, 51–52 (2000).
26. Rabin, *Reassessing Regulatory Compliance,* 2077–79.
27. Lytton, *Tort Claims,* 51–52 (running afoul quote).
28. *Risk and Responsibility: The Roles of FDA and Pharmaceutical Companies in Ensuring the Safety of Approved Drugs, Like Vioxx, Hearings Before the House Committee on Government Reform,* 109th Cong., 1st Sess. 23 (2005) (testimony of Steven Galston, Acting Director, Center for Drug Evaluation and Research, FDA).
29. W. Kip Viscusi, et al., *Deterring Inefficient Pharmaceutical Litigation: An Economic Ratio-*

nale for the FDA Regulatory Compliance Defense, 24 SETON HALL L. REV. 1437, 1447 (1994).

30. Rabin, *Reassessing Regulatory Compliance,* 2077.
31. *Risk and Responsibility Hearings,* 60 (testimony of Steven Galston, Acting Director, Center for Drug Evaluation and Research, FDA)
32. Margaret Gilhooley, *The Effect of Products Liability Litigation on Innovation: Innovative Drugs, Products Liability, Regulatory Compliance, and Patient Choice,* 24 SETON HALL L. REV. 1481, 1490–93 (1994).
33. Benedi v. McNeil-P.P.C., Inc. 66 F.3d 1378 (4th Cir. 1995); Worsham v. A.H. Robbins Co. 734 F.2d 676 (11th Cir. 1984); Wooderson v. Ortho Pharmaceutical Corp. 681 P.2d 1038 (Kan. 1984) (citing cases).
34. Bates v. Dow Agrosciences, LLC, 544 U.S. 431, 451 (2005).
35. Rabin, *Reassessing Regulatory Compliance,* 2080–81; Teresa M. Schwartz, *Prescription Products and the Proposed Restatement (Third),* 61 TENN. L. REV. 1357, 1386 (1994).
36. INSTITUTE OF MEDICINE, SAFE MEDICAL DEVICES FOR CHILDREN 98 (2005); Letter from Patrick Ronan, Assistant Commissioner, FDA, to Hon. Mike Enzi, *reprinted in FDA's Drug Approval Process: Up to the Challenge? Hearings Before the Senate Committee on Health, Education, Labor and Pensions,* 109th Cong., 1st Sess. 75, 79 (2005); *id.,* 24 (testimony of Sandra L. Kweder, FDA); *id.,* 63 (testimony of William B. Shultz, former Chief Counsel, FDA) (good bet); *Ensuring Drug Safety: Where Do We Go From Here? Hearings Before the Senate Committee on Health, Education, Labor and Pensions,* 109th Cong., 1st Sess. 36–37 (2005) (testimony of Raymond L. Woolsey, Critical Path Institute).
37. Salmon v. Parke, Davis & Co., 520 F.2d 1359, 1362 (4th Cir. 1975).
38. Environmental Protection Agency, Benlate and Thiophanate-Methyl; Determination Concluding the Rebuttable Presumption Against Registration and Availability of Position Document, 47 Fed. Reg. 46,747, 46,750 (October 20, 1982) (final warning requirement); Environmental Protection Agency, Preliminary Notice of Determination Concluding the Rebuttable Presumption Against Registration of Pesticide Products Containing Benlate; Availability of Position Document, 44 Fed. Reg. 51,166, 51,169 (Aug. 30, 1979) (1979 proposal); Environmental Protection Agency, Rebuttable Presumption Against Registration and Continued Registration of Pesticide Products Containing Benlate, 42 Fed. Reg. 61,788 (December 6, 1977) (1977 notice).
39. The John Castillo story is drawn from Castillo v. E. I. DuPont de Nemours & Co., 854 So.2d 1264 (Fla. 2003); Jan Hollingsworth, *Telephone Call Brought Back Memory of White Mist,* TAMPA TRIBUNE, May 16, 2005, at 4; Jan Hollingsworth, *DuPont to End Sales of Benlate,* TAMPA TRIBUNE, April 20, 2001; Jan Hollingsworth, *Suits Shed Light on DuPont's Benlate,* TAMPA TRIBUNE, February 25, 2001, at 1; Kara Sissel, *Jury Rules Against DuPont in Benlate Case,* CHEMICAL fiEEK, May 3, 2000, at 12.
40. See Bates v. Dow Agrosciences, LLC, Brief for American Chemistry Council as Amicus Curiae, November 23, 2004.
41. Robert B. Leflar & Robert S. Adler, *The Preemption Pentad: Federal Preemption of Products Liability Claims After Medtronic,* 64 TENN. L. REV. 691, 712 (1997).
42. OWEN, PRODUCTS LIABILITY LAW, 890; Erwin Chemerinsky, *Empowering States: The*

Need to Limit Federal Preemption, 33 Pepperdine L. Rev. 69, 74 (2005); Lyndon, *Tort Law and Technology,* 149–50; Schwartz, *Prescription Products,* 1361; Struve, *FDA and the Tort System,* 612.

43. Owen, Products Liability Law, 890.
44. Lars Noah, *Rewarding Regulatory Compliance: The Pursuit of Symmetry in Products Liability,* 88 Geo. L. J. 2147, 2151–52 (2000); Stewart, *Regulatory Compliance,* 2173–74; Lars Noah, *Reconceptualizing Federal Preemption of Tort Claims as the Government Standards Defense,* 37 William & Mary L. Rev. 903, 966 (1996); Viscusi, et al., *Deterring Inefficient Pharmaceutical Litigation,* 1463, 1470–71, 1478.
45. Noah, *Rewarding Regulatory Compliance,* 2152.
46. Stewart, *Regulatory Compliance,* 2174.
47. Rabin, *Reassessing Regulatory Compliance,* 2075.
48. Troyen A. Brennan, *Environmental Torts,* 46 Vand. L. Rev. 1, 72 (1993); Jayne O'Donnell, *Safety Feud,* USA Today, February 3, 1997, at B1 (field goal quote, quoting NHTSA Administrator Ricardo Martinez).
49. Owen, Products Liability Law, 24.
50. Robert L. Rabin, *Federalism and the Tort System,* 50 Rutgers L. Rev. 1, 8–9 (1997).
51. Restatement (Third) of Torts—Products Liability § 4(b).
52. Rabin, *Federalism,* 17–18.
53. Janet Elliott, *No Flood of HMO Suits in Texas,* Houston Chronicle, July 26, 2001, at A27 (statistics, HMO lawyer quote); Trebor Banstetter, *HMO Bill Puts Focus on Texas,* Milwaukee Journal Sentinel, July 1, 2001, at A8 (Chambers of Commerce quote); Jim Brunner, *So Far, Texans Happy With Patient-Rights Law,* Seattle Times, March 12, 2000, at A1.
54. New State Ice Co. v. Liebmann, 285 U.S. 262, 311 (1932) (Brandeis, J., dissenting).
55. National Academy of Public Administration, Beyond Preemption: Intergovernmental Partnerships to Enhance the Economy iii (May 2006).
56. Richard J. Pierce, *Regulation, Deregulation, Federalism, and Administrative Law: Agency Power to Preempt State Regulation,* 46 U. Pittsburgh L. Rev. 607, 656 (1985).
57. Geier v. American Honda Motor Co., Brief for the Chamber of Commerce of the United States of America as Amicus Curiae, November 19, 1999, at 20.

CHAPTER 10. ENDING THE PREEMPTION WAR

1. James T. O'Reilly, Federal Preemption of State and Local Law 83 (2006); *Note, New Evidence on the Presumption Against Preemption: An Empirical Study of Congressional Responses to Supreme Court Preemption Decisions,* 120 Harv. L. Rev. 1604 (2007).
2. Riegel v. Medtronic Inc., 128 S.Ct. 999, 1008 (2008).
3. O'Reilly, Federal Preemption, 210.
4. National Academy of Public Administration, Beyond Preemption: Intergovernmental Partnerships to Enhance the Economy 2 (May 2006).
5. Chicago & North Western Transportation Co. v. Kalo Brick & Tile Co., 450 U.S. 311 (1981).

6. O'Reilly, Federal Preemption, 82. *See also* Betsy J. Grey, *Make Congress Speak Clearly: Federal Preemption of State Tort Remedies,* 77 B. U. L. Rev. 559, 626 (1997) (tort claims usually have only an indirect effect on federal regulation).
7. Richard J. Pierce, *Regulation, Deregulation, Federalism, and Administrative Law: Agency Power to Preempt State Regulation,* 46 U. Pittsburgh L. Rev. 607, 656 (1985) (regulatory wisdom quote); Nina A. Mendelson, *Chevron and Preemption,* 102 Mich. L. Rev. 737, 767 (2004).
8. National Academy of Public Administration, Beyond Preemption, 5.
9. Margaret Gilhooley, *The Effect of Products Liability Litigation on Innovation: Innovative Drugs, Products Liability, Regulatory Compliance, and Patient Choice,* 24 Seton Hall L. Rev. 1481, 1490 (1994).
10. Shots v. CSX Transportation, Inc., 38 F.3d 304, 308 (7th Cir. 1994).
11. CSX Transportation, Inc. v. Easterwood, 507 U.S. 658, 664 (1993).
12. Lars Noah, *Rewarding Regulatory Compliance: The Pursuit of Symmetry in Products Liability,* 88 Geo. L. J. 2147, 2161–62 (2000); W. Kip Viscusi, et al., *Deterring Inefficient Pharmaceutical Litigation: An Economic Rationale for the FDA Regulatory Compliance Defense,* 24 Seton Hall L. Rev. 1437, 1478 (1994).
13. Buckman Co. v. Plaintiffs' Legal Committee 531 U.S. 341 (2001).
14. 45 U.S.C. § 51–60.
15. 42 U.S.C. § 300aa-11–15.
16. 42 U.S.C. § 2001–2281.
17. 49 U.S.C. § 40101.
18. David C. Vladeck, *Preemption and Regulatory Failure,* 33 Pepperdine L. Rev. 95, 100 (2005).
19. Bates v. Dow Agrosciences, LLC, 544 U.S. 431, 444, 447 (2005); Medtronic, Inc. v. Lohr, 518 U.S. 470, 495 (1996).
20. Silkwood v. Kerr-McGee Corp., 464 U.S. 238, 248 (1984).
21. Hillsborough County v. Automated Medical Laboratories, Inc., 471 U.S. 707, 717 (1985).
22. Sprietsma v. Mercury Marine, 537 U.S. 51 (2002). *See also* Wisconsin Public Intervenor v. Mortier, 501 U.S. 597, 611–14 (1991) (FIFR Act does not preempt the field of pesticides regulation).
23. English v. General Electric Co., 496 U.S. 72 (1990). *See also* Schweiss v. Chrysler Motors Corp., 922 F.2d 473 (8th Cir. 1990) (whistleblower protection provision of Occupational Safety and Health Act).
24. Richard C. Ausness, *Preemption of State Tort Law by Federal Safety Statutes: Supreme Court Preemption Jurisprudence Since Cipollone,* 62 Ky. L. J. 913, 970–73 (2003); Mary J. Davis, *Unmasking the Presumption in Favor of Preemption,* 53 S. Car. L. Rev. 967, 972 (2002); Grey, *Make Congress Speak Clearly,* 565; Susan Reaker-Jordan, *The Pre-emption Presumption That Never Was: Pre-emption Doctrine Swallows the Rule,* 40 Ariz. L. Rev. 1379, 1381, 1428 (1998); Kenneth Starr, et al., The Law of Preemption: A Report of the Appellate Judges Conference of the American Bar Association 48 (1991); Paul Wolfson, *Preemption and Federalism: The Missing Link,* 16 Hastings Const. L. Q. 69, 112 (1988).

25. Geier v. American Honda Motor Co., 529 U.S. 861, 894 (2000) (Stevens, J. Dissenting) (quote).
26. Grey, *Make Congress Speak Clearly,* 617.
27. Silkwood v. Kerr-McGee Corp., 464 U.S. 238, 248 (1984).
28. Grey, *Make Congress Speak Clearly,* 624; Caleb Nelson, *Preemption* 86 VA. L. REV. 225, 277 (2000) (quote).
29. Buckman Co. v. Plaintiffs' Legal Committee 531 U.S. 341 (2001).
30. Nelson, *Preemption,* 276–87; Kenneth W. Starr, *Reflections on Hines v. Davidowitz: The Future of Obstacle Preemption,* 33 PEPPERDINE L. REV. 1 (2005).
31. See Ausness, *Preemption of State Tort Law,* 974; Robert B. Leflar & Robert S. Adler, *The Preemption Pentad: Federal Preemption of Products Liability Claims After Medtronic,* 64 TENN. L. REV. 691, 693 (1997); Sandra Zellmer, *When Congress Goes Unheard, in* PREEMPTION CHOICES (William Buzbee, ed. forthcoming 2009).
32. Sprietsma v. Mercury Marine, Brief for the United States as Amicus Curiae, March 29, 2002, at 18.
33. Leflar & Adler, *Preemption Pentad,* 694.
34. *Id.,* 694; Geier v. American Honda Motor Co., Brief Amicus Curiae Brief of Robert B. Leflar, Robert S. Adler, Michael Green, and Joseph A. Page, October 22, 1999, at 14.
35. Viscusi, et al., *Deterring Inefficient Pharmaceutical Litigation,* 1469.
36. United Construction Workers v. Laburnum Construction Co., 347 U.S. 656, 665 (1954).
37. Geier v. American Honda Motor Co., Amicus Curiae Brief of the Association of Trial Lawyers of America, October 22, 1999, at 6 (ATLA "unable to locate an instance in which a common law product liability damage verdict was accompanied by an order that defendant alter its product").
38. Ausness, *Public Tort Litigation,* 910–11 (concluding that "the costs of public interest litigation probably outweigh its benefits"); W. Kip Viscusi, *Overview,* in REGULATION THROUGH LITIGATION 1, 12–13 (W. Kip Viscusi, ed., 2002).
39. Chevron USA, Inc. v. Natural Resources Defense Counsel, Inc., 467 U.S. 837 (1986).
40. 467 U.S., at 844.
41. Linda Jellum, *Chevron's Demise: A Survey of Chevron From Infancy to Senescence,* 59 AD. L. REV. 725 (2007).
42. RICHARD J. PIERCE, SIDNEY A. SHAPIRO, & PAUL R. VERKUIL, ADMINISTRATIVE LAW & PROCESS 387 (2004) (observing that the Supreme Court itself has applied *Chevron* inconsistently); Linda Jellum, *Chevron's Demise.*
43. Medtronic, Inc. v. Lohr, 518 U.S. 470, 486–98 (1996). *See* Massachusetts Ass'n of HMOs v. Ruthardt, 194 F.3d 176 (1st Cir. 1999) (reading *Lohr* to afford the agency's interpretation an "intermediate" level of deference).
44. Geier v. American Honda Corp., 529 U.S. 861, 833 (2000).
45. Waters v. Wachovia Bank, NA, 127 S.Ct. 1559, 1572 (2007).
46. Mendelson, *Chevron and Preemption,* 778–91.
47. *Id.,* 791–94.
48. *Id.,* 795.

49. Catherine M. Sharkey, *Federalism in Action: FDA Regulatory Preemption in Pharmaceutical Cases in State Versus Federal Courts,* 15 J. L. & POLICY 1013 (2007).
50. Mendelson, *Chevron and Preemption,* 799.
51. Stephen Lubet, *In the Firestone Case, Trial Lawyers Are the Real Heroes,* SAN DIEGO UNION-TRIBUNE, October 11, 2000, at B7.
52. Scott A. Smith & Duana Grage, *Federal Preemption of State Products Liability Actions,* 27 WILLIAM MITCHELL L. REV. 391, 415 (2000).

Index